A Brahms Reader

A Brahms Reader

Michael Musgrave

Yale University Press · New Haven and London

Published with assistance from the Mary Cady Tew
Memorial Fund.

Designed by Sonia Scanlon.
Set in Adobe Garamond type by Rainsford Type/
Binghamton Valley Composition.
Printed in the United States of America by Sheridan Books,
Chelsea, Michigan.

Library of Congress Cataloging-in-Publication Data

Musgrave, Michael, 1942–
A Brahms reader / Michael Musgrave.
p.   cm.
Includes bibliographical references and index.
ISBN 0-300-06804-2 (alk. paper)
1. Brahms, Johannes, 1833–1897.   2. Composers—Germany—
Biography. I. Title.
ML410.B8M865   1999
780'.92—dc21   99-11127
[B]   CIP

A catalogue record for this book is available from the
British Library.

10 9 8 7 6 5 4 3 2 1

For Stephen and Jonathan

Contents

Illustrations follow pages 66 and 194

Preface

The title "Brahms the Ambiguous," coined by Karl Geiringer in 1983 to sum up Johannes Brahms's personality, can be applied to the composer's professional life as well. Despite a growing familiarity with the full range of his music through recordings and writings, disparate images of Brahms persist. It still seems difficult to link the familiar bearded patriarch with the dreamy youth, the master contrapuntist and variation writer with the composer of waltzes and Hungarian dances. Indeed, we are almost led to doubt that Brahms was ever truly young, so strong is the image of control and command established in his later years—an image to which he certainly contributed by destroying most of the working evidence of his youth. And even with growing appreciation of the deep integration of diverse elements in his mature style, it is still difficult to place Brahms historically. The familiar duality of conservative and progressive seems far less appropriate for him than it does for his great contemporaries Wagner and Liszt; at least their innovations were clear in their time and are part of a continuity of technical and generic change that influenced their successors. Yet Brahms offers traditional external forms and styles while offering a new linguistic content as well. Such creative reinterpretation of the past anticipates the musical world in which we live today. Brahms, so easily labeled a conservative in the past, now offers a particular challenge to assessment. Further, not only has Brahms always been seen as a master, he has been seen invariably as an independent master. The image of control obscures the practicalities of earning a living and developing a career, of overcoming difficulties, of fulfilling ambitions for domestic life and family. Even Brahms's executant musicianship itself forms little part of a picture filled with masterworks.

This fragmented view is a result of history. By the time the standard biographies and studies were written in the decades after Brahms's death in 1897, the composer already was losing status in a changing musical world. And the burgeoning scholarly interest of recent years has tended, in the spirit of the time, to take highly specialized routes, with analysts especially finding in Brahms's work a major model in its rich variation of basic principles. Thus we are no closer to forming a full picture of Brahms's work and achievement. Yet his was a single-minded pursuit of a wide range of goals allied by a rounded personality, and his achievements transformed the musical world. His work as a professional musician and scholar—quite apart from his own composition—is extraordinary. Add to all this a full social life, including several deep friendships, through which he engaged with the issues of the time. Thus, the purpose of this book is to offer, at the centenary of Brahms's death, a broader and more integrated picture by the most direct means: a survey of every facet of his life—as composer, performer, scholar, student, and friend—beginning with descriptions of the man as an individual and concluding with a consideration of his career and achievement.

Brahms's avoidance of public statement and his resistance to verbalizing about music naturally influence this book. Instead of relying on extensive excerpts, such as those that can be assembled from the published writings of Wagner, Liszt, and Schoenberg, I had to assemble this text from much shorter and more varied sources—such as his many letters, the reminiscences of his contemporaries, and the observations of later writers with privileged access. Although such an approach might seem to require a greater degree of interpretation on my part, the sources reveal a remarkable consistency of interests and attitudes. Though analysis of the material and music lies beyond the scope of this book, I use the commentary and notes to place the sources in context and to provide accurate attributions. I refer to recent writings that add perspective or a new dimension. I use the biographies by Max Kalbeck and Florence May, who had first-hand access to much material concerning the Brahms circle, to supply the reader with a broader biographical context, but original sources are cited wherever possible. The translations are my own, except when otherwise cited.

Acknowledgments

I acknowledge with thanks the resources of the following libraries and the assistance of their staffs: British Library; University of London Library, Senate House; Goldsmiths College Library, University of London; Royal College of Music Library; New York Public Library; Performing Arts Library at Lincoln Center; Bobst Library, New York University; Archive of the Gesellschaft der Musikfreunde, Vienna; Stadt- und Universitäts-bibliothek, Hamburg; Brahms Archive, Lübeck; Sammlung Hofmann, Lübeck.

The following publishers and individuals allowed me to quote passages from their publications. Every effort was made to trace the copyright owners of extracts not acknowledged here. Ethel Smyth, *Impressions That Remained* (London, 1919); *Female Pipings in Eden* (London: David Higham Associates, 1933); Karl Geiringer, *Brahms, His Life and Work* (London: George Gardiner, 1948); Karl Geiringer, "Brahms as a Reader and Collector," *Musical Quarterly* 19 (1933); Richard Maunder's edition of Mozart's *Requiem* (London: Oxford University Press, 1988); Ronald Taylor, ed. and trans., *Furtwängler on Music* (London: Ashgate, 1991); Theodor W. Adorno, *Philosophy of Modern Music*, trans. A. G. Mitchell and W. V. Bloomster (London: Sheed and Ward, Continuum, 1973); Erwin Stein, *Orpheus in New Guises* (London: Marion Thorpe, 1953); Arnold Schoenberg, *Style and Idea*, ed. Leonard Stein (London: Faber and Faber, 1975); Natalie Bauer-Lechner, *Recollections of Gustav Mahler*, ed. P. Franklin, trans. D. Newlin (London: Cambridge University Press, 1980); Frank Walker, *Hugo Wolf*, 2nd ed. (London: Orion, 1968); Max Graf, *Legend of a Musical City* (New York: Philosophical Library, 1945); *A Future for English Music and Other Lectures*, ed. Percy M. Young (London: Dr. Percy M. Young and Dobson Books Ltd., 1968); J. Peter Burkholder, "Brahms and Twentieth-Century Classical Music," *Nineteenth Century Music* 8 (Regents of the University of California, 1984); Bayan Northcott, "Once and Future Master," *The Independent*, 30 March 1991; Alan Walker, "Brahms and Serialism," *Musical Opinion* 82 (1958); Arbie Orenstein, *A Ravel*

Reader (New York, 1990); Peter Gay, *Freud, Jews, and Other Germans* (New York: Oxford University Press, 1978).

Permission to reproduce illustrations is gratefully acknowledged from the following sources: Gesellschaft der Musikfreunde, Vienna; Royal College of Music, London; Österreichisches Nationalbibliothek (Bildarchiv), Vienna; Wiener Stadt- und Landesbibliothek; Zentralbibliothek, Zurich; Sammlung Hofmann, Lübeck.

Finally, I thank Professor Allen Forte for suggesting that I write this book, though he did so more years ago than I care to admit; the late Edward Tripp of Yale University Press for setting the project on a firm footing; and above all his successor Harry Haskell for his great patience and help in seeing it through to publication. I am indebted to Heidi Downey for her most sympathetic editing of my text. I thank my sons, Stephen and Jonathan, for their constant interest in my work, and my wife, Liza, for her endless patience with it.

Supporting Cast of Characters

In addition to individuals introduced in the course of the text, the following people appear in the Brahms literature and in this narrative.

Julius Allgeyer (1828–1900). A German engraver and photographer based in Karlsruhe whom Brahms met in Düsseldorf in 1853 and who remained one of Brahms's closest friends. Allgeyer was a devotee of Brahms's music and of the painting of their mutual friend Anselm Feuerbach; Allgeyer wrote the critical biography of the painter. Their correspondence includes references to Brahms's interest in operatic composition.

Theodor Billroth (1829–94). The leading German surgeon of his time. From 1867, director and professor of surgery at the Institute of Operative Surgery in Vienna. An amateur string player with wide musical interests, he was one of Brahms's closest friends in Vienna. Their correspondence gives particular insight into Brahms's interest in literature and drama. Brahms dedicated the op. 51 String Quartets to him.

Hans Guido von Bülow (1830–94). The leading German pianist and conductor of Brahms's generation. He was at first devoted to Wagner, conducting the premiere of *Tristan und Isolde* in Munich in 1865, but he later became an enthusiastic supporter of Brahms's. As conductor of the Meiningen court orchestra from 1880–85 he gave the finest performances of Brahms's orchestral works to date.

Hermann Deiters (1833–1907). German writer on music. Beginning in 1861 he wrote widely on Brahms, whom he knew well, in the *Deutsche Musikzeitung* and *Allgemeine Musikalische Zeitung*. His 1880 study of the composer was the first substantial one translated into English.

Albert Hermann Dietrich (1829–1908). German composer and conductor. Court music director at Oldenburg from 1861, where he introduced

Brahms's works early on. He met Brahms in September 1853 in Düsseldorf, where he was a pupil of Robert Schumann's (and there contributed a movement to the collaborative "F A E" Sonata for Joachim). He published important reminiscences of these and later years.

Hans Gál (1890–1985). Austrian-born musicologist and composer who later moved to Scotland. He studied with Mandyczewski at Vienna University in 1908–13; the two men later edited the collected works of Brahms, published in 1926–28. He was director of the Hochschule für Musik and the Conservatory in Mainz in 1929–33, and he taught at Edinburgh University from 1945, producing a study of the composer in 1961.

Josef Gänsbacher (1829–1911). Austrian cellist, teacher of singing, and composer. For some years he taught singing concurrently with practicing law; from 1875 he was a professor of singing at the Vienna Conservatoire and the most sought-after singing teacher in Vienna. He was coeditor of Schubert's collected works.

Karl Geiringer (1899–1989). Austrian-born musicologist who studied in Vienna with Hans Gál and Guido Adler and succeeded Eusebius Mandyczewski as museum curator and librarian of the Gesellschaft der Musikfreunde in 1930. He later moved to the United States. His many scholarly interests included Brahms, and his centenary study draws on unpublished materials in the archive of the Gesellschaft.

Karl Georg Peter Grädener (1812–1883). German cellist, choral conductor, and composer. He founded a vocal academy in Hamburg in 1851 and played a major part in the city's musical life after 1865, when he returned from teaching singing and theory at the Vienna Conservatoire in 1862–65. Brahms knew him well from the 1850s.

Julius Otto Grimm (1827–1903). German pianist, choral conductor, and composer. He was a music director successively at Göttingen and Münster in Westphalia. He met Brahms in Leipzig in 1853, and he and his wife, Philippine, remained close to Brahms throughout life. Grimm was one of the signatories of the Declaration of 1860.

Carl Goldmark (1830–1915). Hungarian-born composer, the son of a cantor, who lived in Vienna from 1850. His operas, including *The Queen of Sheba* and *Merlin*, were very popular, and his *Rustic Wedding Symphony*, Violin Concerto, and some chamber music are still in the repertory.

Eduard Hanslick (1825–1904). A Prague-born music critic active in Vienna, the first great professional in this field. Trained in the law, he was able to turn to music only after the publication of his treatise "On Beauty in Music" (1854). He was appointed the first lecturer in Music History and Aesthetics at the University of Vienna in 1856. As music critic of *Die Wiener Zeitung* and *Die Neue Freie Presse* he was Brahms's most influential supporter. Brahms dedicated the Waltzes, op. 39, to him.

Sir George Henschel (1850–1934). A German baritone singer, composer, conductor, and teacher. In 1881 he became the first conductor of the Boston symphony orchestra, and in 1884 he settled in London, performing much Brahms at his London Symphony concerts from 1886. His reminiscences include a diary of his meetings with Brahms, whom he first met at the Lower Rhine Music Festival in 1874.

Richard Heuberger (1850–1914). An Austrian critic, conductor, and composer, mainly of operettas and choral music that achieved considerable popularity in their day. The operetta *Der Opernball* remains a fixture of the German light operatic repertory. He received informal lessons from Brahms and was much in his company in Vienna from the early 1880s. He based his extensive reminiscences on this experience.

Elisabet von Herzogenberg (born Stockhausen) (1847–92). She met Brahms as a piano pupil in Vienna in 1863, subsequently establishing a close artistic friendship with him after settling in Leipzig with her husband, Heinrich von Herzogenberg (1843–1900; composer and conductor of the Leipzig *Bach Verein*). Possessed of remarkable musicianship, her responses to Brahms's new works elicited revealing views from the composer, who dedicated the Rhapsodies for piano, op. 79, to her.

Gustav Uwe Jenner (1865–1920). German composer. He studied in Hamburg with Marxsen, who passed him to Brahms in Vienna. He was

Brahms's only regular pupil (through the spring and winter of 1888), and he left extensive recollections of the experience. He was music director at the University of Marburg from 1895–1920.

Joseph Joachim (1831–1907). Hungarian-born violinist, composer, and conductor, the leading violinist of the German classical school in the nineteenth century. A protégé of Liszt, he was leader of the Weimar Court Orchestra under him in 1849, director of music at the Court of Hanover from 1853–66, and the first head of the music department of the Royal Academy of Arts, Berlin, in 1868. He led his own string quartet. He was Brahms's closest artistic collaborator.

Max Kalbeck (1850–1921). Austrian music critic, author, poet, and translator. His career as critic began in Breslau in 1875; he moved to Vienna in 1880 on the recommendation of Eduard Hanslick. He became a music critic on various Viennese papers, including *Die Neue Freie Presse* in 1883, maintaining partisan support for Brahms. He was author of the first major Brahms biography and editor of much of the correspondence.

[Fürchgott] Theodor Kirchner (1823–1903). German pianist, organist, and composer. One of Schumann's most gifted pupils, he was active in Switzerland in 1843–73 as organist in Winterthur and concert director in Zurich, later teaching piano and composition in Leipzig, Dresden, and Hamburg. He was a lifelong advocate of the works of Brahms, whom he met in 1856 (giving early performances of the D Minor Piano Concerto), and was a close friend of Clara Schumann.

Hermann Levi (1839–1900). German conductor who studied at the Leipzig Conservatoire from 1855–58. As Hofkapellmeister at Karlsruhe from 1864–72 he became a friend of Clara Schumann's and produced her husband's *Genoveva* in 1869. He also worked closely with Brahms, giving outstanding performances of his works, though their warm relationship cooled with Levi's growing enthusiasm for Wagner.

Rudolf von den Leyen (1851–1910). A Crefeld banker and piano enthusiast who was a key figure in the Brahms circle there. Related to the von Beckerath family, he recorded valuable recollections of Brahms.

Eduard Marxsen (1806–87). Born in Altona, a suburb of Hamburg, he studied first with the Hamburg teacher Clasing and then in Vienna with Ignaz Seyfried (1830) and with Carl Maria von Bocklet, an acquaintance of Beethoven and close friend of Schubert. He taught Brahms piano and composition in Altona from 1843–48.

Florence May (1845–1923). English pianist and biographer, the daughter of the organist and singing teacher Edward Collett May. First trained by her father, in 1871 she traveled to Lichtental, near Baden Baden, to study with Clara Schumann, who introduced her to Brahms. Her two-volume biography of the composer includes personal reminiscences of her lessons and later acquaintance with him.

Walter Niemann (1876–1953). German composer, editor, and writer on music. Born, like Brahms, in Hamburg; his father was born in Wesselburen, where Brahms's father was apprenticed. Niemann studied at the Leipzig Conservatoire from 1898. His often reprinted study of 1920 emphasizes Brahms's north German background.

Adolf Schubring (1817–93). A German music critic, though by profession a judge. His articles, appearing from 1862 in *Neue Zeitschrift für Musik* under the initials D. A. S., were the earliest to claim Brahms's greatness without significant reservation.

Clara Schumann (1819–96). Wife of Robert Schumann and daughter of Friedrich Wieck. She was the leading woman pianist of the nineteenth century and a highly accomplished composer. Trained by her father, she toured widely, especially after the death of Robert, whom she married in 1840. She exerted great influence as a teacher, and her many professional and social connections helped Brahms in his early years. She was his intimate friend for the rest of her life, and their correspondence is one of the central documents of the Brahms literature.

Eugenie Schumann (1851–1938). Youngest daughter of the Schumanns; her *Erinnerungen* is a rich source of information on the Schumann family life and includes extensive references to Brahms. Both Eugenie and her sister Marie helped with the teaching of their mother's pupils.

Robert Alexander Schumann (1810–56). German composer of piano music, songs, chamber, orchestral, and choral music, and one opera. He was one of the leading figures of new music when he met Brahms in September 1853 in Düsseldorf, where he was city music director. Brahms was to know him for only months before Schumann's mental decline, beginning with attempted suicide in February 1854, though his influence in personal and musical terms was profound.

Julius Stockhausen (1826–1906). German baritone singer and conductor. He was equally at home in German song and French opera. He was conductor of the Hamburg Philharmonic concerts from 1862–67; he later taught in Stuttgart, Berlin, and Frankfurt. He gave many recitals with Brahms, inspired many works.

Richard Specht (1870–1932). Austrian music writer and critic. A pupil of Ignaz Brüll, Alexander Zemlinsky, and Franz Schreker, he founded the journal *Der Merker* in 1909. His biographies include studies of Beethoven, Johann Strauss, Richard Strauss, and Mahler. He knew Brahms personally, and his biography of the composer draws on personal acquaintance with the members of his Viennese circle.

Charles Villiers Stanford (1852–1924). Irish-born conductor and composer with strong interest in German music. He was director of the Cambridge University Music Society from 1873, then became professor of music, conductor of the Bach Choir in London, and a professor at the Royal College of Music. A friend of Joachim's, he did much to establish Brahms's music in England.

Joseph Viktor Widmann (1848–1911). Swiss poet, playwright, critic, scholar, theologian, and librettist of Moravian descent. His extensive reminiscences of Brahms, whom he met in Zurich in 1874 (though he first saw and heard him in 1865 and Brahms knew of him thereafter), include further evidence of Brahms's interest in opera, for which he sought to provide libretti. The book includes his poem "Thuner Sonata von Johannes Brahms," inspired by the A Major Violin Sonata, op. 100.

ONE · Brahms the Man

1 · Physical Appearance, Temperament, and Personality

This is the impression made by Johannes Brahms, then in his middle fifties, on the young pianist Adelina de Lara when he walked into her lesson with Clara Schumann. Her comments capture the three features of the composer's appearance noted by all observers: his striking profile and eyes; his stature, much shorter than would be anticipated from his impressive head; and his lack of concern for dress, often coupled with an indifference to manners. But these features were less marked when Brahms was younger. Until the age of forty-five, when he grew a beard, he looked much different, though his height and profile were always noted. He remained youthful looking for his years through his twenties, and when Albert Dietrich met him in September 1853, he recalled the twenty-year-old as "youthful, almost boyish-looking, with his high-pitched voice and long fair hair."[1] In his earlier Hamburg days people had noticed his slightly uncertain gait and the way his body bowed forward a little. Brahms still looked much the same at twenty-eight, when he stayed with the Rösing family at Hamm on the edge of Hamburg, though he had gained some self-assurance. He was observed to be "of medium height and delicately built with a countenance beneath whose high, fine brow were set flashing blue eyes with fair hair combed back and falling down behind, and an obstinate lower lip! An unconscious force would emanate from him as he stood apart in pleasant company, with hands clasped behind his back, greeting those who arrived with a curt nod of his fine head."[2] By his thirties he was beginning to put on weight. J. V. Widmann observed in 1865 that

The door opened and in walked a short stout man. He wore a long beard, and his hair was quite long, swept back from a magnificent brow. His dress had a certain carelessness about it.

the short squat figure, the almost sandy-colored hair, the protruding lower lip which gave a somewhat mocking expression to his beardless young face, were characteristics which were striking and could have been displeasing; but the whole appearance was, as it were, steeped in force. The broad, leonine breast, the Herculean shoulders, the powerful head, often tossed back with energetic move-ments as he played, the fine thoughtful brow, glowing as though illuminated inwardly, and the fiery Germanic eyes and blond lashes revealed an artistic personality which seemed to be charged to the very fingertips with the magnetism of genius. There was also something confi-dently triumphant in his face, the radiant serenity of a mind happy in the exercise of his art.[3]

Brahms took on a completely new aspect in 1878, when he surprised his friends by growing a beard. The singer George Henschel describes coming to Vienna that autumn to give a concert with Ignaz Brüll: "At the end of the concert, [we] were receiving, in the artists' room, the congratulation of friends, when suddenly I saw a man unknown to me, rather stout, of middle height, with long hair and full beard. In a very deep and hoarse voice he introduced himself as 'Musikdirektor Muller,' making a very stiff and formal bow, which I was on the point of returning with equal gravity, when, an instant later, we all found ourselves heartily laughing at the perfect success of Brahms's disguise, for, of course, he it was."[4] Brahms also referred to his beard as "long suppressed," suggesting that he had considered wearing it at an earlier age, as was customary. He said three years later to Widmann that "with a shaved chin one is taken for either an actor or a priest."[5]

With the beard he completely lost his youthful image, and new ac-quaintances were invariably surprised to see that he looked nothing like his portrait, and even less so as the years passed. To the young Gustav Jenner he appeared in 1887 as a "little, plump gentleman."[6] His attire had always been rather casual, though he could dress for the occasion when required. Eugenie Schumann was never happy with this neglect of ap-pearance: "His colored shirts without collars, his little black alpaca coats, and trousers which were always too short were an abomination." But, she added, "the elasticity of his walk, with the weight thrown on the heels, pleased me when I saw him coming along, hat in hand."[7]

Up close, however, the youthful characteristics remained. Henschel, along with everyone else, noticed his eyes: "What . . . struck me most was the kindliness of his eyes. They were of a light blue; wonderfully keen and bright, with now and then a roguish twinkle in them, and yet at times of almost childlike tenderness."[8] A decade later C. V. Stanford was equally impressed: "[They] were of an astonishingly deep and luminous velvet."[9] Another youthful feature was his high-pitched voice. It never fully changed in maturity, so he tried to lower his pitch by speaking with an unpleasant-sounding hoarseness, but his voice tended to break when he was excited. Although Brahms had appeared delicate in his youth, he was actually robust, with a passionate love of the open air and of long walks that exhausted his friends. He had a ruddy complexion and apparently suffered few, if any, prolonged illnesses during his life. Dietrich was impressed by his vigor: "In the company of his equals he was lively, often even presumptuous, robust, and full of mad whims. With the boisterousness of youth, he would run up the stairs, bang on the door with both fists, and storm in without waiting for an answer."[10] Henschel was still impressed by the forty-three-year-old Brahms's physical presence during their holiday on the isle of Rügen:

> His solid frame, the healthy dark brown color of his face,
> the full hair just a little sprinkled with gray, all make
> him appear the very image of strength and vigor. He
> walks about here just as he pleases, generally with his
> waistcoat unbuttoned and his hat in his hand, always
> with clean linen but without collar or necktie. These he
> dons at the table d'hôte only. His whole appearance viv-
> idly recalls some of the portraits of Beethoven. His appe-
> tite is excellent. He eats with great gusto and in the
> evening regularly drinks his three glasses of beer, never
> omitting, of course, to finish off with his beloved coffee.

Henschel and he went swimming, which Henschel greatly enjoyed. "In the water he drew my attention to the possibility of keeping one's eyes open when diving. It is not only possible, he said, but also very agreeable and strengthening for the eyes. I at once followed his advice to try, succeeding immediately, and we greatly amused ourselves by throwing little copper coins into the water and diving for them."[11]

Temperament and Personality

The sense of reserve and quiet detachment mentioned in the earliest descriptions of Brahms was not merely a feature of a self-absorbed artistic temperament. It was a North German mannerism regarded as typical by writers who shared Brahms's background, and it was most apparent when he was emotional. His fellow North German Walter Niemann emphasized this regional trait, summarizing the observations of others: "As so often happens, the older Brahms grew the more noticeable his innate Hamburg, Low German traits, became, even in his way of speaking, curt, abrupt, vigorously rapping out his words, allusive rather than explanatory, with a sharp emphasis on the first syllables, and, in the persistent Low German fashion, still with a thoroughly North German Hamburg intonation, even after long years of residence in Vienna. He was utterly lacking in eloquence—another Low German trait—and he spoke his own words with the greatest difficulty, and in deprecatory and curt terms, rising to heights of positive rage at his own embarrassment. . . . He was apt to fall silent as soon as the conversation turned upon music or a piece of music."[12] But when the subject excited him, he would take a lively part in the proceedings. Eugenie Schumann recalls that when Brahms visited the Schumann household and was in a good humor, whatever was on his mind "really bubbled out of him and gave him a sunny boyishness, even in his later years."[13]

Brahms's frequent reserve in company was a sign of genuine personal modesty. He saw himself as a straightforward professional musician, the son of his father, and affectation was anathema to him. He disliked concerts of his own music, typically commenting that he would prefer to hear music by better composers.[14] By all accounts his modesty was sincere, evidence of his reverence for his greatest German predecessors. He once remarked that the "public in general doesn't understand and appreciate the best things, like the Mozart concertos and this Viotti [the Violin Concerto no. 22 in A Minor] enable the likes of us to earn a living and gain renown."[15] Brahms's humorous and self-deprecating descriptions of his own new works are further evidence of this outlook, as was his aversion to autograph hunters, his reluctance to be photographed, and his disdain for all pretensions to position with colleagues. Richard von Perger quotes him as commenting to his fellow members of an important committee, "Come now, let's have no buffoonery and no stickling for rank here, as if we were at a prince's table; we are all musicians together. You are Herr X and you are Herr Y and I am Herr Brahms."[16]

Brahms's generosity to colleagues and those in need was famous. In his later years he was in a position to be generous, because his earnings vastly exceeded his simple needs. He never lost touch with his background, and he was kind to family beyond the call of duty. He was as loyal to his stepfamily as to his own parents and siblings, and he clearly regarded their well-being as a major obligation. But more surprising was his sensitivity in offering help. For example, he once he hinted to his father with tender understatement that a number of banknotes could be found between the pages of Brahms's score of Handel's *Saul*. "If at any time things go badly with you, music is always the best consolation. Just study my old Saul attentively and you will find something there that will be of use to you."[17] He even pressed money on Clara Schumann for the education of her children. And any musician friends who found themselves in difficulty because of age or sickness (as did the composer Theodor Kirchner in his later years) could always count on him.[18]

A strong sense of humor—quiet and wry, outspoken and elaborate, and sometimes cruel—was a distinctive part of Brahms's personality. His understated manner included a mastery of the droll rejoinder. On hearing of the death of one of the players in the Bayreuth orchestra in 1876, his suspicion of the Wagnerian world prompted the dry response, "The first corpse."[19] And when his Viennese friend Josef Gänsbacher complained during their performance of Brahms's first cello sonata that he could not hear himself play the cello part over Brahms's forceful piano, Brahms laconically responded, "Lucky you."[20] He was fond of practical jokes and liked to deceive his friends by playing in styles other than his own; on one occasion he had music of his own copied in such a way as to suggest that the manuscript was Clara's, and then he presented it to her as a joke.[21] These domestic pranks were quite apart from the deceptions he used to deter prying visitors from his holiday haunts; on one occasion he even assumed a false identity. His circle grew accustomed to intended jokes that were also hurtful: after listening to Max Bruch's *Odysseus,* passionately performed by Bruch himself on the piano, Brahms simply commended him on his manuscript paper.[22]

Had Brahms's sense of humor been simply robust, his reputation would have been different. But in his manner generally there was a failure to control or to integrate the elements of his nature, which intensified his loneliness and perhaps contributed to his bachelorhood. Various reasons for this lack of control have been offered. He may have had difficulty relating his hard upbringing to the privileged world in which he increasingly moved and preserving his integrity in radically changed circumstances. Whatever the reason, his inability to compromise his artistic aims was apparent from a young age. This characteristic was quickly grasped by the violinist Joseph Joachim soon after their first meeting. Two letters show Brahms's two sides, the first in 1854 to Gisela von Arnim:

> Brahms is the most ingrained egoist imaginable, although
> he himself does not realize it, for everything gushes out
> of his sanguine nature quite spontaneously, but at times
> with a lack of feeling (not a lack of reticence, which
> would suit me fine!) that is offensive because it betrays
> lack of education and culture. . . . He recognizes the
> weaknesses of the people with whom he deals and he exploits them. . . . He does not allow anything to disturb
> his musical bliss and belief in a higher world of fantasy—
> and his manner of keeping all the unhealthy sensations
> and possible sufferings of others at arm's length borders
> on sheer genius. He is unwilling to make even the
> slightest sacrifice of his spiritual inclinations.[23]

And two years later: "[Brahms] has two natures: one of essentially childlike genius (it is this one that, because I love it more than I can say, I cannot begrudge a single one of your thoughts) and the other of demoniac cunning which, in icy blast, suddenly breaks forth in a prosaic, pedantic compulsion to dominate. Perhaps, when he gets more recognition, the latter will gradually vanish."[24] It seems not to have done so until the very last years of Brahms's life.

Brahms needed his friends and was devoted to them. But it was difficult to be a friend to Brahms without getting hurt, and not one of his several deep friendships was untroubled by tension, sometimes acute. Though his friends understood the reasons for his outbursts or moods, they were often taken off guard; they never knew just where they stood. His bluntness or detachment could wound deeply even though his need to be alone, even to remain aloof, was respected. He wrote to Julius Allgeyer that he was "accustomed to taking friendships seriously and very simply."[25] Eugenie Schumann recalled that "he was always on the defensive when he was sought after" if he suspected an enquirer's motive: on one occasion he was even led to remark "I have no friends. If anyone says he is a friend of mine, don't believe him."[26] To Clara he wrote, "I always spend feast days in a very lonely fashion, quite alone in my room . . . and very quietly—for my own people are either dead or at a distance. How happy I am when I feel joyfully how love entirely satisfies the human heart! I am indeed dependent upon the outside world; the hubbub in which one lives—I do not laugh at it, I do not join in its deceit—but it is as though the best in one could shut itself off, and only half of oneself go on its way dreaming."[27] On reading Theodor Billroth's complaints of him to Eduard Hanslick (in a letter which had accidentally come into his possession), he resignedly admitted, "It is nothing new to me to be regarded by old acquaintances and friends as something quite different from what I really am (or give myself out to be). I know how in earlier days I used to maintain a scared and wounded silence at such times, but for a long time past I have taken it quite quietly, as a matter of course; this may seem harsh to a kind hearted man like you, yet I hope I have not fallen too far short of Goethe's saying 'Blessed is he who without hatred shuts himself off from the world.' "[28]

He needed distance from the world, the security of self-sufficiency. Niemann comments, "When Philipp Spitta speaks of Brahms's 'noble bashfulness' [edlen Verschämtheit] he has chosen a fine and apt characterization. It is this very idiosyncrasy which had from the outset most thoroughly misled those most unacquainted with the peculiarities of the Low German character in their estimate of him. How often has his transparently sterling and noble character suffered from his offhand, thoroughly North German manner towards those whom he had wounded."[29] He continued, "Nobody tried harder to make amends," often in a touching way, through what Karl Goldmark called his "silent, almost secret tenderness." Goldmark, a close contact of Brahms's during his early years in

Vienna, said revealingly, "In spite of many attacks and many differences, he was at bottom really fond of me. He even had for me a deep, almost secret tenderness and expressed it, except in the company of his North German friends, and then his manner was more than reserved."[30]

Brahms's aversion to letter writing may be another aspect of his unwillingness to be held down to expression. His frequent and pointed business correspondence contrasts with his failure to get to the point emotionally. As Hans Gál puts it, "The fact that he did not always express himself clearly is due to his character, to a certain diffidence which prevented him from showing his true feelings. At times, when he quite incidentally alluded to something as unimportant, even though to him it was actually of prime importance, this almost appears as sham."[31] Brahms commented on these difficulties most frequently to Clara, to whom he confessed as early as February 1855, "I have told you how seldom I succeed in getting my thoughts out of my heart and onto paper." And, in connection with a birthday letter written toward the end of his life: "By the way, I really write in half sentences only, and it is necessary for the reader to figure out the other half for himself."[32]

Brahms's often abrupt manner and sometimes coarse exterior hid a manifest emotionality and sensitivity. He wept easily, whether over artistic experiences or personal events, a tendency that became more marked with the years. Widmann describes how Brahms could be moved by paintings, as on his visits to Italy. In the picture gallery at Parma he "stood long" before a Parmigianino—*The Betrothal of St. Catherine to the Infant Savior.* As Widmann notes, the "graciousness of the many indescribably lovely faces of fair-haired children and girls, a true symphony of sweetness," moved Brahms "almost to tears."[33] Simple tales or affecting poems would have a similar effect, and at the close of a very fine performance of his *Song of the Fates* at Krefeld, "tears of emotion and joy ran down his cheeks," observed Rudolf von den Leyen.[34] Bidding farewell to friends invariably moved him to tears, and he was greatly moved when thanking Hanslick for his friendship on the occasion of the critic's seventieth birthday in 1895.[35] At Clara Schumann's funeral in 1896 he wept "till he could weep no more."[36]

2 · Upbringing and Education

Family Life

Brahms was born on 7 May 1833 in Hamburg to humble circumstances. His family lived at 24 Specksgang (later 60 Speckstrasse) in the Gänge-viertel, or Lane Quarter, in the Dammthor district of Old Hamburg, which was destroyed in World War II. Brahms's English biographer Florence May apparently visited the house in 1903 while working on her study of the composer, first published in 1905.

> The lane quarter exists no longer, but many of the old houses remain and some are well kept and picturesque to the eye of the passer by. Not so No. 60 Speckstrasse. This house does not form part of the main street but stands in a small dismal court behind, which is entered through a close passage, and was formerly called Schlü-ter's Court [Schlütershof]. . . . A steep wooden staircase in the center leads right and left, directly from the court to the various stories of the building. Each of its habitations is planned exactly as every other, excepting that those near the top are contracted by the sloping roof. [The Brahms family] lived in the first floor dwelling to the left on facing the house. . . . The staircase door opens on to a diminutive space, half kitchen, half lobby, where some cooking may be done and a child's bed made up, and which has a second door leading to the living room. This communicates with the sleeping closet, which has its own window, but is so tiny it can scarcely be called a room. There is nothing else, neither corner nor cup-board.[37]

Niemann also appears to have visited the building: "The house is a typical old German timbered building, tall and five-storied, with the windows opening outward and so very close together, low under the eaves, with pots of flowers, canaries and white curtains of the cleanliness worthy of Holland, and thronged with people and children."[38]

Although both May and Niemann also stress the poverty of the environment, it is impossible to draw an analogy between the state of the location at the time of their visits and its state seventy years earlier.[39] In any case, the family moved within a year, and it did so frequently as Brahms's father steadily improved his income, thus lessening the significance of the birthplace as an indicator of family fortunes during Brahms's youth. After Brahms joined the Schumann circle in 1853 he never hesitated to offer accommodation to visiting friends at his parents' home. But when Brahms was born, his parents were still poor. Brahms was baptized in the St. Michaeliskirche into the Lutheran faith; his godparents were his grandfather, Johann Brahms, his uncle Philip Detmering, and Katharina Stäcker.[40] Brahms's father, Johann Jacob Brahms (1806–72), was from Schleswig-Holstein, and his family had lived in the region for many generations. The grandfather, Johann (1769–1839), was an innkeeper and tradesman in the town of Heide, Holstein, and his eldest son, Peter Höft Hinrich (1793–1863), inherited the family business, also dealing in secondhand goods. Brahms's father, born in Heide, was a musician and of more adventurous outlook. After outgrowing the limited musical opportunities in Heide he ran away to obtain music lessons, first to southern Ditmarschen and then to Wesselburen.[41] With his certificate of apprenticeship he traveled to Hamburg to begin working his way up the professional ladder. A competent all-around musician (he played violin, viola, cello, and flute) he soon founded his income on a position in the Hamburg Bürgerwehr as a flügelhornist, though his greatest expertise was subsequently on the double bass, from which he generated much more income through a range of engagements in places of entertainment. By 1863 he had a position as bass player in the Philharmonic Orchestra of Hamburg. Brahms's teacher Edward Marxsen, who met Johann Jacob Brahms in the early 1860s, described him "as of thoroughly upright character, of limited intellect, but of great good nature."[42] He was devoted to his instrument and had a good sense of humor.

Johannes Brahms's mother, Johanna Henrika Christiane Nissen, was seventeen years older than Johann Jacob. She was a native of Hamburg, where she lived with her sister and brother-in-law, for whom she kept house, and their lodgers. According to Marxsen, "She was also of upright character, of no education, it is true, but, as the saying goes, with more native wit than her husband. She had simple piety and soulful, childlike eyes, which Johannes inherited."[43] As she recalled in a letter to Brahms shortly before she died, her upbringing had been simple. She had gone out to sew at the age of thirteen, and she also had helped her mother at home in the evenings, later working as a general servant. She seems to have accepted her courtship with equanimity. "[Your] Father took a room with us and so we became acquainted. He had only been living with us for eight days when he wanted me to become his wife. . . . I could hardly believe it because our ages were so different. Uncle spoke of it again and again, so I took it for destiny."[44]

Christiane's strongest appeal for Johann must have been her excellent skills as housekeeper and seamstress, giving him the prospect of a secure domestic life to support his growing professional status. She had a sensitivity to poetry, which she passed on to her son, though whether she knew Schiller by heart, as Max Kalbeck claims, has been disputed.[45] Despite her lack of education, her family origins were socially superior to those of her husband. Her family was named in the *Ahnentafel berühmter Deutscher* (Genealogy of distinguished Germans) published in 1929; her mother was of gentle birth, and her father's family was traceable to the fourteenth century and included burgomasters and clergymen.[46] By her father's generation that status had been lost; he was a tailor, and his trade obviously determined the occupation of his daughter.

Christiane and Johann had three children: Elizabeth Wilhelmine Luise (Elise), Johannes, and Fritz Friedrich (Fritz). Elise suffered headaches that lasted for days on end, and she was little help in the hard-pressed household. Fritz had striking musical gifts and became a pupil of Marxsen (apparently on Johannes's advice).[47] But Fritz lacked his brother's determination and dedication to work—and felt wronged by his success. He left Hamburg in 1867 for Caracas, Venezuela, returning in 1870 to Hamburg as a sought-after, highly paid piano teacher after Brahms had left. But he was known inevitably as *"der falsche Brahms"* ("the wrong Brahms").

The marriage of Brahms's parents had lost its intimacy by the 1860s, and they separated in 1864. The age difference had begun to tell: on Brahms's visit in 1863 he found his mother greatly aged but his father still youthful and vigorous. Brahms's mother died in 1865, and a year later his father remarried. His new wife was a widow, Karoline Schnack, who came from Neustadt in the Bay of Lübeck. She was eighteen years his junior and would long outlive him. This marriage was happy if brief, and Brahms always acknowledged his affection to his stepmother verbally and with financial support, which he also extended to the son of her first marriage, Fritz Schnack, a watchmaker from Pinneberg.[48]

Brahms's relations with his siblings were not close. Henschel recalls him saying in about 1876 that "with his sister he had little in common: their interests had always been too far apart. Between his brother, whom he had likewise supported, and himself, there existed no intercourse whatever."[49] Brahms was not close to his brother, who had refused to help him support their aging father. Although they were brought together at their father's deathbed in 1872, the reconciliation did not last. Brahms did have a relationship of sorts with Elise. She was clearly still an acknowledged part of his family when he moved to Vienna (for Hanslick wrote to her in 1864), and they maintained contact mainly through letters in which she showed some affection toward him.[50] But she could share little from her mundane world with her brother: her chief pleasure had been to make him good meals. Her marriage to a widower of sixty with six children when she was about forty at first displeased Brahms, who thought the responsibility too great, though the marriage was happy and Brahms contributed to the family's support. Although she was clearly attached to her brother, they met only rarely after their father died.

With his parents he was on much closer terms. Whatever he felt about the limited circumstances of his early life—and he was not always philosophical—he appears to have been a loving and loyal son. A sense of duty and respect for the home emerges from a recollection to Henschel: "Only once in my life have I played truant and shirked school, and that was the vilest day of my life. When I came home my father had already been informed of it, and I got a solid hiding." Brahms had affectionate memories of his father in later years, describing him as a "dear old man, very straightforward and most unsophisticated."[51] A letter written in 1865 concerning his father's intention to remarry confirms his warmth of feeling: "Dearest father, when I opened your letter and found three hand-written pages, I looked with some trepidation for the news that caused you to write that much. I was indeed greatly surprised that I had not suspected it before. Dearest father, a thousand blessings and the warmest wishes for your well-being also accompany you from here. How gladly would I sit at your side, press your hand, and wish you as much happiness as you deserve, which would be more than enough for one earthly lifetime. This step is nothing but a fine testimonial to yourself and tells us how much you have deserved the happiest of family lives."[52] Brahms took great pleasure in sharing with his father his own pleasures when he began to become independent in Vienna. In 1867 he invited him to visit:

> Come to Vienna. Don't think it over for too long; only
> consider that at your age traveling becomes more difficult
> and less enjoyable with every year, and that with every
> week this summer is getting hotter and hotter and Vi-
> enna less agreeable. . . . It goes without saying that this
> journey will cost you nothing, not even the loss of op-
> portunities in Hamburg. Of course, we will arrange every-
> thing for you so that this will not be too tiring for you.
> You must not and cannot refuse and you are not to
> think this over for too long. It would be best for you to
> start, if possible, this very night. . . . I beg you, dearest fa-
> ther, kiss mother good-bye at once and give her a kiss
> for me too. Off you go. You will enjoy yourself thor-
> oughly and you will give me the greatest pleasure. I am
> waiting impatiently for your word that you have left.[53]

Jacob came and the visit was a great success, the father even writing to Brahms to describe how he had impressed his friends by claiming to have climbed the Scharfberg in the Salzkammergut.[54] Brahms wrote to a close friend, "Through the visit of my father and the little trip we made together, I found the most delightful uplifting of spirit that has come to me for a long time. No small part of my joy was due to the pleasure my father had, especially from everything new he saw. . . . My dear father has no idea how much good he did me. I almost went back with him to Hamburg."[55] After his father died in 1872 Brahms wrote to his stepmother:

> My dear mother, many a time have I put out the paper
> in order to write to you. For I have truly thought of you
> most affectionately, and always further and further back
> into the past—but it could hardly be put into writing,

nor the words of consolation. And even now I can't attempt to console you. I know too well what we have lost, and how lonely your life has become. I hope, however, that now you are doubly conscious of the love of others . . . and finally mine, which is entirely and wholly yours. Here I have received so many marks of sympathy that you would have been happy to see how father was valued by all who knew him. . . . I am sending you 1,000 thalers. Of that you can give Elise her share. May I ask you to write when, and in good time, how much money I shall send? Simply the sum you need. . . . Now my most heartfelt greetings and as you assuredly know how I loved my father, so be sure that I shall always, and for all time, in truest and most grateful love be, Yours Johannes.[56]

He kept this relationship with his stepmother until his death.[57] Brahms's relationship with his mother is less well documented, and he later destroyed his letters to her, though hers to him emerged after his death.

Brahms's affection for his father clearly surmounted the fact that Johann Jacob could never really grasp his son's achievement as a composer. He is recorded as appearing overwhelmed by his son's success, and matter-of-fact over his triumph with the first performance of *A German Requiem,* his major choral work, in Bremen on 10 April 1868: just a curt acknowledgment—"quite good."[58] The fact that Brahms could not speak emotionally of his mother and the fact that he seems to have memorialized her in the work suggest that his feelings were too intense to express in words. Perhaps part of his grief was that his mother did not live to see his greatest achievements, of which the *Requiem* was one.[59] But she had suffered a great deal, had poor health, was small and plain, and had a bad limp; by her later years, according to one of Jacob Brahms's colleagues, she "had faded into a little withered mother who busied herself unobtrusively with her own affairs, and was not known outside her dwelling."[60] Just as he acclaimed his father's professional skills, Brahms proudly acknowledged his mother's great skill as a seamstress. He was clearly the center of her life, and she took great interest in his well-being, not least when he met Joachim. But the surviving letters are almost all of practicalities.[61]

Education

From the age of six Brahms attended an elementary school run by H. V. Voss, by the Dammthorwall near his home, and from 1842–48 a progressive *Bürgerschule* operated by J. F. Hoffmann in the A B C Strasse. By the age of fifteen he had gained a basic education, which included some French: when he was thirteen he was able to send his parents a Christmas greeting in the language.[62] It seems likely that his education helped him most by providing contact with literature and the Bible.[63] At age fifteen he was confirmed in the Lutheran faith.[64] As a working musician's son, Brahms was destined to receive a practical musical education. He learned to play piano, horn, violin, and cello. For a young musician of the lower economic class, regular professional performance at local dances, receptions, and restaurants would have been normal.[65] Most of his income appears to have come from teaching piano. As he recalled later, "See, now I have given lessons ever since I was twelve years old, and you will certainly believe me when I say that such a young lad was hardly likely to have pupils entrusted to him who could give him any particular pleasure. And yet I stood it all well enough; indeed, I would not on any account have missed this period of hardship in my life, for it did me good and was necessary to my development."[66] Piano teaching assumed a more pleasant aspect when his father arranged for the fourteen-year-old Brahms to teach the daughter of a musical contact at Winsen an der Luhe, a few miles outside Hamburg.

It seems likely that Brahms's first study of the piano was something of a concession by his father, because he could probably have commanded a better living with an orchestral instrument. He must have impressed his father at an early stage, wherever it was that he had access to a piano.[67] In 1841 he began lessons with Otto Cossel, who devoted himself to Brahms's training from the first.[68] On 1 January 1842, Brahms wrote a letter to his "beloved master" pledging his commitment to his lessons.[69] Cossel's only reservation concerned Brahms's desire to compose and arrange, which he felt took time from his playing. The pianistic fare was limited, largely to the studies of Czerny, Clementi, Cramer, and Hummel. At the age of ten Brahms played a concert that included a piece by Henri Herz. An agent attended this concert and wanted to take Brahms on a tour of the United States. Although his parents seem to have been attracted by the offer, Cossel resisted it. For this Brahms was appreciative all his life. In 1843, Cossel sent Brahms to his own teacher, the leading Hamburg teacher Eduard Marxsen, who later recalled:

> In the year 1843, my pupil Cossel—an outstanding
> teacher of technique, and as such greatly loved and es-
> teemed—brought me the ten-year-old boy, who was at
> that time attending the ordinary popular school, which
> he continued to do up to the time of his early confirma-
> tion, so that I might test whether he really possessed mu-
> sical aptitude. He played me a few studies from Cramer's
> first volume thoroughly well. Cossel praised his diligence
> and wanted me to give him lessons if I saw ability in
> him. At first I refused, for the instruction he had hith-
> erto received was most competent and would be suffi-
> cient for some time to come. A few months later the
> boy's father came to repeat the request in his own and
> Cossel's name; whereon I consented so far as to devote
> an hour a week to the boy, on condition that he was to
> continue his lessons with Cossel as usual. And so things
> contrived; but less than a year later, Cossel pressed me to
> undertake the boy's entire instruction from that time on-
> ward, for he was making such progress that Cossel could
> not trust himself to criticize him in any way. His pro-
> gress was indeed remarkable, but not such as to give evi-
> dence of exceptional talent, only the results of great
> industry and unremitting zeal. Accordingly, from that
> time onward I undertook his whole instruction, and that
> gladly, for two reasons: on the one hand because I had
> already taken a liking to the boy, and on the other out
> of consideration for his parents, who were unable to
> make any sacrifices to continue his education. His studies
> in the practical side of playing made excellent progress,
> and his talent became more and more evident.[70]

Marxsen had much evidence of Brahms's musical skill, such as his performance of Weber's E flat Rondo. Marxsen had assigned him to learn
the piece, and after Brahms played it faultlessly he said, "I have also

practiced it in another way . . . and played me the right-hand part with the left hand."[71] Brahms's first public concert took place on 21 September 1848, when he was fourteen, with the assistance of Marxsen's friends Madame and Fraulein Cornet; his contribution included movements by Rosenhain, Döhler, and Marxsen himself, an etude by Herz, and, conspicuously, a "fugue by Sebastian Bach," surely reflecting Brahms's personal taste. By the spring of 1849, Brahms was ready to give another concert. It was held on 10 April, and the program began boldly with Beethoven's *Waldstein* Sonata and included Thalberg's Fantasia on Themes of *Don Juan* as well as Brahms's own Fantasia on a Favourite Waltz.[72] But though the concert was successful, the time was not ripe for a young musician to make headway: the Revolutions of 1848 had drawn many foreign musicians to the city. Brahms was left to continue his professional routine and live his creative life internally: teaching, accompanying, making arrangements of popular pieces for piano. But he did not expose himself as a player in public. Marxsen wrote, "During the last few years before he left Hamburg he did not appear in public, for this time seemed to me too precious, as interludes of this kind often upset study very considerably. At any rate, the press always spoke of these first attempts with great appreciation."[73] It was a rare period of absorption for Brahms, who took in what the city had to offer; which included the concerts of the Philharmonic orchestra and the Singakademie conducted by F. W. Grund; Carl Voigt directing the Cäcilienverein; and G. D. Otten conducting an annual series of subscription concerts.[74]

This anonymous existence was given new stimulus in 1848, when the leading violinist Joseph Joachim visited Hamburg: though only two years older than Brahms, he was already an international figure. This event was of great importance for Brahms, who later spoke to Joachim of the "very chaos of emotion" he experienced through music and its performance. From this moment Brahms was vulnerable to such influence of other musicians and ready for change and opportunity when it came. As it happened, change came through a youthful acquaintance of Joachim's, the Hungarian violinist Eduard Reményi. An ensuing partnership took Brahms and Reményi on a recital tour of the Hamburg region in the spring of 1853. For Brahms's parents, the partnership seemed to be the beginning of a proper career for Brahms, for Reményi was a distinguished player who had come to the city as a political exile in 1848. Their view of the tour emerges clearly from the reply of Brahms's mother on 11 June to his letter home:

> Your letter surprised and moved us so much that we
> could hardly read it, and when we came to the end we
> said: happy Johannes, and we his happy parents. Surely,
> yes, this exquisite feeling, not for all the treasures of
> earth would we miss it. Now Johannes dear, your life re-
> ally begins, now you will reap what you have sown with
> toil and diligence here. Your great hour has come. You
> must thank Divine Providence which sent an angel to
> lead you out of the darkness into the world where there
> are human beings who appreciate your worth and the
> value of what you have learned. How much we should
> love to be with you a few hours, to see your happy face,
> and tell each other how happy we are. Alas it is impossi-
> ble. We will pray to God for your health, which, how-
> ever, you must not overtax, and you must not stay up
> too late at night.[75]

Although the partnership did not outlast the tour, it brought Brahms into direct contact with Joachim at Hanover that June. When Brahms and Reményi split up after playing to Franz Liszt at Weimar, it was to Joachim that Brahms turned, and Joachim invited him to stay at his lodgings at Göttingen.[76] The termination of the tour and the stay with Joachim worried Brahms's parents. They were so concerned that they offered Brahms his brother Fritz's savings, which he refused, eliciting this response from his mother: "You have not written plainly enough about your circumstances. For example, [you say that] you need no money. Even if you have free lodging, food and drink, you must have clean linen, your boots wear out, and, after all, how can you live away from home without money? If you have to get every little thing from Joachim you will be under too great an obligation to that gentleman. You had better write to Herr Marxsen. He can advise you in everything. But you must write the exact truth, otherwise the same thing will happen as with Reményi. You understand people too little and trust them too much."[77] Their anxiety eased when Joachim himself allayed their fears.[78] Only then, and when

Brahms met the Schumanns, did they perhaps begin to comprehend the measure of eminence that lay ahead for their son.[79]

3 · The Critical Stages of Brahms's Life and Ambitions

Had circumstances been different, Brahms probably would have stayed in Hamburg and pursued a career as a teacher and performer. He was building contacts in the city in order to establish a senior position in its musical life. But his relationship with Reményi set off a series of events that rapidly shifted Brahms's attention elsewhere. The concert tour took them through towns close to Hamburg: Winsen, Luneburg, and Celle. By the end of May they had arrived at the court of Hanover, where Joachim was kapellmeister. It was not the flamboyant Reményi who impressed Joachim, however, but the young pianist:

> The dissimilar companions—the tender idealistic Johannes and the self-satisfied, fantastic virtuoso—called on me. Never in the course of my artist's life have I been more completely overwhelmed with delighted surprise than when the rather shy-mannered, blond companion of my countryman played me his sonata movements of quite undreamed-of originality and power, looking noble and inspired the while. His song "O versenk dein Leid" sounded to me like a revelation, and his playing, so tender, so imaginative, so free and so fiery, held me spellbound. No wonder that I not only foresaw but actually foretold a speedy end to the concert journey with Reményi. Brahms parted from him soon afterward, and, encouraged before long by an enthusiastic recognition, marched proudly onward in his own path of endeavor after the highest development.[80]

Reményi's presence at Hanover had attracted the attention of the police, and the partners had to flee so that Reményi could remain free. They headed for Weimar, where Liszt was responsible for the music of the court: Brahms carried Joachim's introduction, for he was still a close friend of the composer.[81] Brahms's indifference to Liszt affected more than his relationship with the composer: Reményi was furious because Brahms's coolness undermined his own interest in meeting Liszt, a fellow Hungarian. Reményi then disassociated himself from Brahms and left. Brahms recalled Reményi's reaction in a letter to Joachim (he spoke through his artistic persona, Johannes Kreisler, Jr., derived from the writings of E. T. A. Hoffmann): "If I were not named Kreisler, I should now have well-founded reasons to be somewhat dispirited, to curse my love of art and my enthusiasm and to retire as a hermit . . . into solitude. . . . Reményi is leaving Weimar without me. It is *his* wish, for my manner could not have given him the slightest pretext for doing so. . . . I really did not need such another bitter experience: in this respect I had already quite enough material for a poet and composer. . . . May I pressingly ask, dearest Herr Joachim, to fulfill if possible the hope you gave me in Göttingen, of establishing me in the life of an artist."[82]

Brahms spent several months in Göttingen, an entirely new environment, getting to know his new friend and sharing for the first time the world of a fellow spirit. Although he extended his visit, he could not stay at Göttingen indefinitely. The whole point of the tour had been to make contacts. With some money made through a recital with Joachim, he set off in August to explore the west, including a long-anticipated walking tour through the Rhine, eventually taking Joachim's suggestion and going to Bonn. Here he introduced himself to the conductor, Joseph von Wasielewski. "Toward the end of the summer I was delighted by a visit from an attractive-looking, fair-haired youth, who delivered me one of Joachim's visiting cards, on the reverse side of which was his own humorously written signature. It was Johannes Brahms. Coming from the direction of Mainz, he had traveled the Rhine Valley on foot, and presented himself staff in hand and knapsack on back. His fresh, natural, unconstrained manner impressed me sympathetically, so that I not only bade him a friendly welcome but invited him to stay a day or two with me, to which he then consented."[83]

Wasielewski was impressed with Brahms's playing and compositions, and he quickly introduced Brahms to the music-loving Deichmann family at Mehlem, where he met such eminent musicians as Ferdinand Hiller,

Karl Reinecke, and the young Franz Wüllner.[84] But the greatest significance of the visit for Brahms was becoming acquainted with the music of Schumann. Brahms had imagined that the Schumanns would rebuff him: a parcel of compositions that he had sent to Schumann on his visit to Hamburg in 1850 had been returned unopened.[85] Now he followed Joachim's advice and visited Schumann at Düsseldorf, where he had been music director since 1850. Brahms arrived on 30 September and was immediately welcomed. On October 1, Schumann noted in his diary "visit from Brahms—a genius,"[86] and he expressed his feelings for Brahms's art soon after in "New Paths" in the *Neue Zeitschrift für Musik*.[87] In their studio, Schumann and his wife listened "enthralled" to Brahms's work.[88] Brahms never forgot their supportiveness, and after Schumann died he wrote, "To me Schumann's memory is holy. The noble pure artist forever remains a model and ideal. I will hardly be privileged to love a better person."[89]

Aside from providing an artistic impact on Brahms, the Schumanns helped fulfill his desire for tangible professional achievement, and Schumann recommended his publications to Breitkopf & Härtel, the major publisher in Leipzig. Brahms joined a new circle of young musicians that gathered around the Schumanns. The most important of his new acquaintances was Schumann's composition pupil Albert Dietrich:

> Soon after [Brahms's] arrival in September [1853], Schumann came up to me before the commencement of one of the choral society rehearsals with a mysterious air and pleased smile. "Someone is here," he said, "of whom we shall one day hear all sorts of wonderful things; his name is Johannes Brahms." And he presented to me the interesting and unusual-looking musician, who, seemingly hardly more than a boy in his short gray summer coat, with his high voice and long fair hair, made a most striking impression. Especially fine were his energetic, characteristic mouth and the earnest deep gaze in which his gifted nature was clearly revealed.[90]

Brahms quickly formed a friendship with Dietrich (one that would last a lifetime), and he shared his new experiences with Joachim:

You will have received a letter from the Schumanns telling you of my being here. I need not, I think, tell you at length how inexpressibly happy their reception, kind beyond expectation, has made me. Their praise made me so happy and strong that I can hardly wait for the time when at last I can settle down to undisturbed working and composing. . . . What should I tell you about Schumann; should I burst into praises of his genius and character, or should I lament that people still so badly misjudge a good man and a divine artist so freely and respect him so little. . . . And myself, for how long did I commit this sin? It is only since I left Hamburg, and especially during my stay at Mehlem, that I got to know and admire Schumann's works. I should like to ask a pardon from him.[91]

At Christmas Brahms wrote to Schumann with his compositions: "I take the liberty of sending you your first foster-children (which are indebted to you for their world citizenship) very much concerned with whether they may still enjoy from you the same indulgence and affection. To me they look in their new form much too precise and timid, almost philistine indeed. I cannot accustom myself to seeing the innocent sons of nature in such decorous clothing. . . . I am looking forward immensely to seeing you in Hanover and being able to tell you that my parents and I owe the most blissful time of our lives to you and Joachim's too great affection."[92]

After visiting his parents at Christmas to show them his new compositions, Brahms returned to Hanover at the beginning of 1854 with Joachim. In Hanover he met Joachim's friend Hans von Bülow, who responded warmly to Brahms's music and personality.[93] But Brahms's new professional self-confidence was checked by Schumann's attempted suicide on 27 February. Brahms spent the two years in complete if psychologically confused devotion to Clara and her family. When Schumann finally died, at Endenich, Bonn, on 29 July 1856, Brahms faced a future that was in many ways unclear. Writing from Heidelberg to Julius Otto Grimm, a friend he met in 1853 in Leipzig, he describes Schumann's death:

I shall surely never again experience anything as moving as the reunion of Robert and Clara. He lay first for some time with closed eyes, and she knelt before him with greater calmness than one would think possible. But later on he recognized her, and he did again the next day. Once he clearly wished to embrace her and flung one arm around her. Of course, he was past being able to talk any more, one could only make out single words, perhaps only in imagination. But even that must have made her happy. He often refused the wine offered to him, but he sucked it from her finger sometimes so eagerly and long, and with such fervor that one knew for certain that he recognized [her]."

Brahms had to leave the Schumanns to meet Joachim, who was traveling from Heidelburg, and they arrived half an hour after Schumann's death. Brahms continues: "He looked calm in death. . . . What a blessing this was! . . . I wish I could write you just what I feel but this is impossible, and if only I set down the crude facts, you can imagine for yourself how sad, how beautiful, how deeply touching this death was. We (Joachim, Clara and I) have put in order the papers Schumann left behind. . . . With every day one thus spends with him one gets to love and admire the man more and more. I shall again and again plunge into them. . . . Next time [I'll write] more, and more calmly. . . . Frau Clara is as well as can be expected, though not as one could wish.[94]

Professional Ambitions: Hamburg and Detmold

The stark professional realities that confronted Clara after Schumann's death also confronted Brahms. She needed money to support her family and could earn it best by touring. He likewise had to earn an independent living, so after three years in the Schumann circle he began his adult life in earnest. His new friends had contacts far beyond those in Hamburg: Joachim in Hanover, Grimm in Göttingen, and Dietrich in Bonn. Through Clara's recommendation a modest position became available at the court of Lippe-Detmold, near Hanover. From 1857–59, Brahms spent October, November, and December teaching piano to the Princess Frederike and her ladies in waiting, giving recitals, conducting a choir, and conducting the court orchestra (but only when a choral work was involved, so as not to offend the aging conductor, Clemens August Kiel, though this restriction contributed to Brahms's resignation).[95] The income was modest, and Brahms continued to teach piano in Hamburg the rest of the year. But the experience was valuable, and Brahms, whose mornings were free of formal responsibilities, was able to use the court's and the town's facilities for study, to gradually engage in chamber music performance, and to make firm friendships with contemporaries. His compositions from the time reflect these influences. He described his professional situation at court to Joachim:

> The recreations of their excellencies leave me no time to think of myself. So I am glad that they occupy me thoroughly and that I can derive advantages from a great deal that I have so far missed. What a small amount of practical knowledge I have! The choral rehearsals have shown me many weak spots: they won't be a waste of time for me. My things are written far too impractically. I have rehearsed various items with them and fortunately from the outset with sufficient boldness. . . . Bargheer [the leader of the orchestra] is, as you may imagine, most pleasant to me here. Otherwise there is a complete lack of musical friends, except for a few ladies. I don't want to tell you at length about the pleasant and unpleasant experiences I have had here. I even refrain from talking to myself about them: it's better so. But I live most comfortably (in the room where you stayed), and I hit it off with Kiel somewhat better than not at all. . . . How is life in Hanover? It's really just as if I had emigrated, as though I had already become rusty as a Detmold conductor. Don't let us leave such long gaps between our letters. It pains me.[96]

When he finally returned to Hamburg, he felt out of place:

> Dearest Joseph,
>   I was most delighted to see your handwriting, unluckily now so rare. I can only reply by letter. Frau Musica is

really ungracious to me. I can't send you a friendly greeting from her. . . . I have to openly complain that I make a living here just as in a kitchen . . . and that I can no longer enjoy a walk, or even take one, as I used to when a boy, since I have grown unaccustomed to the big city. You can imagine that it would create difficulties, on account of my parents, if I were to live here by myself. So I shall have to leave merely out of delicacy, and yet I should really like to make my home here. I am a regular son of Hamburg. . . . I have often made big plans to entice you to Hamburg. . . . There are some lovely rooms here outside the gates, so beautiful that I often look longingly at them. . . . However, I am content to let things take their course from day to day (only not as concerns your arrival). I am also busy teaching; one girl always plays better than the other, and some play still worse.[97]

A senior professional position in Hamburg remained his goal. Finally, such a position became a real prospect. Friedrich Wilhelm Grund, the aging conductor of the Philharmonic Concerts, was to retire, and Brahms spoke with influential Hamburg friends about the possibility of succeeding him. But the job was offered to Julius Stockhausen.[98] Brahms's response shows how much the position would have meant to him, and it reveals the broader problems of working as a creative musician—problems that Schumann also had experienced. He wrote to Clara from Vienna on 18 November 1862:

For me this was a much sadder event than you could possibly imagine, perhaps even sadder than you can understand. I am a rather old-fashioned character, not at all cosmopolitan, and am attached to my native city as to a mother. . . . Now along comes this enemy of a friend— and probably for good—pushes me aside. How rare it is for one of our kind to find a permanent position! How happy I would have been to find one in my native city! Now even here, though there is so much beauty . . . to enjoy, I still feel very keenly and always will that I am a stranger and cannot find repose. If I can't find hope here, where shall I? Where may I and can I? You experienced it with your husband and know full well that they would prefer to let us go altogether, to have us fly around in empty space. And yet one craves to belong to and to earn that which makes life really worth living: one dreads loneliness. Working in close harmony with others—the happiness of family life—who is so inhuman as to not have a longing for all this?[99]

Life in Vienna

Brahms never fully recovered from what he regarded as rejection by his native city. Though he had already decided to spend time in Vienna, traveling there in September 1862, his desire for advancement remained focused on North Germany. It would be the end of the decade before he regarded Vienna as home. In 1862, however, Vienna was somewhat known to him through contacts. They included one of the members of his Hamburg Frauenchor (Hamburg Ladies' Choir), Bertha Porubszky, who was a Viennese and had just moved back to the city.[100] After his move he made many friends and found the city increasingly conducive to work. He wrote to Grimm at about the same time he wrote to Clara: "Well, this is it. I have established myself here within ten paces of the Prater and can drink my wine where Beethoven drank his. Since I can't have it any better, I find things quite cheerful and attractive. Of course, hiking through the Black Forest with one's wife is not only more cheerful but also more beautiful."[101] He wrote his parents about his first Vienna concert, arranged through friends associated with the Vienna Conservatoire: "I had much joy yesterday. My concert came off very well. The Quartet [the Piano Quartet in A] was well received, and I had extraordinary success as a pianist. Each number won rich applause. I sensed much enthusiasm in the audience. . . . I played as unconcernedly as though I were at home among my friends. The public here is much more responsive than ours at home. You should see their attention and hear their applause! I am very glad I gave the concert."[102] In March he reflected on his first few months in Vienna to Adolf Schubring, a leading supporter of his music.

I have spent the whole winter here, very much at a loose end but rather enjoyably and cheerfully. I regret above all things that I didn't know Vienna before. The gaiety of the town, the beauty of the surroundings, the sympathetic and vivacious public, how stimulating all these are to the artist! In addition we have in particular the sacred memory of the great musicians of whose lives and work we are daily reminded. In the case of Schubert especially, one has the impression of his still being alive. Again and again one meets people who talk of him as of a good friend; again and again one comes across new works, the existence of which was unknown and which are so untouched that one can scrape the very writing-sand off them. . . . I am suffering in a somewhat old-fashioned way from homesickness and so, when the spring is at its best, I shall probably leave and visit my old mother.[103]

Brahms still needed a permanent position. After visiting his family in Hamburg in May 1863 (a visit that revealed to him growing domestic tensions) and working on a new composition in the suburb of Blankenesee, he was invited to conduct the Vienna Singakademie, a recently founded and prominent choral society. After some indecision he accepted the invitation. The first concert took place on 15 November 1863. He stayed for only one season, 1863–64. Despite Brahms's characteristic resistance, Clara was realistic about the importance of the position: "Before you dampen my ardor almost immediately by saying that you don't think you will keep the post, I can't think why you think Dietrich's or Stockhausen's positions enviable. . . . In view of the small appreciation he gets in Hamburg, Stockhausen's position is on the whole not enviable, for the public there is not nearly ripe for good orchestral performances. . . . Once more I can plainly see what a difficult position you would have had there as a native of Hamburg, and as so young a man. Your wings would soon have drooped with irritation. How different things must be in Vienna."[104] In fact, the Singakademie experience was salutary. Brahms had done well but was not quite at ease with the responsibilities. Yet he continued to hanker after such positions as Dietrich's and Stockhausen's, and his friends kept him informed of possible openings. He considered positions in Dessau and later in Cologne and Düsseldorf. He wrote again to Schubring in 1865:

> I had almost forgotten to write to you about Kapellmeister position. It now looks as though I may get rid of involuntary life as a vagabond. Dessau is not the only city that gives me a bit of a nod. Going by the map, the locality doesn't please me too much, and the neighborhood, of which you boast, is not at all to my liking. What else is to be said about it? Should one be addressed as Conductor No. 2? Does one have to accept for life? Does one get decent things to bite? Isn't it possible that your theater is as unbearable as your concerts certainly are not? Yet I am by no means uninterested in such proposals and should be grateful if you would write me more about them.[105]

His interest was natural for a German musician. Most of the leading figures of the period had worked as court or theater music directors at some point. In 1869, Hiller invited Brahms to direct the Cologne Conservatory,[106] and even in 1876, having completed his work at the Gesellschaft der Musikfreunde, Brahms expressed interest in a position at Düsseldorf to Theodor Billroth:

> You will have heard from Faber that I have received a call to Düsseldorf. I have wished so long and so earnestly for such a position, and regulated activity, that I now must give it serious attention. I am reluctant to leave Vienna, and I have a great many objections to Düsseldorf. . . . [Because of this] I have made up my mind to come out with a symphony. I thought I'd have to produce something decent as a farewell to the Viennese. I dislike writing far too much, otherwise I would now go into detail about how the manner and the form of the invitation to Düsseldorf pleased me very much. . . . My principal reasons for not going are of a rather childish nature and

must remain secret. Perhaps the good eating places in Vienna, [perhaps] the poor, uncouth manners of the Rhinelanders (especially those of Düsseldorf)—and in Vienna one can remain a bachelor without difficulty; in a small city an older bachelor is a caricature. I no longer wish to marry, yet I do have some cause to fear the fair sex.[107]

Retirement

Brahms expressed his plan to retire from composition in December 1890, when he wrote to his publisher, Simrock, that the op. III quintet that he was sending would be his last work: "With this slip, bid farewell to notes of mine."[108] He had reached a reflective stage and often commented about leaving tasks to younger people. Perhaps the offer of the directorship of the Hamburg Philharmonic Concerts in 1893, when he was sixty, had seemed symbolic to him. In his reply to Senator Scheumann he showed his long-held reserve toward the city: "There is but little I have desired so long and so ardently in its time—that is, at the right time! It has taken a long time before I got used to the idea of having to go along other paths. If things had gone according to my wishes I would perhaps be celebrating an anniversary with you today. But in that case you would still have to look around for a younger capable talent. May you find him soon and may he serve you with as much good will, passable competence, and complete devotion as I would have. Your very respectful J. Brahms."[109]

But the course of events was interrupted. After hearing the principal clarinetist of the Meiningen orchestra, Richard Mühlfeld, in the later 1880s, his outlook changed, and he produced four final chamber works (the Clarinet Quintet, Clarinet Trio, and two clarinet sonatas). But he did not change his general pattern of tidying up and slowing down. His lifelong interest in folksongs climaxed with the publication of his *49 Deutsche Volkslieder* for solo voice, chorus, and piano. He could not resist pointing out that one of them, "Verstohlen geht der Mond auf," was also used in his first published opus, the Sonata in C. "Did you notice that the very last of these songs also occurs in op. 1? Did it mean anything to you? It should really say something; it should represent the snake that bites its own tail; thus it says symbolically: the story is now finished, the circle closed."[110] He wrote in almost exactly the same terms to Simrock, more explicitly saying, "[Do you know that] I have now expressly said farewell as a composer?!"[111]

In October 1895 his *Song of Triumph* was given in the same program as Beethoven's Ninth Symphony at the opening concert of the newly constructed Tonhalle in Zürich, where he had many friends. His own portrait looked down from the ceiling with other masters he so revered.[112]

4 · Professional Outlook and Relationships

Brahms's upbringing gave him a professional outlook from the first: he had to live by his earnings. Whether working as an entertainment pianist, a recitalist, a teacher, or a composer, he knew how to evaluate his own worth and demand recompense. Thus his humorous request for a higher fee from his publisher Fritz Simrock for the lengthy variation movement of the op. 87 Trio: "[because] in the trio are variations, and the public has come to expect them."[113] Brahms's relentless criticism of his compositions and his need to prove a work ready—he never worked to commission—led him to continue teaching, concert playing, and touring well into middle age. It was years before Brahms could survive just from the money he made composing. Thus there existed a tension between the young composer's own artistic desires and his family ethos, most obvious when he had compositions ready for performance. Gaining publication was a matter of family obligation for the twenty-year-old Brahms, who had to prove his worth as a professional before that as an artist. Thus he wrote to Joachim in June 1853, "I cannot return to Hamburg without anything to show, although there I should feel happiest with my heart tuned from C–G sharp. I must see two or three of my compositions in print so I can cheerfully look my parents in the face."[114]

His first works were published through Schumann, who wrote directly to Breitkopf & Härtel in Leipzig after his first meeting with Brahms. He recommended the works he thought most worthy of publication: the two Sonatas in C Major and F sharp Minor, and a group of songs and the Scherzo in E flat Minor, which became opp. 1–4 by December 1853.[115] The company published the works, and Brahms went to Leipzig to collect his fee. Breitkopf & Härtel also took opp. 7–10, which Brahms sent them on his own. He also had approached Senff, which took opp. 5 and 6. Rieter Biedermann in Winterthur took opp. 11–15; the first work taken by Simrock was the Serenade, op. 16.; Simrock also took the works to op. 21 and the instrumental works opp. 25, 26, 36, 38, and 40. By op. 46 Simrock was virtually Brahms's sole publisher.[116] But Brahms resisted pressure to overcompose for the eager publisher, which was steadily building its business on the immense popularity of Brahms's works in dance form for popular media: the waltzes, Hungarian dances for piano duet, and *Liebeslieder* for piano duet and vocal quartet. His letter to Simrock in 1870 reveals the tension between the craftsman-composer and the romantic artist:

> Leave off driving your composers. It might prove to be
> as dangerous as it is generally unnecessary. After all, com-
> posing cannot be turned out like spinning or sewing.
> Some respected colleagues (Bach, Mozart, Schubert) have
> spoilt the world terribly. But if we can't imitate them in
> the beauty of their writing, we should certainly beware of
> seeking to match the speed of their writing. It would
> also be unjust to put all the blame on idleness alone.
> Many factors combine to make writing harder for us (my
> contemporaries), and especially for me. If, incidentally,
> they would use us poets for some other purpose, they
> would see that we are of thoroughly and naturally indus-
> trious dispositions. . . . I have no time: otherwise I should
> love to have a chat on the difficulty of composing and
> how irresponsible publishers are.[117]

A year earlier he had complained about Simrock's request for a sequel to the *Wiegenlied*. "As regards the trifle you asked for, I have by degrees supplied enough examples of this item and would rather participate in another capacity in this matter, which, after all, can be considered from other standpoints. I am afraid that this is a terribly pensive sigh. But I really should have to find some amusing words to set if I am once more to help rock other people's children to sleep."[118] Simrock also asked in 1888 to purchase Brahms's early works, originally published by Breitkopf & Härtel. Brahms commented ironically:

I am touched by your kindness, but I find it exceedingly improvident that you buy things from Härtel—I can't think at what expense—which may have cost them about 100 Louisdors and which in a very short time won't be worth a thing. . . . In order to show you my sympathy, or rather my compassion for your kindness, I should like to propose right now, seriously and truly, that henceforth I receive no further payment from you, but instead . . . that a credit account be opened up against which I can draw in case of need, and which will simply expire at the time of my death. You know my circumstances (better than I do) and are therefore aware of the fact that I can get along perfectly without the need of further honorarium. And that I will, according to the un-Wagnerian nature of my requirements.[119]

In spite of Brahms's desire for just reward—he often asked for high fees—he had no real interest in money. He had become secure by the 1870s, and he left it to Simrock to handle his affairs. When his trusted Simrock lost 20,000 of his marks in investment, Brahms took it lightly. His response reveals his values in other ways too: "Do not make an unnecessary fuss over this famous bankruptcy above all—if you were [going to replace] the loss to me—ridiculous. . . . Of course I haven't bothered a moment about the matter—except when I wrote you. Only one thing would have made me angry: if it had been my fault, if it had been my wish to buy those shares. . . . I should be ashamed and very vexed if I had wanted to earn money that way. But if a good friend makes a mistake, I am sorrier for him than for myself—no, sorry for him only, because I think only of money while I am talking about it."[120]

Notable Professional Relationships

In spite of his many friendships with people in other fields, Brahms restricted his creative relations largely to music. He held his professional positions only briefly (at Detmold, 1857–59, the Vienna Singakademie, 1863–64, and Gesellschaft der Musikfreunde, 1872–75) and seems to have had no sustained desire to involve himself in administration. But certain individuals played a vital role in relation to his composing, advising him and supporting and promoting his work. Among those who advised him were Clara Schumann, Joseph Joachim, and, later, Hans von Bülow.

Brahms's respect for Clara Schumann was enormous, and her advice was critical for Brahms, especially in the early years. He even once counseled a friend by saying, "When you write something, ask yourself what a woman like Clara Schumann would think, and if doubtful, strike it out."[121] She was an early performer of his music and the senior artistic figure in his world. After Robert Schumann's death Brahms looked to Clara for advice on the new professional world into which he was moving, and she knew about all his new works. He solicited her response to some new songs: "Please write me whether you like anything in them or whether one or another arouses your dislike. Especially if the latter is the case, perhaps I'll hearken and thank you. But don't judge things harshly at first reading; do read a poem twice if you don't like it first time, for example "Das Mädchenfluch," which perhaps might frighten you. Forgive me, I am just afraid of being scolded."[122] But he by no means regarded her as the only judge. In fact, Clara Schumann found aspects of Brahms's music uncongenial, but he was always tactful if he did not agree with her view. Her real compositional model was Mendelssohn, and her own works show his influence.

Although Brahms first knew Joachim as a player, it was his skill as a composer that the young Brahms admired most. Although Joachim was not a major figure, his spiritual, earnest character was a major stimulus to the young composer looking for an ally. He writes of a performance of one of Joachim's overtures: "What you write about the [bad] reception of your overture [in Leipzig] was quite unexpected by me. I had dreamed of immense acclaim, encores, and travels [of the overture] through the whole of Germany in the shortest possible time. One should not venture to experience more sublime and more pure emotions than the public. You can see from my case that if one dreams merely the same dreams and puts them into music, one gets some applause. The eagle soars upwards in loneliness, but rooks flock together: may God grant that my wings grow strongly and that I belong one day to the other kind."[123] And within a year later: "What can I write or later say about your splendid *Variations* [op. 10]? What else than that they are just what I expected and as your overtures promised? Your works affect me just as Beethoven's do. When I got to know a new symphony or overture, it absorbed me completely for a long time. Everything else just formed arabesques round the beautifully great picture."[124] Brahms's admiration was partly based on his perception of Joachim's greater technical experience, and he turned to him in the early years for precise guidance in orchestral composition; even as late as the late 1870s he sought his advice on the solo part of the Violin Concerto.[125]

The third great artistic relationship of Brahms's life, with Hans von Bülow, did not come about until Brahms had become an established master. In Brahms's youth Bülow had belonged to the world of Wagner and Liszt, and it was not until the late 1870s that they really grew closer. It was the November 1877 performance of the First Symphony in Hanover that made the difference: Bülow proclaimed the work "Beethoven's Tenth," thereby designating Brahms, as had Hanslick, the successor of Beethoven.[126] When Bülow was appointed musical director to the ducal court of Meiningen in 1880, he transformed the orchestra into one of world renown and offered Brahms the opportunity to rehearse his new works. The Meiningen orchestra became the greatest instrument of the propagation of the Brahms symphonies in Germany. Bülow wrote to his fiancée: "You know how much I think of Brahms; after Bach and Beethoven he is the greatest, the most exalted of all composers. I consider his friendship my most priceless possession, second only to your love. It marks an epoch in my life; it is like a moral conquest. I believe that not a musical heart in the world, not even that of his dearest friend Joachim, experiences so deeply, has immersed itself so far in the depths of his soul as mine."[127]

Under both Bülow and his successor, Fritz Steinbach, Brahms's larger instrumental works were presented regularly in Meiningen. On 3 February 1884 the Third Symphony was performed twice in the same concert (an idea of Bülow's), and on 25 October 1885 the Fourth Symphony started its career at Meiningen being conducted by Brahms and then Bülow. Although Brahms made the most of every opportunity to conduct, he always regarded Bülow as the master.[128]

Through the years Brahms worked with many conductors in the course of promoting his orchestral and choral work. He conducted his own early choral works himself, at Detmold and Hamburg. Though he premiered his own choral and piano music as soloist and chamber player, he entrusted his first orchestral works—the First Piano Concerto and the Serenades—to Joachim. In Vienna, Brahms made new contacts for performances of his Serenades. First among these was Otto Dessoff, the young director of the court opera house and the Philharmonic Concerts given by the opera orchestra, who premiered the A Major Serenade in Vienna.[129] On the basis of this contact Brahms entrusted the first performance of the First Symphony to Dessoff, who had become court music director at Karlsruhe in November 1876. "It was always my cherished and secret wish," Brahms said, "to hear the thing first in a small town that possessed a good conductor, a good friend, and a good orchestra."[130] Brahms and Dessoff remained firm friends, and after Dessoff's sudden death in 1892, Brahms commented to Clara that "he was an excellent man and as a musician exceptionally sensitive and scholarly."[131]

At about the same time as he met Dessoff, in 1864, Brahms also met Hermann Levi. Levi was the director of the opera house in Karlsruhe and had long known Brahms's music. After Brahms had spent some time in Karlsruhe at the music festival, Levi wrote to Clara Schumann that "the close contact with Johannes has had, I believe, a deep and lasting influence on my whole character such as I cannot remember having experienced at any other period of my musical life. In him I have seen the image of a pure artist and man, and that is saying much nowadays."[132] And in 1866: "He alone knows how to free himself of all earthly entanglements, to remain uncontaminated by the grime and misery of life, and soar to ideal heights where we can only gaze after but not follow him."[133] For his part, Brahms wrote to Joachim of the festival that "the whole affair . . . was made bearable by the company of Hermann Levi, the musical director there. This young man, despite all his theatrical upbringing, is so lively and looks up with such bright eyes to the greatest heights, that everything done [with him] is a pure joy."[134] Levi directed the D Minor Concerto in Mannheim in 1865, the first performance at which the composition received its due. He also gave fine performances of *A German Requiem* at Karlsruhe, and Brahms entrusted him with other performances as well.[135] But their relationship faltered, chiefly because of Levi's growing enthusiasm for Wagner, which Brahms could not understand in the deeper sense. He took it as a betrayal, despite Levi's protests. Bülow had deserted the Wagnerian world but Levi was drawn to it, giving the first performance of *Parsifal,* in 1882. Thus Brahms lost a conductor, and his place in Brahms's esteem was taken eventually by Bülow. But in the meantime, another rising young conductor appeared: Hans Richter, who successfully participated in both worlds. Richter, who had given the first complete performance of *The Ring of the Niebelung* in 1876, now commanded attention as an exponent of Brahms's music. He gave the first performance of the Second Symphony in December 1877 and of the Third in December 1883.[136]

When Brahms moved to Vienna in 1862 the leading choral conductor there was Johann Herbeck, director of the Gesellschaft der Musikfreunde. Herbeck gave the first public partial performance of *A German Requiem* on 1 December 1867, advising Brahms as to its unsuitability to full performance there. For its subsequent full performance (still in six movements) in Bremen on 10 April 1868, preparation passed into the hands of the Cathedral organist Carl Martin Reinthaler. Reinthaler took great pains to commend the work to his singers, and the success was partly his when Brahms conducted the successful first performance of the composition. During the preparations Brahms had written to him, "I wish from all my heart that your people would maintain their zeal. I confess, I would have to admire you if we could be quite happy in Holy Week (when the work was given). My work is, after all, quite difficult, and in Bremen they attack the high A rather more cautiously than in Vienna."[137] Brahms long maintained contact with the conductor. Even when, in later years, Reinthaler became implicated in the decline of Bremen music, Brahms remained loyal to him. "There still remain some twenty years during which I can accept that he worked most honorably and diligently—and against what stupidity, indifference, brutality, and foolishness!—and quite single-handedly in this daily fight. How do you think Richard Strauss, for example, would look after being interned in Bremen . . . for thirty years?"[138] Though Brahms generally handled the first performances of the other big choral works himself (the first part of *The Song of Triumph* in Bremen, *The Song of Destiny* in Karlsruhe, the *Song of the Fates* in Basel, and *Nänie* in Zurich), his friends in these places played their part. The difficult unaccompanied choral motets became something of a speciality, however. Eduard Kremser did op. 74 in Vienna, and Franz Wüllner the motets op. 110 in Cologne. Wüllner (whom Brahms had known since 1853) later held positions in Munich and Dresden as well.

5 · Brahms's Mode of Life

Brahms's early life in Hamburg had been circumscribed by family ties. Even after his return from Detmold in 1858 at the age of twenty-six, social conventions made it difficult for him to live independently: independence in Hamburg was associated with a future professional position. When he went to Vienna, his indecision regarding a long-term professional future was mirrored in his frequent changes of residence. From 1862 to 1865 and from 1867 to 1871 Brahms lived in at least seven different apartments, always within the first and second districts. From December 1871 he took rooms at 4 Karlsgasse, fourth district, in the third-story apartment of Fraulein Vogl and afterward of her successor, Frau Celestine Truxa. This location, close to the Gesellschaft der Musikfreunde, became his permanent residence. Brahms, increasingly resigned to his bachelor existence, had no desire to move from a situation that offered all he needed. Niemann, drawing on many sources, has vividly re-created the accommodation.

> We stand before the plain three-storied old Viennese, middle-class residence in the classical style of the late Empire, dating from about 1830. Crossing the vestibule with its wooden floor and closed French windows, with gaudily colored glass, opening on to the garden, we stumble up the dark, worn winding stone staircase to the third floor. There is no plate, no name, only a no. 8 on the door, a little letter box, and a peephole. . . . A short passage with two windows and a kitchen on the right leads, in typical Viennese style, straight into Brahms's bedroom. . . . Rohrbach's Johann Sebastian Bach above the bed, the bust of Haydn in the old Viennese biscuit china on the tiled stove, the simple wooden music stand which he used in conducting the concerts of the Gesell-

schaft in the left hand corner, at once show us who lives
here. . . . The chief pieces of furniture in the music room
are the Streicher grand piano, which had soon replaced
that of Schumann, besides an old square piano supposed
to have belonged to Haydn, the simple writing table,
with Calamatta's engraving of Leonardo's mysteriously
smiling Mona Lisa hanging over it, and an engraving of
Rietschel's medallion of Robert and Clara Schumann,
with a beautiful personal inscription, a simple breakfast
and reading table standing before the brown leather sofa,
with Steinle's engraving of Raphael's Sistine Madonna
hanging above it, and a carved rocking chair beside it.
On the piano, which was always open, a volume of the
great collected edition of Bach's works was usually open.
The cover of the piano was used as a show table: here
lay in exemplary order a pile of notebooks, writing tab-
lets, calendars, cigar cases, spectacles, purses, watches,
keys, souvenirs of his travels, portfolios, recent books and
musical publications. The rest of the artistic adornment
of the room consists of an engraving by Klinger, the portrait of Cherubini by the French classical painter Ingres,
with a Muse characteristically shrouded in a veil crown-
ing him with a laurel, an engraving by Schütz of the
Stefansdom in Vienna in 1792, Turner's mezzotint of
Hogarth's Handel, Morgen's engraving of the young
Mendelssohn at the piano, busts of Beethoven and Bismarck. . . .

Opening off it at the side was the library, whose array
of books showed that this was the haunt of no ordinary
mere musician but one exceptionally well read in the
whole sphere of the arts and sciences, and with a commanding grasp of the vast field of literature from the re-
motest times onwards. For, though not very large,
Brahms's library—contained in a bookcase with five sections, which occupied the whole of one long wall of the
room—was rich in precious old books on music,

autographs, curiosities, copper engravings, etchings, portfolios of pictures, etc. . . . The simple furniture of the library is completed by the composer's upright desk,
Cornelius's "Horsemen of the Apocalypse" hanging between the windows, and his travelling trunk and valises,
which always stood ready under the window packed
ready for instant use. The windows of the music room
and library, which were always shut—looked out over
the broad Karlsplatz and the copper green dome of Fischer v. Erlach's handsome Baroque Karlskirche; his bed-
room, whose windows were open day and night, looked
out over the neglected gardens of the neighboring houses
and the "Technik" (technical school), above which tow-
ered a great walnut tree, the higher branches of which almost rose as high as Brahms's rooms. It was only in the
music room that the old-fashioned floors of polished
wood blocks were covered by a few small rugs.[139]

Many musicians visited Brahms in these quarters, though few were as
mindful of the details as the young Gustav Jenner, his only real pupil,
who recalled the situation that arose when a visitor called:

As soon as we caught sight of such a visitor through the
curtain of the glass door from our seat on the grand piano, Brahms would flee with great bounds into the library, where I gave a signal by means of prearranged
signs as to whether he should put on a jacket or not. He
always did so when a lady came by. It would be untrue
if I were to say that Brahms was always polite to his visitors. On the contrary, I have often witnessed embarrass-
ing scenes, particularly in the case of visits by unknown
artists in whom he had no interest. If he felt that someone was coming out of curiosity, or that someone wanted
something that he was not inclined to give, or perhaps
even wanted something unreasonable, then he knew how
to dispatch the visitor in a stunningly short time.[140]

The Working Pattern

Brahms's workday in Vienna was regularly ordered. He arose at dawn, then worked steadily through the morning until about noon, after which he went out. Jenner asserts that Brahms could almost certainly be found at home in the late morning and that he often received visitors then.[141] His regular midday meal was at the inn Zum Roter Igel (The Red Hedgehog),[142] which he reached by midday or 12:30 P.M. He seems to have taken coffee there and then gone for a walk, or to have gone to another restaurant, where he read the papers. The walk, in the Stadtpark or the Prater, or possibly the Wiener Wald, was an important part of his day. At about six he returned to his room to write letters or do other work. Niemann summarizes:

> In the evening, often after a visit to a concert or to the opera, he would seek out his regular table in the low-ceilinged back room of the Roter Igel—which was, he was firmly convinced, the best and cheapest of the old inns in Vienna between the Wildpretmarkt and the Tuchlauben, and was, moreover, sacred in the eyes of musicians owing to a tradition that Beethoven had visited it, because of the hall on the first floor which belonged to the Gesellschaft der Musikfreunde from 1831 to 1869. Here he would meet his few but carefully chosen intimates, Hanslick, Kalbeck, Door, Pohl, Brüll, Rottenberg, Nottebohm, and others. If he was not to be found at the Roter Igel he would be sitting—at least between 1875 and 1881—at the habitués table at the Gause's Pilsener Bierhalle in the Johannisgasse. Though Brahms had a good appetite and stood his drink well, he was moderate, simple, and frugal in both what he ate and what he drank. As Jenner expressly tells us, thereby disarming in advance all spiteful gossip, his midday meal, including a quarter liter of red wine and small glass of pilsener beer, seldom cost more than seventy or eighty kreuzer.[143]

Brahms's routine when away on holiday is described by Widmann in the period 1886–88, when the composer established his summer residence at Hofstetten on Lake Thun, not far from Widmann's residence at Bern:

> Wide awake at the first break of dawn, he brewed his
> first breakfast on his Viennese coffee machine. A faithful
> lady admirer from Marseilles . . . furnished him excellent
> mocha for it, and in such abundance that from the very
> beginning he was able to share it with the household,
> thereby indulging in the simple pleasure of being simul-
> taneously host and guest while visiting us at Bern. The
> morning hours were devoted to work, which, in his
> quarters in Thun where a large arbor and a lodging of
> several spacious rooms permitted him to walk about pen-
> sively and undisturbed by anyone, turned out particularly
> well. . . . For his noon meal Brahms went to some out-
> door restaurant whenever the weather permitted. He al-
> ways disliked eating at the Table d'hôte and avoided it
> whenever possible for the simple reason that he did not
> like to get dressed up. He felt most comfortable in a
> striped wool shirt without collar and without a necktie.
> Even his soft felt hat was more often carried in his hand
> than worn on his head.[144]

The Social and Private Man

Brahms's most regular social contact was with other musicians. When he first arrived in Vienna, it was musicians he had first met, especially those connected with the musical institutions, the Conservatory of the Gesellschaft der Musikfreunde and the Philharmonic Orchestra. With the establishment of his compositions, the critical fraternity also opened up to him, beginning with Hanslick, whom he knew from earlier years, his stoutest supporter. In later years, when Brahms's concert traveling was less frequent, his social life found a particular focus in the activities of the Wiener *Tonkünstlerverein,* which he helped to found in 1885, the social meetings of which took place on Friday afternoons: Geiringer describes it thus:

> He was elected honorary president . . . in December 1886
> and took a keen interest in its development, believing

that the performances of the *Tonkünstlerverein* were an important influence in the training of the younger generation of musicians. The social side of the activities, however, pleased him more than the artistic. He never failed to attend the pleasant sociable meetings of the *Verein,* and there were many of its members whom he was glad to see on Sundays, and accompany on excursions into the Wienerwald. Only those, however, who could keep up with his rapid gait were welcome; as, for example, his old friends Julius Epstein, Ignaz Brüll, and Carl Goldmark, with the sensitive composer Robert Fuchs and distinguished piano teacher Anton Door; and of the younger generation the composers Richard Heuberger and Ludwig Rottenberg, with Richard von Perger, subsequently the conductor of the Gesellschaft der Musikfreunde, and above all the master's particular *famulus,* Eusebius Mandyczewski.[145]

Brahms was characteristically an outsider. Though he maintained a strong social context for his life in the city, he always went home alone as he had done in the early years, when he was still contemplating marriage. He simply grew more stoic and independent with the years. He also needed a periphery of friendships and social activity. The same applied to his preferred vacation locations: on the outskirts of Ischl, of Pörtschach and of Thun. Whether he was also lonely is a different issue. He seems to have come to terms with his choice and to have been prepared to defend it. As to Billroth, to whom he wrote in 1887, "It always seems to me a bit melancholy when you write of your feeling of being lonely. I have a thorough understanding of that and hope that you are going to be careful. For I am that too. For a long time—or for all time—I have been a bit of a shocking 'outsider'—and still am!"[146]

This all accorded with a stoic and reflective attitude to existence, which is also present in his religious and artistic outlooks. The sense of being on the edge of things emerges strongly in his religious views. "Nothing made Brahms angrier than to be taken for an orthodox church composer on account of his sacred compositions" was observed of him by Kalbeck.[147] This was presumably a regular assumption in view of the large number of his works using biblical texts. But Brahms was suspicious of religious dogma and was not a churchgoer. His position was that of a freethinking German Protestant, closer to a humanist in today's terms. Brahms appears to have had only passing interest in philosophy, not least that of his time; he was introduced to the writings of Arthur Schopenhauer in 1863 and later those of Friedrich Nietzsche, who took a brief interest in his music.[148] His attitude to Roman Catholicism was apparently severe, though he was moved by the simple piety of the faithful he saw at their prayers on his visits to Italy.[149] He rather regarded the Bible, which he knew intimately, as a repository of wisdom and experience as well as of great literature and he often chose texts from outside the "official" texts of the Old and New Testaments, referring to his "heathen" tendencies in so doing.[150] Of his German Requiem, which begins with one of Christ's Beatitudes from the Sermon on the Mount, he commented "I will admit that I could happily delete the [word] 'German' and substitute instead 'Human.' "[151]

6 · Brahms and Women

Marriage and Family Life

There was nothing in Brahms's youth that predicted his bachelor existence. Along with desiring a permanent professional position, he expected to marry and have children. He assumed a settled future, even if he was already doubtful of his deeper capacity for commitment, as seems to emerge from his response to Joachim's engagement:

> Lucky man! What else can I write but some such exclamation! If I set down my wishes they appear almost too solemn and serious. Nobody will appreciate your good fortune more than I do just now, when your letter found me in just the mood to be deeply affected. For I cannot leave off wondering whether I, who ought to be on my guard against other dreams, ought just to enjoy everything here, as one, or to go home and have the same thing, namely be at home, and give up everything else. Now you break in on these thoughts and boldly pluck

for yourself the finest and ripest apples of paradise. . . .
May things proceed according to my most heartfelt
wishes and I shall look forward to the time when, in
your home, as in that of many a faithless friend, I can
bend over a cradle and forget to ponder while looking
over a dear smiling baby's face.[152]

Some of Brahms's reasons for never marrying emerged in a conversation with Widmann many years later, in the late 1870s. Widmann recalls
Brahms as saying

I missed my chance. When I still had the drive, I
couldn't have made the right offer to a woman. . . . At
the time when I was still wishing to get married, my
compositions were whistled at and received with hisses or
at least with icy silence in the concert room. I was perfectly able to put up with this because I knew exactly
what they were worth, and that the picture would eventually change. And when after such a failure I would return to my lonely lodgings I was by no means
discouraged. On the contrary! But if at such moments I
had to face a wife, her questioning eyes anxiously meeting mine, and had to tell her that, again, "nothing," that
I could not have endured. For no matter how much a
woman may love an artist who is her husband and, as
the saying goes, have faith in him, she can never know
the full certainty of eventual victory that dwells in his
breast. . . . And if she had tried to console me—a
woman's commiseration for her husband's failure—bah! I
would rather not think what a hell on earth that would
have been, at least that is the way I feel about it.[153]

The responsibility of raising children would certainly not have deterred
Brahms. Numerous recollections show his delight in their company and
the easy relationships he formed with them. He was attracted by their
loyalty and directness. As he acknowledged to Clara Schumann, "I cannot
go out without my heart rejoicing, and feeling refreshed as if by a cooling
draught, if I have embraced a few darling children."[154] His physicality

came out in games with children, and he even ran Widmann's five-year-old daughter on his shoulders through the streets of Bern.[155]

But the binding commitment of marriage was obviously too daunting for Brahms, and, in any case, his attitude to women was seemingly ambivalent. He related his quandary to a musical problem about which he could also never reach a decision, citing his resolution no more to attempt opera or marriage.[156] He appears to have classified women in two ways: as idealized, unattainable figures or as playthings. Ethel Smyth, a radical social reformer, noted his misogynistic and chauvinistic side when she met him in the circle of Elisabet von Herzogenberg in Leipzig:

> Brahms, as artist and bachelor, was free to adopt what
> may be called the poetical variant of the "Kinder, Kirche,
> Küche" axiom, namely that women are play-things. He
> made one or two exceptions, as such men will, and chief
> among these was Liesl [Elisabet von Herzogenberg], to
> whom his attitude was perfect . . . reverential, admiring
> and affectionate, without a tinge of amorousness. . . . It
> specially melted him that she was such a splendid Haus-
> frau. His ways with other womenfolk . . . were less admi-
> rable. If they did not appeal to him he was incredibly
> awkward and ungracious; if they were pretty he had an
> unpleasant way of leaning back in his chair, pouting out
> his lips, stroking his mustache, and staring at them as a
> greedy boy stares at jam tartlets. People used to think
> this rather delightful, specially hailing it, too, as a sign
> that the great man was in high good humour, but it an-
> gered me, as did also his jokes about women, and his ev-
> erlasting jibes at any, excepting Liesl of course, who
> possessed brains or indeed ideas of any kind. I used to
> complain fiercely to her about this, but her secret feeling
> was, I suspect, that of many anti-suffragist women I have
> known, who, for some reason or other on the pinnacle
> of man's favours themselves, had no objection to the rest
> of womankind being held in contempt—the attitude of
> Fatima, the Pride of the Harem. . . . She was of her ep-
> och and intensely German.[157]

The Relationship with Clara Schumann

Any discussion of Brahms's relationships with women must include the relationship with Clara Schumann. Apart from his mother, she had the most powerful female influence on his early life, and she indeed became an artistic mother figure as well as an intimate friend and companion. Perhaps the magnitude of the change from his culturally circumscribed upbringing to the inspiring artistic world of the Schumanns was so great that he could not imagine any other relationship: she remained his star even after the ardor of romantic youth had cooled (even before Schumann's death) and life had made other demands. In Gál's phrase the relationship was the "decisive, tragically fateful experience of his younger years,"[158] and it was destined never to work out satisfactorily for either party. They both were sensitive to their independence and identity in different ways, Clara as much as the more obviously taciturn Brahms. It always seems to have been he who wished most to break free, preserving his creative independence, and he hurt her deeply by leaving in 1856 and distancing himself emotionally. But she insisted on making the concert tours that economic necessity forced on her, and she refused the financial support he wanted to give.[159] In spite of all the surface tension, he loved her and could not bear to lose her. His life was entwined with hers.[160]

As early as May 1856, Brahms had written to her: "My dearest Clara, I wish I could speak to you as tenderly as I love you, and do as many good and loving things as I would like. You are so infinitely dear to me that I can't express it in words. I should like to call you darling and lots of other names, without ever getting enough of adoring you." He continued: "I regret every word which does not speak of love. You taught me and are every day teaching me to recognize and marvel at what love, attachment and self-denial are. . . . I wish I could always write to you from my heart, to tell you how deeply I love you, and can only beg you to believe it without further proof."[161] To Joachim the nature of the feelings had been vouchsafed more specifically two years earlier, when Brahms was still using a formal address in letters to Clara: "I believe that I do not respect and admire her so much as I love her and am under her spell. Often I must forcibly restrain myself from just quietly putting my arms around her and even—I don't know, it seems to me so natural that she would not take it ill. I think I can no longer love a young girl. At least I have quite forgotten about them. They but promise heaven while Clara reveals it to us."[162]

But the harsh realities of both their lives changed this idyllic relationship, which was so deeply grounded in their needs: his for an artistic mentor, especially since Schumann's illness, hers for support and for artistic exchange. Soon after Schumann's death Brahms left for Hamburg and an independent life. It was a difficult time for Clara. Some indication of how she viewed this emerges from the recollections of her daughter Eugenie Schumann:

> I did not know at that time just what Brahms's friend-
> ship had meant to my mother during this most difficult
> period of her life; it was not until several years after my
> mother's death that I saw the words which, like a legacy,
> she had set down in her diary for us children to read,
> words in which she bound us to a lifelong gratitude to
> him who had sacrificed years of his young life to her. . . .
> After our father had fallen ill, Brahms was filled with
> that enthusiastic devotion to our mother which guided
> his entire being and to which he consecrated—not sacri-
> ficed, since he followed his own deepest and most heart-
> felt inclination—several years of his existence. The
> realization was inevitable, however, that a task awaited
> him which demanded his entire strength and which
> could not be reconciled with an exclusive dedication to
> any single friendship. To recognize this and immediately
> seek a way out were acts in keeping with his strongly
> pronounced masculinity. Even the fact that this was done
> in a brusque way was inherent in his nature and perhaps
> in the nature of the entire situation. But it is certain that
> he fought a hard fight in order to steer his ship of fate in
> a different direction, and that the knowledge of having
> hurt my mother at that time long haunted him and of-
> ten manifested itself in his abrupt behaviour, especially
> since the wrong could no longer be righted. This at least
> is what we children came to believe.[163]

Whatever Brahms's hopes, and whatever the assumptions of Clara's children, there was also an element of the maternal in Brahms's relationship with Clara, a feature several times observed, as by Smyth in the late 1870s: "He behaved as might a particularly delightful old-world son."[164] His devotion to his own mother may have subconsciously prevented him from facing the demands of a lover. This seems implicit in the interpretation of Hübbe inspired by Widmann's observations:

> I cannot refrain from appending a remark to Widmann's
> important communication [on the subject of Brahms's
> bachelorhood]. . . . Though one may accept the answer
> given by Brahms to Widmann on this point as quite
> valid, yet I would venture to supplement it by conjec-
> ture. Just as there are instances of great men having been
> deterred from marriage by devotion to their mother, so it
> has often struck me that Brahms may have found a simi-
> lar obstacle in his particular relation to his so warmly re-
> vered maternal friend Clara Schumann. Widmann's
> words on the subject have confirmed me in the supposi-
> tion that this relation was a factor—though possibly un-
> recognized—in determining Brahms's abstention from
> marriage.[165]

For her part, Clara seems to have assumed the maternal role as the years passed, advising him in 1867 that "you should establish a household of your own soon. Take some well-to-do young lady of Vienna (surely you can find one whom you can learn to love) and you will become again brighter and, despite some worries, of course, get to know joys to which you were a stranger till now; and then you can embrace life with renewed vigor. The concept of earthly happiness is, after all, bound up with life in the home. I wish you would create one for yourself. The time for it is ripe."[166] Whatever her personal feelings, Clara knew what was best for him and continued to encourage him.

But for all her closeness to him, Clara was not spared Brahms's moody nature. Like others, she never quite knew how to take him; but they at least on occasion were frank with each other. In 1868 he wrote, "I am conscious of only one offence in regard to my friends; awkwardness of behaviour. . . . I feel that I may by my manner, by nothing else, have deserved the great pain of your estrangement from me."[167] In later years she even complained to Kalbeck that Brahms was still as mystifying and strange as he had been many years earlier. On this occasion the reason was associated with her own sensitivities, however: the editing of Schumann's works for her complete edition, about which she was extremely possessive.[168] Even later, a year before his death, in connection with the publication of Schumann's letters Brahms wrote to Hanslick, "Confidential intercourse with women is difficult. . . . The more earnest and confidential, the more difficult."[169]

Brahms's hardness, which so hurt Clara, is most apparent in his destruction of letters. In 1887 the two agreed to return one another's letters in order to destroy them, and Clara wrote in her diary: "On the 16 October Brahms passed through here. . . . We discussed the return of his letters, which was extremely hard on me. . . . He has now given me back my own letters and it is only right that I should return his. . . . I had wanted to extract from them everything concerning his life as an artist and a human being, because they provide a more comprehensive portrait of him and his work than any biographer could possibly hope for. I had intended to compile all this prior to the destruction of the letters; but he did not want this, and I have let him have them today, with sad tears."[170]

Clara did manage to retain a few letters to which she was especially attached, and these were preserved. Brahms threw the rest into the Rhine, whereas Clara burned only a part of her own. "In her work of destruction," writes her daughter Marie, "she was fortunately interrupted by me. She gave in to my urgent plea to preserve the letters for us children."[171] Despite all the tensions in their friendship, Brahms still wrote to Clara in later years: "I love you more than myself and more than anything else in the world."[172] He could not bear to lose her. In April 1896, Joachim notified Brahms that Clara had suffered a stroke. Brahms's reply reveals his admiration for her: "Now then—I cannot consider sad what your letter mentions. I have often thought that Frau Schumann might outlive her children as well as myself—but I have never wished it for her. The thought of losing her can no longer frighten us—not even my lonely self, to whom all too few still remain alive. Once she has gone from us will not our faces light up with joy whenever we think of her? This glorious woman whose presence we have been privileged to enjoy for a long lifetime—to love and admire ever increasingly? Only this way can we mourn her."[173] Clara died on May 20. Her decline seems to have impelled the completion of the *Four Serious Songs*. He wrote to Marie:

> If shortly you receive a book of "serious songs" please don't misunderstand my motives in sending it. Quite aside from the dear old habit of writing your name at the heading, these songs concern you particularly. I wrote them during the first week of May. Similar texts have often haunted me. I had been in hopes of not having to expect worse news of your mother. Yet in the depth of the soul something may speak, and urge you on almost unconsciously, and that something may materialize as poetry or music. You cannot play through the songs now because the words would be far too distressing for you. But I beg you to consider them as a very personal offering to the memory of your beloved mother and keep them as such.[174]

For all the stoicism expressed in Brahms's remark to Joachim, his life had been bound with Clara's. He outlived her barely a year, seeing this work into print less than a year before his death in April 1897.[175]

Other Relationships

The fateful relationship with Clara to which Gál refers prevented Brahms from establishing permanent relationships with other women: his tie to her engendered feelings of guilt, responsibility, and obligation. But whatever lay in the future, the young Brahms sought to move boldly on with his life. Within two years of leaving Clara he became engaged to Agathe von Siebold, the pretty daughter of a Göttingen professor.[176] Brahms often visited Göttingen because Grimm was a director of music there. Clara, visiting at the time, heard of the engagement and departed without taking her leave of Brahms. She wrote later: "I spent difficult days in Cassel, and the thought of Agathe and of a great many things kept haunting me. I constantly saw the poor, abandoned girl, and lived through all her sufferings with her. O dear Johannes, if only you had not allowed things to go that far."[177] The affair had become small-town gossip, and Brahms had to make a decision about his commitment. Grimm had subtly attempted to pressure Brahms to formalize the relationship. Brahms wrote to Siebold: "I love you, I must see you again, but I am incapable of bearing fetters. Please write me again whether if I may come again to clasp you in my arms, to kiss you and to tell you that I love you."[178] Siebold later married happily, and in her autobiographical novel she indicated that she forgave Brahms.[179] Brahms never saw her again, but he conferred immortality on her by encoding her name in the String Sextet in G Major, op. 36. Gänsbacher confirms Brahms as saying of the quote, "Here is where I tore myself free from my last love."[180]

Brahms never again allowed things to go that far, but he remained very attracted to pretty women, though he seems to have been generally relieved when the situation resolved itself without the need for his commitment. One early exception was Clara's own daughter Julie. When she became engaged to Count Marmorito, Clara commented in her diary, "He seemed not to have expected anything of the sort and to be quite upset." And later, "Johannes is quite altered. He seldom comes to the house and speaks only in monosyllables when he does. And he treats Julie in the same way, though he always used to be specially nice to her. Did he really love her?" Brahms arrived at the house on the wedding day with the autograph of one of his most misanthropic works, the Alto Rhapsody, referring to it ironically as his "Bridal Song," a work in which Clara immediately noted the "depths of despair in both words and music."[181]

After the Siebold episode, Brahms's involvements were almost always with attractive singers who responded to his music. The first of these he met while still in Hamburg. Bertha Porubszky, a Viennese, was a temporary member of Brahms's Hamburg Ladies' Choir and the daughter of the minister of the Protestant congregation. She was one of Brahms's links to Vienna, and she encouraged him to move there. Brahms seems to have been relieved to hear of her engagement when he arrived in Vienna: "When I first saw her, she looked very pale and sickly and my conscience was greatly relieved when I shortly received her formal announcement with a few words added."[182] Bertha Faber, as she became on marriage, and her husband, Arthur, remained among Brahms's closest friends in Vienna, and he acknowledged the birth of their first child in the "Wiegenlied."[183] At about the same time a genuine German with Viennese connections attracted his attention: the singer Luise Dustmann, who was born in Aachen and had moved to Vienna to sing in the opera. Her forthcoming and unaffected manner appealed to Brahms, whom she always referred to as "Hansi," a Viennese familiarity for children, often signing herself "Fidelio," one of her famous parts. It was again a combination of music and charm, and she too became a lifelong friend but with no attachment. Once in Vienna, Brahms was hardly unaware of attractive women, not least in the choral context. An outstanding voice in the Sunday choir, which met at the house of the von Asten family, was that of Ottilie Hauer. Later he was to write to Clara "of a very pretty girl with whom he, God knows, would have made a fool of himself if, as luck would have it, someone had not snatched her up." She became engaged to Dr. Eduard Ebner at Christmas 1863, and the Ebners likewise remained lifelong friends.[184]

Brahms came to terms with his bachelorhood, and he seemed with the years to become much more uninhibited in his response to young, pretty women, cultivating a slightly rakish manner. Edward Speyer, who was married to Antonia Kufferath, an old acquaintance of Brahms's, recalled greeting Brahms as he arrived by train at Frankfurt: "The train rolled in, and I ran to the compartment which Brahms had already opened. He flung his arms about me, then shoved me back with the words 'Oh, forgive me, I thought you were your wife.'" Gál comments that "Brahms acted as though he gladly remained single out of conviction." According to Widmann, "He generally spoke facetiously about his bachelorhood and liked, especially when confronted by inquisitive ladies, to use the formula 'Unfortunately Madam, I am still unmarried, Heaven be praised.'"[185]

But one by one his male friends married, beginning with Joachim, then Hanslick and his father, and Bülow (for the second time). At fifty, Brahms carried on a lively flirtation with Hermine Spies: so friendly were they that, according to Elise Brahms, their engagement had been expected in Viennese circles.[186] A dedicated lieder singer—in itself a new phenomenon (she was a pupil of Julius Stockhausen)—who had worked on Brahms's songs long before she met him, the pretty and light-hearted Spies made a great impact on him, and he was always carefree in her presence. He helped with her career, and she was his favorite performer of the Alto Rhapsody, clearly inspiring other works too. For her part she openly admitted to a "Johannes passion" as late as July 1887, as in correspondence with their mutual friend Klaus Groth, the poet: "What a splendid fellow is Brahms! Once more I was absolutely overwhelmed, enraptured, enchanted, carried away. And what a dear he was! In a really happy, youthful summery mood! He is eternally young." She wrote to the daughter of Albert Dietrich, "What I value most particularly is to have now enjoyed Brahms as a man. How charming he was with us when we were making and guessing riddles. What delightful hours we spent in your congenial home. For me that was the happiest day of the whole journey. Of course, I now only play Brahms the livelong day. It was a real rest for me to make music for my own pleasure after all the compulsory music on the platform. At Christmas I received all Brahms's works, and am now really reveling in these lovely things."[187] She also left a vivid record of his way with children. Her early death at thirty-six in 1893 was one of a series of losses that gave Brahms's last years such a backcloth of sadness.

But some years before her death, after the relationship had cooled, her place in the affections of the sixty-year-old composer had been taken by an Italian singer of striking "classical beauty" and remarkable artistic accomplishment: Alice Barbi. Brahms wrote to Clara in February 1890 that many things could not be performed more beautifully than by Barbi. He even appeared as her accompanist for her farewell concert (she retired when she married) when he no longer appeared on the platform.[188] But he never got beyond the stage of paying court—he was detached, uncommitted. But she retained a special place in his circle, and because no women family members or old friends survived, she was the only woman at the head of the funeral procession.[189]

One relationship stood apart from this pattern, though it began in a similar way and shared features of some other relationships. During Brahms's first winter in Vienna his pupils included the young Elisabet von Stockhausen, daughter of the ambassador of Hanover to Vienna and a pupil of Dessoff. She had the fatal combination of gifts, beauty, and musical intelligence: she was an excellent pianist and could retain a new orchestral work after a single hearing. Brahms soon confessed a fear of his feelings for her to male friends and entrusted her instruction on piano to Julius Epstein. As with some other relationships, this one was resumed in a different, safer context. Brahms met her again in 1874 after she had married Heinrich von Herzogenberg, a leading figure in Leipzig's musical life. Brahms and Elisabet now developed a remarkable relationship: Brahms's music became the focus of her interest, and the two shared a correspondence that reveals much about her insights and his reactions.[190]

He fitted easily into the social setting she offered, so adversely observed by Smyth. On one occasion he wrote to her, "It was so beautiful with you. I still feel it today, as an agreeable warmth, and I should like to shut it up and lock it in, so as to keep it for a long time."[191] Clara apparently was sensitive about the place Elisabet held in his regard.

One other relationship is notable for standing outside Brahms's musical and social circle. Mathilde Wesendonck is primarily associated with Wagner, who immortalized her in his conception of the part of Isolde in *Tristan und Isolde.* In the period after Wagner's cooling toward her Mathilde showed great admiration for Brahms. She met him in Zurich in 1866, and this gave Brahms the opportunity to study Wagner's treasures at first hand. Moreover, she placed Wagner's former lodgings by the lake at Brahms's disposal, writing at the time of the Zurich Festival in June 1867: "During the Festival the Stockhausens are going to be our guests; unfortunately I shall be absent. The little green nest nearby with its hermit's gate will remain untouched. Before I leave for St. Moritz I am going to see to it that at any time a light-hearted swallow can find a modest shelter there." Brahms did not accept the invitation, but she wrote again the following year: "Your rooms are always ready. For the New Year, let me tell you all that you ought to have known long ago, and do know now, don't you. I should not have liked to have lived in this century without at least giving you a friendly and pressing invitation to join us at our fireside." She repeated the invitation again in December.[192]

TWO · Brahms the Composer

7 · The Young Composer's Outlook

Brahms's reluctance to discuss his own works, apparent from early years, reflects not only his essentially private personality and artistic self-sufficiency but also his response to the artistic climate of his life. He was deeply suspicious of the public polemic concerning the nature and future of music; this theorizing would prevail throughout his lifetime. Ironically, his impatience with this climate led him in 1860 to make the one public outburst of his life: his published "Declaration" against the claims of the so-called Music of the Future.[1] He had long been concerned with the fundamental issues of musical progress, which were of primary concern to a young composer working in a world dominated by the writings of Wagner and then Liszt. Schumann's reference to the "quiet obscurity" in which Brahms had lived in Hamburg certainly did not apply to his intellectual life.[2] On the contrary, he had obviously been seeking his own path, an effort that can be traced through his vast reading and his attitude to his teachers.

To his own

compositions he

alluded only on the

very rarest occasions.

Before meeting the Schumanns in September 1853—and apparently even before coming to know much of Schumann's music[3]—the young Brahms had independently explored Schumann's poetic world. He had allied himself with Schumann's hero E. T. A. Hoffmann, styling himself in letters and on manuscripts as "Johannes Kreisler, Jr.," in emulation of Hoffmann's character Kapellmeister Kreisler.[4] Most significantly, Brahms assembled his thoughts on art in a series of little anthologies of literary quotations that he had begun in his teens and continued up to September 1854 under the title *Des Jungen Kreislers Schatzkästlein,*[5] apparently emulating the quaint title of Hoffmann's 1810 collection *Johannes Krei-*

sler, des Kapellmeisters, musikalische Leiden. Brahms's 645 quotations range from aphorisms to passages several pages in length and show the range and trend of his thought, as well as the impact of his new idols, Joachim and Schumann. Hoffmann created a romantic inheritance for composers through his interpretations of Haydn, Mozart, and especially Beethoven. Later composers—notably Weber, Wagner, and above all Schumann—responded by acknowledging the importance of his writing. Although Hoffmann may have been a spiritual mentor, for his anthology Brahms drew almost nothing from his writings. Rather, the two poets who shared Hoffmann's obsession with music dominated Brahms's outlook: Jean Paul (Brahms's greatest source by far) and Novalis.[6] But the range of the collection is extremely wide, and many other writers are represented as well, some reflecting Schumann's choices in texts and many offering only a few passages. They include Rückert and Eichendorff, Arnim, Chamisso, Hebbel, Geibel, Kerner, Kulmann, Tieck, Wackenroder, Hölderlin, and Büchner. There is a strong overall emphasis on the earlier, pre-Romantic generation, with Goethe (almost rivaling Jean Paul in number of quotes), Lessing, and Schiller substantially represented, along with Klopstock and Kleist. Writers who influenced German Romanticism through translation also figure prominently, especially Byron, Bulwer-Lytton, Macaulay, Bishop Percy, Pope, and Shakespeare. But there are a fair number of quotations from French and Italian authors, and several from the Greeks. One also notes the presence of texts from other fields: religion (the Bible and Luther), Bismarck (politics), and Moses Mendelssohn (philosophy). This was not a collection for setting, so it includes few texts that Brahms later used in his songs.

Brahms's Romantic credentials are clear in his view of the nature of music and the arts. His quotations stress the indefinite quality of music, its otherworldliness, as in a quote from Jean Paul: "O Music! Echo from a distant harmonic world. Angelic sighing within us!"[7] Novalis views music as a voice of nature, anticipating Brahms's later solo song on the subject, "An eine Aeolsharfe," op. 19/5: "Nature is an Aeolian Harp, a musical instrument, whose notes are now keys, now again notes of more elevated chords within us."[8] Hoffmann's view of the superiority of instrumental over vocal music through its greater immateriality finds expression in a quote from the fourteen-year-old Elisabeth Kulmann: "O tones without words, when you speak into the heart, you arouse power-fully the depths of soul within me."[9] And from these sentiments it follows that poetry and music must be in union, as expressed by Novalis: "Music and poetry may well seem rather as one, and perhaps likewise belong together like mouth and ear, since the first is only an active and answering ear."[10] Brahms's view of the composer as an artist with a unique respon-sibility emerges from quotes attributed to other composers or associated with them. An entry ascribed to Schumann's notebook captures the spirit: "Whoever places life before art will never be an artist."[11] Clearly Brahms's contact with Joachim influenced his thinking, as is evident in a sequence of aphorisms, including the following: "Artists should not be servants but priests of the public."[12] Beethoven states his outlook and values more precisely: "I can never follow the fashion in my work. . . . The new and original give birth to themselves without my thinking about them."[13] Ironically, one of the clearest of these statements comes from a composer with whom Brahms later disagreed but whose radical views on the future of opera Brahms had now read: Wagner. "The generator of the artwork of the future is none other than the artist of the present, who anticipates the life of the future and longs to be contained in it. Whoever cherishes the longing within himself already lives in a better life, but only One can do this: the Artist."[14]

The young Brahms was seeking freedom in his work and allying him-self with fellow spirits; he emphasized the creator more than the work. But equally striking are his comments showing concern over the basic issues of compositional value. He was preoccupied with the larger general statements about the role of technique, the relation of form and content, the discipline of craft. Later emphasis in other books in such underlined passages as "the artist must discipline himself in order not to dissipate his efforts" is anticipated in a quote from Carl Friedrich Zelter showing the importance of early discipline (no. 539): "The technique of an art must be systematically learnt from the earliest years. When the spirit starts to emerge from within, the concern with presentation must be set aside."[15] But technique was not to be taken too seriously. "Theory and practice constantly interact with one another," Goethe wrote.[16] Adolf von Menzel gives a slightly different emphasis to the relationship: "Between theory and practice, rule and example, law and freedom there always remains a residual gap, and perhaps it is just this gap which is of more value than the whole. For perhaps the beautiful would be no more so if someone unravels its secret."[17]

The biggest concern for the young composer was the relationship between ideas and their formal expression. This, the most elusive quality of art, was the gift of the individual artist only, the unique quality of genius to which Beethoven and Goethe alluded. Thus, in Goethe's *Zur Farbenlehre:* "If one considers art in the highest sense, one would wish that only masters would contribute to it, that pupils be given the strictest examinations and that amateurs feel a certain happiness in approaching it fearfully. For the work of art should spring from genius, the artist should summon form and content from his deepest essence."[18] The concept of a natural originality was basic to Brahms's outlook, best expressed in a later underlining in *Zur Farbenlehre:* "We are original only because we know nothing," suggesting that originality in the least valuable sense is the product of ignorance.[19] Brahms viewed it more broadly, however. A quotation from J. P. Eckermann makes the same point, again reinforced by Goethe. The deepest experiences are beyond the "original": "Form is something achieved over a thousand years by the most advanced masters, and every successor cannot make it his own quickly enough. It would be the highest stupidity of a misunderstood originality if everyone who came along sought through his own devices to search out that which is already so fully to hand."[20]

The variety in these quotations reflects the conflicts—or at least the alternatives—regarding the lines of development that lay open to Brahms, essentially the Romantic and the Classic. His concern with the nature of musical form draws attention to the composition instruction that he received and his reaction to it—indeed, these quotations might be responses to his learning experiences. His comment that "from Marxsen I learnt nothing"[21] was not a criticism of Marxsen as much as a reflection on the gap between the vast discipline that Brahms felt he needed and the capacities of the teacher. It must be taken in light of another comment in which he sees himself not as a pupil but as a master. In his later years he remarked to Heuberger that "neither Schumann nor Wagner nor I learnt. . . . Schumann took one path, Wagner the other, I yet a third. Yet none of us actually learnt properly. None of us passed through a systematic school. In truth it was afterwards that we learnt."[22] And likewise, to the philologist Gustav Wendt, "Mendelssohn had a great advantage compared with us: the excellent school. What indescribable efforts it has cost me to recover this lost ground as a man!"[23] That Brahms saw his position in such broad terms should put his reactions to Marxsen's teaching in perspective, not least in the context of Brahms's extraordinary ambition and capacity for self-discipline. Surely no one could have taught Brahms beyond the preliminaries: he was self-taught throughout his life. Rather, it almost seems that he is using Marxsen's limitations to stress his own achievement, which was otherwise manifest in the virtual litany of his later years—"Few have worked as hard as I"[24]—through which he sought to stress the virtues of craft in a world of shifting musical values.

Marxsen was the most famous teacher in Northern Germany, and the loyal and appreciative Brahms stayed in contact with him over the years. The evidence of Brahms's affection is most clearly recalled by Josef Sittard to La Mara: "Brahms regarded his teacher with touching gratitude, and when at the height of his creative powers still continued to send his compositions, before their publication, for Marxsen's critical inspection. Nothing is more indicative of the intimate relation between the two men than the letters (from Brahms to Marxsen) that I was permitted to see years ago." Brahms's gestures included publishing a set of variations by Marxsen in which Brahms had taken great interest, and he surprised Marxsen with a parcel of proof sheets for checking and an affectionate letter. And he dedicated to him the greatest work of his mature virtuosity: the B flat Piano Concerto.[25]

Sittard's accounts show that Marxsen emphasized certain principles, all of which influenced Brahms. First, Marxsen had great belief in the individuality of talent, and he encouraged talent to emerge. Second, he believed in classical form and the organic whole, attained through the study of the classics. May summarizes:

> As a teacher of free composition, and especially of the art
> of building up the forms which may be studied in the
> works of Haydn, Mozart and Beethoven, he was great—
> the more so that he did not educate his pupils merely by
> setting them to imitate the outward shape of classical
> models. He began by teaching them to form a texture,
> by training them radically in the art of developing a

theme. Taking a phrase or a figure from one or another of the great masters he would desire the pupil to exhibit the same idea in every imaginable variety of form, and would make him persevere in the exercise until he had gained facility by perceiving the possibilities lying in a given subject, and ingenuity in presenting them. Pursuing the same method with the material of the pupil's own invention he aimed at bringing him to feel, as by intuition, whether a musical subject was or was not suitable for whatever immediate purpose might be in view. The next step was that the idea should be pursued not arbitrarily, but logically, to its conclusion—a conclusion that was not, however, allowed to be a hard-and-fast termination. Marxsen's pupils were taught to aim at making their movements resemble an organic growth, in which each part owed its existence to something that had gone before. "Unity clothed in variety" might have been his motto.[26]

Sittard knew Marxsen and believed that "Brahms had the rare good fortune of being trained under a teacher whose like does not fall to the lot of many young musicians. Pledged to no particular artistic creed, sworn to no particular tendency or party, Marxsen had interest to bestow upon every important development of musical art. He never gave instruction on an inflexible scheme but allowed himself to be guided by the separate requirement of each case. He was careful not to interfere with the individuality of young talent, not to meddle with the distinctive peculiarities of his pupil's creative ability; he only guided them within artistic confines."[27] There is little record of Brahms's earliest training. His first teacher, Otto Cossel, who died before Brahms's greatest fame outside North Germany could be fully anticipated, was concerned solely with the piano. Indeed, it was as a pianist that Brahms first attracted attention. His fellow Hamburger Luise Japha, with whom he had close musical contacts, speaks of hearing him play a sonata of his own composition when he was about eleven. She had found him practicing at Schroeder's pianoforte house. Cossel, responsible for Brahms's progress as a piano player, is said to have been anxious at his pupil's spending too much of his time in these youthful attempts.[28]

Marxsen became interested in Brahms's broader musical intelligence early in their relationship, though he took notice of his pupil's urge to compose only when it could not be restrained. After a while he began to teach Brahms theory, and he later told La Mara, "I was captivated by his keen and penetrating intellect, and though his first attempts produced nothing of consequence, I perceived in them a mind in which, as I was convinced, an exceptional and deeply original talent lay dormant. I therefore spared myself neither pains nor trouble to awaken and cultivate it, in order to prepare a future priest of art, who should proclaim in a new idiom through his works, its high, true and lasting principles." Thus Brahms's sudden acknowledgment by Joachim and the Schumanns was actually anticipated by Marxsen: "There was probably but one man in the world who was not surprised—myself. I knew what Brahms had accomplished, how comprehensive were his acquirements, what exalted talent had been bestowed on him, and how finely its blossom was un-folding. Schumann's recognition and admiration were, all the same, a great, great joy to me; they gave me the rare satisfaction of knowing that the teacher had perceived the right way to protect the individuality of the talent, and form it gradually to self-dependence."[29]

The meeting with Joachim in May had been powerful, providing a major stimulus to the young musician's imagination. But it is impossible to overstate the impact of Brahms's meeting with the Schumanns in Sep-tember 1853. Since their marriage in 1840 they had become the outstand-ing musical couple in Germany: Clara was one of the most accomplished pianists of her generation, and Robert was rapidly attracting attention with his strikingly individualist musical spirit. After the disappointment of having his compositions returned unopened when the Schumanns vis-ited Hamburg in 1850, Brahms suddenly found both his compositions and his playing hailed as unique and prophetic. Even allowing for Schu-mann's enthusiasm toward many young musicians, the remarks with which Schumann sought to "lighten his first steps in the musical world" were unreserved and forceful.[30] The remarks appeared in the *Neue Zeit-schrift für Musik* (founded by Schumann and edited by him until 1844) on 28 October under the title "Neue Bahnen" (New Paths):

Years have passed—almost as many as I earlier devoted to the editing of these pages—ten indeed—since I have made myself heard in this place so rich in memories. . . . Many new and significant talents have appeared: a new strength seemed to announce itself in music, as is proved by many artists of recent years, even though their works are known only to a comparatively limited circle. . . . It seemed to me, who followed the progress of these chosen ones with the greatest sympathy, that in these circumstances there must inevitably appear a musician called to give expression to his times in ideal fashion: a musician who would reveal his mastery not in gradual stages but like Minerva would spring fully armed from Kronos's head. And he has come; a young man over whose cradle Graces and Heroes have stood watch. His name is Johannes Brahms and he comes from Hamburg, where he has been creating in quiet obscurity, though instructed in the most difficult statutes of his art by an excellent and enthusiastically devoted teacher. A well-known and honoured master recently recommended him to me. Even outwardly he bore the marks announcing to us: "This is a chosen one." . . .

Should he [in addition to his piano compositions] direct his magic wand where the powers of the masses in chorus and orchestra may lend him their strength, we may look forward to even more wondrous glimpses of the secret world of spirits. May the highest genius strengthen him to this end. Since he possesses yet another facet of genius—that of modesty—we may surmise that it will come to pass. His fellow musicians hail him on his first step through a world where wounds perhaps await him, but also palms and laurels; we welcome him as a strong champion. . . . There exists a secret bond between kindred spirits in every period. You who belong together, close your ranks ever more tightly that the Truth of Art may shine ever more clearly, diffusing joy and blessings everywhere.[31]

Brahms had an "earnest deep gaze in which his gifted nature was clearly revealed," recalled Albert Dietrich. Pencil sketch of the twenty-year-old Brahms, made at Schumann's request after Brahms's arrival in Düsseldorf, by J. J. Bonaventura Laurens in autumn 1853.

Brahms approaching age thirty. Photograph made before his departure for Vienna by F. König of Hamburg in 1861–62. (Brahms Institut, Lübeck, Sammlung Hofmann)

Newly established in Vienna. This 1864 picture shows an early version of the canon "Göttlicher Morpheus," dedicated by Brahms to Frau Ida Flatz, a member of the Vienna Singakademie, whose husband supported Brahms's appointment to the conductorship in 1863. (Gesellschaft der Musikfreunde, Vienna)

Brahms at about forty in 1872, the year he became artistic director of the Gesell-schaft der Musikfreunde. Photo by Adèle, Vienna. (Royal College of Music, London)

The mature master in his fifties. Royal College of Music, London

Brahms's parents, photographed in the same Hamburg studio in 1862. Brahms's mother, Johanna Henrika Christiane Nissen Brahms (1789–1865), at seventy-three. Brahms's father, Johann Jacob Brahms (1806–1872), still in his vigorous middle fifties. (Österreichisches Nationalbibliothek, Vienna)

Brahms's birthplace at Schlütershof, 24 Specksgang (at the time of this photograph, 60 Speckstrasse) in Hamburg, at the turn of the century. It was destroyed in 1943. The family's dwelling was in the first floor above ground to the left.

The house at 4 Karlsgasse, Vienna IV. Brahms's apartment was on the third floor. He lived there from December 1871 until his death. Watercolor by R. Schmidt.

Brahms's music room. Note the coffee machine on a table, to the left; the Streicher piano, always closed with books on the lid, by the window; a bronze of Bismarck with laurel wreath and a bust of Beethoven on the facing wall; and the Sistine Madonna at center. (Gesellschaft der Musikfreunde, Vienna)

A view of the Elizabeth-Brücke by Franz Alt (1872) in a chromolithograph from a watercolor. In the distance at left is the recently erected Gesellschaft der Musikfreunde building (1870); Karlskirche is at right. (Gesellschaft der Musikfreunde, Vienna)

Ein deutsches Requiem ("A German Requiem"), the work that made Brahms's international name. Movements 1–3 were first performed on 1 December 1867, Grosse Redoutensaal, Vienna; movements 1–4 and 6–7 were performed on 10 April 1868, Bremen Cathedral. Movement 5 was then added, and the whole work was performed on 18 February 1869, Leipzig Gewandhaus. Pictured is the first edition of the Piano Duo score. (Leipzig and Winterthur, Rieter-Biedermann, 1869)

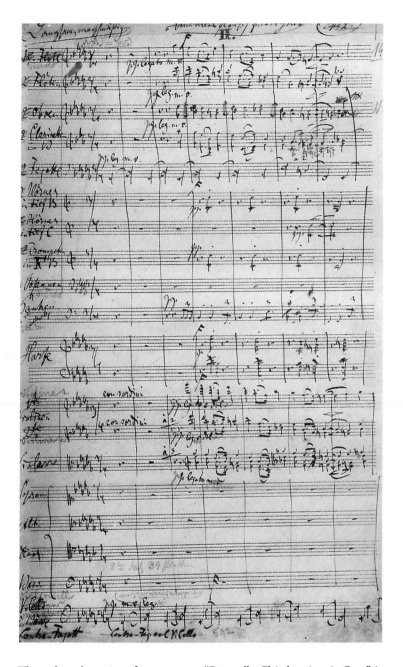

The orchestral opening of movement 2, "Denn alles Fleisch es ist wie Gras," in Brahms's autograph full score. Gesellschaft der Musikfreunde, Vienna

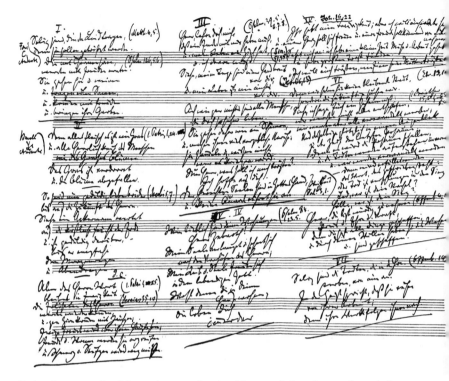

Brahms's autograph of the entire text, showing his second thoughts on the ordering of the fourth and fifth movements. (Wiener Stadt- und Landesbibliothek)

Text

für das

Geistliche Concert

am Charfreitag 1868

in der Domkirche zu Bremen.

Bremen.

Druck von Heinrich Strack.

1868.

Gesellschaft der Musikfreunde.

Zweites
Gesellschafts-Konzert

Sonntag, den 1. Dezember 1867,

Mittags, präcise halb 1 Uhr,

im k. k. grossen Redouten-Saale,

unter der Leitung

des artistischen Directors Herrn **JOHANN HERBECK,** k. k. Hof-Kapellmeisters,

und unter Mitwirkung der ausübenden Gesellschafts-Mitglieder

(SING-VEREIN),

des Fräulein **Helene Magnus** und der Herren: Direktor **Hellmesberger**, k. k. Konzertmeister, und Dr. **Panzer**, k. k. Hofkapellensänger.

PROGRAMM:

Brahms Johannes Drei Sätze aus: „**Ein deutsches Requiem**", für Solo, Chor und Orchester. (Manuscript, zum 1. Male.)

Schubert - - — Aus der Musik zu dem Drama „**Rosamunde**", für Solo, Chor und Orchester.
1. Entreact — H-moll.
2. Balletmusik   G-dur. (1. Konzert-Aufführung.)
3. Entreact — H-moll mit Geisterchor. (1. Konzert-Aufführung.)
4. Ouverture — C-dur. (2. Konzert-Aufführung.)
5. Romanze — F-moll.
6. Balletmusik — H-moll. G-dur. (1. Konzert-Aufführung.)
7. Entreact — B-dur.
8. Hirtenchor — B-dur

Druck von J. B. Wallishausser in Wien.   Verlag der Gesellschaft der Musikfreunde.

The program of the Vienna performance of movements 1–3 in the Grosser Redoutensaal, when the work shared the program with the *Rosamunde* music of Schubert.

II.

The opening of "Denn alles Fleisch" in the first English edition of the vocal score. (Leipzig and Winterthur, Rieter-Biedermann, 1872)

More second thoughts. The opening of the Fourth Symphony, op. 98, in Brahms's autograph
full score. The markings direct the copyist to take in four preliminary bars of introduction
that Brahms notated elsewhere in the score, but he then decided to leave them out. (Zentralbibliothek, Zurich)

MAX KLINGER
zugeeignet

VIER ERNSTE GESÄNGE

für

eine Bassstimme

mit Begleitung des Pianoforte

von

JOHANNES BRAHMS

Op. 121.

English text adapted by Paul England.

Ausgabe für Alt oder Baryton.

Ausgabe für Sopran oder Tenor.

Aufführungsrecht vorbehalten.
Verlag und Eigenthum für alle Länder
von
N. SIMROCK G.m.b.H. BERLIN.
Copyright for the British Empire by SCHOTT & C.º
5/58 Berners Street,
LONDON, W.
Copyright 1896 by N. Simrock, Berlin

The last opus number published in Brahms's lifetime. *Vier Ernste Gesänge,* op. 121 (Four Serious Songs), published in July 1896 by Simrock of Berlin. The first edition is dedicated to the artist Max Klinger, who made many drawings and engravings inspired by Brahms's works, some of which were used to decorate Brahms's publications.

Brahms at his upright work desk (*Stehpult*) in the library of his Vienna lodging.
(Gesellschaft der Musikfreunde, Vienna)

Such an introduction would have been enough for even the most confident artist to cope with. For the self-critical and studious Brahms it must have posed as much a problem as an opportunity as he took stock of his achievements in 1853. He wrote to to Schumann, whom he addressed as "revered master," from Hanover on 16 November 1853: "The public praise which you have bestowed upon me will have so extraordinarily increased the expectations of the musical world regarding my work that I do not know how I shall manage to do even approximate justice to it. Above all it will compel me to exercise the greatest caution in my choice of pieces for publication. . . . You will naturally understand that I am straining every nerve to bring as little as possible disgrace to you."[32]

For the moment, however, the prophesied symphonies were to wait. For Brahms was no epigone of Schumann. The path he needed to travel was one he could discover only by himself.

8 · The Years of Study

The New Discipline

Brahms had explored many musical fields before meeting the Schumanns. Though the piano and song had dominated his compositions, it seems that he wrote chamber music prior to the first known works, and his earliest named piece was for chorus.[33] But with the Schumanns a broader musical and literary world opened up to him, including access to more music of earlier periods than he had known—not merely of the Baroque period but also the Renaissance. But Schumann's encouragement was above all to compose, and Brahms did so intensely in 1853–54. But by 1855, whether for artistic reasons or because of the trauma of Schumann's suicide attempt, Brahms sought musical discipline by emphasizing counterpoint, chorale harmonization, and variation. By early 1855 Brahms was studying counterpoint on his own, telling Clara about his prowess in canonic writing. But study soon became intimately tied to his friendship with Joachim, which deepened through their similarity of outlook and shared responsibilities in the Schumann tragedy. Joachim, still a composer but feeling increasingly overshadowed by the vast talent of Brahms, became the agent of his friend's discipline. Brahms wrote to him in February

1856: "I also want to remind you and request you that at long last we carry out what we have long discussed; to send each other contrapuntal studies. Each fortnight, each to send the other back their work with criticism (therefore [to reply] in eight days), together with some work of his own; and let us so continue for a really long time until both of us have become really adept. Why shouldn't we two intelligent and serious people be able to teach one another better than any professor could? . . . I am hoping, and looking forward to your first packet. Let's start in earnest. It would be so lovely, good and productive."[34]

Work began in earnest a month later, when Brahms wrote: "I am enclosing two short pieces as a beginning of our shared studies. If you still have the inclination, I would like to lay down a few rules which I consider useful. Every Sunday some work must go either back or forth. If, for example, you send me something one Sunday, I will return it the following week with some work of my own, and so forth. And whoever misses the day, i.e., sends nothing, will be fined one thaler, with which the other can buy himself some books!!! One is excused only when, instead of the exercise, he sends some compositions, which will be then all the more welcome . . . double counterpoint, canons, fugues, preludes or whatever it may be."[35] Brahms had greater interest in the work than his friend, who soon lapsed and needed prompting, several times being eagerly encouraged by Brahms to send more.[36] Part of the reason for Brahms's commitment to Joachim involved his admiration for him as a composer and, in matters orchestral, as a mentor. But Joachim appreciated the exchange, as he revealed to Gisela von Arnim: "Some time ago I started a kind of musical correspondence with Brahms—we send each other assignments of considerable difficulty. This kind of musical relationship with him means a great deal to me; I remain in intellectually close contact with someone in whom I take a heartfelt interest. My younger friend is already very accomplished in the manipulations of this kind of composition, whereas I never occupied myself with it beyond the basic grammatical necessities. In this way I also acquire some artistic stimulation."[37]

Brahms's interest in the writing of canons remained particularly strong, though he kept it in perspective, as in his comments, "I am again returning my canons for the last time. Quite apart from the skills in them, are they good music? Do the artifices make them more beautiful and valuable? I am also enclosing some short canons. I particularly want to request your opinion on the four-part round. I add yet another work which I found difficult, and which I ask you, or rather, give over to you, to complete; the canonic imitation (rather free) on a C[antus] F[irmus]. Please save all the music sheets which you sent me. I will do the same; then perhaps, after a long while, we can look at them together again and, I hope, note great progress." Joachim replied, "To keep my word, here are the desired contrapuntal solutions on a given theme. . . . It was a difficult task, and compared with your characterful and purposeful ones, my canons are rather muddy and unsure in their rhythmic as well as their melodic execution. I must repeat: have patience with my lack of rudimentary skill in such matters."[38] Brahms never lost his interest in counterpoint, claiming, "When I do not feel like composing I write some counterpoint."[39] An inevitable consequence of canonic preoccupations was interest in fugue, of which Brahms produced some remarkable examples for keyboard and chorus. Brahms's interest in counterpoint naturally led him into choral music, and he explored a range of sources to gain a vast knowledge of the literature that was reflected in his many choral works of the period.

Another vital thrust was Brahms's concern for the principles of variation and thematic development. Brahms's love of variation goes back to his earliest works, in which some slow movements are variations on simple melodies, and he devoted a lengthy set to a theme of Schumann, which had intimate associations for Clara.[40] But his rapidly developing awareness of musical form and technique led him to see the limitations of his inherited methods and manner, not least as displayed by Schumann himself. Thus in 1856 he wrote to Joachim: "I occasionally reflect on variation form and find that it must be kept stricter, purer. The [old composers] retained the bass of the theme, their actual theme, strictly throughout. In Beethoven, melody, harmony and rhythm are so beautifully varied. But I sometimes have to admit that the newer composers (both of us!) rather (I don't know how to put it) rummage around the theme. We keep anxiously to the melody, but we do not treat it freely, do not actually create anything new from it, but only load it down. Thus the melody is barely recognizable." He expressed himself similarly more than twenty years later to Elisabet von Herzogenberg: "I wish that people would distinguish between the title: Variations and everything else, like fantasy variations, or whatever we may choose to call the greater variety of modern writings in the form. I have a particular affection for the variation form and consider that we could achieve much more from it with our talents and energies. Beethoven treats it with unusual severity and one can rightly translate them as 'alterations' [*Veränderungen*]. All the later ones by Schumann, Herzogenberg and Nottebohm are something very different. I am of course objecting to neither the form nor the music. I only wish for some distinction in name to denote the character of each."[41]

Despite his disclaimer, Brahms's interest in variation was strict. He explored it thoroughly in the following years, gaining a preeminence in the form rivaled only by Beethoven. His use of it involved retaining the length of the model and its essential harmonic skeleton but freed him to create freely from it. An essential part of this was his new attitude toward the melodic theme itself, which now became a source for motives that inspired completely new themes. The music itself gives all the evidence needed of his stimuli—chiefly from the Beethoven and Bach keyboard variations, though he never referred to them directly.

Broader Compositional Models and the Challenge of the Medium

In the years following 1855, Brahms's technical discipline was remarkable and his acquisition of method profound, impressing on him the sheer distance he had to travel in order to restore the classic tradition in the instrumental forms. Thus he began to explore in many directions. His immediate concerns were the problems of large-scale composition—the relation of ideas to form and of form to medium. From the moment he began to think in terms of instruments other than the piano, especially for the full orchestra, he lacked confidence. The problems with medium began with his first known orchestral attempt: the symphony that he sought to create from a two-piano sonata, which eventually became a piano concerto. Beethoven remained central as a model of formal mastery, but Brahms possessed a growing knowledge of Bach, Handel, Mozart, Haydn, and other contemporaries. And he began to explore the vital new stimulus of Schubert in about 1860. His interest extended to dramatic music, particularly to Beethoven's *Fidelio,* and to French opera, notably Méhul and Cherubini.

By March 1854 Brahms had written three movements of a two-piano sonata.[42] He was expanding the scope of the three preceding piano sonatas, the third of which stretches the capacity of the solo player to give the piece adequate force and control. By summer Brahms had begun to orchestrate the first movement, and, later, to speak of the work as a symphony to Robert Schumann. On 7 February 1855 he wrote to Clara that he had dreamed of the work as a three-movement concerto comprising the first movement, a scherzo, and the finale, and he followed this scheme. By April 1856 he had sent the first movement to Joachim, and by 1 October 1856 Clara spoke of a "splendid" concerto movement.[43] On 12 December Brahms sent the rondo movement to Joachim, and by 30 December he had written to Clara that he was writing an adagio—"a tender portrait of you"—which he then sent to Joachim in early January 1857.[44] Until after the first performance, on 22 January 1859 in Hanover, Brahms was revising and seeking advice, chiefly from Joachim, on both orchestration and form.

Problems of medium had prompted Brahms to change from his original two-piano format. On 19 June 1854 he wrote to Joachim, "I wish I could leave my D Minor Sonata alone for a long time. I have often played the first three movements over with Frau Schumann and find that they require even more than two pianos."[45] But Brahms never considered the orchestrated version of the first movement a success, even after extensively revising the eventual concerto version. Nor have even sympathetic critics spared it, either. For Gál, "the orchestra does not have instruments with the necessary brute force to do justice to the neighing, awe-inspiring trills of the theme. Brass instruments would be too strident. One must simply take the will for the deed and do his best to achieve the desired effect; this is almost possible with a sufficiently large string section."[46] The composer was fully conscious of the problems, but they were not easily solved. And quite apart from the orchestration, the change to concerto format must have involved inventing and deleting material, since the character of the sonata's first movement no doubt differed considerably from the concerto's movement, even allowing for its symphonic spirit.

He leaned heavily on Joachim. "A thousand thanks for having studied the first movement in such a careful and sympathetic manner," Brahms wrote. "I have already learnt a great deal from your remarks. As an artist I really have no greater wish than to have more talent so that I can learn still more from such a friend." The revisions continued. On 24 February 1858, Brahms still wrote, "I cannot cut as much as I should wish; it has all grown so interwoven." The second movement created fewer problems in the execution, though Brahms still expressed concern to Joachim in January 1857: "I wish I could rejoice over a really effective adagio. Let me know your opinion. If you like it, show it to our dear friend [Clara Schumann], but not otherwise." The finale, however, was as troublesome as the first movement. In the same letter to Joachim he said guardedly, "You are surely not troubling to make deeper and deeper cuts in the rondo, [though] I know they are quite necessary."[47] By 20 April he wrote to Joachim that "I am sending you the rondo once more. And just like the last time, I beg for some really severe criticism. Some parts have been quite changed—for the better, I hope—some merely altered. The ending especially has been improved; it was too sketchy and did not achieve what it set out to do." By 9 December Brahms seemed to have lost interest, remarking to Clara that "I have been thinking about my Concerto lately. You cannot imagine the trouble it has given me. It is one botch from start to finish and bears the hallmark of amateurishness. I am trying to get rid of this and finish with the work for good." But it was not to be easily finished, despite the support of his friends. On 26 November 1858, after the final rehearsal for the first performance—to be held in Hanover on 22 January 1859—he reported to Joachim that "my head was full of improvements, but I have forgotten them. Shouldn't much in the orchestration still be changed, also before the big performance?" Even after the second public performance, in Leipzig on 27 January, Brahms continued to reflect and to make changes before publication.[48]

The Piano Quintet in F Minor, op. 34, also was developed in three stages, though this time Brahms first wrote a string quintet and then recast it as a two-piano sonata. But since his ideas were essentially those of chamber music rather than symphonic music, he did not proceed to orchestration but sought a compromise in a quintet for piano and conventional string quartet. The original quintet, for the Schubertian ensemble of two cellos, one viola, and two violins, was finished in August 1862, though its finale was added later. It was well received in Brahms's circle, especially by Clara, who wrote on 3 September 1862 on receipt of the first three movements: "I do not know how to begin to tell you quietly the great delight your quintet has given me. I have played it over many times and am full of it! It grows on me, more beautiful and magnificent. What inner strength and what riches there are . . . and what an adagio, rapturously singing right to the last note! I am constantly playing it over and over and never wish to stop. I like the scherzo also, but I am inclined to think the trio a bit too short? When will the last movement be ready?"[49]

On 18 December she responded to the finale: "I think the last movement rounds off the whole thing splendidly, full of swing; the introduction is beautiful, the second motiv is a fitting contrast to the first, and the interplay of themes in the working out section is most ingenious. In short, the work is masterly." Joachim, though just as keen on the music in his letter of 5 November 1862, sounded a warning on the performance aspect: "This piece of music is certainly of the greatest importance and is strong in character. The movements taken separately unite well as a whole. . . . The quintet is difficult, and I am afraid that without vigorous playing it will not sound clear." After rehearsing the work he was more blunt: "I am unwilling to let the quintet pass out of my hands without having played it to you. That would be the best, indeed the only, way to help you. I do not wish to dogmatize on the details of a work which, in every line, shows some proof of overpowering strength. But what is lacking, to give me pure pleasure, is, in a word, some charm. After a time, on hearing the work quietly, I think that you will feel the same as I do about it."[50]

Brahms revised passages noted by Joachim and had the work performed with him in Vienna. He then concluded that he had miscalculated in the use of instruments, and he recast it for two pianos and played it with Carl Tausig to great effect. Clara was captivated, having studied the version with Hermann Levi, but she now felt that it needed an orchestra: "The work is splendid . . . but it cannot be called a sonata. Rather it is a work so full of ideas that it could have—must have—an orchestra for its interpretation! Even the most beautiful ideas go for nothing on the piano; they are only to be recognized by a musician and do not exist for the general public. The first time that I tried the work, I had the feeling that it was an arrangement, but, thinking I might be prejudiced, I kept quiet. But Levi was quite decided about it, without saying a word. But please . . . remodel it once more!"[51] Levi felt this even more strongly, and Brahms then rewrote it for piano quintet, receiving Levi's confirmation of its success in a letter of 9 November 1864: "The quintet is beautiful beyond words. Anyone who did not know the earlier forms of string quintet and piano sonata would not believe that it was not originally thought out and designed for the present combination of instruments. It does not contain a single note leading me to suppose it is an arrangement: all the ideas are rich in color. You have turned a monotonous work for two pianos into a thing of great beauty . . . a masterpiece of chamber music, the like of which we have not seen since the year 1828." But Brahms did not discard the second form of the quintet. He obviously felt that it had a special quality, and it was published as op. 34b, with the designation "after the quintet op. 34." He wrote to his publisher on 22 July 1864: "I still think we must keep the work in mind as a sonata for two pianos. It appeals to me in this form and appeals to everyone who has played it over or heard it. It might prove an interesting and acceptable composition for two pianos."[52]

The characteristic force of the many ideas of the piano concerto and piano quintet is such that the piano was essential for their full expression. But the piano could play no role in the creation of a genuine symphonic texture. When Brahms created his first truly symphonic allegro—the first movement of the First Symphony (completed in a form related to the one we know by 1862)—the texture was independent and markedly contrapuntal in parts. But this stage was not reached immediately. The Serenade in D Major "for large orchestra," completed in 1859 and published as op. 11, shows Brahms approaching the composition of orchestral music by thinking about textures rather than ideas. Much of the musical language is overtly classical in reference, Brahmsian by inflection rather than concept, only rarely touching the intensity of the concerto and quintet. The origin was in chamber music of a different kind: the classical semi-chamber combination of wind and strings used by Mozart and Haydn in divertimenti and by Beethoven and Schubert in their septet and octet, respectively. Brahms's work was first apparently an octet or nonet, with flute, two clarinets, horn, bassoon, and three or four string parts.[53] Joachim first heard it on the piano in September 1858 in Göttingen (Brahms began it in Detmold). Joachim knew it at that time by its outer movements, its adagio non troppo and a "trio." In December came "two new trios and a minuet." He now sought to expand the scoring, commenting, "I see that the work is a hybrid; it is not right."[54]

The Serenade was given in its version "for small orchestra" on 28 March 1859. When Brahms sent the score to Joachim in December in its version "for large orchestra" he now described it as a "Symphony-

Serenade." On receiving the first movement he wrote to Brahms: "What a magnificent surprise. Your orchestration is almost everywhere effective and in many places even beautifully original: only little will have to be changed. Some of the passages must be played through before one can come to a decision. . . . So much after a first reading. Do continue and finish it happily."[55] Joachim performed the version in Hanover on 3 March 1860.

These were works openly discussed by Brahms. But there were other works, with deeper problems, of which he rarely spoke. Those problems took years to resolve. Most protracted was the piano quartet in C sharp minor that he began in 1855 and finally published in 1875 as the Piano Quartet in C Minor, op. 60. The time he spent on the First Symphony is unknown, but is at the very least before 1862–77 (Brahms made revisions after the first performance, on 4 November 1876).[56] In both cases the primary issues seem to have been formal. There are strong grounds for suggesting Brahms's rearrangement of the movements of the eventual op. 60 piano quartet in addition to its change of key from C sharp minor to C minor. In the First Symphony the late adjustment of the middle movements, involving a remodeling of the second movement in ternary rather than rondo form after the first performance, suggests a concern with formal totality that must have centered on the creation of an adequate finale, so original is the surviving text.

9 · The Mature Compositional Outlook

The Brahmsian Ethos

Brahms's mature attitude toward compositional technique and values emerges chiefly from his occasional teaching and advising of young composers. For only when he was asked to pass on his values did he have occasion to express them, to reveal his very critical view of the musical world of his time. His comments sharpen and elaborate tendencies apparent from years of study, adding valuable evidence. Moreover, the expressions of the mature composer carry the vital coloring of his youthful experiences: of the sense of struggle to overcome youthful disadvantage, and of some resentment, characteristics that were an essential part of the mature man. This sense of struggle manifests itself most strongly in his concern with basic valucs, with his striving to achieve things of worth, however simple. Jenner witnessed how Brahms still regarded his hard upbringing as a point of reference for values: he retained a loyalty toward it and a modesty over his own achievements. " 'It is not easy to find someone who has had as tough a time of it as I have,' he said to me once as I sat alone with him on his birthday in the Hedgehog; and then he recalled sad events which were partly known to me already through Klaus Groth's accounts. 'If my father were still alive,' Brahms said, 'and I were sitting at the orchestra in the first desk of the second violins, then at least I could tell him that I had achieved something.' He could speak with justifiable pride, for everything he was he had accomplished through his own efforts."[57]

Brahms's belief in solid achievement recurs in his comments. And as a self-educated man who had acquired his great knowledge though practical application, he had reservations about formal academic training. Both facets find touching expression in Florence May's description of Brahms's reaction to the gifted young daughters of Hugo Conrat, who "paying the master a visit in his rooms, had been encouraged to talk about the progress of their [apparently academic] studies. 'You must know these things, which are very important; but I will show you something to be learnt of still greater consequence,' and he fetched from a drawer an old, worn, folded tablecloth. 'Look here,' said he, showing the girls some exquisite darning. 'My old mother did this. When you can do such work you may be prouder of it than of all your other studies.' "[58] The many young composers who beat a path to Brahms's door for advice got essentially the same response: a no-compromises confrontation with the harsh necessity for complete craft, a reality that was interpreted by some as simply discouragement, especially when accompanied by his familiar put-down, "So, young man, go on amusing yourself in this way."[59]

In evaluating a work he was above all concerned with getting to the point of the composer's task. This required a dedication to deriving from the material everything it had to offer, however long that might take. Henschel received the classic statement of the Brahmsian ethos in connection with some songs he brought for the composer: "He took up the one in E flat, 'Where Angels Linger,' and said, 'Now there is a charming song. In some of the others you seem to me too easily satisfied. One ought never to forget that by actually perfecting one piece one gains and learns more than by commencing or half-finishing a dozen. Let it rest, let it rest, and keep going back to it and working at it over and over again, until it is completed as a finished work of art, until there is not a note too much or too little, not a bar you could improve upon. Whether it is *beautiful* also is an entirely different matter, but perfect it *must* be. You see, I am rather lazy, but I never cool down over a work, once begun, until it is perfected, unassailable.' Thus he continued speaking, drawing, in the most amiable way, my attention to this little defect, that little blemish, so that I sat happy and silent, careful not to interrupt this, to me, so precious lesson."[60]

Brahms's concern for the "little blemishes" in someone else's work reflects his great capacity for concentration. He gave serious study to the work of his young composers when possible, even though his manner was sometimes brusque and ironic and his advice depressing. Jenner recalls him as "minutely prepared, down to the tiniest detail" for their sessions, and the English composer Walford Davies recalls even a hurried meeting at Ischl to inspect his work: "He read quickly and attentively, pausing only occasionally to note something."[61]

Counterpoint

Counterpoint was at the basis of Brahms's art, and he regarded it as a fundamental area of knowledge for all composers. But he had little occasion to talk about it, for he sent would-be students to other teachers for this basic training. His words to Jenner capture the spirit of his advice: "First look for a teacher who will instruct you in strict counterpoint; you will find the best are among the cantors in the villages; he doesn't need to be someone as famous as Mr. X (here he gave a well-known name). It is absolutely essential that you see the world through these spectacles for a good time to come. You will have plenty to do for several years. But write to me." Mr. X was doubtless Eusebius Mandyczewski, the outstanding young theorist who became the librarian of the Musikverein and a close friend in Brahms's later years. In earlier years Brahms recommended Nottebohm to students of counterpoint, telling Elisabet von Herzogenberg: "I can strongly recommend him as a teacher. I send everyone who comes my way, and have often had occasion to be delighted with the results."[62] And we can gain a good idea of the kind of books

Brahms esteemed on the subject from Mandyczewski's record of the contents of Brahms's library. He lists many venerable eighteenth-century sources: Marpurg, Mattheson, Kirnberger, Kellner, C. P. E. Bach.[63]

Brahms's own attitude to counterpoint was formed through his teaching of the harmonic aspect of the simplest of free compositional assignments—strophic song—which also provides a focus for his rigorous attitude to tonality, modulation, and inner coherence. Through this channel and that of form we get to the core of Brahms's attitude to musical values. Henschel, Jenner, and the composer Richard Heuberger were direct recipients of these values. Contrapuntal factors dominated even the simplest song, as he declared to Henschel: " 'In writing songs,' he cautioned me, 'you must endeavour to invent, simultaneously with the melody, a healthy, powerful bass. You stick too much to the middle parts. In that song in E flat, for instance,' he again referred to 'Where angels linger,' 'you have hit upon a very charming middle part, and the melody, too, is very lovely, but that isn't all, is it? And then, my dear friend, let me counsel you: no heavy dissonances on the unaccentuated parts of the bar, please! That is weak. I am very fond of dissonances, you'll agree, but on the heavy, accented parts of the bar, and then let them be resolved easily and gently.' "[64]

The last comment implies a further emphasis on the counterpoint of the outer voices, for the bass is less able to make a strong line with dissonances on the weak beat. Brahms's demonstration of the point to Jenner was more precise.

> Sometimes he used a drastic but surprisingly simple
> means to open my eyes and make me really perceive that
> under that rich and gleaming cloak lay hidden something
> pitiable, insufficient, and meager, which could not possi-
> bly expose itself naked. [Brahms] covered the upper stave
> of the piano accompaniment with one hand and, point-
> ing to the vocal line and the bass, said with an expressive
> smile: "I only read this." In this way, the artificiality of
> the invention was not infrequently presented to me "ad
> ocolos," as it were; I no longer grasped how I could have
> arrived at such a dull melodic line and such boring
> basses, unless it were that I had actually been engrossed

in the figuration of the accompaniment and had
therefore not been free. The governing role of the melody and with it definite, good contrapuntal basses were a
basic requirement with him, one that also remained in
force even in the most artful shaping of the design of the
whole song.[65]

Brahms insisted on the clarifying role of the bass to Heuberger as well, suggesting that the bass "must be a kind of mirror structure of the upper voice."[66] So, as Jenner intimates, Brahms's attitude toward the basic counterpoint of a setting had obvious implications for the character and details of the accompaniment, of the desire to see everything serving the central purpose. He had no interest in novel effects as such, but only in the organic whole. "It should be apparent that Brahms was not one to be impressed by a few 'interesting' phrases or by complicated and 'atmospheric' accompaniment figures. His eye remained sharp. . . . But if, however, [only] scanty crumbs from the piano accompaniment are allocated to the vocal part, then Brahms could never permit such inferior work to be give the title 'song.'" This sense of the underlying logic of a piece reemerges when Brahms discusses the handling of tonality and of modulation, of the deeper unity of the parts to the whole. Jenner continued:

The location and form of the cadences is intimately associated with the course of the modulation. Here Brahms
called for the tightest possible reins and the most extreme
consistency. Even in a very long song, with extended, en-
closed secondary sections, the principal key had always to
be fully expressed, and its mastery over all the secondary
keys maintained through clear relationships, so that, as
one might put it, the sum of all the keys employed in
the piece appeared as a picture of the main tonality in all
its activity. . . . It was in order to help me acquire a reliable sense of the unified character of the modulation that
Brahms made me imitate . . . the modulations from Adagio movements of Mozart or Beethoven. "If Beethoven
goes from C major to E major, you do the same; I have
often done so in the past," he told me. As regards the
overall course of the modulation, with the exception of

individual digressions, the guiding principle was: the straight path is the best.[67]

Theory

Brahms's approach to teaching musical form and to the values of craft and practical experience inherent in it inevitably attracts interest to his view of formal teaching and music theory: that is, theory apart from the basic principles of counterpoint. Brahms's reserve in offering himself as a teacher was based not just on a temperamental disinclination to teach the basics nor on the time commitments for someone so heavily involved in creative work and performance. It also was based on an apparent aversion to the formalized theory that was such a strong part of it: that is, theory conceived of as the systematic elaboration of a method or as a speculative concept. He seemingly opposed the formulation of systems, preferring to acquire good models, especially those from the past. As he put it to Heuberger, it was not theory books that helped him around his lack of a "good school" but good models and rigorous application. "You would not believe what I had to put up with from incompetent textbooks and how I had to unlearn everything," he told the theorist Hugo Riemann. In connection with practice of modulation he remarked to Eugenie Schumann, "Though a knowledge of harmony is of course very useful . . . I can't think what benefit anyone would derive from years of study in harmony." That this was no throwaway remark seems clear in this exchange with Gustav Jenner: "After a severe examination of everything that I had done up to that time, Brahms said, 'You see, you haven't really learnt anything basic about music; for everything you tell me about theory of harmony, attempts at composition, instrumentation and the like, is worthless in my opinion.' Then he asked me how old I was, and when he heard that I had just completed my twenty-second year, he did not disguise his misgivings that it might be too late."[68]

Brahms's low opinion of formal teaching reemerges at about the same time in his comments to Elisabet von Herzogenberg about Vienna: "Our Conservatory is in a terrible state as regards the teaching of composition. You need only see the teachers and not, as I often do, the pupils and their work."[69] His solution was to recommend individual teachers, especially Nottebohm and Mandyczewski. But they, like Brahms, were steeped in musical literature and interested in didactic traditions, the more so since they seemed so threatened in the modern musical world. Although his comment to Hugo Riemann reflects his ambivalence toward being offered the dedication of Riemann's "Kleine Kompositionslehre" (which he finally did accept with reluctance), he remained interested in the subject.[70] His analytical turn of mind is recorded not only by Jenner but by Riemann and Bülow, and he certainly appreciated good critical writing.

However deep Brahms's interest in speculative concepts of music may have gone—in theories of coherence, for example—it was on the practical examples of problemsolving in the works of predecessors that he placed his emphasis. In his collection of parallel octaves and fifths in works of the great masters he balanced the basic rules of counterpoint against the evidence of the ear.[71] The collection surely indicates the way he worked, for such examples could come only from constant examination of the music of others. Some writers have seen the collection as a theory in embryo. This is certainly not impossible, though Brahms's lack of commitment to formal theory makes it unlikely. But the collection had real purpose in allowing to broaden his field of possibility: he comments on the examples as "good fifths, bad fifths," "beautiful," "ugly," and so on, indicating a recognition of when and how a rule could be broken.

Attitude to Song

Brahms's most pointed comments on individual genres chiefly concern the field in which he was very active—song—and one in which his aspirations were never realized—opera. But insights into the field of Brahms's most extended mastery, the instrumental forms (especially the sonata and its variation), remain obscured beyond the generalities of principle already noted, though much can still be drawn from them. Because song offers the most accessible free compositional exercise and was one of Brahms's favorite musical genres, detailed information on his outlook survives. The strictness of Brahms's aesthetic outlook affected his approach to song composition in his treatment of the text itself. His position was the consequence of musical considerations of the natural possibilities and limitations of word setting—he tended to regard poems as self-sufficient or as being music in themselves. To Henschel he stated, "Schubert's 'Suleika' songs are to me the only instances where the power and beauty of Goethe's words have been enhanced by the music. All other of Goethe's poems seem to me so perfect in themselves that no music can improve them."[72] But poems by Daumer, Groth, and others could be lifted to a higher artistic level than they formerly possessed by adding music. Brahms's choice of verse has been criticized, but not by all composers and performers of his culture. The young Henschel said that the "sources—individual or national—from which he drew his inspiration have in themselves been, to a greater or lesser degree, inspired. All his songs, duets, quartets, etc., are set to beautiful, significant, worthy poems." Brahms always defended his choices vigorously, as he defended Ludwig Hölty to Adolf Schubring.[73]

Brahms's emphasis on the quality of Goethe's words as set by Schubert implies more about the process of setting than simply the expressive response of the composer. It acknowledges the formal identity and integrity of the poem, which were central to any Brahms setting. Jenner recalls that Brahms first demanded that his composer "know his text precisely. By this he naturally also meant that the construction and meter of the poem should be thoroughly clear to him. Then he recommended that before composing I should carry the poem around in my head for a long time and frequently recite it to myself, paying precise attention to everything, especially the declamation. I should also specially mark the pauses and observe these later in the work. 'Just imagine to yourself that Lewinsky were reciting this song,' he once said as we were discussing a song with almost no pauses; 'Here he would certainly stop for a moment.' "[74]

Heuberger reported that Brahms "took a fresh sheet of paper and began to write in my text in blank measures, so that each word had its proper accent." In his opinion this was an excellent method for beginners to find the exact coincidence of musical and verbal rhythm.[75] He found this vital correspondence best exemplified in the songs of Schubert, Jenner recalls:

> When he discussed a song with me, the first thing he
> considered was whether the musical form matched that
> of the text throughout. He censured mistakes of this
> kind especially sharply as indicating a lack of artistic
> sense, or as the consequence of insufficient absorption of
> the text. In general he demanded that if a text allowed
> strophic treatment, this should be adopted. In order to
> be clear which texts were to be treated in strophes and

which not, he recommended a close study of the complete songs of Franz Schubert, whose sharp discrimination of these things was apparent even in his most unassuming songs. "There is not one song by Schubert from which one cannot learn something."

Given Brahms's poetic predilections and formal inclinations, his musical preferences emerge clearly: "I have always retained the impression," declares Jenner, "that of all song forms, Brahms valued strophic songs most highly."[76]

Once the overview had been achieved, Brahms focused on punctuation, phrase structure, and cadence:

> It mattered here above all to understand the combination and opposition of the three great factors of music— rhythm, melody, and harmony: to understand, for example, that a cadence which is harmonically and melodically perfect will have a weaker effect if it does not occur simultaneously with the rhythmic cadence. . . . Occasionally Brahms showed me passages where the cadence was not well motivated rhythmically and from this he proved beyond doubt that the cadence had been placed there because the imagination had flagged. Often in such cases, a six-four chord appears like a secure armchair in which the exhausted imagination can prematurely repose. "Draw a line under every six-four chord and examine closely whether it is in the right place," Brahms said.

This comment substantiates Brahms's remark to Henschel on the placement of dissonances on strong parts of the bar.[77]

Brahms also stressed the role of pauses and irregularity of phrasing in giving flexibility to a setting. Heuberger recalls his comment that "you can make irregularities, but they must always be grounded in the piece itself and really have meaning. If you make a three- or five-bar phrase, always be sure that you come to the correct rhythmic position again." For Jenner, who received similar advice, this was an "unmistakable sign that the composer is an artist who creates with freedom and assurance, not a dilettante groping in the dark, influenced by every chance occurrence." He had clearly absorbed Brahms's own view. Jenner observed a distinct attitude toward textual expression in Brahms's teaching:

> Brahms could never be satisfied if there was nothing but a pretty, well-accompanied melody. In one instance, when my melody did not seem to suffice for the text, he said, "Write yourself another text underneath that." Brahms strongly believed in what one can term "word expression" (*Wortausdruck*). One often will find in his songs striking melodic turns of phrase that have obviously been brought about by certain individual words in the text. But rather than disturbing the melodic flow, these phrases seem to be essential components of the melody, which gave it a particular appearance. Indeed, they often resemble the kernels of motives from which the whole melody seems to grow. . . . However, he never composed any so-called "mood poems," which subsist merely as an accumulation of such kinds of word-paintings. If the melodic line followed a particular verbal expression too closely, he would criticize it with the words: "More from the whole." And with that he got to the core of the thing.[78]

Brahms directed Henschel's thought toward contemporary trends in song composition, though the sentiment reemerges in connection with opera: "There are composers who sit at the piano with the poem before them, putting music to it from A–Z until it is done. They write themselves into a state of enthusiasm in which they see something finished, something important in every bar."[79]

With the publication of the "Declaration," 1860 was a year of truth for Brahms. He commented to Clara Schumann that "song composition is today sailing along so false a course that one cannot sufficiently remind oneself of the ideal: and that for me is the folksong."[80] Brahms had included folksongs in his free compositions from the first, and by this time he had arranged many German folksongs for chorus, set folk poems in a folklike musical idiom, and provided piano accompaniments to folksongs for Clara's children. This commitment strengthened throughout his life. He provided his favored folk poems with original music, often drawing closely on originals. His collection *49 Deutsche Volkslieder,* which he published in 1894, was the richest flowering of this interest. His seemingly flippant comment to his publisher gains value when contrasted with his fierce self-criticism in other areas: "This is the only part of my work which has really given me pleasure."[81] That is, one may surmise, that he found the relation between concept and execution is closest in such perfect miniatures. And he was greatly pleased when others could link his original melodies with those that had inspired them. "Those who hear and see them declare that they are my own and very like my work."[82] The sense of continuity from his earliest musical tendencies was grasped with special intimacy by Joachim, writing on 27 September 1894: "One cannot sufficiently admire the skill of the accompaniment which conceals with wonderful art and vivid expression. How beautifully are the final repetitions accommodated at the cadence and how rich in modulation you manage to make them. Pictorial and yet only suggestive, they are perfectly adapted to the folksong. Not a single one with all its many verses was too long for me."[83]

The very importance that Brahms attached to these settings enables us to see deeper into his musical character. For these settings were the occasion for a musical controversy that nearly rivaled that surrounding the "Declaration" of 1860. Much as he loved them, many of Brahms's sources were not original but were relatively recent composed pieces from the collections of Kretschzmer-Zuccalmaglio and of Nicolai.[84] Brahms's choices placed his scholarly friends in a difficult position, especially Max Friedländer, who recalled that "Brahms refused to believe that there existed in his time a real folkmusic. When I pointed out to him in the eighties that such songs still flourished on the Lower Rhine, in Hesse, in Thuringia and in Silesia, he answered: 'Ah, you are far too idealistic and optimistic about it! Believe me, the so-called people sing only the street songs of the moment now.' "[85]

Brahms obviously had no interest in scholarly facts when it came to the authenticity of his favored melodies. To Hermann Deiters he wrote, "I got over the dispute about their genuineness very easily. The editors Erk and Böhme collected their songs in Pomerania, Mecklenburg, etc., Zuccalmaglio and others in the Rhine valley before the days of railways. They are therefore equally to be believed alike, or . . . equally to be suspected alike of arranging."[86] But, as Friedländer commented, "not one-hundredth part of the songs collected by Erk came from Pomerania or Mecklenburg, though on the other hand, his collection contains many fine examples from the Rhine, since he was himself half a Rhinelander."[87] Brahms always acknowledged his debt to Kretzschmer-Zuccalmaglio, whose collection he spoke of in the same letter: "There are books which are much abused, in my opinion wrongly, which continue to interest me. Friedländer comments, 'Thus it was that words and tunes, altered and colored artistically, adapted to a higher standard of culture or even forged, if only they were in his style, received his applause and approval, and genuine and original songs remained in a minority.' "[88]

For once, Brahms failed to give the work of a genuine scholar its due, making no distinction between the pioneering work of Erk and the undiscriminating editorial contribution of Böhme in the *Deutscher Liederhort*, Erk and Böhme's collection of more than two thousand songs that appeared in 1893.[89] The collection "triggered all of Brahms's pent-up irritation against the wholesale system of folksong research." Brahms had intended to write an article against "this whole class of folksong farmers." He later remarked, "I was in deadly earnest about the polemic. . . . While I was writing so strongly and so zealously, I was thinking of my old, favorite songs." The intended polemic was never issued. Instead, Brahms let music speak for him, though the matter was probably the trigger to final editing and publication of the collection: "For a long time, Erk and Böhme have set this very narrow-minded fashion, and my collection is definitely in opposition to them." Artistic value, he believed, would overcome everything. "My songs are not the songs the workmen sing on the street corners," he wrote. "These songs will dazzle the philistines of Berlin like a ray of bright sunlight." He never lost faith in his sources, even when he had to admit that not everything in Kretzschmer-Zuccalmaglio was original: "Ah well, so we have one good composer the more, and for him I do not have to apologize as for myself."[90]

Music and Drama

The extent of Brahms's interest in theater and its consequences for his operatic ambitions are stressed by Widmann. He was especially well placed to observe them, since his close friendship with Brahms was based largely on shared literary enthusiasms, and Widmann was a prospective librettist for Brahms.

It is well known that Brahms was an indefatigable thea-
tergoer and that dramatic pathos could powerfully affect
him. And the fact that (especially in the last two decades
of his life) he, on the whole, avoided operatic performances, affords no real reason for questioning the keen interest he took in the opera: on the contrary, does not
this rather point to the fear of rekindling long-buried
wishes? At any rate, he was always particularly animated
when speaking of subjects relating to the theater; as, for
instance, when he once pointed out to me the total absence of any true dramatic spirit, the vaudeville character
demonstrated in the first act of the libretto of *Fidelio,*
which is generally considered particularly good. Possessed
of an extraordinary dramatic instinct, it gave him keen
pleasure to analyze any scheme for a dramatic work.[91]

In earlier years he had followed everything by his contemporaries and
had taken an interest in performing their music while he was director of
the Gesellschaft der Musikfreunde. After attending Max Bruch's *Hermoine*
in 1871 he wrote to Simrock: "I am always thankful for novelties and
therefore naturally rejoice at *Hermoine*."[92] He took a similar interest in
Hermann Goetz's *Francesca da Rimini* in 1877, attending the first performance.[93] But it was mainly the older operas that attracted him in later
years. Despite his admiration for Wagner's work and perpetual interest in
the problems of operatic composition, he was never interested in modern
through-composed structures." Even Weber's *Euryanthe* or Schumann's
Genoveva (works by composers closer to him in idiom) interested him
less than more distant works, such as the operas of Cherubini, especially
Medea (1797), and Méhul, in whose *Uthal* (1806) he took great interest.
Thus, when he discovered that the conductor Felix Mottl had staged a
performance of *Uthal* in Karlsruhe in 1891, he commented, "But that is
actually *my* work. Years ago I gave the material to [Edward] Devrient and
[Hermann] Levi. . . . Mottl then found [it all] and went ahead and produced it."[94]

Brahms's operatic preferences emerge from his own aesthetic position,
which defined clearly individual roles for music and drama, as Widmann
recalled:

It seemed to him that to compose music for the whole
drama was unnecessary, even harmful and inartistic: only
the climax, and those parts of the action where words
alone cannot suffice, should be set to music. By these
means, on the one hand, the librettist gains more space
and freedom for the dramatic development of the subject, and, on the other, the composer is not hindered in
devoting himself exclusively to the demands of his art,
which can best be fulfilled when he has musically complete mastery of the situation as, for example, in a jubilant ensemble. Besides, he held it to be a barbarous
demand to expect musical accentuation to accompany a
purely dramatic dialogue all through several acts.[95]

Although we have only hints of how Brahms developed as a dramatic
composer—in such works as the cantata *Rinaldo* or the Alto Rhapsody,
effectively a dramatic scene with chorus—the continuous style of these
works suggests the influence of Wagner and points to creative tension, as
between musical style and dramatic ideal.

Wagner's influence is but one of many factors that affected Brahms's
decision regarding opera composition. The others include a disinclination
toward being involved in the practical world of the theater, as well as
unwillingness to provoke comparison with Wagner, and lack of commitment. But his interest continued for years. Widmann, who gives no hint
of the inherent musical problems of opera for Brahms, was convinced
that the composer was resistant because he could not find an appropriate
libretto. Had he known the history of the issue, perhaps Widmann would
have been less optimistic. Brahms had been searching for a libretto since
the eighteen-sixties with his friend Julius Allgeyer. But Brahms always
found something wrong with them. From Vienna in January 1869 he
wrote to Allgeyer:

I have little courage and inclination to reach into the
wide blue sky and snatch at opera librettos by some new
poet or other. If I were to come to Winterthur in the
spring, I certainly would not fail to have a thorough chat
with W[idmann]. By the way, I am not too encouraged

by your liking for his *Iphigenie* [in Delphi] and by his finding subjects in Celtic myths. I would rather that his *Der geraubte Schleier* ("The Stolen Veil") were not inspired by Musaeus and went straight to one's heart. But this is all by the way. Above all, men like myself stand so far removed, not only from the theater but from all other practical activities, that it is altogether desirable that the second partner in such an undertaking be versed in the usual routine. As a kind remembrance, your text does not leave my nearest drawer—but I've hardly looked at it.[96]

By the following year he had grown more encouraging to his would-be librettist:

I shall not fail to ask as urgently as possible not to give up looking about (for libretti) on my behalf. . . . Do send me the book of *Uthal*. . . . I am now pondering over the Jewish liberation from Babylon, though an oratorio would be less acceptable to me than an opera, but I cannot find a satisfactory ending (possibly a reference to Christ). The only thing I can arrive at after such hard thinking is always a "No." For instance, Kleist's *Kätchen von Heilbronn* has often attracted me, and now when I have a decent libretto of it in front of me, all I have learned from it is not to use any text at all, where we, so to speak, only obscure the music of the words by cloaking it with our music. . . . Let me hear from you from time to time—if only sporadically—what you are reading on my behalf.[97]

In fact, despite his criticism of the libretto, it was not Allgeyer but Widmann who was closest to the potential Brahms opera. As their friendship grew, the libretti became a natural focus of discussion, and Widmann immersed himself in his speciality on Brahms's behalf, as he recalls of *König Hirsch, Der Rabe, Das laute Geheimnis*.[98] These topics reemerged several times before fading from Brahms's view.

Instrumental Music

The demonstration of Brahms's general principles concerning song and dramatic composition was relatively straightforward, but the complex balances and organic aspects of the instrumental forms in which he excelled received little verbal expression. Indeed, Jenner's recollections of Brahms's reactions to his attempts at sonata and rondo forms are rare and valuable. Brahms's sense of a whole—of the logic of connections, of the avoidance of curiosities in favor of the direct and sensible—is clearly his prime concern in scrutinizing Jenner's piece.

> In the first movement of the trio there was much turning of pages to and fro. With devastating precision Brahms pointed out to me the illogicality of the structure; it was as if in his hands the whole thing fragmented into its individual parts. With growing horror I saw how weakly and loosely they hung together; I realized that the bond which was supposed to hold them together was much more external than internal: it was nothing more than the scheme of the sonata form. The essence of form gradually began to reveal itself to me and I suddenly grasped that it was not enough to have a good idea here and there; that one has not written a sonata when one has merely assembled several such ideas through the outward form of the sonata, but that, on the contrary, the sonata form must emerge with necessity from the ideas. I was already making the discovery that precisely those passages from which I had expected the most hardly seemed to interest Brahms at all. At such enthused of passages, where my heart beat faster, he calmly and coldly criticized "sleepy and lazy" basses, pointed out weak harmonies, suggested replacing a few notes with others that were more logical and thus allowed the idea that had, as it were, become hidden by my harmonies, and lost its ability to develop, so to speak, to emerge clearly and strongly. . . . Sentences such as "that could just as well mean something else" already gave me . . . much to think about. . . . Brahms showed me how my

eye . . . had focused on inessential things, while the essential things that made all the difference remained unnoticed. Naturally those deficiencies showed up most strongly in the slow movement. . . . For all my discomfort, however, which Brahms probably sensed, he offered only the dubious consolation that "such a long adagio is the most difficult thing of all."[99]

Brahms's early awareness of "misguided originality" (as quoted from Eckermann in *Des Jungen Kreislers Schatzkästlein*) had obviously lost none of its force when he taught Jenner. "In the Scherzo I had tried to be 'original.' . . . Unfortunately it did not hold up either; this originality was surely and slowly transformed into simple nonsense. We came to the end of the movement remarkably quickly, and Brahms said well-meaningly, 'Of course, you will promise not to write anything like this again.' "[100]

Brahms's reference to Beethoven as an exemplar in modulation is symbolic of his reverence for the composer in formal matters. From the youthful literary and musical quotations to the completion of the First Symphony—with his famous comment "I will never write a symphony. You don't know what it's like for the likes of us to hear that giant's footsteps . . . marching behind"[101]—his efforts were overshadowed by Beethoven. Yet in declaring at a difficult rehearsal of one of the A major orchestral serenades under Dessoff, "Gentlemen, I know I am not Beethoven, but I am Johannes Brahms,"[102] he shows his ability to put himself in perspective without losing his admiration for Beethoven. Certainly no composer of Brahms's generation is as openly Beethovenian as is Brahms in the D Minor Concerto, parts of the Serenades and First Symphony, to say nothing of the chamber music. But the First Symphony is misunderstood if seen only as a tribute to Beethoven. When Clara observed that the middle movements of the First Symphony sounded more like serenade movements,[103] she was touching on one important and different aspect of Brahms's development as a symphonist. As stated, the first of the two orchestral serenades (op. 11, his first purely orchestral music) was briefly titled "Symphony Serenade" when scored for full orchestra in 1859. Its previous conception as chamber music and for small orchestra relates to the eighteenth-century tradition of serenade and divertimento music as well as symphonies. He took interest in the performance of Mozart serenades by the wind players of the Detmold orchestra and brought scores of Haydn symphonies from Hamburg in the hopes that the court orchestra would rehearse them.[104] Classical symphonies and serenades remained an important source of the Brahms orchestral style.

The original form of the serenade in D throws light on another stimulus of Brahms instrumental style: chamber music. For throughout the symphony's development Brahms's major achievements were in chamber music. Although the main influence on the String Quartet in C Minor that appeared shortly before the symphony (seemingly the earlier of the two quartets, op. 51) was Beethoven's, the background to the more unusual genres of string sextet and (as with the original version of the piano quintet) string quintet was Schubert's. The model for the two cellos of the quintet was obviously the Schubert Quintet, an influence that also permeates the two sextets. This super-chamber medium was the province of Schubert. Though Brahms made no direct analogy, his view of Schubert was unequivocal and he obviously represented the essential counterpoise to Beethoven in Brahms's development. He referred to more than songs when he said of Schubert, "He plays in a region, at a height to which the others can in no way aspire."[105]

10 · Attitude to Contemporaries

Brahms's reactions to his own achievements and to the works of his contemporaries were colored by his reverence for the great composers of the past. For him, none of the achievements of modern composers bore real comparison, and his devotion emerges repeatedly in his comments, as to Henschel: "How must those Gods Bach, Mozart, Beethoven have felt, whose daily bread was to write things like the *St. Matthew Passion, Don Giovanni, Fidelio,* [the] *Ninth Symphony!*" May recalls that "Brahms disliked to hear anything said which could possibly be interpreted as depreciation [sic] of either of the great masters."[106] This sensitivity also extended to any undue familiarity with the composers, as to Henschel: "To twaddle about Bach or Beethoven, as is done in the letters [of Hauptmann] to Hauser, in a chattering, feuilletonistic way, is wholly unnecessary: they are too great for that kind of thing."[107] The qualities that ensured this greatness were the yardstick by which Brahms measured everyone else's work. Only in this context can Brahms's almost notorious aversion to flattery be understood, particularly the claims that Brahms was another Beethoven: "What I cannot understand is how people like myself can be vain. As much as we men, who walk upright, are above the creeping things of the earth, so these Gods are above us. If it were not so ludicrous, it would be loathsome to me to hear colleagues of mine praise me to my face in such an exaggerated manner."[108] And this was no pious devotion: Brahms admired the music with passion, and contact with it reinvigorated him. On hearing the close of the slow movement of a Mozart symphony in rehearsal he remarked to Elisabet von Herzogenberg: "I'd give all my stuff [*kram*] to have written that one Andante."[109] And even in the gloom following the near silence that greeted the second public performance of the D Minor Piano Concerto he could comment, "My rather ill-humoured and sober mood soon vanished when I heard the C Major Symphony of Haydn and Beethoven's 'Ruins of Athens.'"[110] The power of this slant in the attitudes of the developing composer is caught in his reaction to the death of Louis Spohr in October 1859, when he wrote to Bertha Porubszky:

> Spohr is dead! Truly the last of those who still belonged
> to a more beautiful artistic period than the one through
> which we now suffer. In those days one might well have
> looked around eagerly after each fair to see what new
> and beautiful things had arrived from one composer or
> another. Now things are different. For a long time I have
> hardly seen a single collection of music that gave me
> pleasure, but a great many that almost caused me physi-
> cal distress. At no time has any art been so mistreated as
> is now our beloved music. Let us hope that somewhere
> in obscurity something better is emerging, for otherwise
> our epoch would go down in the annals of art as a dung
> pit.[111]

It was therefore inevitable that his view would bring him into conflict with those very contemporaries who were blazing the modernist trail. Within a matter of months the nascent conflict came to a head.

Liszt and the Declaration of 1860

The music of Liszt had become the focus of Brahms's antipathy toward modern trends in the later eighteen-fifties, and he never expressed himself with such persistent vehemence about any other composer. The antipathy is an essential backdrop to the Declaration of 1860 (discussed below), Brahms's only public statement on the contemporary musical scene. Although Brahms was still a minor figure in relation to his contemporaries, his statement crystallized and politicized the diverging musical attitudes in Germany. Liszt certainly had had no reason to receive Brahms less warmly than he did all young artists when the twenty-year-old Brahms arrived at his home with Reményi, carrying a letter of introduction from Joachim, in June 1853. Much has been made of this meeting in light of later events, Brahms depicted as having dozed off during Liszt's performance of his new piano sonata after Liszt had "amazed and delighted" Brahms by playing his Scherzo in E flat Minor and part of his Sonata in C at sight, maintaining a sympathetic commentary as he played.[112] Whatever caused Liszt to leave the room abruptly at the end of the performance had no apparent effect on their relationship, because Brahms stayed another three weeks at Weimar and met him again happily the following year. But the incident does appear to indicate that Brahms's antipathy to Liszt's music and presentational manner was formed at this early meeting. When the composer looked for the "special interest and sympathy of his listeners" at an expressive part that he "always imbued with extreme pathos," Brahms apparently was insufficiently attentive.[113] But Brahms was also capable of distinguishing between manner and technical quality, stating in later years that "whoever has not heard Liszt has not even heard piano playing. He comes first and then for a long space nobody follows. His playing has something unique, incomparable, and inimitable."[114] But Brahms seems to have felt that Liszt's gifts were misdirected, and he told Mandyczewski in later years that "the prodigy, the itinerant virtuoso, and the man of fashion ruined the composer before he had the chance to develop."[115]

In the years that followed his first meeting with Liszt, Brahms's attitude toward the claims of the Weimar school, as broadcast through Liszt's writings in *Neue Zeitschrift für Musik,* intensified. By 1859 his restlessness was growing uncontrollable. In the summer he wrote to Joachim in England: "The Weimarites continue their uproar. . . . My fingers often itch to start a fight and to write something anti-Liszt. But who am I? I can't even write greetings to my dearest friend because I don't know what to write—or whatever other excuses my inherent laziness dictates to me. But it would be wonderful if you were to remain in Germany in the summer, to compose wonderfully and to strike these people dead with a few flying shots, whilst I sat near you, rejoiced, and helped to write music."[116]

Joachim's views on Liszt were similar to Brahms's but more circumspect. "The people in Liszt's camp are far too well versed in writing, too much on guard, too coarse, and too sophistical. Liszt knows only too well how to arouse enthusiasm and how to exploit it for his own ends; consequently, an honest fight with these bacchantes and sycophants is not possible. And it is really not necessary—their uncouth fanaticism and their false harmonies will dig their own graves for them."[117] When Liszt finally appeared on the program of the Hamburg Philharmonic under G. D. Otten, Brahms could not contain himself. He wrote to Clara, "Yesterday Otten was the first to introduce works by Liszt into a decent concert: 'Loreley,' a song, and 'Leonore' by Bürger, with melodramatic accompaniment. I was perfectly furious. I expect that he will bring out yet another symphonic poem before the winter is over. The disease spreads more and more and in any event extends the ass's ears of the public and young composers alike."[118]

It would have been better for Brahms had his reservation remained private. For his attack on the New German School inevitably drew attention to him as representing a distinct tendency. He quickly became intimately involved in composing a Declaration against the "so-called Music of the Future," a reference to the claims of the Liszt school through Brendel's *Neue Zeitschrift für Musik.*[119]

Brahms seems to have been at the heart of the Declaration, since his is the address given for signatories. But he was hardly alone in his antipathy: the new tendencies and the claims of their proponents were the subjects of constant discussion among musicians and were irritations to younger as well as older composers not of the Liszt camp. The composer and conductor Ferdinand Hiller, for example, had already written a polemic in 1857. But for such an overt public rebuke on behalf of artistic values to have effect, it needed considerable support. Many prominent musicians were approached, and by the time of its publication there were more than twenty supporters, including Hiller, Woldemar Bargiel, Albert Dietrich, Franz Wüllner, Karl Reinecke, and Theodor Kirchner.[120]

But many weighty names were needed, not least those named by Schumann as progressive figures in commending Brahms in "New Paths." Joachim had sought support for the Declaration from several artists, including Robert Franz: "We felt that we had been slack, if not actually cowardly, in not protesting long ago against those who in their vanity and arrogance regard everything great and sacred which the musical energy of our people has created up to now as dung for the rank, miserable weeds growing from Lisztian fantasias. The word Liszt is out, hard as I find it to connect this name, which evokes memories of many a fine and admirable deed in the old days, with a public protest against the artistic clique bound to it; but, 'Amicus Liszt, magis amicus Musica.' The consequence of what he is doing, and which he must abide by, have become too ruinous. . . . Strengthen our protest with the weight of your name." The reluctance of those sympathetic to the statement comes through in Franz's response, rather tendentiously dated "21 March (Bach's birthday)" 1860. But private inclination was one thing: public antagonism toward the remarkable and sociable Liszt was another. Franz's equivocation must have been typical: "I hear that for some time past, in consequence of many bitter experiences, L[iszt]'s world has collapsed—certainly a fresh blow would cast further gloom on his condition."[121]

The premature publication highlights the difficulty of the venture: time was against it. There was the overwhelming task of writing so many letters and obtaining responses, to say nothing of responding to likely requirements for revision. Even Brahms and Joachim had differing views, with Joachim cautious and Brahms wishing to differentiate between the works of Wagner and Berlioz on the one hand and Liszt's "productions" on the other. And there was every chance that the circulating document could go astray. For a reason never explained the Declaration was leaked, and a parody of it appeared in the *Neue Zeitschrift für Musik* on 4 May 1860, two days before the actual statement was published in the musical paper *Berliner Musik-Zeitung Echo*, where it carried just four names, seemingly those suggested in Joachim's letter as "I, friend Brahms, and several others"—Brahms, Joachim, Julius Otto Grimm, and Bernhard Scholz.[122] Because the statement was ridiculed before it even appeared, its effect was lost. The actual text is brief and to the point, its rather censorious tone suggesting a public duty to maintain values that may well have struck a false note with those required to support it. It appeared with the preface "circulating among local musicians with the address of Herrs Brahms, Joachim, and Grimm in which they send to the party of the music of the future a letter of refusal which they invite their artistic colleagues to sign." The Declaration reads

> The undersigned have long followed with regret the ini-
> tiatives of a certain party, whose organ is Brendel's Zeit-
> schrift für Musik. The above journal continually spreads
> the view that musicians of more serious endeavor are
> fundamentally in accord with the tendencies it represents,
> that they recognize in the compositions of the leaders of
> this group works of artistic value, and that altogether, es-
> pecially in Northern Germany, the arguments for and
> against the so-called Music of the Future are concluded,
> as the dispute settled in its favor.
>
> The undersigned regard it as their duty to protest
> against such a distortion of fact, and declare, at least for
> their own part, that they do not acknowledge the princi-
> ples avowed by Brendel's Zeitschrift, and that they can
> only lament and condemn the productions of the leaders
> and pupils of the so-called New German School, which
> on the one hand apply those principles practically and
> on the other necessitate the constant setting up of new
> and exorbitant theories which are contrary to the very
> nature of music.
>
> Johannes Brahms, Joseph Joachim, Julius Otto
> Grimm, Bernhard Scholz[123]

The rapid appearance and the tone of the parody suggest a history of underlying tensions—if not from 1854 then certainly from Joachim's estrangement from Liszt, which was recalled years later by Wagner as the "defection of a hitherto warm friend, the great violinist [initiating] a violent agitation . . . against the generous Franz Liszt." The parody ascribes to "the undersigned" a protest against the whole spirit of the new music and an offer of "brotherly association for the advancement of monotonous and tiresome music," in the name of J Fiddler (Joachim), Hans

Newpath (Brahms, after the title of Schumann's article), and other derogatory names.[124]

Of the four signatories of the Declaration, only Brahms and Joachim were significant figures, and the publication left all four publicly embarrassed rather than enhanced by an authoritative statement on behalf of traditional values. Even potential supporters were perplexed. Thus, Hans von Bülow, who had been sympathetic to both tendencies long before his Meiningen connections with Brahms, found easy fault with the statement. He wrote to Louis Köhler from Berlin, where the statement was published: "The Declaration of the Hanoverians has not made the least sensation here. They have not even enough wit mixed with their malice to have done the thing in good style, and to have launched it at a well chosen time, such as the beginning or the end of the season."[125] For the moment nothing significant showed in terms of polemic exchange; rather, Brendel sought to reconcile the opposing parties.[126] But the battle lines had been drawn. Brahms's private views grew more vehement over the years, and by the end of the decade he had attached them to choral works and even to a judgment of the audience, as in April 1869 to Hermann Levi of Liszt's *St. Elizabeth,* performed under Herbeck in Vienna: "The public here may well be praiseworthy, but being a child it needs strict discipline: its schoolmasters, our worthy colleagues, disclosed their utter shabbiness so completely at the new swindle by Liszt that I hid my head in shame." And to Reinthaler in December 1871: "On the 30th we will have to live through Liszt's *Christus,* and the whole thing is so monumentally boring, stupid, and senseless that I can't understand how all the necessary swindle will be carried off this time."[127]

Brahms and Wagner

It is the consistency of Brahms's admiration for Wagner's achievements that confirms the integrity of his view of Liszt. For that view was not based on reactions to Liszt's lifestyle; moreover, Brahms was to receive more insults from Wagner than from Liszt. Though both composers were roughly twenty years Brahms's senior, Wagner was established long before Brahms's first published works were even composed; he was a figure to whom Brahms naturally looked as a young composer interested in everything. In contrast, Liszt's orchestral works were contemporary with the early works of Brahms; in addition, they represented an incursion into a field that he regarded as the natural territory for his work. But if Brahms's interest in operatic composition was strong and lasting, he made no secret that his approach differed from Wagner's. And Brahms's approach seems to have become more defined after the 1860s: "This much I know: in all other things that I attempt, I follow on the heels of predecessors, who make me self-conscious. Wagner would not in the least make me self-conscious about tackling an opera with the greatest desire."[128]

Brahms's independence from Wagner was evident in his willingness to support the performance of *The Mastersingers* in Vienna in 1863 by helping with the copying of parts, a task undertaken by many musicians: he might well have held aloof. He was at this stage on easy terms with Wagner, and Wagner, for his part, invited Brahms to play his Handel Variations at a gathering at Penzing, Vienna, that Wagner hosted early in 1863. Wagner declared that something could still be done in the old forms "when someone who understands how to handle them comes along."[129]

The difficulties attending Brahms's independent outlook were clear in this ironic comment to Joachim: "Wagner is here and I shall probably be considered a Wagnerian largely because of the contradiction to which any intelligent person must be provoked by the irresponsible manner in which musicians here rail against him." And of the influence of Liszt, "I am also particularly in touch with Cornelius and Tausig, who claim not to be, nor ever have been, followers of Liszt and who moreover can accomplish more with their little fingers than other musicians with their heads and all their fingers."[130] (Cornelius and Tausig were both sympathetic to Wagner, however.) It was Wagner's totality of conception, his lofty and individualist imaginative aspiration, and his "amazing clarity" of thoughts that attracted Brahms.[131] And in acknowledging this, Brahms's own circle was as much to be corrected as the followers of Wagner when any suspicion of a partisan response arose. Thus he writes to Widmann in 1888: "If the Bayreuth theatre were in France it would not require anything as grandiose as Wagner's works to make you and [Gustav] Wendt and all the rest of the world to undertake pilgrimages there and be inspired by such ideally inspired and created things."[132] But it was as a stage composer that Brahms most admired Wagner and felt that his works should be judged. He told Leyen, "One cannot do a greater disservice to Wagner than by bringing his music into the concert hall. It is created solely for the theatrical stage and that is where it belongs."[133]

Brahms greatly enjoyed such set pieces in Wagner as "The Ride of the Valkyries," and his preference seems to have been for works that contained musical elements to which he could relate. He regarded *The Flying Dutchman* as "the best thing that Wagner has done" in conversation with Eugenie Schumann,[134] though his most enthusiastic comments were for *The Mastersingers,* the one mature work with which he, like so many musicians, could naturally establish the closest connection through its subject and musical content. Thus he rebuked Specht: "Do you think me so narrow that I, too, cannot be enchanted by the gaiety and grandeur of *The Mastersingers?* Or so dishonest as to conceal my opinion that a few bars of this work are worth more than all the operas that have been composed since?"[135] But once Wagner's music was considered outside what Brahms thought of as its proper context, he reacted sharply. He rated the funeral march in Handel's *Saul* above Siegfried's funeral march in *The Twilight of the Gods* because it served not only dramatically but as self-sufficient music: "Wagner's march belongs unquestionably to the drama; the other has value on its own."[136]

The sense of context seems to have been at the root of his aversion to Wagner's imitators. Within Brahms's repeated claim to be the "best of all Wagnerians" lay a detailed knowledge not only of the music and the theories but of the context: a concern with dramatic purpose, not mere effect, that prompted him to criticize empty partisanship based on the character of the musical style. This was the "misunderstood Wagner," and Brahms rounded as much on his own circle when they indulged in such partisanship. Kalbeck received the classic rebuke when he opined at Wagner's expense, as Specht recalls: "I had noticed that Brahms had grown increasingly animated. Suddenly he banged his fist on the table and shouted at Kalbeck, 'For God's sake, Kalbeck, stop speaking of things you don't understand.' "[137] Perhaps the force of this reaction was impelled by the fact that he had also told Kalbeck on another occasion, "It is only when one sees Wagner's imitators that one learns to appreciate Wagner himself."[138] Just what Brahms really thought about the size of Wagner's claims and theories is not recorded. His failure to visit Bayreuth, after attending at Munich several times, was not through lack of interest but because of the political aspect. He could never quite make up his mind about the first complete *Ring* cycle in 1876 or about the first performance of *Parsifal* in 1882, chiefly because of the partisan character of Wagnerian support, which ruined the occasion for him.

But if Brahms was moved to defend a fellow artist against superficial criticism, to acknowledge his achievements and enjoy that part of his music that he did enjoy, he could only go a certain distance. Perhaps his very enjoyment of the set pieces made them problematic, part of the broader resistance to the sheer length and slowness of external action. Even *The Mastersingers* prompted reservations about the "spinning out of the strongly defined pieces" of which he often tired. He described "The Ride of the Valkyries" as a "taxing pleasure." It is hardly surprising that he should have recommended taking a box in the theater so that one could move around or take a drink.[139] Brahms's fundamental equivocation on Wagner's ultimate artistic achievement is strongest when addressing Clara, even allowing that he had to speak with care in view of her Wagner aversion. In 1870 he wrote from Vienna: "The Mastersingers had to put on and off five times. Now, however, every additional performance causes as much trouble. This in itself, of course, prevents the audience from waxing enthusiastic, for which a certain momentum would be required. I find the public much more apathetic than I had expected. I myself am enthusiastic neither for this work nor otherwise for Wagner. Still, I listen to it as intently as I can, i.e., as often as I can stand it. I confess that it provokes one to talk."[140]

Part of the discussion concerned subject matter. Brahms, a keen student of German literature and an experienced vocal composer, took a professional interest in text and its setting, quite apart from his admiration of the theatrical conception: he did not just accept Wagner's treatment of familiar subjects without response. We catch the flavor of Brahms's attitude in his responses to Henschel's enthusiasm for *The Ring*, especially concerning the text:

> I had just spoken of some, to me, especially beautiful
> places in the first act of "The Valkyrie," and of the fresh
> and breezy song of Siegfried in Siegfried[:] "From the
> wood forth into the world fare." "Certainly," he said,
> "these are fine things, but I cannot help it, somehow or
> other, they do not interest me. What you just hummed

... is no doubt beautiful; and when Siegmund in "The Valkyrie" pulls the sword out of the tree, that's fine, too; but it would, in my opinion be *really* powerful and carry one away, if it all concerned—let us say, young Bonaparte, or some other hero who stands nearer to our sensibilities, has a closer claim to our affection. And then that stilted, bombastic language." He took a copy of the textbook. "Listen," ... he recited the words with greatly exaggerated pathos ["Am Brünnhilds Felsen fahret vorbei. ... "So-werf' ich den Brand in Walhalls prängende Burg."] "If I read this to a counting-house clerk I am sure it would make a tremendous impression: "So—werf' ich den Brand—" ... *I* do not understand this kind of thing. What really happens with the ring? Do *you* know? And those endless and tedious duets![141]

By the time of *The Ring* in 1876, years after Brahms had made his name with *A German Requiem,* Wagner's attitude toward Brahms had turned vitriolic. Despite Wagner's attacks, Brahms remained detached, complaining that he did not understand why Wagner attacked him so.[142] That he looked up to Wagner is confirmed by the fact that Wagner's manuscripts became part of his passion for autograph possessions, to the extent of doggedly retaining a manuscript score of part of Wagner's *Tannhäuser*—it had come to him through Cornelius without Wagner's permission. Perhaps Wagner's venomous remarks reflected his incredulity at the opposing direction of Brahms's development and the threat posed by the younger man's great achievements.

German Contemporaries of His Own Persuasion

Although Brahms expressed himself strongly about trends in music, he had little to say about the minor figures of his own circle or persuasion. His responses are more notable for providing examples of his caustic social wit than for their insights into his views. But whatever his reservations, he was prepared to give his contemporaries their due in the most direct way when he became artistic director of the Gesellschaft der Musikfreunde: through performance. He gave Bruch's *Odysseus,* Dietrich's Violin Concerto, Volkmann's *Konzertstück* for Piano and Orchestra and Cello Concerto, and works by Goldmark, Rietz, Rheinberger, Rubinstein, Hiller, Scholz, and Bargiel. Of the established figures of Brahms's earlier years, the most prominent and prolific was Ferdinand Hiller. He was a contemporary of Schumann and friend of Clara's who had written many symphonic works and had an aversion to Lisztian modernism. Brahms thought him routine and was never at ease in his company.[143]

Two younger figures interested him in earlier years: Carl Goldmark and Max Bruch. He admired both and was close to them at first, though he was disappointed with their lack of development. Goldmark was the leading younger composer in Vienna when Brahms arrived in late 1862. Thereafter, he increasingly lived in Brahms's shadow, though Brahms openly acknowledged having the "deepest respect" for Goldmark's gifts. Brahms could never really bring himself to admire Goldmark's operas, which had considerable success in Vienna, though he attended regularly and even dragged himself to the premiere of *Das Heimchen am Herd* in his last days. He saw little beneath the accomplished surface of these works and felt that they owed much to Wagner, though Brahms could be enthusiastic, as he was over *Merlin*.[144] But he could also pay Goldmark a genuine compliment, as when a fellow listener at a rehearsal of *Das Heimchen am Herd* exclaimed of the two bars containing the "Zwei Sternlein," "Why, that is a folksong!" Brahms, sitting next to her, replied, "Not yet, but it may become so." He rightly assessed the *Rustic Wedding Symphony* as Goldmark's finest work: "that is the best you have done . . . clear-cut and faultless, it sprang into being a finished thing, like Minerva from the head of Jupiter." In summary, "I do not care for all of Goldmark, but I would never deny him the deepest respect."[145]

A similar pattern arose with Bruch, whose interests—large-scale symphonic, concerto, and choral works—were much closer to Brahms's than were Goldmark's. Not being a Viennese resident, Bruch was not part of Brahms's social circle, and the relationship had nothing to hold it together. Yet Bruch knew about the incomplete First Symphony in 1870 and dedicated his own First Symphony to Brahms. Bruch's lack of development over the years was remarked by Brahms when the death of Philipp Spitta brought the composers together briefly. Brahms wrote to Clara in 1895, "Bruch has just published his 'Moses' and Herzogenberg his 'Birth of Christ.' If only one could feel a spark of joy at all these things. They are in every way weaker and worse than their earlier works. The only pleasant thing about it all is if one can, as I think I can, thank God for having preserved me from the vice, the sin and the bad habit of mere note-writing."[146] Perhaps even more revealing of Brahms's attitude is his reaction to Bruch's Second Violin Concerto, a work that begins, atypically, with an adagio. The piece was very well received at its first performance, and Bruch was warmly congratulated by all present—except Brahms. Bruch recalls that he said, " 'My dear Bruch, how can one commence a violin concerto with an adagio?' Not content with this, he followed me round during the afternoon and kept on tugging at my coat tails and repeating the words 'How can one commence a violin concerto with an adagio?' An insupportable fellow."[147]

Three Austrian Contemporaries: Bruckner, Strauss, Fuchs

Only rarely did Brahms express strong feelings about his German or Austrian contemporaries, especially those active in Vienna. Of Anton Bruckner he was highly critical; of two, Johann Strauss, Jr., and Robert Fuchs he was enthusiastic. Brahms was bound to have judged any new symphonic composer severely, and if he felt that the claims of such a composer were advanced by means other than the purely musical, he would have been even more resistant. This feeling colored Brahms's perception of Bruckner, who was seen as naive and as a follower of Wagner. Specht, who admired both composers, saw the issues clearly.

> [Bruckner's] devout faith struck him as priest-ridden bigotry, and he rated his vast symphonic structures as the amateurish, confused, and illogical abortions of a crafty rustic schoolmaster. To their inward inevitability, different from his own, and even to the wonderfully rich and ecstatically devotional adagios of Bruckner, he could, with the best will in the world, gain no access. (But: had he the best will?) What he said to me, approximately, was this. "Bruckner? That is a swindle that will be forgotten a year or two after my death. Take it as you will, Bruckner owes his fame solely to me, and but for me nobody would have cared two hoots for him. Of course, I had nothing to do with it: in fact, it happened very much

against my will. Nietzsche once declared that I had become famous through a mere chance, because the anti-Wagner party required me as an anti-Pope. That is mere nonsense, for I am not the man to be placed at the head of any party whatsoever. I must go my way alone and in peace, and I never crossed that of others" (I did not at that time dare ask the sick master, what of the Declaration?). But in Bruckner's case it was so. That is to say, after Wagner's death his party naturally had need of another pope, and they had nothing better than Bruckner. Do you really think that anyone in this immature crowd has the least notion of what these symphonic boa-constrictors are about? And do you not think that I am the musician who knows and understands Wagner's works best today, certainly better than any of his so-called followers, who would like nothing better than to poison me? And Bruckner's works "immortal" and perhaps even "symphonies?" It is ludicrous![148]

Only the most partisan of Brahms's supporters went along with this judgment. Indeed, it seems unlikely that Brahms could ever really have been so unresponsive to the traditional beauties of Bruckner's music. Specht's niggling suspicion of Brahms's disingenuousness is seemingly borne out in Mandyczewski's suggestion that it was actually the *context* that deterred Brahms—the nature of the musical whole. The work in question was Bruckner's Fourth Symphony, which the younger man had just found Brahms earnestly studying: " 'Look,' exclaimed Brahms, pointing to the first pages of the score. 'Here this man composes as though he were a Schubert.' " Brahms then indicated the unisons and the chromatic passages in the closing section and said, "Then he suddenly remembers that he is a Wagnerian and everything goes to the devil."[149]

Brahms wrote to Elisabet von Herzogenberg on 12 January 1885 to offer his opinion after obviously withholding it in a previous letter: "I understand. You have sat through the roaring of Bruckner's symphony once, and now, when people talk about it, you are afraid to trust the recollections of your own impressions. Well, you may safely do so. . . . Moreover, but one symphony and quintet of Brucker's have been printed.

I advise you to get them to look at, with a view to steeling your mind and your judgement. You will not want me! . . . With supreme ill-humour . . . yours J Br."[150] Brahms himself always studied the scores before making a judgment. He had known Bruckner's work from his early days in Vienna, and he owned copies of Symphony 8 and the Te Deum.[151] In fact, we know that he could be moved by the music on occasion: an example is the Mass in F Minor, whose more stylized nature perhaps made it more acceptable to him. It certainly lacks the qualities that he objected to in the symphonies. But when he was most moved by a Bruckner work (the adagio of Symphony 7) it was apparently because of the event: Bruckner's own funeral. "I will be the next," said the ailing Brahms.[152]

It is ironic that the one composer of his circle for whom Brahms felt almost unreserved admiration—Johann Strauss the Younger—was actually more drawn to the music of Bruckner than to his own. Despite their friendship and Strauss's admiration for Brahms's achievements, he could not warm to Brahms's music as he did to that of his fellow Austrian. Although enthusiasm for Strauss began to sweep musical Europe in the 1860s and affected musicians of widely differing persuasions, Brahms's admiration was based on Strauss's mastery of specific technical skills, as well as his interest in the dance. In Brahms's eyes, Strauss perfectly achieved what he set out to do—and something entirely in Brahms's own vein and in which he too was preeminent: popular music of the highest class. And he did it in a genre that Brahms loved—the waltz—showing the utmost refinement and imagination with its simple forms. He was the perfect Brahmsian composer, and it is impossible to divorce Brahms's own waltz development from this influence.[153]

Brahms met Strauss in 1862 at the house of the critic Richard Pohl, and the composers kept frequent contact thereafter. Brahms was a regular guest at the Strauss home in Vienna and at the Strauss villa in Ischl in the summer. He was invited to family events and was pictured with their circle as well as with husband and wife. Their acquaintanceship moved to friendship in 1871 at Baden Baden, a favorite place for Brahms and a common summer locale for the Waltz King.[154] Attending Strauss's performances in the spa gardens at Baden was one of Brahms's favorite recreations there. He would walk from his lodgings in Lichtental the mile or so into town. The English pianist Florence May, who was living there to study with Clara, once caught him on his journey: "He delighted in the music of Strauss's band, which was engaged to play daily . . . through some weeks of the season . . . and he used to walk over every evening to hear it. 'Are you so engrossed' said a voice behind me one evening as I was standing in the Lichtental village street with a friend, looking at the performances of a dancing bear. In turning round, I found Brahms, hat in hand, smiling with amusement at our preoccupation, himself on his way, as usual at that hour, to listen to the delicious music." And doubtless he would have responded physically to the music, as he was elsewhere recalled as "exuberantly rapping his umbrella on the table—a little boy with a gray beard" to the music of the Viennese *Schrammeln*.[155]

By this time, Brahms's view of Strauss's music had become clear. To Bülow he confided, "He is one of the few colleagues I can hold in limitless respect."[156] Even when he found the content thin or sentimental—as with *Jabuka*—he loved the overall effect, and he repeatedly praised Strauss's orchestration. In 1887 he told Heuberger, himself a master of operetta, that "there is now no one as sure as he" when it comes to orchestration[157]; elsewhere he compared him with Mozart. Brahms even set himself against adverse criticism of Strauss's work, as in the case of *Cagliostro in Wien,* which premiered at the Theater an der Wien on 27 February 1875. Brahms was enraptured by the score, which he first heard played by Strauss on the piano at Strauss's home. To the writer Paul Lindau he was enthusiastic: "What can one single out. It is all equally wonderful! The man oozes music! He always comes up with something—in that he differs from the rest of us."[158] He attended many Strauss first performances. In 1887 he was so captivated by *Die Fledermaus* that he attended multiple performances in the Schänzli Theatre. Only one work yielded a less enthusiastic response, as when he wrote to Simrock that *Das Spitzentuch der Königen* was "recht langweilig" (really tedious).[159] Strauss reciprocated this artistic endorsement by dedicating the waltz "Seid Umschlungen Millionen" to Brahms.

If Brahms was prepared to acknowledge major masters in the field, he also hailed the minor masters, including the Viennese composer Robert Fuchs. Fuchs, fourteen years Brahms's junior, came to know the older composer well in Vienna, and they often were in each other's company. Brahms saw in Fuchs both artistic sensitivity—"charming within limits"—and a mastery of the smaller instrumental forms and opera. He commented (in connection with an operatic scheme), "Fuchs never goes deep—[a little deeper] here and there in the symphonies," though Brahms also made an exception of the Trio dedicated to him. "What I specially like is the way in which in opera he gives only the [musical aspect of] the text and does not worry about the action, dialogue, etc."[160]

Younger Germans and Austrians: Richard Strauss, Gustav Mahler, and Hugo Wolf

The outstanding younger figures of Brahms's musical world in his later years were Richard Strauss and Gustav Mahler. Both soon came to epitomize the new directions in music against which Brahms increasingly reacted; Hugo Wolf embodied similar tendencies in the composition of lieder, though Brahms did not come to know his work until later. Strauss was first on the scene. Though four years younger than the others, his privileged musical background brought his talents rapidly to the fore. And since his father, Franz Strauss, was an influential figure in orchestral music, and averse to the newer developments, it was natural that he should have come into contact with the Brahmsian world. Strauss was appointed Bülow's assistant with the Meiningen Orchestra in 1885, just when Brahms was visiting Meiningen to conduct a concert of his own works.[161] To Strauss's surprise, Brahms was also present in Meiningen at the rehearsal of his Symphony in F Minor, which Strauss conducted himself. During that visit Strauss drew advice from Brahms that he valued thereafter: "I was eager to hear his opinion. In his dry manner he said to me 'Quite nice,' but appended a considered lecture: 'young man, look carefully at some Schubert Dances and get an experience of writing simple and eight-bar melodies.'" Strauss commented that "above all I thank Brahms that, since then, I no longer felt ashamed of taking into my work popular melodies." Brahms continued: "Your symphony contains too much thematic working. This piling up of themes that are barely contrasted rhythmically on a triad has hardly any value." It was then, Strauss observed, that he realized that counterpoint is justified only when prompted by a poetic necessity (though this is not, seemingly, the point that Brahms was seeking to make).[162] To Heuberger, Brahms elaborated: "He writes a richly-worked good movement, well scored: but his work has got the same characteristic that almost all the young people have. It is a barely unbreakable uniform drawn from the spirit which covers up everything personal and lets only the formal outline come through." But when Strauss moved on to symphonic poems, Brahms was outraged. "Truly dreadful" was his reaction in 1890; and of *Also sprach Zarathustra* in 1896, "Have you seen the end? B major and C major together. I'd have nothing against it if something were to come of either tonality . . . something that fulfilled the implications of either. But so!"[163]

He was even more outraged by the music of Gustav Mahler, though his first meeting with Mahler was positive. In 1887, Mahler was conducting Mozart's *Don Giovanni* in Pest, where Brahms had been taken by Hans Koessler and Viktor von Herzfeld. Brahms, who was typically critical of everything, was in no mood to be convinced on this occasion: he had been dragged there, and he actually declared at the front of the theater that "no one does Don Giovanni the way I like it. If I wish to enjoy it I lie down on the sofa and read the score." But he soon changed his mind, commenting in the first act "Excellent! Splendid! Magnificent! Yes, that's it finally. What a devil of a fellow!" Immediately after the first act Koessler and Von Herzfeld had to guide him to the stage, where he embraced the young conductor and, beaming, declared this the best performance of *Don Giovanni* that he had heard.[164] But it was different with Mahler's own music. When he first heard it, apparently a performance of the Second Symphony, his reaction was sharp: "Previously I thought that Richard Strauss was the leader of the Revolutionaries. Now I know that Mahler is the King of the Insurgents." But he was clearly not insensitive to its quality, judging the scherzo (second movement) a work of "genius."[165]

Brahms's views on Hugo Wolf have been obscured by the polemics of the time. Brahms actually saw merit in Wolf's early work, and Wolf initially admired Brahms's symphonies. Our knowledge of Brahms's appraisal comes through Kalbeck, with distorted details of Brahms's and Wolf's first meeting in 1879, when Wolf was just nineteen. The composer had come to Brahms with his compositions, and he clearly received the customary treatment. Kalbeck relayed his version of Brahms's reaction to Wolf's visit in his biography as follows:

> Brahms had just sat down at the piano when he heard a
> suspicious noise at his glass door. At the same time he
> saw in the blind the shadow of a man, who seemed to

be occupied with the lock of the door. Brahms rose at length and opened it. He had some trouble to get his strange visitor to come into the room, as the latter could not be got away from the door latch, which he kept on kissing. "The compositions which he brought to me," related Brahms, "did not amount to much. I went through everything thoroughly with him, and drew his attention to many things. Some talent was certainly forthcoming, but he didn't take the matter seriously enough. I then told him quite earnestly what it was he lacked, recommended contrapuntal studies and referred him to Nottebohm. That was enough for him and he did not return. Now he spits poison and gall." This story was modified to the foregoing after a legal dispute. In the original version Kalbeck quotes Brahms as having said, "My God, that's a wretched, needy fellow, A Musikant come to grief, who won't learn anything. He once came to see me when he was not to be got away from the door; he kept on kissing the latch out of respect. Disgusting!"[166]

Years after Brahms's death Kalbeck admitted that so dismissing Wolf was an error on Brahms's part.[167] For Brahms the problem was that Wolf ignored the principles that he cherished. He commented of Wolf's songs in 1889, "Yes, if one doesn't worry oneself too much with the music but only with the words, then declamation is easy." And again, ironically, "The Wagnerians present Hugo Wolf as a great song writer, as discoverer of the 'symphonic song' whereas Schubert, Schumann and Brahms can only write songs 'as with guitar accompaniment.' " But Brahms did record admiration of one work: "Der Feuerreiter."[168]

Non-German Composers: Dvořák, Smetana, Grieg, and Tchaikowsky

Heuberger notes that "of the newer masters Brahms loved above all Bizet, Dvořák, Smetana, Verdi."[169] His admiration for Dvořák was by far the most strongly expressed, if only because Dvořák's musical style related most closely to his own. His bond with Dvořák's music was immediate and lasting. Even before moving to Vienna, Brahms had shown an interest in the musical resources of Bohemia and Hungary. But for all his enthusiasm he could hardly have anticipated the appearance of a composer with the originality and technical mastery of Dvořák. And once introduced to Dvořák's early music, Brahms stopped at nothing to advance Dvořák's career through his own publisher, Simrock. No contemporary received as direct a testimony of Brahms's allegiance as Dvořák: Brahms helped him obtain grants, he proofread for him, and he eventually put his wealth at Dvořák's disposal. Even the inevitable Brahmsian caveats were offered with uncharacteristic gentleness. Brahms admired Dvořák's spontaneity and technical assurance, and even when speaking independently of the qualities essential to composition for the young, he cited Dvořák as possessing the "decisive talent" necessary to achievement. "He is never at a loss for an idea like the rest of us," Brahms wrote. He was enthusiastic over the Orchestral Variations, a work perhaps inspired by his own "St. Antoni" Variations: "It is so beautiful and so refined, so natural." Of the D Major Rhapsody he noted, "So musical."[170]

Brahms discovered Dvořák's music through Hanslick, who sent Brahms the Moravian Duets. In recommending them to Simrock as moneymakers, Brahms cited their "delicate and piquant charm."[171] When Dvořák wrote to dedicate the D Minor Quartet to Brahms in acknowledgment of his support, Brahms overcame his normal reticence in letter-writing: "To occupy myself with your things gives me especial pleasure. I would like to have the time to talk with you about many details. You write somewhat hurriedly. When you fill in the necessary sharps and flats, look rather more closely at the notes themselves and at the part-writing etc. Please do forgive me. It is very presumptuous to express such wishes to a man like you over such matters. I nevertheless accept the works just as they are."[172] Brahms seems to have responded similarly to all the succeeding orchestral and chamber works. He was not without criticism; he told Eugenie Schumann "it was a pity and a great sadness to him that Dvořák had published "many inferior things."[173] Brahms was aware that Dvořák knew little literature and little other music. Even in a major work like the G Major Symphony, whose formal originality prompted some reservations ("too fragmentary, neighbouring ideas push each other . . . no big form"), he still acknowledged "everything fine, musically fashioned and beautiful . . . what delightful music."[174] By comparison he had only trifling reservations about the E Minor Symphony, and he was overwhelmed with the compositional talent in evidence and the sheer sound of the work. Dvořák sat in Brahms's box for the Vienna premiere of his New World Symphony, and he responded with special enthusiasm to the Cello Concerto, commenting to the cellist Robert Hausmann: "If I had known that it was possible to write a cello concerto like that, I would have done it years ago."[175] The only areas of real reservation were opera and oratorio, with the text again taking his attention, as with *St. Ludmilla*, which he regarded as written for the English choral market.[176]

Brahms's knowledge of Smetana was based on the operas, which he heard in Vienna, though there are few surviving comments to illuminate Heuberger's claims of Brahms's enthusiasm. But apparently Brahms praised the works at a time when they were little known outside Prague. Of the opera performed as *Das Geheimnis (Tajemskvi)*, which was given on 22 March 1895, he commented that there was "so much text, and the music was so broken up"and belonged not in the big ceremonial opera house but the small, bohemian theater.[177]

In light of Brahms's enthusiasm for newer composers outside the German tradition, one views his contacts with musicians of more distant cultures with interest. Though he was reluctant to travel too widely, many important contemporaries from other countries came to him, as visits to Germany and Austria were mandatory. Leipzig in particular was a music center. Brahms first met Grieg there in 1878–79, and in 1885 they met again at the house of the Herzogenbergs. Their next meeting was in 1887, this time in the company also of Tchaikowsky. Despite his declining health in his last year, Brahms took an interest in Grieg and his companion Julius Röntgen, entertaining them at the Red Hedgehog and even visiting Grieg three times when was ill with influenza. Grieg shared Brahms's box at the Gesellschaft, where he heard Nikisch conduct Brahms's Fourth Symphony, and Brahms attended the Grieg concert at which Busoni played the Piano Concerto. Grieg saw Brahms frequently in the last year of Brahms's life. They both were devoted to simple song and dance forms, and both had folklike accents in their music, but neither seems to have been significantly drawn to the other's music. In 1888, when Grieg played his Norwegian Bridal Procession and Brahms his G Minor Rhapsody, Röntgen commented, "I got the impression that neither of them liked the other's piece." On the other hand, he continued, "Brahms spoke very warmly to me of Grieg's Ballade [op. 24]."[178] His admiration likely was for the treatment of the form: despite the title, the form of the work is that of variations structured into an effective whole through the poignant return of the theme at the close.

The Brahms-Tchaikovsky relationship is much more clearly defined because it was strongly antipathetic. Both had years to form an impression of the other's work. Tchaikowsky had no direct contact with German culture but for years had to hear Brahms being touted as the successor to Beethoven without impinging comparably on German awareness of his own works; his was naturally the stronger-held view: it was characterized by his response to the First Symphony. "He has no charms for me. I find him cold and obscure, full of pretensions, but without any real depth."The composers met at the home of the violinist Adolf Brodsky on 31 December 1887 when Tchaikowsky, arriving early, was invited to attend a rehearsal of Brahms's Trio, op. 101. Tchaikowsky had ventured to comment to Brahms on the "skill of the execution of the relative tempo 2–3 [of the third movement], remarks which were well received by the composer." But when Brodsky asked Tchaikowsky whether he had enjoyed the work, he had to admit, "Do not be angry with me, . . . but I did not."[179] In his diary, he noted, "Brahms's manner is very simple, free from vanity, his humour jovial, and the few hours I spent in his society left me with a very agreeable recollection. I was forced to confess that . . . I only respect in Brahms an honorable, energetic musician of strong convictions; but, despite all efforts to the contrary, I never could, and never can, admire his music."[180] Tchaikowsky heard the Gewandhaus performance of the Double Concerto on the following evening, 1 January 1888, and Brahms attended the rehearsal of Tchaikowsky's Suite, op. 43, earlier that morning. Tchaikovsky reported that he later heard through Reinecke (though Brahms had made no encouraging remarks) that Brahms was "very pleased with the first movement, but did not praise the rest, especially the 'Marche Miniature.' "[181] But Brahms clearly maintained some interest, for when the Fifth Symphony was performed in Hamburg in 1889, he delayed his journey in order to hear the rehearsal. It was no doubt a professional interest in another symphonist: Tchaikowsky noted that afterward at lunch Brahms responded "very frankly and simply" that it had pleased him on the whole with the exception of the finale.[182] Specht's observations seem to summarize Brahms's reaction: "Brahms was unable to make a relation with him and silently dismissed him." His work struck him as "worldly and cosmopolitan rather than indigenous, from the drawing room, not the soil."[183]

French and Italian Composers

In spite of his political antipathy toward France, especially after 1870, Brahms had a clear sense of the importance and value of French musical tradition. His critical yardstick was the reference to an older tradition, especially as embodied in the work of Cherubini. Brahms believed that the school of which Cherubini was part existed in France until the 1890s. He commented to Heuberger in 1896: "Cherubini was the great master from whom everything had proceeded, beside him the excellent Halévy, then Auber, who also mastered his craft to a remarkable degree; eventually even Thomas who still had a good schooling."[184]

The newer French composers were judged by this standard, and the great success was Georges Bizet. If Brahms's admiration for *Carmen* was hardly unique—it fascinated a wide range of artists—it was certainly based on intimate knowledge. For Brahms, Bizet was part of the continuity: "Yes, the French still have a school! Bizet certainly seeks in many places to loosen or broaden the rules, but always as one who knows what's right." And the racy music had, as Heuberger observed, a powerful attraction to the strongly Protestant North German. But Brahms never seems to have attended a performance. About the Bizet works he did attend—*La Jolie Fille de Perth* in Vienna 1883 and *Djamileh* in Berlin in 1892—he had reservations. Though he loved the "wundervolle musik" of *Djamileh,* he did not immediately warm to *La Jolie Fille de Perth:* "The new opera is so without interest that I earnestly beseech you to go to the operetta tomorrow," he advised Billroth; however, when changes were made he warmed to it somewhat. Only one other modern French composer, Delibes, seems to have survived the Brahms criticism.[185] Brahms classified Delibes' work with Bizet's in quality, though he offered no comment. The others fell victim to Brahms's reverence for classic German texts. In the cases of Gounod and Massenet, Brahms was struck by what he regarded as the inadequacy of the music to the text: the diminishing of its power through simplification of action and sentimentalization of music—"French sugarbread," as he repeatedly put it.[186] Specht's perspective on his indignation at the injury to a great work was slightly different, however. "He was furious about Massenet's 'confectioner's music,' to a childishly watered-down version of Goethe's *Werther,* and he resented the fact that Max Kalbeck undertook the translation of opera librettos of this kind, because a critic, he thought, ought not to identify himself with such trash."[187]

Of all his older French contemporaries, Brahms seems to have had greatest respect for Berlioz—not surprising in view of his admiration for Cherubini. Brahms had met Berlioz in the late 1850s, when Berlioz had obviously taken a liking to him. Not that Berlioz's spirit was akin to Brahms's, and doubtless Brahms shared the reservations of Schumann and others of his persuasion. But Brahms's feeling for some pieces was genuine, and he was prepared to own them as early on as 1857, even in the face of Clara's disinclination. Thus of *The Childhood of Christ:* "I knew exactly that Berlioz's 'Flight into Egypt' would make the impression upon you that you say it has. One is however too prone to stigmatize as affected and coquettish this kind of simplicity in a man like Berlioz, who is inclined to be hard on one's ears. I have often heard it and it has always enchanted me. I really like it best of all Berlioz's works."[188] One might deduce from the almost ecclesiastical character of the music a connection to another work in which Brahms felt sufficiently interested to include in a Gesellschaft concert program: *Harold in Italy.* And the "Queen Mab Scherzo" also drew his attention, though, as with Wagner's set-pieces, context was his touchstone.[189]

Though he had many opportunities to hear Italian opera in Vienna, Brahms had even less to say about Italian opera than French. Widmann confirms his lack of interest, even when in Italy, noting that Brahms never attended a Verdi opera.[190] His dismissal of Mascagni's *Freund Fritz* at the Hofoper in 1892 as "dreadfully wretched" led him to refuse to attend the more important premiere of Leoncavallo's *Pagliacci* the following year: "There have been so many terrible operas recently." Although Heuberger lists Verdi as one of Brahms's favorites, he had little to say: only on *Simon Boccanegra* did he comment, though again it is the libretto that dominates the issue. Of the music he stated "with especially animated appreciation 'there is a great deal of talent there,' but of the libretto: 'the textbook condemns it. After some time one gives up on what it all means.' "[191] But the measure of his enthusiasm comes through in his reaction to criticism of the *Requiem,* in the speed with which he was prepared to defend Verdi against the criticism of a close friend and supporter. Hans von Bülow had written a scathing criticism of the Mass, characterizing it, from a Germanic standpoint, as "Verdi's greatest opera" after one of the original performances. Brahms heard of this while in Zurich. His friend there, the conductor Dr. Friedrich Hegar, related his response: "Brahms went immediately to Hug's music shop (in Zurich), and obtaining the pianoforte score, read it through. When he had finished it he said, 'Bülow has made a fool of himself for all time; only a genius could have written that.' "[192] To his credit, Bülow then revised his opinion and responded to Verdi with equal spirit, to which Verdi in turn responded positively.[193] We have stronger evidence of Brahms's response to Verdi the man. According to Widmann, Brahms entertained great respect for the Maestro Verdi, dwelling with pleasure on the fact that in his habits of life—early rising, simplicity of clothing, and unostentatious demeanor—Verdi resembled himself. Brahms's great predilection for Verdi was chiefly a result of the fact that, like himself, Verdi was a true "child of the people." Heuberger echoes this in recalling how Brahms found Verdi's "full-blooded nature attractive."[194]

II · Brahms Reflects on His Achievement

Though Brahms's characteristic dismissal of his own works was almost invariably associated with his allegiance to the classics as exemplars, it should not be assumed from its frequency that it was morbid in character. Smyth, who was quite capable of exposing Brahms's weaknesses, found his outlook balanced, observing that "one of his finest characteristics was his attitude to the great dead of his own art [though] he knew his own worth—what great creator does not?"[195]

Jenner approached the nature of self-esteem and the difficulty Brahms had in its expression:

> On this subject it was harder than ever to understand
> him. He was quite aware of the value of his own works,
> but his nature, with its manly restraint, made it incredi-
> bly difficult for him to talk about himself. He often tried
> to escape with a joke, but of course this was not always
> understood, so a difficult atmosphere could easily de-

velop. Usually when he spoke seriously about himself it was with embarrassment, which was often mixed with anger if someone pressed him whom he felt had no right to do so. If, as was normally the case, he did not feel confident of being understood from the outset, he was capable, unless constrained by some personal regard for the individual concerned, of deceiving them mercilessly and with perfect ease. The saying "since truth is a pearl, cast it not before swine" as Theodor Storm puts it, was sacred to him, and there were few individuals who were not from time to time numbered among the swine. But if someone succeeded in winning his confidence . . . then he was capable of finding that person worthy of the truth.[196]

One such person was Georg Henschel. His recollections of his holiday with Brahms on the Isle of Rügen give unique insight into Brahms on his own music. He recalls "the other day I happened to hum the theme of the andante from his Quartet in C Minor [op. 60]. He seemed to like my doing so, for when it came to the place [bb. 34–35] he accompanied my humming with gentle movements of the hand, as if beating time to it. At last he smilingly said, 'I am not at all ashamed to own that it gives me the keenest pleasure if a song, an adagio, or anything of mine, has turned out particularly well.' . . . [He] remarked that he considered the agitato from his still unpublished Quartet in B flat the most amorous, affectionate thing he had written."[197]

Brahms's mature attitude to his own works falls into interesting perspective in light of his youthful behavior. Evidence has already been shown of his awkwardness and seeming superiority as a young man. Henschel's record shows Brahms's own attitude toward his manner: "Taking up the volume of Hauptmann's letters I had lent him, he said, 'Just look: d'you see those asterisks instead of a name?' I did, and read the whole sentence, which described a certain composer, indicated by the asterisks, as a rather haughty young man. 'That's me,' said Brahms amusedly. 'When I was a very young man, I remember playing, at Göttingen, my Sonata in C to Hauptmann. He was not very complimentary about it, in fact he had much fault to find with it, which I, a very modest youth at the time, accepted in perfect silence. I afterwards heard that this silence had been interpreted and complained of as haughtiness.' "[198]

If Brahms appeared modest and sincere in the intimate company of fellow musicians, the larger context of his self-evaluation was always a threatening one. For the sentiments apparent in his response to Spohr's death in 1859 had only accelerated in the course of his lifetime. His emphasis on craft, on a good school of composition, and on the avoidance of novelty for its own sake appears to be a way of defying confrontation with the natural extension of artistic possibilities. Hard as Brahms tried to appear an independent artist, he invariably became an "anti-pope" figure—first to Wagner, then to Bruckner. And, characteristically, it was Brahms to whom the younger generation were first drawn through the more accessible instrumental tradition, moving subsequently to Wagner and the greater physical resources of music drama. But Brahms did not go out of his way to endear himself to them. When discussing with Mahler at Gmunden the impending end of music as he saw it, they came to a stream running into Lake Traun: "Suddenly Mahler seized him by the arm, and with his other arm pointed excitedly down into the water; 'But look, Herr Doctor, look': 'What is it?' asked Brahms. 'Look, there goes the last wave.' Whereupon Brahms retorted, 'That's all very well, but perhaps the real point is whether the wave flows into a lake or into a bog.' "[199]

Brahms seems an embattled figure. Indeed, his wry comment "My fate will be that of Cherubini"[200] shows him passionately acknowledging that his very efforts to strengthen his own musical education and build his work on the foundations of a real "school" would now work against him: that his fight against the trends of the 1850s had been in vain. What he could not have envisaged was that his values would be revived and that one young Viennese composer would increasingly come to view Brahms as a model of deep creative integrity and therefore "progressive": Arnold Schoenberg.[201]

THREE · Brahms the Performer

12 · Brahms the Pianist

Although Brahms the composer dominates any consideration of his achievement, it was as a performer that he made his name. Broad skills were central to the career of musical director, which he held until well into his maturity. The skills were those of choral and orchestral trainer and conductor, piano accompanist and chamber player, and piano soloist. But Brahms the performer was much more than an aspiring kapellmeister: he was an exceptionally fine musician for whom the piano was the central means of communication even after he gave up playing professionally. Robert Schumann gave the first and most vivid description of Brahms's playing after their first meeting in September 1853:

He began to disclose

wonderful regions to

us.

Sitting at the piano, he began to disclose wonderful regions to us. We were drawn into ever more enchanting spheres. Besides, he is a player of genius who can make of the piano an orchestra of lamenting and loudly jubilant voices. There were sonatas, veiled symphonies rather; songs, the poetry of which would be understood even without words, although a profound vocal melody runs through them all: single piano pieces, some of them demoniac in spirit while graceful in form: again sonatas for piano, string quartets, every work so different from the others that it seemed to stream from a separate source. And then, rushing like a torrent, they were all united by him into a single waterfall, the cascades of which were overarched by a peaceful rainbow, while butterflies played about its borders accompanied by the voices of nightingales.[1]

In this famous passage Schumann captured the essential relationship between the player and the composer. Brahms gave his listeners a unique experience of singing quality allied to a powerfully orchestral character. These characteristics emerge repeatedly in the recollections of his listeners throughout his life. But along with the originality were limitations and inconsistencies that were as disconcerting as the strengths were inspiring and reveal another dimension of the relationship between the player and the composer which became stronger through the years. Albert Dietrich (slightly his senior, a pupil of Schumann since 1851) recalls his playing "soon after Brahms's arrival at the house of the music-loving family Euler": "Brahms was asked to play and executed Bach's Toccata in F, and his own Scherzo in E flat Minor with wonderful power and mastery; bending his head down over the keys, and, as was his wont, in his excitement humming the melody aloud as he played. He remained detached from the torrent of praise with which his performance was greeted. Everyone marveled at his remarkable talent, and above all, we young musicians were unanimous in our enthusiastic admiration of the supremely artistic qualities of his playing, at times so powerful, or, when occasion demanded it, so exquisitely tender, but always full of character."[2]

Walter Hübbe, who often heard Brahms in Hamburg in the 1850s, is more direct about the nature of the individuality: "He does not play like a consummately trained, highly intelligent musician making other people's works his own (like, for instance, Hans v. Bülow) but rather like one who is himself creating, who interprets the works of the masters as an equal, not merely reproducing them, but rendering them as if they gushed forth directly and powerfully from his heart." The Viennese critic Eduard Hanslick was also struck by this composer-oriented quality when he attended Brahms's first public recital, in Vienna on 29 November 1862:

> Brahms's playing stands in close and most beautiful relationship with his artistic individuality in general. He only wishes to serve the composition, and he avoids almost to the point of shyness any semblance or suggestion of self-importance or show. He has a highly developed technique which lacks only the final brilliant polish, the final muscular self-confidence required of the virtuoso. He treats the purely technical aspect of playing with a kind of negligence, as when, for instance, he shakes octave

passages from a relaxed wrist in such a way that the keys
are brushed sideways, rather than struck squarely from
above. . . . He has too many important things in his head
and heart to be constantly concerned with his external
personal appearance. [But] his playing is always heart-
winning and convincing.[3]

Three years later Josef Viktor Widmann, who had not yet met Brahms,
was struck by similar physical characteristics: "Not only by his powerful
playing, with which no merely brilliant virtuoso's display could compare,
but also in his personal appearance, Brahms, then in his thirty-third year,
at once impressed me with a powerful individuality. . . . There was something confidently triumphant in his face. The radiant serenity of a mind
happy in the exercise of his art."[4]

Florence May first heard Brahms in 1871, when she studied with him.
Her recollections are valuable, given her observation that a decade later
his playing would be much changed: "Brahms's playing at this period of
his life was, indeed, stimulating to an extraordinary degree, and so *apart*
as to be quite unforgettable. It was not the playing of a virtuoso, though
he had a large amount of virtuosity (to put it moderately) at his command. He never aimed at mere effect, but seemed to plunge into the
innermost meaning of whatever music he happened to be interpreting,
exhibiting all its details and expressing its very depths. Not being in
regular practice, he would sometimes strike wrong notes—and there was
already a hardness arising from the same cause, in his playing of chords;
but he was fully aware of his failings, and warned me not to imitate them."[5]

The orchestral effect was partly a result of the dynamic range of his
playing, which was noted by many observers. As well as the capacity to
draw orchestral effects from the instrument, Gustav Ophuls observed that
Brahms could be "full of deep feeling and poetic dreaminess." His concern for a full tone was characteristic of his style, and he emphasized its
importance when teaching the young or responding to new pianists. In
Brahms's later years, Clara's pupil Adelina de Lara vividly recalls his quick
response to her playing of the E flat minor scherzo: " 'No, no, it is too
fast, you must draw it out more, like this.' . . . His hands seemed to rest
quietly on the keyboard and brought out a depth and volume of tone,
even in the most quiet *pp*." Clara's grandson Ferdinand Schumann recalls

Brahms commenting in the same period on a pupil playing Schumann's "Prophet Bird" (Vogel als Prophet), one of Anton Rubinstein's great solo items. Brahms said that, in comparison with Rubinstein, "the good players of the present day have no touch." He shared Clara's belief in creating a beautiful tone by coaxing the sound from the instrument. "Force as such had no place in his playing," Leyen wrote. "Indeed he never demanded more of an instrument than it was capable of giving without overstepping the bounds of artistic beauty."[6]

These observations are important in relation to Brahms's own piano writing, which makes immense demands. Although his pianism obviously exceeded that of Clara—and admitting his own comment that his D Minor Concerto (whose passages of octave scales and double trills require great force and energy) required a pianist of the "modern school"[7]—he apparently never believed in the sheer force associated with the performances of Liszt and his followers. Ethel Smyth's description complements Willi Beckerath's familiar drawing of Brahms: "The veins of his forehead stood out, his wonderful bright blue eyes became veiled and he seemed the incarnation of the restrained power in which his work is forged. For his playing was never noisy and when lifting a submerged theme out of the tangle of music he used jokingly to ask us to admire the gentle sonority of his 'tenor thumb.'" But with the passing of the years, the "gentle humming to himself and trembling with inward excitement" that Dietrich had noted in the 1850s had matured as well. Smyth adds: "I like to think of him best at the piano, playing his own compositions or Bach's mighty organ fugues, sometimes accompanying himself with a sort of muffled roar, as of Titans stirred to sympathy in the bowels of the earth." By 1894, Ferdinand Schumann heard this accompaniment as "a sort of gasping, grumble or snoring."[8]

After Brahms gave up recital playing in the 1870s, his technical inconsistencies became more troublesome to listeners not prepared for them, or not sympathetic towards him. He rarely interpreted the music of others after the mid-1870s, and his performances became much less technically secure. Many of the negative comments were sparked by the B flat Piano Concerto, surely the most demanding concerto for piano written up to that time. The English composer Charles Stanford, visiting Hamburg in the winter of 1880, heard Brahms when the work was still very new.

His piano playing was not so much that of a finished pianist, as of a composer who despised virtuosity. The skips, which are many and perilous in the solo part, were accomplished regardless of accuracy, and it is no exaggeration to say that there were handfuls of wrong notes. The touch was somewhat hard and lacking in force-control; it was at its best in the slow movement, where he produced the true velvety quality, probably because he was not so hampered by his own difficulties. But never since have I heard a rendering of the concerto, so complete in its outlook or so big in its interpretation. The wrong notes did not really matter, they did not disturb his hearers any more than himself. He took it for granted that the public knew that he had written the right notes, and did not worry himself over such little trifles as hitting the wrong ones. His attitude at the piano was precisely that in Professor Von Beckerath's sketch. The short legs straight down to the pedals, which they seemed only just to reach, the head thrown back and slightly tilted as if listening to the band rather than to himself, the shoulders hunched up and the arms almost as straight as the legs and well above the keyboard.[9]

Bülow, who conducted the performance that Stanford heard, was impressed with Brahms's performance: "His new piano concerto is absolutely first rate and sounds wonderful, and, moreover, he plays it with matchless beauty—with clarity, weight and richness." But Florence May was less impressed, at least at the rehearsal the previous afternoon. "I did not think Brahms's playing what it had been. His touch in *forte* passages had become hard, and he did not execute difficulties, which he had mastered with ease." She would have preferred Brahms to have conducted and Bülow to have played. Eugenie Schumann recalls that her sister Marie responded to another performance of the work, seemingly given at around the same time, as a "spirited sketch," adding that "in later years he hardly ever played anything except his own compositions—when it didn't matter whether he reached technical perfection or not."[10]

Brahms's aim in performance was apparently for an overall view, a broad reading in which no special technical feature drew attention to itself—a significant fact in an age of emerging and competitive pianistic technique. However, if one feature was memorable to his listeners, it was Brahms's rhythmic precision and intensity. It is obvious in the B flat Piano Concerto (the first two movements especially), and it is the major feature of Brahms's first instrumental work, the Scherzo in E flat Minor, op. 4, of 1851. The early impression that he made on Schumann, Dietrich, and others remained. The young Adelina de Lara was overwhelmed by his rhythm, precision, and intensity: "He played all the octaves ... with a tremendous rhythm which burnt itself into my memory. Even when I got to know him better, it was always with a jolt that I heard him play." Fire was certainly something he sought in a player, as when he evaluated a performance of the B flat Concerto by another of Clara's pupils, Leonard Borwick. "He played it with all the fire and passion that Brahms had imagined, even in his most sanguine moments."[11] Added to Brahms's rhythmic energy was great power of the left hand in taking wide leaps.

Although Brahms's inaccuracies were of minor significance for many listeners, there was another, more serious dimension to his limitations: a detachment and reticence of expression. Hanslick was clearly struck by this at Brahms's first Vienna recital, in November 1862:

> It may appear praiseworthy to Brahms that he plays
> more like a composer than a virtuoso, but such praise is
> not altogether unqualified. Prompted by the desire to let
> the composer speak for himself, he neglects—especially
> in the playing of his own pieces—much that the player
> should rightly do for the composer. His playing resem-
> bles the austere Cordelia, who concealed her finest feel-
> ings rather than betray them to the people. The forceful
> and the distorted are thus simply impossible in Brahms's
> playing. Its judicious softness is such, indeed, that he
> seems reluctant to draw a full tone from the piano. As
> little as I wish to gloss over the minor shortcomings, just
> as little do I wish to deny how insignificant they are
> compared with the irresistible spiritual charm of his play-
> ing.[12]

Before he grew close to the composer, Bülow was less charitable, referring to the playing of the "brooding Brahms." Brahms was in fact often moody about playing in private, and he could be inconsistent. May recalls that "he seemed forced and self-conscious . . . as it were, outside the music" at Clara's one afternoon, "but . . . the very next evening it was entirely different," giving a Scarlatti piece "as though he were inspired." Eugenie Schumann also noted that "he played my father's E flat [piano] quartet" very badly, though she added, perhaps out of loyalty, that "this did not happen very often." She adds another side to this sense of unease with the instrument: "I never gained the impression that Brahms looked upon the piano as a beloved friend, as did my mother. He seemed to be in battle with it . . . when he played passionate parts, it was as though a tempest were tossing clouds. Then he made one feel the limitations that the instrument placed upon him." This failure under certain conditions for the two sides of his creative personality to meet perhaps reflects the depth of his struggle for independence from the piano. The young Brahms thought entirely through the instrument, but the mature composer forged a powerfully independent sound world. Characteristically, Brahms himself had no illusions about his playing. He admitted to his limitations and often had to be goaded into practice for pubic performances.[13]

Interpretation at the Piano

Although the most vivid impressions of Brahms the pianist emerge from his playing of his own compositions, accounts also survive of his teaching of basic keyboard repertory. All reports stress the preeminence of J. S. Bach as the keyboard companion of his private hours. A volume of the "Forty-Eight" was invariably open on the piano in his apartment. When Henschel noticed it, Brahms commented, "With this I rinse my mouth every morning." And when Brahms sat down to play to others, it was invariably the "Forty-Eight" that came to his mind. When improvising, it was with the style of Bach that he most often deceived the uninitiated. His famed facility in transposition was also frequently deployed in the performance of Bach, and he played "fugues of Bach and other works for his own edification in various transposed keys when at the height of his mastership." Florence May described Brahms's playing and teaching of the music of others, especially Bach. May recalls that his interpretation of Bach was always unconventional and quite unfettered by traditional theory, and he certainly did not share the opinion, which has had many distinguished adherents, that Bach's music should be performed in a simply flowing style. In the movements of the Suites he liked variety of tone and touch, as well as a certain elasticity of *tempo*. His playing of many of the preludes and some of the fugues was a revelation of exquisite poems, and he performed them not only with graduated shadings but with marked contrasts of tone effect. Each note of Bach's passages and figures contributed, in the hands of Brahms, to form melody which was instinct with feeling of some kind or other. It might be deep pathos or light-hearted playfulness and jollity; impulsive energy or soft and tender grace; but sentiment (as distinct from sentimentality) was always there: monotony never. "Quite tender and quite soft" was his frequent admonition to me, whilst in another place he required the utmost impetuosity.

Brahms particularly loved Bach's suspensions. "It is here that it must sound" he would say, pointing to the tied note and insisting, whilst not allowing me to force the preparation, that the latter should be so struck as to give the fullest possible effect to the dissonance. "How am I to make this sound?" I asked him of a few bars of a subject lying for the third, fourth and fifth fingers of the left hand, which he wished brought out clearly, but in a very soft tone "You must think particularly of the fingers with which you play it, and by and by it will come out" he answered."[14]

In correspondence with Clara Schumann he discussed his performance of ornaments in Bach. "I am always very punctilious about ornamentations, although slovenly editions of the works often force one to follow one's own taste in these matters. . . . I often regard prolonged mordents . . . as trilled notes and I do not take the small notes before the principal note, as I do with simple mordents. . . . Altogether I do not treat mordents, trills, and small runs in Bach as ornamentations. Not leggiero (that is, except when it is especially called for), but I think one ought to accentuate the trilled note in such cases, as was probably necessary with the old weak pianos."[15]

Less information survives concerning his playing of Mozart, especially his performances of the piano concertos during his years at Detmold. But May records interesting remarks on the F Major Sonata during her lessons, where his "delicate shading" was noted, as also in Haydn:

> He taught me that the music [of Mozart] should not be performed with mere grace and lightness, but that these effects should be contrasted with the expression of sustained feeling and with the use of the deep legato touch. Part of one of my lessons was devoted to the Sonata in F Major [K.533 bb 1–2]. Brahms let me play nearly a page of the first movement without making any remark. Then he stopped me. "But you are playing without expression," and imitated me, playing the same portion in the same style, on the upper part of the piano, touching the keys neatly, lightly, and unmeaningly. By the time he left off we were both smiling at the absurd performance. "Now," he said, "with expression," and he repeated the first few bars of the subject, giving each note its place as an essential portion of a fine melody. We spent a long time over the movement that day, and it was not until the next lesson, after I had two, perhaps even three, days to think myself into his conception, that I was able to play it broadly enough to satisfy him. At the close of the first of these two Mozart lessons I said to him, "All that you have told me today is quite new to me." "It is all there," he replied, pointing to the book.[16]

May continues:

> Brahms in fact recognized no such thing as what is sometimes called "neat playing" of the compositions of either

Bach, Scarlatti or Mozart. Neatness and equality of finger were imperatively demanded by him, and in their utmost nicety and perfection, but as a preparation, not as an end. Varying and sensitive expression was to him as the breath of life, necessary to the true interpretation of any work of genius, and he did not hesitate to avail himself of such resources of the modern pianoforte as he felt helped to impart it; no matter in what particular century his composer may have lived, or what may have been the peculiarities or excellencies and limitations of the instruments of his day.

Whatever the music I might be studying, however, he would never allow any kind of "expression made easy." He particularly disliked chords to be spread unless marked so by the composer for the sake of a special effect. "No arpége" he used invariably to say if I unconsciously gave way to the habit, or yielded to the temptation of softening a chord by its means. He made very much of the well-known effect of two notes slurred together, whether in a loud or soft tone, and I know from his insistence to me on this point that the mark had special significance in his music.[17]

Brahms's comment that "it is all there" points to a vital aspect of his attitude to performance: the status of the text. He had reservations about adding to the original, and this concern was probably behind a comment to May about ignoring the features of Czerny's edition of Bach's *Forty-Eight* save its fingering.[18] His concern is clarified by a comment on the playing of Beethoven, which makes an interesting comparison with earlier comments on the nature of his interpretations. "When I play something by Beethoven, I have absolutely no individuality in relation to it; rather I try to reproduce the piece as well as Beethoven wrote it. Then I have (quite) enough to do." Similar comments emerge elsewhere, as does the commitment to a good fingering by an established master of technique. Unfortunately, few descriptions of his playing of other composers survive. Hanslick's warm response to his playing of the Schumann Fantasia in C at his first solo recital in Vienna was inspired partly by its breadth and directness. May refers to him playing a "wild piece by Scarlatti as I have never heard anyone play before . . . and I never thought the piano capable of it."[19]

Technical Training

Brahms's own prodigious technique began to be formed when, at the age of seven, he received his first piano lessons from Otto Cossel. After establishing "a good hand position and free movement of the fingers" he proceeded to the etudes of Czerny, Cramer, and Clementi, classical sonatas and Bach keyboard works. When he began studying with Eduard Marxsen in 1843 he could play some studies from Cramer's first book "very capitally."[20] Brahms's pianistic background emerged clearly in his public concerts, which began in 1847; he played a mixture of Beethoven and Bach, variations on popular songs, and studies in the bravura style of the time. There is no Chopin.[21] Florence May had become Clara's pupil during her visit to London in winter 1870–71 and was invited to study with her in Baden in the following spring. She arrived in May, and her lessons with Brahms took place thereafter. Her reflective accounts of this time complement the down-to-earth reports of Eugenie Schumann, stresses Brahms's technical approach in the following:

> He took a great deal of trouble in the training of my fingers. He had thought about such training and about technique in general much more than my mother, who had surmounted all technical difficulties at an age when one is not yet conscious of them. He made me play a great many exercises; scales, and arpeggios as a matter of course. He gave special attention to the training of the thumb, which, as many will remember, was given a very prominent part in his own playing. When the thumb had to begin a passage he flung it onto the key with the other fingers clenched. As he kept his wrist loose at the same time, the tone remained full and round, even in a fortissimo. Considerable time was daily given to . . . exercises for the passing under of the thumb. . . . I had to

take the note on which the thumb was used on the wing
[so to speak] and accentuate the first of the four notes
strongly. Then I had to play the same exercise in triplets,
with strong accents on the first note of every triplet.
When I could play the exercises faultlessly in keys without the black notes, I played them, always beginning
with the thumb, in C sharp, F sharp, A flat, E flat, and
D flat. Then followed the common chords with inver-
sions through three and four octaves, also in groups of
four notes and in triplets, beginning with the accent on
the first note. When I had played this about ten times, I
changed the accent to the second, then to the third note
of each group, so that all the five were exercised equally.
I practiced these arpeggios alternately as triplets and sex-
tuplets, and had to distinguish clearly between twice
three and three times two notes. Brahms also made me
practice trills. In all exercises he made me play the non-
accentuated notes very lightly. I practiced the chromatic
scale with the first and third, first and fourth, and first
and fifth finger, and repeated the two consecutive notes
where the thumb was passed under. They were all, in
fact, quite simple exercises; but carefully executed, first
slowly, then more rapidly, and at last prestissimo. I found
them extremely helpful for the strengthening, suppleness,
and control of my fingers. I also played some of the difficult exercises published later as "Fifty-One Exercises for
Piano by Brahms," in which he did not include the easier and musically less valuable ones. With regard to studies Brahms said: play easy ones, but play them as rapidly
as possible. He thought very highly of Clementi's "Gradus ad Parnassum" and made me play a great number of
these.[22]

Florence May also stressed his care about fingering from the very start
of her lessons.

After hearing me play through a study from Clementi's
"Gradus ad Parnassum" he immediately set to work to

loosen and equalize my fingers. Beginning that very day
he gradually put me through an entire course of technical training, showing me how I should best work, for the
attainment of my end, at scales, arpeggi, double notes,
and octaves. He not only showed me how to practice: he
made me, at first, practice to him during a good part of
my lessons, whilst he sat watching my fingers; telling me
what was wrong in my way of moving them, indicating
by a movement of his own hand, a better position for
mine, absorbing himself entirely, for the time being, in
the object of helping me. He did not believe in the util-
ity for me of the daily practice of the ordinary five-finger
exercises, preferring to form exercises from any piece or
study upon which I might be engaged. He had a great
habit of turning a difficult passage around and making
me practice it, not as written, but with other accents and
in various figures, with the result that when I again tried
it as it stood the difficulties had always considerably di-
minished, and often entirely disappeared.[23]

The Chamber Player and the Accompanist

Brahms's large output of chamber music and songs gave him many more
opportunities to play his own works than did his often taxing solo compositions. Early on he engaged in chamber playing with his circle and
acquired an intimate knowledge of the classical and romantic repertory.
It was as a chamber player in partnership with Eduard Reményi that
Brahms made his first professional tour and established his credentials in
transposing at sight. He transposed the piano part of the Beethoven C
Minor Sonata up a semitone in their concert at Celle because the piano
was below pitch.[24] He invariably introduced his own chamber works as
pianist, and he debuted in Vienna in this capacity with the piano quartet,
op. 26; his private rehearsals were a regular feature of the life of his musical
circle.[25] The decline in his own playing standards over the years naturally
affected his playing of chamber music in public. Clara Schumann advised
him to engage a professional to introduce his final works with clarinet
rather than play them himself.[26]

Brahms's closest chamber music partnership was with Joseph Joachim, with whom he had played since 1853. They were especially noted for the Beethoven violin sonatas. Brahms's playing reportedly took on a new beauty of tone during their tour of Switzerland in autumn 1866, apparently in response to Joachim's sound and classical poise of interpretation.[27] Brahms grew to have great sensitivity and control in the case of the D Minor Sonata, written with Joachim in mind in 1888. Eugenie Schumann recalls a performance of the work with Brahms at the piano. "There is a 'tranquillo' at the end of the third movement, and our mother always said that there one walked on eggs. Marie and I were most anxious to hear how he would get safely across. When it came he took the 'tranquillo' so unbelievably slowly that nothing could happen."[28] Toward the end of his life Brahms expressed reservations over how the piano and the string instruments related in chamber music; he preferred the clarinet. Ferdinand Schumann recalls Brahms commenting that the tone of the clarinet was "much more adapted to the piano than string instruments. The tone character of the latter was quite different." He continued: "The clarinet, as a solo instrument as well as in chamber music, should be more cultivated than it had been."[29] At his best, Brahms was a master player of chamber music, not least his own. Max Graf recalled the first performance of the revised version of the Piano Trio in B, op. 8, with the Rosé Quartet: "He played in the powerful and tightly woven classic style which was so characteristic of him and as usual introduced thundering basses. Upon this ponderous structure a magnificent and uniform building was erected. In the great climaxes of the composition ran the undertone of subterranean rumbling like the echo of a remote earthquake which served to remind listeners that beneath the heavy boulders of classic form the romanticism of Brahms's youth was buried."[30]

Because of his vast output of solo songs, Brahms was probably more active as pianist in this capacity than in any other, though fewer records of it survive. His greatest professional partner in lieder was Julius Stockhausen. Their earliest joint recitals in Cologne and Bern were the year of their meeting, 1856, and their performances caused a sensation. The quality of Brahms's accompaniment was often noted thereafter in their chief repertory—Schubert, Schumann, and Beethoven. Stockhausen inspired many of Brahms's most characteristic baritone songs, and Brahms dedicated to him the "Magelone Lieder," his most extensive single work for voice and piano, dating from 1861. The only other singer to rival Stock-

hausen in Brahms's affection was the tenor Gustav Walter, who Graf
claimed was the first singer in Vienna "to appear as a soloist in a concert
at which no other artist was programmed . . . Walter was especially well
known for his charming renditions of Brahms's semi-classical songs, such
as "Ständchen" and "Wiegenlied." Brahms, whose hands were heavy, experienced some difficulty in adapting his accompaniment to Walter's hov-
ering 'pianos.' "[31] In later years Brahms rarely appeared with any other
singer, though he greatly enjoyed accompanying the young female singers
who took up his songs or the singers of his own circle, including Antonia
Kufferath.[32] He also accompanied the mezzo-soprano Alice Barbi, whose
beauty and rich voice impressed all who heard her, at her farewell recital
in Vienna on 14 May 1895. Graf recounts the event: "Finally the door to
the stage opened and Barbi came out dressed in one of the simply cut
white gowns she always wore, her black hair knotted softly, and behind
her to our surprise, and the surprise of the whole audience, in the place
of the usual accompanist, came Brahms. He was somewhat at a loss and
came on the stage with the awkwardness of a great Newfoundland dog
following its mistress. Later we were told that Brahms appeared unan-
nounced at the singer's dressing room and astounded her by saying that
he wished to accompany her at the piano. That night the audience not
only heard Brahms's most beautiful songs sung by Barbi, but played by
the composer himself."[33] Graf adds definition to his observation of
Brahms the chamber player:

> Brahms never accompanied in the manner to which we
> are accustomed today [c. 1945]. Accompanists of great
> singers perform in the same manner as lackeys laying a
> carpet at the feet of their mistresses. They are in the
> background, obsequious and bending to the whims of
> the artist and never step forth to attract attention. But
> not Brahms. He was still a great musician as an accom-
> panist. At this concert there were two musicians perform-
> ing with an equally distributed effort and attention. The
> singer was not the main feature, the song was important,
> and both singer and pianist worked toward the same goal
> in the service of the composer. . . . Brahms's accompani-
> ment had a strong foundation of basses, even in sweet

songs like the *Wiegenlied,* the accompaniment of which is usually sublimated and pampering. Brahms himself always used firmness in the basses. His hand was somewhat heavy and his playing was devoid of the complicated shading and nuances of colours which characterize players of the Liszt school. He was simple and strong. There was spiritual and musical potency in his playing—no nervous over-sensitiveness running amuck in hundreds of little colour patches. When Brahms played, the design was important and not the colours themselves. . . .

There was another trait in Brahms's accompaniments which is no longer found. He built up his accompaniment like a symphonic composition. There was unity, gradation and development. The music reached its climax from within by virtue of the musical forces. When he played his songs he was the creator of great symphonic forms, used in the development of a vast musical composite of several ideas, which grew like petals to form a single beautiful flower.[34]

13 · Brahms the Conductor

You have a gift for conducting such as no other possesses.

The Place of Conducting in Brahms's Career

Although Brahms held his professional conducting positions for only several years at a time at most, he conducted regularly throughout his life. At the age of fourteen he proved himself "astonishing competent for the role" when he was asked, on short notice, to conduct the male choir of the musical community at Winsen. He "inspired such confidence and sympathy" that he was invited to assume conducting responsibilities for the duration of his stay there.[35] He founded his own Ladies' Choir at Hamburg in 1859, and in his later years he conducted many of his own works. He gave first performances of all his major choral works with the exception of the *Alto Rhapsody* and the complete *Song of Triumph* (A

German Requiem, Rinaldo, Nänie, Song of the Fates, Song of Destiny, Song of Triumph [first movement]). Of the orchestral works he gave the first performances of the "St. Antoni" Variations and the Fourth Symphony, and he played the first performances of both the piano concertos. He conducted the two concertos in which he was not soloist (violin concerto and double concerto) when they were first performed. He performed until the end of his life, last appearing in Vienna with the students' orchestra of the Conservatory. He took an obvious pleasure in conducting and put great energy into it. But there was a conflict between the pressures associated with training and organizing choirs and orchestras and the internal drives of the composer. Moreover, Brahms did not cut a striking figure as a conductor, and he was certainly not as memorable in this role as in that of pianist. It was perhaps out of loyalty on the part of his friends that there are so few vivid accounts of the conductor in action, though he was captured in the drawings of Willy von Beckerath. But Brahms's profound musicianship and care in preparation were evident, and his achievements were real if not always fully acknowledged.[36]

Brahms's three professional conductorships were coincident with the three professional posts he held. His responsibilities at the princely court of Lippe-Detmold in October, November, and December of the years 1857–59 were for teaching piano to Princess Frederike, for conducting the choral society, and for performing as pianist in the court concerts. The conducting of the orchestra was in the hands of the aging Clemens August Kiel: Brahms appeared as orchestral conductor only when the choir was involved, as in a performance of Beethoven's *Choral Fantasia* in the 1857–58 season.[37] While at Detmold he was able to try out works, learn conducting as well as choral compositional technique, establish his artistic principles in repertory planning and historical emphasis. Brahms maintained his musical connections with Hamburg, where he organized his Ladies' Choir after the end of the second Detmold season; he wanted to focus more directly on his musical interests as a composer and performer. The stimulus for establishing the choir was the wedding of a pupil of Karl Grädener, where choral music for unaccompanied women's voices was performed. Soon more than forty singers were assembling every Monday morning to rehearse, and some lasting friendships were created. The choir continued until 1862, when Brahms left for Vienna.[38]

Brahms took his first Viennese position, with the Vienna Singakademie, after he had been in the city for about a year. He soon found the responsibilities onerous, and he declined the invitation to continue for a second year. But he made valuable contributions to the city's musical life during his tenure. He served as director of the concerts of the Gesellschaft der Musikfreunde, Vienna's most prestigious musical institution, in 1872–75. But after three years of extensive concert-giving and administration he resigned, never to take a formal position again. He was then free to promote his own works and rehearse them where he found the situation congenial (as through von Bülow with the Meiningen orchestra in 1884–85). Brahms's work as conductor gives insight into his creative nature and values, adding an essential dimension to his musical personality and complementing his life as a composer.

Programming and Organization

Prior to the Detmold appointment, Brahms had had little opportunity to conduct. Of the pieces he wrote to perform at Winsen, none of which survive, one was described as displaying "a feeling for independent part-writing."[39] This characteristic was to predominate in his exploration of the repertory through library study of early scores. But once at Detmold, Brahms boldly took every opportunity to introduce works that interested him, including his own. In his first year his programs included Rovetta's "Salve Regina," Praetorius's "Maria zart" as well as Handel's *Messiah;* the second year included Bach's Cantatas 4 and 21, as well as the preparation of Palestrina's *Missa Papae Marcelli,* though it was not performed.[40] Such unusual pieces inevitably caused problems in a small musical establishment. There were not enough singers, especially tenors, and in his last season Brahms had to ask the prince's permission to recruit singers from town.[41] As in the Schumann years, Brahms was observed at Detmold as quietly self-absorbed and determined: "When engaged in the performance of his duties, he was always quiet and serious, and would stand, before the commencement of a choir practice or a court concert, at the extreme end of the long room in which the functions took place, speaking to no-one, perhaps looking through a piece of music or a letter."[42] But because the position offered no senior responsibility and provided no future, Brahms's eye was on Hamburg.

Brahms's Hamburg choir was essentially for private performance but gave ad hoc public performances in churches. In this more relaxed context Brahms had more freedom to pursue his artistic goals, and he had far better singers at his disposal that he did at Detmold, including his own piano pupils and other cultivated musicians in the city. The choir became a tool for testing his intense compositional studies during these years, first manifest in choral works, and it enabled him to explore further the repertory in performance. As a conductor he had an easy manner with his singers, combining friendliness and humor with a commitment to high standards and discipline, as is evident in the quaintly humorous prospectus he drew up as earnest of intentions. Its five points begin as follows: " 'Avertimento': 'Pro primo, it is to be remarked that the members of the Ladies Choir must be there. . . . By which it is to be understood that they must oblige themselves to be there. Pro secundo, it must be observed that the members of the Ladies Choir must be there; which is meant that they must be there at precisely the appointed time."[43]

The principle of fining as a penalty for nonfulfillment of conditions recalls Brahms's exchanges of counterpoint exercises with Joachim. Works performed by the Ladies' Choir included one piece from the Detmold concerts (the "Angel Chorus" from *Messiah*); the rest was unfamiliar to his singers: duets from the Bach Cantatas 79 and 80; German sixteenth-century motets, including Eccard's "Übers Gebirge Maria geht"; Gallus's "Ecce quomodo"; Hassler's "Mein G'mut ist mir verwirret"; Isaac's "Innsbruch, ich muss dich lassen"; Italian sixteenth- and seventeenth-century motets—Caldara's "Peccavi," Lotti's "Vere languores nostros," Palestrina's "Gaude Barbara beata" and "Princeps gloriosissime"; and, most unusual of all, an English sixteenth-century canon, Byrd's "Non nobis Domine."[44]

Brahms's conductorship of the Vienna Singakademie in 1863–64 was of an entirely new order of importance in his professional life, and he used the opportunity to make a much more influential statement of his artistic commitments, as well as to gain professional prestige, for he still wished to establish himself in Hamburg or elsewhere in the north.[45] Although he left after a year, he won respect and laid valuable groundwork for his artistic links with the city in the future. He was required to give three concerts in the first season—in November, January, and March— the last a single performance of a major choral work.

His programs show his pioneering spirit. He took over some items from earlier concerts—Bach's Cantata 21, Isaac's "Innsbruch," Rovetta's "Salve Regina"—and added other pieces by these composers: two more German folksongs set by Isaac: "Es ist ein Schnitter heisst der Tod," "Ich fahr dahin"; Bach's Cantata 8, Eccard's "Des Christen Triumphlied," as well as completely new and equally obscure ones: Schütz's "Saul, Saul, was verfolgst du mich," Gabrieli's "Benedictus" in 12 parts, Stobäus's "Auf's Osterfest," a Bennet madrigal, and a Morley "Dance Song." J. S. Bach's *Christmas Oratorio* was hardly better known, as only two Bach Passions were regularly performed. Even compositions by more recent composers were obscure: Beethoven's *Opferlied* and *Elegischer Gesang,* Mendelssohn's "Mitten wir im Leben sind." Only a few instrumental items, duets and folksongs arranged by Brahms, were familiar; Schumann's *Requiem für Mignon* was the only choral piece with orchestra. The sources reflect his scholarly explorations: the *Bach Gesellschaft* edition, which was begun in 1851, Winterfeld's *Johannes Gabrieli und sein Zeitalter,* and other sources were to be found only in rare editions from which he had made copies.[46] Such works were tremendously challenging to his public, and reception was mixed. But such music was not likely to please Viennese audiences, and attention was focused as much on his conducting skills as his choice of works.

The audience's response to the first concert, on 15 November, which included Bach's Cantata 21 ("My Spirit Was in Heaviness"), was very favorable. The press commented that the concert was "not only excellent in itself, but was with the exception of the first performance in Vienna of Bach's *St. Matthew Passion,* by far the most noteworthy achievement in the record of the Singakademie, and gave us the opportunity of recognizing Brahms's rare talent as a conductor." The cantata was rendered with "splendid colouring and spiritual insight," and the three Volkslieder "opened all hearts," the audience insisting on a fourth as encore. But Brahms's conducting drew implied criticism: clarity of the beat "could hardly have been expected of an artist who has shown himself, in his creations and performances, so essentially a romanticist and dreamer."[47]

At the second concert the program was less well prepared, and there were technical deficiencies in the performance. The second item broke down at one point because of mistakes by the accompanist; the piano sent in lieu of the organ was too high in pitch. Again Brahms's folksongs emerged as the most popular items. The choir began to desert in droves, and critical reaction became unfavorable. Hirsch speaks of a "ship-wrecked" performance, and Hanslick of the performance of some numbers that they had "the character of an improvisation or a practice rather than a concert production."[48] In the third concert, the Christmas Oratorio, receiving its first performance in Vienna, was unfavorably compared with the *St. John Passion,* given some time earlier by the Singverein of the Gesellschaft der Musikfreunde under the well-established Johann Herbeck.[49] But many members of Brahms's choir admired him; he took great care in preparation, and his musical gestures drew a sensitive response. Loyal members of the choir organized another concert as a result of the decline in interest in the second and third concerts. The program was entirely of Brahms's music, which was generally well accepted. Although the more perceptive musicians and critics appreciated Brahms's importance, he was too ambitious for the resources at hand and for the critical climate. He was obviously discouraged, though he had achieved much in his high-profile post. Clara sought to encourage him, citing the problems now faced by Stockhausen in Hamburg and stressing Brahms's "splendid success."[50]

Although many of the same kinds of problems would remain when Brahms became director of the Gesellschaft der Musikfreunde in 1872 and conductor of the concerts—much of his preferred music was not favored by the public—their effects were mollified by the higher standards of the choir and orchestra and by Brahms's status as Vienna's leading musician. By now his appetite for the musical possibilities of a conductorship had returned, and he could give even greater expression to his artistic commitments. He came to the task in a positive frame of mind. Billroth recalls on 25 October 1872 that "he is all enthusiasm over the direction of the choral society and enraptured with the voices and the musical talent of the choir. Should the results be favorable I think he will persevere; a failure might suffice to discourage him so much that as to deprive him of all inclination for the work."[51] His responsibilities were for four concerts between November and April, with two extra concerts for choir and orchestra, at least one of which was to be a large oratorio work.

Brahms now approached his task in a more radical manner than previously, and he immediately set about reorganizing the orchestra.[52] He began by replacing some of the amateur members with members of the court orchestra. He also began a second weekly rehearsal for the choir and allowed the more difficult passages to be studied by different groups at a time. His work was marked, as usual, by careful preparation. One member of the choir, Frau Gugler, recalled rehearsing under Brahms: "[He] was always businesslike in rehearsals, *yet at the same time, kindly and patient, never rude or coarse.* The singers enjoyed working under him. . . . Brahms had the singers read through the music first and concentrated for a time on fundamentals, almost *al fresco* before turning to the working out of rhythmic and dynamic detail. . . . [His leadership] was distinguished and enormously stimulating."[53] Brahms spent three months preparing the *St. Matthew Passion* for his last concert, a degree of care that was noted by Henschel, who was to sing the part of Christus.[54]

Brahms's programs combined little-known music with the familiar, and works of the new generation with those of his contemporaries. In program content the first season showed a continuity from the public concerts at Detmold and the Singakademie. In the first year Brahms retained "Übers Gebirge Maria geht," "Innsbruch, ich muss dich lassen," Bach's Cantatas 4 and 8, and "Ecce quomodo." He later added Bach's Cantatas 50 and 34 and the *St. Matthew Passion.* Of other earlier works, he included Palestrina's "Haec Dies," Lassus's "Aus meiner Sünden tiefe," as well as comparative performances of two harmonizations of one chorale, "Est ist genug," by J. R. Ahle and J. S. Bach.[55] There were major works by Handel, the first season opening with the *Dettingen Te Deum* and the Organ Concerto in E flat; later seasons included *Alexander's Feast* and *Solomon.* The first season also included Bach's Prelude and Fugue in E flat, BWV 552, for organ. His interest in early and obscure works remained strong in the second year, and the outstanding pieces were the newly discovered offertorium "Venite Populi" by Mozart and an aria from Mozart's cantata "Davidde Penitente." Little-known Schubert included, in the first season, Joachim's orchestration of the Grand Duo as a Symphony in C, and later "Ellens zweiter Gesang" (arranged by Brahms), the overture to *Fierrebras,* and an aria from *Die Zauberglocken* as well as the "Kyrie" and "Credo" from the Mass in B flat, at that time unpublished.

He gave good representation to an increasing proportion of established works and to new works by his contemporaries. The established works include Cherubini's Requiem in C Minor; a chorus from Beethoven's *The Consecration of the House;* Beethoven's Choral Fantasia; Mendelssohn's *The First Walpurgisnacht;* the overture to "Camacho's Wedding"; Schumann's "Des Sängers Fluch," Fantasie for Violin and Orchestra, and *Manfred;* and Hiller's Concert Overture in D. Works by his contemporaries include Volkmann's Concertstück; Rheinberger's Prelude "The Seven Ravens"; Goldmark's *Frühlingshymne;* Dietrich's Violin Concerto; Rietz's Arioso for Violin; Rubinstein's overture "Dmitri Donska"; Joachim's *Hungarian Concerto;* Bruch's *Odysseus;* and a work by a composer outside his circle, though admired by Brahms: Berlioz's *Harold in Italy.* Of his own works he gave the *Song of Destiny* and the Alto Rhapsody, and he also appeared as soloist, in the Beethoven E flat Concerto.[56]

If Brahms's work with the Singverein had been controversial, the sheer range of works performed—not least of what would be termed "early music" well into the next century—helped to create an ethos of which the society would become ever more proud. To this day the society regards Brahms's work as representing a significant period in its history, and many features introduced by him were prophetic of later years. Structuring programs into tighter and more integrated entities than was customary, and devoting an entire evening to one work, were traditions continued by Friedrich Hegar and Wilhelm Furtwängler.[57]

But when Brahms began, opinions were not entirely in his favor; many recalled the problems with the Singakademie. Despite the challenging programs, the first-year concerts were on the whole well received, and any lingering doubts over Brahms's abilities disappeared. It was rather the choice of an orchestral piece that prompted criticism: Joachim's orchestration of the Grand Duo of Schubert. The first extra concert—with Amalie Joachim in an aria from Gluck's *Alceste* and the Mozart "Offertorium" for double chorus and orchestra in its first performance—were enthusiastically received, as was Brahms's *Song of Triumph.* The second concert suffered a series of misfortunes, though not of Brahms's making. Hiller had problems with the percussionist in his Overture in D Major, and there were misunderstandings between soloists and the harpist in Schumann's "Des Sängers Fluch." But the second extra concert, devoted to Handel's *Saul,* was an unreserved success. Apart from some audience unease at the opening of Bach's Cantata 4 "Christ lag in Todesbanden," the 23 March concert went well, with keen response to Brahms's folksong settings. The last concert, of Bach's Cantata 8 and Cherubini's Requiem in C Minor, had to be repeated by request two days later. Two additional concerts given at the end of the second season were well received. One featured Handel's *Solomon,* about which a critic commented, "We can only thank the conductor for bringing this work forward; the performance was ideal."[58] Hereafter, with the exception of an inadequate performance of the Beethoven E flat concerto by Brahms himself, the concerts pass without criticism, and there was a warm response to a performance of *A German Requiem,* which overshadowed the appearance of Wagner in Vienna conducting excerpts from *The Ring of the Niebelung* several days earlier.

The Conductor at Work

Although Brahms's commitment to the choice and preparation of the music he performed with his choirs and orchestras was never in doubt, opinions were clearly divided over the effectiveness of his technique. This disagreement also reflects varying critical values in relation to the conductor's art. It seems significant that the highest praise was offered only by his close friends and in private. Thus the comment of Hermann Levi, who appears to be responding to Brahms's or someone else's critical reserve: "I saw in Karlsruhe, and with unprejudiced eyes, that you have a gift for conducting such that no other possesses."[59]

Brahms is vividly described at the podium by Geheimrat Wichtgraf, a relative of Billroth's, at Essen: "His manner of conducting is extremely vigorous and exciting. When he wants a *pianissimo* he bends forward, while for a *fortissimo* he draws himself up erect, but always with a perfectly natural movement, without any theatrical striving for effect. One can see from the expression on his face, from his every movement, how he throws himself into every note. The passion which emanates from him communicates itself automatically to the members of the choir and orchestra." Bernhard Vogel praised the commanding intelligence and energetic will with which Brahms conducted, and his terse, definite directions which were uttered in a clear, powerful voice. Ferdinand Schumann stressed Brahms's undemonstrative aspect while conducting the *Academic Festival Overture* in Frankfurt in 1894: "I shall never forget his conducting—the concise, calm gestures, the serious expression of the face, the amiable directions to the different instrumental groups."[60]

But things did not always go easily, especially with new and difficult works. Ethel Smyth recalls that "there had been a good deal of friction" in the first rehearsals of the Second Symphony at Leipzig in 1878, adding that she "had the impression that rehearsals had not gone altogether smoothly." Specht summarizes some of the views that emerged in the press, especially in relation to the choral performances with the Vienna Singakademie and Singverein of the Gesellschaft der Musikfreunde, which he could corroborate from his own observation. First, observers said that Brahms lacked the necessary manual dexterity and flexibility of the wrist to quickly communicate or to adjust in performance. His signs were not clear enough to communicate his meaning to the singers. "Already in the second concert" with the Singakademie "he had to intervene" by stopping the performance for lack of response, apparently because his reserved attitude on the podium put off the choir. Specht comments that his unhistrionic competence was mistaken for pedantry, and one critic compared his "dreamy pensiveness" with that of Schumann.[61] And Brahms's capacity to take in everything at a glance must have been compromised by his extreme nearsightedness, which, even if it did not necessarily affect his capacity to recall his own music or that of others, is unlikely to have inspired full confidence.

But when the situation was right, he could realize all the qualities admired by his friends. This happened most often in performances of his own music. Stanford describes his technique in the first movement of the D Minor Piano Concerto: "His conducting of the D Minor Concerto threw an entirely new light on the whole composition, especially as regards the rhythmical swing of the first movement. Written in the troublesome *tempo* of 6/4, most conductors either take it too quickly by beating two in a bar or too slowly by beating six. Brahms beat it in an uneven four . . . which entirely did away with undue dragging or hurrying, and kept the line of movement insistent up to the last note." Stanford's account is also revealing of Brahms's attitude to tempo: "His *tempo* was very elastic, as much so in places as Von Bülow's, though more restrained, but he never allowed his liberties with the time to interfere with the general balance: they were of the true nature of *rubato*. He loathed having his slow movements played in an inexorable four-square. On one occasion at a performance of his C minor symphony he was sitting in a box next to a friend of mine, and in the Andante, which was being played with a metronomic stiffness, he suddenly seized his neighbour by the shoulder and ejaculating 'Heraus!' literally pushed him out of the concert room." In a separate account of this experience Stanford makes it clear that the conductor with the Vienna Philharmonic was Hans Richter.[62]

This outlook naturally affected Brahms's attitude toward the use of the metronome, which was growing popular with performers. He commented to Henschel in 1880: "I think here as well as all other music, the metronome is of no value. As far at least as my experience goes, everybody has, sooner or later, withdrawn his metronome marks. Those which can be found in my works—good friends have talked me into putting them there, for I myself have never believed that my blood and a mechanical instrument go well together."[63] The presentation of new works might require changes to the score, though only temporary ones, as Brahms indicates in his comments to Joachim on the Fourth Symphony.

> I have marked a few modifications in the score with pencil. They may be useful, even necessary for the first performance. Unfortunately they often find their way into print (with me as well as others) where, for the most part, they do not belong. Such exaggerations are only necessary when a composition is unfamiliar to an orchestra (or to a soloist). In such a case one often cannot do enough pushing or slowing down to produce even approximately the passionate or serene expression I want. Once a work has become part of flesh and blood, then in my opinion nothing of that sort is justifiable any more. In fact, the more one deviates from the original, the less artistic the performance becomes. With my older works I frequently find that everything falls into place without much ado and that many marks of the above-mentioned type become entirely superfluous![64]

In other instances, performance traditions actually led Brahms to change his mind regarding his markings. In the First Symphony, at the conclusion of the first movement, he asked his publisher to change the marking from "piu sostenuto" to "meno allegro" because he thought that conductors were taking it too slowly.[65] In the *German Requiem* he removed the metronome marks, which had been incorporated into the first edition even though they were meant to guide the preparation of only the first performance. Prior to the appearance of the first edition he had already altered the marking of the timpani part at the beginning of the pedal fugue of the third movement from "ff" to "fp," since the timpanist had ruined the Vienna part-performance of 1867 with his unrelenting volume on the pedal note. In later years Brahms admitted to wishing to revise the dynamics of the opening choral passage of *A German Requiem*. The choral conductor Siegfried Ochs, with whom he discussed the work in the 1890s, states that "Brahms wished to have the first three bars sung in the softest pianissimo, despite having written 'p.' He regarded it as an oversight that the choir was not thus indicated, as it is in the orchestral entry at the third bar of the choral passage."[66] Brahms was always sensitive to the needs of performers in securing effective performances of his works, which were technically challenging. The singer Georg (later Sir George) Henschel recalls a request to Brahms concerning a particularly high note in the baritone part of the *Song of Triumph*. He could not reach the note because of a cold and so "asked Brahms if he would object to my altering that note into a more convenient one . . . and he said: 'Not in the least. As far as I am concerned, a thinking, sensible singer may, without hesitation, change a note which for some reason or other is for the time being out of his compass into one which he can reach with comfort, *provided always that the declamation remains correct and the accentuation does not suffer.*' "[67]

FOUR · Brahms the Music Scholar and Student
of the Arts

14 · Reading and Scholarship in Brahms's Life

A Scholarly Disposition

Brahms's response to the appearance of further volumes of the complete works of Schütz (all but unknown to the general public) in 1891 and of Bach reflects the range of his interest in the music of the past. His absorption in such music extended to lengthy study, and even to a profound influence on his own works. Though no composer of his time was untouched by the music of the past, Brahms soon gained a purely technical knowledge of both music and sources that rivaled that of the newly emerging class of musicologists. Indeed, he was effectively one of them, spending as much time in their company as he did with performing musicians or literary figures. His devotion to the early composers, on whose music so much of modern musical life has been built, makes him seem more a figure of the twentieth century than of the nineteenth. Brahms's interests can be traced through three broad areas: his scholarly contacts, fields of interest, and collecting in Hamburg, Detmold, and Vienna; his work as a professional editor; and the connections between these activities and his creative output as a composer.

A new volume of Schütz lies here; one of Bach is expected.

Brahms was from the first an avid reader. Even at the age of fourteen he spent much time reading for himself, as well as reading to Lieschen Giesemann, whom he had been hired to teach piano while at Winsen. Throughout his lifetime books remained an important part of his friendships, as with the scholar and theologian J. V. Widmann. When staying close to Widmann at Thun, Switzerland, in 1886–88, he would "wander over to his friend . . . with a large leather travelling bag in which to abduct as may books as possible."[1] He early discovered the second-hand bookstalls located in the Jewish quarter of

Hamburg, where he spent much of his meager resources, and he quickly made use of a lending library during the Winsen stay.[2] Brahms visited libraries in Hamburg as a youth, and it can be concluded from this that early on he felt the need to go beyond the confines of the literary and musical resources of his teachers Cossel and Marxsen. At Düsseldorf he had access to Schumann's library, which he rearranged, as he himself wrote, "with the greatest delight." He gladly undertook the task of arranging its books and music in order to become acquainted with its contents.[3]

Brahms's passion for German literature was complemented by his purely musical interests. The earliest evidence of this passion came in 1848, when he wrote his name and the date on a used copy of David Kellner's 1743 treatise *Treulicher Unterricht im General-bass,* in which a copy of Mattheson's *Die Kunst, das Klavier zu Spielen* was bound.[4] Over the years he added a number of eighteenth-century books to his collection. In order to get to know obscure music he had no choice but to make his own manuscript copies.[5] The first copies were from the collection *Musica Sacra,* published by Schlesinger of Berlin (c. 1852): namely Durante's "Miserecordia Domine," Lotti's "Vere languares nostros," Corsi's "Adoramus te Christe," and the "Crucifixus" from Palestina's *Missa Papae Marcelli.* Copies of other works were also commissioned for him by friends, notably Clara Schumann. His access to the Schumanns' library in 1853 must have added greatly to his knowledge of both literature and music, and in Detmold he discovered in the court library eighteenth-century scores, including "the Haydn and Mozart Symphonies and Cassations," as well as much music literature.[6] In addition, the town had a good public library, which he used. Brahms's growing professional circle clearly appreciated his interests—for example, members of the Philharmonic Society of Karlsruhe gave him carefully copied scores of all five volumes of Georg Forster's *Ein Ausbund Schöner Teutscher Liedlein* in appreciation of the first performance there of *A German Requiem,* in 1869.[7] He also received presents of music books from others, including Clara.

By the time Brahms left Hamburg for Vienna in September 1862 he had already assembled an impressive collection of books. But the move quickly extended his knowledge by giving him access to music and musicians and allowing him to explore music for his own concerts, though the immediate possibilities with the Singakademie actually were short-lived. Certainly the opportunity to be near the materials of his art was not the least of the attractions of Vienna when Brahms made his first visit. He wrote to Adolf Schubring of the "many interesting people, the libraries, the Burgtheater, and the picture galleries. All these give one quite enough to enjoy outside one's own room."[8]

Scholarly Contacts in Hamburg and Vienna

Brahms's deep interest in musical literature naturally led him to seek greater contact with the leading musical figures of Hamburg as well as further afield. Once he had made a name for himself through his contact with the Schumanns in 1853 he received easier access to the musical circles of the city, which included the elderly conductor of the Philharmonic, F. W. Grund, his successor Georg Dietrich Otten, and the composer Karl Grädener. But he was equally interested in musicians with scholarly, historical, and even antiquarian interests. Two individuals were to be of special importance in stimulating these interests before Brahms left for Vienna, one little known to history, one familiar: Theodor Avé Lallemant and Friedrich Chrysander. Outside Hamburg, Brahms had cultivated important links with two other figures: the critic Adolf Schubring, resident in Dessau, and the scholar Otto Jahn, resident in Bonn. Brahms knew Avé Lallemant from at least 1854, and he was invited back to Hamburg by Avé Lallemant in 1878 for the fiftieth anniversary of the Philharmonic. His house was a focus of the city's cultural life; events included regular meetings of a group that met to read Shakespeare and other authors. But musicians were prominent as well, so Brahms had added reason for his regular visits there, and he often played, first mentioning one of these occasions to Clara Schumann in October 1854.[9] Avé Lallemant had a collection of music books, and the young Brahms received various books and scores from him, including Keiser's *Divertimenti Serenissimi* (in 1855), Winterfeld's *Johannes Gabrieli und sein Zeitalter* (1858), Karl Meister's collection *Das Katolische Deutsche Kirchenlied* (in about 1862), and a score of Gluck's *Alceste* of 1776. Adolf Schubring was a judge by profession in Dessau, an enthusiastic musical amateur, and, most notably, a music critic. Brahms knew him from at least 1853. Whereas Avé Lallemant's interest was in scholarship and teaching, Schubring's interest lay more in the domain of new music, and he was one of the first to evaluate Brahms's work in the press and identify his stature. He is one of the few to whom Brahms spoke of the creative process, and one of the few people outside the Schumann circle to whom Brahms confided from Vienna, including his acquaintance with the unpublished music of Schubert.[10]

In contrast, Chrysander and Jahn were figures of international stature in the world of music, scholars of the new generation who were interested in assembling and documenting musical materials and sources rather than compiling biographies and reminiscences, which had characterized earlier work in the field. Chrysander lived near Hamburg and provided a link to Brahms's world there. For Brahms, Chrysander's devotion to the study of earlier music was an opening into a new musical world. He published pioneering articles on a range of composers, including C. P. E. Bach, J. S. Bach, Buxtehude, Carissimi, and Corelli. Handel was the center of his work, and in 1856 Chrysander founded the *Handel Gesellschaft,* which published, between 1858 and 1894, the first complete edition of Handel's works. Chrysander traveled frequently to England for this work and encouraged Brahms to visit as well. He was active as an editor, first of *Allgemeine Musikalische Zeitung,* in 1868–71 and 1875–82, later of the short-lived *Jahrbuch für Musikalische Wissenschaft* (1863–67) and, with Spitta and Adler, of the *Vierteljahrschrift für Musikwissenschaft* (1885–95). He and Spitta founded *Denkmäler Deutscher Tonkunst,* of which he was general editor. The first volume appeared in 1892 with Scheidt's *Tabulatura Nova,* a work of great interest to Brahms. Though Chrysander was an unconventional individual and notoriously uninterested in modern music, Brahms kept contact with him and his work, subscribing to the complete edition, and became involved in important new editing through him. Chrysander invited Brahms to prepare realizations of the continuo parts of the Handel Italian Duets and Trios, which appeared in volume 32 of the complete edition. Brahms also edited Couperin's "Pieces de Clavecin" for Chrysander's own *Denkmäler der Tonkunst,* which appeared in 1871. In 1892, Brahms, with Bülow, organized a fund to enable Chrysander to publish a facsimile edition of Handel's *Messiah.*[11] But Brahms was not interested in everything Chrysander published: uncut pages in his copies of the *Vierteljahrschrift für Musikwissenschaft* suggest that he was less than comprehensive in his reading of its contents.

Otto Jahn moved to Bonn in 1855 and was professor of classical philology and archaeology at Bonn University. He also was director of the art museum, a position he held until he died in 1869. Brahms apparently met him at the Lower Rhine Music Festival of 1856, which Brahms visited as part of the Schumann circle. At that festival he met many other individuals destined to remain his longtime friends, including Hanslick, Theodor Kirchner, Stockhausen, and Klaus Groth. Though not primarily a musician, Jahn knew this circle and attended chamber music evenings.[12] Jahn was also a friend of the poet Klaus Groth, a North German who became a close friend of Brahms, and of Hermann Deiters, one of his philology students and a future member of the Brahms circle and author of an early book on the composer. In 1856, Jahn was the·major music scholar in Germany. He wrote the definitive biography of Mozart (1856–59), which went into two additional editions in Brahms's lifetime, the second edited by Deiters.[13] Such was his status that no less a work than the Köchel catalogue was dedicated to Jahn. Brahms had two copies of the biography in its first edition by 1863. Jahn had wide interests in music, writing essays on such composers as Berlioz and Wagner. Brahms stayed in contact with Jahn until his death in 1869, sometimes taking issue with him in matters of Mozart scholarship.

With his life in Vienna, unparalleled resources became available to Brahms. Vienna had a much broader and more cosmopolitan musical culture than did Hamburg: it possessed (in the archives of the Philharmonic Society) major manuscripts of the Viennese classical composers, as well as many other unique musical documents; other libraries added to the treasures at hand. Other vital sources of information were the manuscript owners and publishers. Brahms already knew J. P. Gotthard, then the manager of the publishing house Spina.[14] Through him and others Brahms became acquainted with the completely unknown Schubert manuscripts that had come from Schubert's brother Ferdinand.[15] As in Hamburg, Brahms's involvement with performing musicians was complemented by his interest in scholars, and he soon got to know those with whom he could share his scholarly commitments.

First and senior of these was Gustav Nottebohm, whom he met almost immediately on his arrival though Gotthard. Nottebohm was the leading Beethoven scholar of his time, and his "important researches into the work of Beethoven and Schubert were a source of inexhaustible interest to an artist of so strong a historical bias as Brahms."[16] He was one of the first experts in textual criticism, and Breitkopf & Härtel asked him to revise Beethoven's works for a complete edition; his work resulted in a thematic catalogue in 1868. He was the first to study Beethoven's manuscripts for compositional process, and his work resulted in editions of the Beethoven notebooks, a monograph, and a set of studies. He also produced, in 1874, the first thematic catalogue of the works of Schubert, a work that remained a standard source until the appearance of the Deutsch catalogue in 1950.[17] Although he also edited music by Bach, Handel, and Mendelssohn, he was also interested in much earlier music. Soon after their meeting Nottebohm allowed Brahms to transcribe from his collection items by Zirler, Walter, Forster, and Senfl. After Nottebohm's death in 1882 Brahms inherited six volumes, mainly in manuscript form, of *Alte Instrumental Compositionen,* a gigantic compendium of instrumental works chiefly from the sixteenth century.[18]

Another factor in cementing the friendship was the fact that Nottebohm had known many important figures, including Mendelssohn and Schumann. Indeed, Brahms's comment to Elisabet von Herzogenberg on variation writing in 1872 includes Nottebohm's name with that of her husband and of Schumann. Nottebohm's works included sets of variations, including one on the theme of a Bach sarabande for piano duet.[19] He thus was for Brahms a special model: a scholar of composers of particular interest to Brahms, and a composer himself. It was no doubt for this reason that he was Brahms's first choice in recommending young composers for counterpoint tuition.

Carl Ferdinand Pohl, born in 1819, had become librarian and archivist to the Gesellschaft der Musikfreunde through the influence of Jahn, Köchel, and others in 1866. It was then that a close relation between Pohl and Brahms developed. The focus of Pohl's work was the listing of the Society's extensive library holdings and his studies of Mozart and Haydn. He produced a monograph on the history and extent of the collection, and collaborated with Haberl and Lagerberg in Eitner's *Bibliographie der Musiksammelwerke* of 1877. His work on Haydn and Mozart had taken him to London in 1863–66, resulting in his study of the composers' relationship with the city. At Jahn's suggestion he undertook a Haydn biography. He did not live to finish it, but it became the basis for much later work.[20] He was in tune with Brahms's musical philosophy as well as his interests, and had a strong belief in traditional compositional disciplines and values. As with Nottebohm, these values drew them into a close friendship from the moment Pohl arrived at the Gesellschaft. He could not welcome Brahms often enough to the library: "Properly speaking, there ought to be a footbridge, leading from St. Charles's, across the Wienfluss, straight to our music building. It ought to be called the Brahms Bridge, and only the person of that name should have the key." Brahms learned much of Haydn through his contact with Pohl's work, and this knowledge directly influenced his own work. Brahms treasured the pen with which Pohl wrote the last chapter of the second volume of his unfinished three-volume biography of Haydn, and his sudden death in 1887 was a great shock to the composer.[21]

Eusebius Mandyczewski in 1887 succeeded Pohl as director of the Gesellschaft archives, as director of the orchestra in 1892, and as professor in the conservatory. Brahms met him in 1879, and they formed a close friendship that became especially important to Brahms in his latter years, Mandyczewski acting as a secretary and even an amanuensis. Mandyczewski represented the next generation of musicologists, having been a pupil of Hanslick and Nottebohm and a student at the University of Vienna, and Brahms admired his vast knowledge. His primary work was on the complete edition of the works of Schubert, which appeared between 1887 and 1897; it comprised ten volumes of songs, impeccably edited with printed variants. Mandyczewski also edited the second volume of Nottebohm's *Beethoveniana*. Their joint work included editing Brahms's *49 Deutsche Volkslieder* for voice and piano. Mandyczewski's role as coeditor, with Hans Gál, of the complete edition of Brahms's works (published 1926–28) provides a last link to the Brahms era.[22]

Philipp Spitta was the major German music scholar of Brahms's later years. He became professor of music history at the University of Berlin and director of the Berlin Hochschule für Musik. Whereas Nottebohm had made giant steps with Beethoven research, Spitta reflected the growing scholarly interest in music of earlier eras, especially that of Bach and Schütz. His great work was a two-volume biography of Bach, the first volume of which appeared 1873. Trained as a classical scholar with a strong interest in history as well as in music, he approached his subject with an emphasis on historical context and critical source study. His editions were of Buxtehude organ music (1876–77), and he edited the complete edition of Schütz (1885–94). His many contributions made a lasting impact on the new discipline of musicology, and, with Chrysander and Adler, he founded the *Vierteljahrschrift für Musikwissenschaft*. He also gave great support to the *Denkmäler deutscher Tonkunst*. Spitta, eight years Brahms's junior, grew to musical maturity with Brahms's music as one of his greatest influences. He first heard Brahms's music while participating in a performance of the *Begräbnisgesang* in 1860. They met in 1864, and Brahms advised Spitta through Grimm to study music history. They corresponded regularly on scholarly matters, though a dispute concerning the function of church music threatened their friendship: Brahms almost withdrew the dedication of the motets op. 74 as a consequence.[23]

Brahms the Collector

By the end of his life Brahms had assembled a library of great value. As well as reflecting his profound sense of historical continuity, it also suggested a sheer love of collecting. He once remarked to Reinthaler, "Yesterday I bought the manuscripts of six Haydn quartets! . . . Would you not also have a pleasant feeling of inner warmth and quite some emotion if you held something like this in your hands and called it your own?" The valuable library, with its complete editions, autographs, and numerous scores and music books, was left by Brahms to the Gesellschaft der Musikfreunde.[24] In the centenary year of Brahms's birth the librarian of the Gesellschaft, Karl Geiringer, summarized a collection that seemed even more remarkable then than now, for so much of the historical background to his work was little known.

> The quantity of music Brahms collected is immense. Its foundation stones are the full sets of the complete editions of Bach, Handel, Schütz, Chopin, Schumann, and Mendelssohn, to which were added a number of magnificent first editions of works of Johann Sebastian and Carl Philipp Emanuel Bach, Domenico Scarlatti and Gluck. Scarcely to be counted are the works of Mozart, Haydn, Beethoven and Schubert that Brahms possessed, some of them also in valuable first editions. So numerous were these—especially in the cases of Beethoven and Mozart— that he suffered no loss in not acquiring the monumental complete editions of these composers. Brahms was particularly fond of the dainty little pocket chamber-music

scores published by Heckel in Mannheim, which had been given to him by Clara Schumann and Joseph Joachim; numerous marginal notes in his own hand show how carefully he used them. Among his contemporaries, his friends were naturally very well represented. But the presence in his library of compositions of Joachim, Herzogenberg, Dvorák, Bruch, Goldmark, Reinthaler, Grädener has in a way less to do with Brahms's musical convictions than with the circumstances of his life. This is particularly true as regard the examples he possessed of Rubinstein, Liszt and Wagner.[25]

In addition to scores, Brahms's extensive holdings of music books, biographies, and treatises provide a key to his musical mind: "Brahms's music books are naturally of particular interest to us. First and foremost are the older theoretical works of Adlung, Forkel, Fux, Gerber, Hiller, Marpurg, Mattheson, Walter and the rest, which Brahms began assembling as a very young man. Then came the great musicological and critical works of his own contemporaries which we should the more expect to find, since . . . Brahms was . . . at least acquainted with most of the authors. Jahn's 'Mozart,' Chrysander's 'Handel,' Spitta's 'Bach,' Pohl's 'Haydn,' Nottebohm's 'Beethoveniana' and thematic catalogs."[26]

But the autographs were especially attractive to Brahms:

Unquestionably the most precious part of Brahms's collection is its autographs. The jewel among these is the score of Mozart's great G Minor Symphony, which Brahms received from the Langravine of Hesse as a token of thanks for the dedication of his Piano Quintet. Of particular value also are the daintily penned scores of Haydn's six "Sonnenquartette" [op. 20], and the unique document of two sheets, the first of which bears Beethoven's song "Ich liebe dich so wie du mich" and the rest a Schubert andante for piano in D minor (later transposed into G minor and used in the E flat Piano Sonata), and upon which Brahms has immortalized himself as the third in this great company. There are several Beethoven and Schubert autographs. Brahms owned more than sixty sheets of Beethoven sketches, five with composition exercises, besides various transcripts (one of them of *Missa Solemnis*) and proof sheets with notes in the master's own hand. Of original Schubert manuscripts he possessed a number of songs, among them the "Wanderer," several fragments and sketches, and 24 pages with various dances. Schumann, thanks to the intimate friendship of Brahms with himself and his wife, is also represented by larger works, such as the first version of the D Minor Symphony, the overture to Schiller's "Bride of Messina," the orchestral suite "Overture, Scherzo and Finale," the Davidsbündler dances, and others. Brahms naturally owned a number of his friend Joachim's larger works, such as the overtures to "Hamlet," "Henry IV," and "Demetrius." Among the smaller compositions of other masters are Berlioz's "La Mort D'Ophélie," Chopin's E minor Mazurka and A flat major Prelude, Mendelssohn's motet "In the Midst of Life We Are in Death," the closing scene of Strauss's *Ritter Pazmann,* and the concert ending to Wagner's opera *Tristan and Isolde.*[27]

Brahms the Editor

Brahms's extensive involvement in the pioneer editing of music from before his own time emerged from more than simply interest and knowledge. Brahms had an editor's instinct. An examination of the books in his library shows how keenly he spotted misprints and that he made marginal corrections. He was a born student, scholar, and analyst of style. These skills, however, should not lead to the supposition that Brahms was an editor in the modern musicological sense. Indeed, he never claimed to be. He found the formal process daunting, as he indicated in this comment to Clara in 1891: "I have often enough tried my hand at it, and brought love and diligence to bear, but it is impossible for me to give myself a testimonial for such work and I have to confess that others are far better fitted for the task."[28] Although he made this comment while in the midst of particularly delicate editing project—he was contributing to Clara Schumann's complete edition of Schumann's works—it was true. Even with his own music, which he saw through the press and for which many of his corrected first editions exist, there are inconsistencies that give scholars the basis for different editorial decisions. But similar license seems to have been applied in the preparation of the complete editions of then classical masters of the past. As Brahms's reputation grew in Hamburg and Vienna, and as he displayed his historical allegiances in performance, the invitations came: to edit individual pieces, then to contribute to series, and finally to be involved with the editorial board in connection with most of the complete editions that appeared during his own career (Handel, Mozart, Schubert, Chopin, Schütz, and Schumann).

The appearance in 1851 of the first volume of the Bach Gesellschaft edition of the works of Bach (published by Breitkopf & Härtel) was the major musicological event of Brahms's youth and clearly ranked with Bismarck's creation of the German Empire in 1871 as a major national event of his life.[29] He was too young to have been involved in its preparation, though he became a subscriber in 1857 and obtained the preceding volumes as a gift from Princess Frederike of Lippe-Detmold. The edition was to be of vast importance to Brahms. Its early volumes, which included the choral cantatas, opened up a new world, and Brahms drew on it for performances of these pieces at Detmold, with the Vienna Singakademie, and with the Singverein of the Gesellschaft der Musikfreunde. Numerous scholarly problems arose as a consequence of this first major exploration of sources, and Brahms found himself involved in issues of scholarly debate, for he was regarded as an authority on matters of style. A notable example concerned the question of the authenticity of a setting of the Passion according to St. Luke, which had been attributed to J. S. Bach. This work was held to be authentic by Philipp Spitta, the foremost Bach authority of the day. Brahms disagreed, and his was the view most widely held thereafter, for the work remains outside the Bach canon.[30]

Apart from arrangements that Brahms made for his own choral performances, the only editing of the music of a member of the Bach family is of the music of his sons. Brahms began editing when the Hamburg firm of Cranz asked him in November 1858 to edit concertos 1, 4, and 5 of "VI Concerti per il Cembalo" (Wq. 43) by C. P. E. Bach. He did these anonymously, and they were published in 1862. For Rieter-Biedermann he edited, again anonymously, the Violin Sonatas in B Minor and C Minor (Wq. 76, 78) by C. P. E. Bach and the sonata for two claviers in F major (Falck 10) by W. F. Bach, both appearing in 1864.

Brahms's devotion to Handel was not as great as to Bach. He commented to Mandyczewski, "When the new Handel edition comes out and is sent to me, I put it in my library and say 'as soon as I have time, I will look it over.' But when a new Bach edition appears, I let everything else go, for there is nothing as important to me as studying the volume. I know that I shall learn something new." However, he had more opportunity to become involved in editing both because the complete Handel edition began later, in 1858, and because of his early contact with Chrysander, who soon got to know the measure of Brahms's interest.[31] Brahms's involvement falls more under the classification of arrangement than textual editing, however, since it provided a realization of the figured bass for various Italian Duets and Trios of volume 32. The volume contained thirteen items, two duets, and eleven trios of 1710–12 and was published in 1870. Chrysander's preface to the 1870 volume states that most of the realizations—apart from the third duet, realized by Joachim—are by "J Brahms."[32] The revised edition included six more trios in 1880–81. For his performances of Handel at the Gesellschaft der Musikfreunde concerts, Brahms added expression marks and organ parts, though these were never published. The extent of his interest in the background to the works emerges, however, in relation to the Dettingen *Te Deum,* which he performed in 1872. He was familiar with Chrysander's new *Denkmäler der Tonkunst* series, volume 5, which included Urio's *Te Deum,* and he wrote enthusiastically to a friend: "on the first two pages compare Handel's *Saul* and *Te Deum:* extraordinarily striking."[33] The contact with Chrysander also allowed him to edit Couperin as part of the same short series of *Denkmäler der Tonkunst* of 1870–71. He invited Brahms to edit Livres 1 and 2 of the "Pieces de Clavecin" in volume 4, which appeared in 1871.[34]

Mozart, Schubert, Chopin, and Schumann

Brahms's work on Mozart was much more extensive, reflecting the great knowledge that he had begun to acquire through early study and through playing the concertos, sonatas, and chamber works. Brahms's knowledge of Mozart's output and sources increased with the publication of the

Köchel catalogue in 1862 and the supplements that soon followed. He had received a copy of the catalogue as a present from Joachim in 1863. He made corrections on the basis of his own knowledge, that were taken into the second edition of 1905 and retained in the third of 1937: he mainly corrected names and orthological errors. As a result of his connection with Köchel's collection Brahms discovered an unknown work, the Offertorium de Venerabili Sacramento ("Venite Populi") for double four-part chorus, organ, and two violins "ad libitum," composed in Salzburg in 1776. He gave its first performance with the Gesellschaft, for which he wrote his own organ part, but he withheld this when sending the manuscript to Gotthard for its first publication, and he made no changes and gave no editorial authorship with the edition.[35]

The plans for a complete edition provided a focus for Brahms's expertise. His advice was first sought in 1880 concerning series 7, "Concertos for one wind instrument with orchestra," when the editor, Ernst Rudorff, wrote to Brahms for his opinion concerning a corrupt passage in the rondo of the second concerto. Brahms consulted the parts in the Gesellschaft library and made suggestions that were adopted for the new edition.[36] Brahms's biggest Mozart challenge came with the edition of the *Requiem* that he provided for the complete edition. It was his major piece of work on Mozart, undertaken in 1876 for the 1877 edition. The Revisionsbericht containing his editorial commentary did not appear until 1886.[37] The state of the surviving score posed many problems. It is described as follows by its most recent editor, Richard Maunder:

> In the autograph score the vocal parts and figured bass
> are complete as far as the end of the "Hostias," except
> for the "Lacrymosa," where Mozart had written only the
> first eight bars. The first movement ("Requiem aeter-
> nam") is fully orchestrated, but elsewhere only a few or-
> chestral bars are filled in, often just the first violin part,
> though occasionally inner parts and woodwind as well.
> . . . [Franz Xavier] Süssmayr said that he orchestrated
> Mozart's movements (though in fact he copied Eybler's
> version some of the time), completed the "Lacrymosa,"
> and composed the "Sanctus," "Benedictus" and "Agnus
> Dei" himself.[38]

Henschel, who was working with Brahms at the time, describes the extreme care which Brahms took in the work. "We went together through the full score of 'Mozart's Requiem,' which he had undertaken to prepare for a new edition of that master's works. I admired the great trouble he had taken in the revision of the score. Every note of Sussmayr's was most carefully distinguished from Mozart's own." And to Joachim Brahms wrote, "I have just got a difficult editing job out of the way. The Requiem of Mozart. I hardly cease peering at the two manuscripts."[39] Brahms edited the work as whole rather than simply the problematic parts, marking the score and explaining how only by an exact presentation of the manuscript could he give a true indication of how Mozart left the work and how after his death his pupil completed it. His marking went to individual parts in individual bars to give the most precise account of the relative attributions.[40]

The editorial task in relation to Schubert's music was significantly different from that of the works of other composers. Research was much less advanced, and many important works were still only recently published or little known. Although Brahms had apparently known some Schubert piano music in his early years, it was the publication of Schubert's later works, in the 1850s, and Brahms's contact with the Schubert circle in Vienna that gave his passion wing. He wrote to Schubring: "Again and again one meets people who talk of him as of a good friend, again and again one comes across new works, the very existence of which was unknown and which are so untouched that one can scrape the very writing-sand off them." And again later to Schubring: "My love for Schubert is of a very serious kind, probably because it is not just a fleeting infatuation. Where else is there a genius like his, which soars with such boldness and certainty to the heavens, where we see the very greatest enthroned? He impresses me as a child of the gods who plays with Jove's thunder and occasionally handles it in an unusual manner. But he does play in a region and at a height to which the others can by no means attain."[41]

At about this time Brahms was approached by several publishers to edit some of these unknown or little-known works: first by Spina to edit 12 Deutsche Tanze, op. post. 171, which appeared in 1864; by Rieter Biedermann for Drei Klavierstücke, D 946, which appeared in 1868; by Senff for the Quartetsatz (Quartet Movement) in C Minor, which appeared in 1870. His edition of the song "Der Strom," of which he owned the manuscript, appeared in 1877 through Fritzsch in Leipzig.[42] He later became heavily involved in the edition, though he recommended the involvement of Mandyczewski for the song volumes. Brahms undertook the symphonies in 1884–85 for series 1, volumes 1 and 2, though it is impossible to ascertain his editorial principles, because the Revisionsbericht merely describes the manuscript; Brahms is listed only as a committee member with others.[43]

Although Brahms's involvement with Breitkopf & Härtel's complete edition of the works of Chopin of 1878 seems less to be anticipated than in other editions (for he appears to have included no Chopin in his recitals), he was in fact more extensively involved in the whole undertaking. The publisher had planned the edition after the completion of the Mozart edition, and Clara Schumann was enthusiastic about it and about Brahms's participation. But Brahms resisted and suggested the involvement of Bargiel and Rudorff. But he remained responsible for volumes 3 (mazurkas); 4 (nocturnes); 8 (sonatas opp. 35 and 58); 10 (various works); 11 (piano and stringed instruments); 12 (piano and orchestra); and 13 (posthumous works). There are no editorial remarks, but extensively marked proof copies survive, illuminating the editorial process.[44]

Of all the music that Brahms edited, he had the greatest emotional attachment to that of Schumann, which he had known in its most authentic context since youth. He was early involved in the work: in 1857, the full score, vocal score and parts of *Vom Pagen und der Königstöchter* for Rieter-Biedermann; in 1866, the Scherzo in F Minor for Piano (from the sonata op. 14) and the Presto Passionato for Piano (from the sonata op. 22), again for Rieter-Biedermann; and in 1873, the five discarded variations of the Etudes Symphoniques for piano for Simrock. But his involvement in the complete edition of Schumann's music was difficult. Clara Schumann, in whose name the edition first appeared in 1881, became very protective of her husband's works and asserted her belief in how the texts should appear, based on her view of their meaning.[45] Brahms undertook two major editorial tasks, though he seems to have participated in much else: first, the original version of the Symphony no. 4, in April 1891; and then the posthumous volume of piano works chosen by him for series 14.

They disagreed about the publication of the original version of the D minor symphony. In April 1888, Brahms wrote to Clara, "But a much more valuable possession to me [than the "Jugendlieder" and F sharp Minor Sonata] is the first version of the D minor symphony. I have now added the finest copies to the printed score and bound them together. . . . Everyone who sees it agrees with me that the score has not gained by being remodelled; it has certainly lost in charm, ease and clarity. Unfortunately, however, I cannot make any thorough trial anywhere. In Cologne the hall prevents me. . . . In this new (or rather old) version one will find no difficulty, only enjoyment . . . and a change, and a refutation of the usual manner of orchestration." Later he wrote, "[I am enjoying looking at] two beautiful double scores (in which the two versions are printed on opposite pages). . . . I have long been of the opinion that the work must appear in this form." Alluding to Clara's resistance he continued, "I do not wish to enlarge upon my reasons for liking and admiring it and for considering its publication necessary. But I have no doubt that you will ultimately agree with me about it if only tacitly." The edition was subsequently published as part of the complete edition, though not under Brahms's name.[46]

The supplementary volume to series 14 (nine posthumous works) contained the following preface: "A few things were found among Robert Schumann's papers which on account of their value, or of some special interest ought not to be omitted from this collection. The theme with which the volume concludes is, in a quite peculiar sense, Schumann's last musical thought. He wrote it on 7 February 1854 and afterward added five variations, which are withheld here. It speaks to us of a kindly greeting spirit (genius) and we think with reverence and emotion of the glorious man and artist."[47]

Creative Consequences in Original Compositions

The ultimate confirmation of the depth of Brahms's historical studies lies in the extent to which they permeated his own composition. Brahms studied to learn, but as early technical imitation yielded to a deeper affinity with his sources, the past posed bigger and more fundamental technical and aesthetic challenges. Brahms's public performances as pianist and conductor give the first indication of this trend, which gradually extended to vocal and orchestral works. So profound is this relationship that it generally defies detailed analysis. In some cases, however, evidence of style or of specific origins serves to reveal the kind of influences and processes that lay beneath much of his work.

Viewed overall, the most striking feature of the output of the years of technical development (1855–60) is the extent of its choral music and how much of this clearly draws on the Renaissance and Baroque models rather than on the classical or romantic. Brahms's preoccupation with canonic writing is notable. By 1856 he had written several movements of a setting of the Latin Mass entirely in canonic form, though the work was never published in his lifetime.[48] He continued with this genre in *Drei Geistliche Chöre,* published as op. 37 in 1864. From this period date numerous canons, some simple, some intricate and constructed at unusual intervals. What applied to canons applied to fugues and to many other technical devices drawn from the study of early models rather than textbooks, as, for example, in Brahms's application of the tenorlied technique of German sixteenth-century music to folksongs in his settings published in 1864. Such devices come to more extended and original use in the motets opp. 29 and 74. Counterpoint appears for itself, as in the canon by augmentation between the outer parts in the first section of op. 29/2, or in combination with the chorale melody, as in the chorale fantasia first movement of op. 29/1, in which the chorale cantus firmus appears in augmentation within the fugue based on it. Part of the motet op. 74/1 draws from *Missa Canonica* and concludes with a chorale harmonization that subtly transforms Bach's settings of the melody. The motet op. 74/2 is cast as a set of strict variations on the model of Bach's Cantata 4 (which Brahms performed at Detmold and with the Singverein) "per omnes versus," using a modal chorale melody.

These elements find their greatest fulfillment in the one work that sums up the early years of choral experience: *A German Requiem.* All the technical features are found there: canon, fugue, contrapuntal and harmonic variation, modal harmonic effect. Brahms handles these resources with a flexibility that denies their technical self-sufficiency, however. Intricate devices are as likely to be found in the "free" passages as in the fugues, which become free in the application of their strict devices. The thematic material would, however, seem to be freely invented, were it not for a comment by Brahms to the choral conductor Siegfried Ochs to the effect that the work was based on a chorale melody: "if you can't hear it it doesn't matter much. In the first measures and in the second movement you can find it. It is a well known chorale."[49]

These features relate to the medium of the solo song with accompaniment less naturally. The repertory of unaccompanied choral music contains a large representation from earlier periods, whereas solo song with piano accompaniment is a product of the nineteenth century and the rise of the piano. But even in this repertory Brahms integrated some earlier "historical" material, and not merely where he reset a choral piece, as in the archaic style of "Vergangen ist mir Glück und Heil," which appears as op. 48/6, or in the quotation of a chorale for symbolic effect, as in "Auf dem Kirchhofe," op. 105/4. In one case Brahms drew with a stated purpose on a religious folksong: the "Geistliches Wiegenlied," op. 91/2. This song uses the carol "Josef, lieber, Josef mein" in its instrumental introduction (for viola and piano), from which Brahms evolves a new melody by inversion to sustain the vocal verse. He quotes its source in the score. The piece was intended as a present to Joachim and his wife on the birth of their first child, hence the use of the melody.[50] In another case, Brahms cites in the published score the composer Scarlatti as author of the material in the piano introduction from which he builds his song "Unüberwindlich," op. 72/5.

In the keyboard music as a whole, however, Brahms moved more purposefully toward a conscious synthesis of old and new. His early organ works had already shown the creative response to Bach, whose music he had included in his very first recital in 1848: a single fugue by J. S. Bach. The Fugue in A flat Minor, written in 1856 and published only as an example of compositional craft in *Allgemeine Musikalische Zeitung* in 1864, offers the full range of devices in the most didactic of keys. Brahms's first major set of variations employing his new approach to the form, based on Beethoven, the Variations and Fugue on a Theme of Handel, op. 24, is on a very obscure theme that he may have had from Chrysander: it was taken from a suite for keyboard published in London by Walsh in 1723 of which no modern edition existed at the time. Moreover, the work is full of canons and devices imitative of historical style. The inclination toward poetic and Schumannesque canonic writing in the earliest variation yields here to a thoroughgoing test of his technique, methods taken even further in the Variations on a Theme of Haydn ("St. Antoni Chorale"). This work has the added interest of a second set of variations, in the form of a passacaglia coda on a five-bar bass figure that reintroduces the first theme of the work and thus unites bass with melody. In this case the melody was totally unknown, for it had been discovered by C. F. Pohl in the Gesellschaft der Musikfreunde library in a divertimento for wind instruments attributed to Haydn; Pohl made a copy for Brahms, who three years later wrote his variations on it.[51]

The technique of variation, and especially that more restricted model offered by the ground bass in the finale of the "St. Antoni" Variations, provides a link to the climax of Brahms's symphonic career in the finale of the Fourth Symphony, which features thirty-two variations on a bass that appears in various positions, thus opening a wide field of harmony for the variations. It also falls into a three-section form, appropriate to the finale of a symphony in its suggestion of a sonata form design with recapitulation. Brahms knew many such works from the Baroque, and they may all have played a part in the background, particularly the violin chaconne in D minor by J. S. Bach, which so inspired Brahms through the vast world it created from restricted means that he arranged it for piano left hand, to simulate this effect. But his interest went beyond the form in its historical perspective. He justified his decision by citing the precedent of the finale of the *Eroica* Symphony: "not to compare content and value, but purely with regard to form."[52] More significantly, Brahms drew his material from Bach. The bass theme is a transformation of that of the chaconne of the Cantata 150, "Nach Herr Gott verlanget mich." The source was identified by Siegfried Ochs, who was with Brahms in the company of von Bülow, whom he accused of having scant knowledge of the cantatas. Pointing to the last section of Cantata 150, Brahms remarked, "What would you say to a symphonic movement based on this theme one day? But it is too straightforward, too lumpish. It would have to be chromatically altered in some way." The eight-bar theme that Brahms employed as the foundation of the finale of the Fourth Symphony shows how he resolved the problem.[53]

15 · A Student of History and the Arts

Brahms the Self-Educated

Brahms's interest in the music of earlier centuries was part of a historically oriented outlook that manifested itself in many ways, not least in his continuing interest in German politics and international current affairs. Likewise, the sensitivity to literature extended into a growing interest in drama and visual art. Although his formal education was limited, Brahms had a deep desire for knowledge, and he worked assiduously to cultivate his knowledge over the years. He befriended many leading figures in the cultural world of Vienna, and he could hold his own in any company. Widmann found in Brahms a man of "clear ideas and firm principles not only in all that concerned art and literature, but also in other fields."[54] Though Brahms wasted no words, he could suddenly come alive when an issue excited his interest or provoked him to argument. Karl Geiringer, the successor to Mandyczewski at the archive of the Gesellschaft der Musikfreunde, describes Brahms's cultural and intellectual stature.[55]

> Rarely has the honorary title of Doctor of Philosophy been bestowed upon an artist with such well founded justification. . . . When in 1879 the University of Breslau named him "doctor honores causa," it was for the great composer that the distinction was intended. The faculty probably did not know that they were simultaneously conferring the honor upon a man who was also entitled to it through the exceptional breadth and profundity of his culture. Brahms, whose regular schooling had ceased in his fifteenth year, strove from his earliest youth with uncommon fervor to deepen and extend his knowledge. By his thirst for information and his never-flagging industry, this son of a poor musician became an authority esteemed not only by his fellow artists but among men of science as well. It was no mere chance that Brahms's circle of friends and acquaintances included scholars like Spitta, Nottebohm, Pohl, Chrysander, Jahn, and Mandy-

czewski, the music historians, Wendt the philologist, and the famous physicians Billroth and Engelmann.[56]

The evidence lay further in the contents of his library, its range, and the extent to which he was acquainted with its contents: "Yet all this conscientiousness in Brahms's reading did not ill accord, as might have been the case, with the sudden outbursts of a lively temperament manifested by frequent marginal entries in the books in his library. At one point in the 'Butterflies' of Spitteler, the Swiss poet he so much admired, he wrote, 'Beautiful.' On the other hand, at a sugary passage in Suess's "Progress of Mankind" he says, "a better example might have been chosen: Sentimental!"[57] Despite his keen intellect and vast knowledge, he never strove to be a society intellectual or to cultivate a coterie of admirers, though he was inevitably lionized in his musical circle. Hanslick contrasts him with Liszt, pointing out that Brahms preferred to hide his learning, whereas Liszt would throw off references to famed writers of whom he had scarcely read a chapter.[58] But it is difficult to know how Brahms would have been received in intellectual circles had he not been Brahms. Indeed, it is interesting to place the image suggested by Geiringer into the perspective of acquaintances from outside his circle, especially among those meeting him for the first time, as in the case of the Polish pianist Paderewski. "I had not the impression he was a very communicative or a very learned man. But he knew a great deal in many ways, I think. . . . But I think he was interested in politics. I had that impression, though I had no opportunity to approach the subject with him."[59] Ethel Smyth came to know Brahms much better through her contact with the Herzogenbergs in Leipzig in the later 1870s. She was much less sympathetic to the social Brahms. Though her criticisms were certainly enhanced by her objection to his attitude to women, they reflect the impression he made and the position he held among friends and admirers.

> Young and enthusiastic though I was, it was impossible
> for me to join in the chorus of unmitigated admiration
> that prevailed in that world. For one thing, I never fath-
> omed wherein lay the intellectual supremacy Brahms was
> credited with, and suspected it was a case of subscribing
> to a gradually built-up legend. Sayings of his were

quoted and handed round with exclamation points, in which I failed to see anything so very wonderful. Professor Wach . . . often let fly splinters of wisdom, of shrewd criticism, of humorous reflection on life that seemed to me far more striking than anything one ever heard Brahms say. Or again, many a remark of Ed[w]ard Grieg—as modest, golden-hearted, natural a creature as ever breathed—had exactly the fresh, fascinating quality of his music.

Smyth does not disguise his bluntness of expression in society, which Brahms clearly made no attempt to overcome.[60] In one other dimension his efforts at self-improvement never came to fruition: the mastery of languages. Geiringer continues: "Brahms was anything but a linguist. Various well-worn French and Italian grammars in his library bear witness to his strenuous efforts to master those languages. Nor did the Italian translations of German classics, presented to him (after their journey to Italy together) by Billroth in the hope of inducting Brahms pleasantly and easily into the secrets of the foreign tongue, achieve their purpose. Brahms's disinclination to desert German-speaking territory (the trip[s] to Italy excepted) and more particularly his opposition to receiving the honorary doctor's degree from Cambridge, were doubtless connected with this weakness."[61]

History and Current Affairs

As Paderewski intimates, one area in which Brahms became easily vocal was politics, and especially German politics. Brahms spoke with an authority based on extensive study of German history, as well as deep interest in the events of his own time. His library reflects his interests. In addition to Bismarck's letters and speeches (a volume of which he often carried on journeys), there are books on the War of 1870, Treitschke's *Historische und Politische Aufsätze*, Exner's *Über Politische Bildung*, and other volumes of this sort, stressing his conservative stance. His books of German history included Sybel's seven-volume *Die Begründung des deutsches Reichs durch Wilhelm I* and Haüsser's four-volume German history. Of general histories he possessed Müller's three-volume *Allgemeine Geschichten . . . der Europäischen Menschheit* and other such volumes, including a modern edition of Herodotus's history. His interest in society is reflected in Haufen's *Das Causalitäts-Gesetz in der Socialwissenschaft.* And his interest extended to aspects of the modern world of science and technology so manifest in the Vienna of his day. His contact with pioneers of medical science kept him abreast of the latest developments. His close friendships with Billroth and Engelmann account for his owning a copy of Billroth's *Chirurgische Briefe* (*Surgical Letters*) and Engelmann's *Über den Einfluss des Blutes* (*Experiments on the Microscopic Changes in Muscle Contraction*): indeed, he would observe, along with the students, Billroth's pioneering surgery at the university hospital in Vienna. The worlds of scientific invention earned his attention as well, and he was interested in the introduction of electricity in Vienna and the development of the Edison recording system.[62]

Brahms's interest in scientific progress and his involvement in a broad culture made him a part of the *Grossbürgerthum* (high bourgeoisie) of his day, despite his humble background, which no one in his circle shared. The prevailing attitude of this class, which was at its peak during Brahms's years in Vienna, was liberal and tolerant, naturally stimulated by the wide racial and national mix of residents there. In this attitude he stood apart from those who held a more romantic view of history and from the often racist outlook of the Wagner circle. Many of Brahms's friends were Jews, and Brahms is recorded as disdaining the anti-Semitism of Georg Ritter von Schoenerer and Karl Lueger, which was gaining currency at the time of his death.[63] But, like so many in his class, he greatly admired Bismarck and took pride in the creation of the German Empire, a view of his maturity that entailed contradictions in relation to his background. As Gál observes, "His years of development coincided with a period of increasingly Austrian-Prussian tension and rivalry within the loose-knit German confederation. At that time the scion of a free Hanseatic city of Hamburg had no sympathy for the Prussian cause, and when open conflict erupted in 1866, he was equally critical of both sides. The patriotic fervor of 1870, however, engulfed him just as it did all Germans at the time, and his deep veneration for Bismarck the unifier of the nation and creator of the German Reich stemmed from this period."[64] Brahms remarked, "So great was my enthusiasm . . . that after that first great defeat, I firmly resolved to join the army as a volunteer fully firmly convinced that I should meet my old father there to fight side by side with me.

Thank God it turned out differently."[65] But after 1870 his attitude changed. Niemann summarizes thus:

> Brahms was a great patriot and an ardent admirer of the great creator of German unity. "What *he* says to me is enough; that is what I believe," he once said to Rudolf von der Leyen. He never forgot to put Bismarck's speeches or letters in his travelling bag. In speaking of the "absolutely passionate patriotism of this earnest, virile soul," his Swiss friend Widmann coined the apt phrase "the faithful Eckart of the German people." True to this character, he not only, like his great countryman [Friedrich] Hebbel, took the liveliest interest in the questions of the day and what went on in political life, but kept an anxious and watchful eye on affairs, which he took seriously to heart when they seemed to him ominous and likely once again to imperil the German unity created by Bismarck. He was capable of flying into a furious rage at the incredible political vice of Germany—namely, jealousy, criticism, dissension, when, as he once wrote to Widmann, "the factions in parliament begin bargaining and criticizing over the great achievements of the heroic days which that very generation had experienced, but seemed so soon to have forgotten."[66]

But Brahms's resolutely pro-Bismarck stance inevitably caused problems with friends who saw the issues in a broader perspective. His deep friendship with Widmann was once threatened by an argument over the advantages and disadvantages of the monarchical and republican forms of government. Widmann appealed to Gottfried Keller as arbiter. In his reply to Widmann, Keller commented ironically on the German Empire under Bismarck, "Now only eighteen short years later, this son of a free city now clings pathetically to the emperor and his house, as was scarcely ever the case in the great old days." As Niemann observes, "We see that Brahms's ideal of the State was the conservative Bismarckian one— namely a united German Empire, with Prussia as the North German predominant power. In this too he represented the middle-class ideal of his day." Niemann continues: "He was mortally offended at any criticism of the German emperor—whether the old emperor or the young one—even on the part of his best friends."[67]

But the aging man never changed his position and continued to regret that he had never done military service as a young man. When Brahms's pupil Gustav Jenner, a fellow North German, joined his regiment at Schleswig, Brahms took leave of him at Hamburg with the words: "I cannot say how I envy you. If I were only as young as you are I should go with you at once, but that too I missed."[68] This intense national pride found musical expression in his celebratory works. Niemann comments on such works as the *Fest-und Gedenksprüche* and the *Song of Triumph*, written to celebrate the victory of 1870, that they were for him "no mere occasional pieces. It was with no self-seeking retrospective patriotism that he chose patriotic subjects for his compositions, as so many German composers unfortunately did during the Great War, but to him love of his country and people, his emperor and army, were an inward necessity, a matter of the heart. When he wrote patriotic music it was the immediate reflection of the patriotic emotions and feelings, joys, foreboding, and alarms, which were always strongly alive in him. In one respect alone they are immensely different from those of Hebbel; not only were they thoroughly conservative, monarchical and imperialist, but they know no doubts or hesitations."[69]

Literature, Drama, and the Visual Arts

These three fill one's heart and home . . . and it is indeed no mean age in which one can enjoy such a trio, to whom can be added . . . Freytag, Keller and Heyse . . . and Menzel.

Brahms's appreciation of the work of the painters Feuerbach, Böcklin, and Klinger, in addition to that of the poets and painter mentioned above, indicate his absorption in the world of artistic expression apart from music.[70] This is particularly clear in his central interest, literature. Widmann stresses how thorough a reader was Brahms: "He would tend to read the same book several times over rather than new things . . . but though decidedly conservative in taste . . . [this] did not prevent him from at least getting to know all that was written. He read modern literature in the hope of finding it good and great." His library is well represented with modern literature. Of the collection as a whole Geiringer observed:

"Brahms's interests and learning come to focus, as it were, in his own collections. His books, his music, his pictures are like bits of himself. But although he had a passion, deep rooted and perhaps inherited from a paternal relative, for acquiring musical and literary works, ancient and modern, collecting was for him always a means, never an end. Nothing that failed to advance or enrich his experience did he consider worth keeping. Of the endless amount that Brahms heard, read, and saw in the course of his life, he desired to possess comparatively little; thus these collections . . . enable us to look deep into his mental life."[71]

Brahms was able to draw freely from memory on his sources, not least in the case of Shakespeare, as Billroth noted. His pleasure in annotating his books is another aspect of this complete involvement. His wide knowledge of German history and myth gave him an authoritative view in relation to the increasing interest in this literature stimulated by Wagner's music dramas. His interest in collecting the texts that he had chosen for setting offers an uncharacteristic example of the pride he took in his achievement. This pride may reflect the facts that the knowledge had been gained in a field outside his own profession and that its acquisition had involved much effort.[72]

By upbringing and preference Brahms had the greatest love for some of the most traditional German literature of his time: that contained in Luther's Bible and in folksongs and folk literature. The Bible apparently was one of the first and most powerful experiences of his early schooling, providing the foundation of the intimate knowledge that enabled him to draw out exactly which texts suited his musical needs, particularly in the case of the *German Requiem*. He owned several copies of the Bible, of which one dated from 1665. Luther's writings are further represented in *Von guten Zwecken* and *Tischreden*.[73] His knowledge of the literature of hymnody must also have dated from his early years and experience in the church. His collection of folk poetry included some important texts, such as the *Lieder der alten Edda, Deutsche Sagen*, and *Kinder und Hausmärchen* by the Brothers Grimm, *Liederbuch aus dem 16 Jh.* by Goedicke, and "Des Knaben Wunderhorn" by Arnim and Brentano (Brahms met Bettina von Arnim in 1853 through Joachim). He was interested in all folk poetry that was available to him in translation. Niemann includes with these sources Herder's *Stimmen der Völker* as forming "the most important nucleus of his library [which] exercised a decisive influence on a large part of his work," and he possessed other works by Herder. Another translator on whom he drew widely (and whom he sought out and met) was Friedrich Daumer, from whose collection "Polydora" he drew a number of texts for setting.[74]

Brahms's love of the German Romantic poets also seems to have blossomed very early. As Geiringer observes, "True child of his time, in the field of belle lettres Brahms first learned to know the Romantic poetry of the Germans; witnesses to which youthful inclination are the works we find in his library of Eichendorff, [Achim von] Arnim, Novalis, Hölderlin, Mörike, and especially his favorite poets, Jean Paul [Richter] and E. T. A. Hoffmann."[75] In this he was doubtless stimulated by the example of musical settings, not least those of Schumann, which he came to know fully from 1853, and he was helped by his circle—especially by Clara, who gave him many books as presents. Clara gave him the complete works of Jean Paul for Christmas in 1854; it was to become thoroughly annotated. He also owned the complete works of Hoffmann, again thoroughly annotated, and a separate copy of volume seven of the complete writings—*Phantasiestücke in Callot's Manier*—which he purchased in 1854. He also possessed the complete poems of Eichendorff by 1854, and he wrote enthusiastically to Clara of the spirit of "Eichendorff [being] let loose upon me." Other items were the writings of Novalis edited by Tieck and Schlegel, the complete works of Hölderlin, and the *Märchen* of Mörike. His interest in Arnim was stimulated by his meeting with his widow (the former Bettina Brentano) in 1853. Brentano gave him the collected works, which he annotated comprehensively, especially volume 8. He wrote to Clara: "I am reading a lot of Arnim now and like him immensely. I cannot understand why Arnim is not more read (by intelligent people). He is one of the authors I like and respect most, and the more deeply I learn to understand and grasp him the more I like him. You must have Waldemar with you. Read it. You will be particularly surprised by the first part and the calm way in which it progresses and grows more and more interesting episode by episode. Did I not give you a number of his plays to take away with you?"[76]

But literary enthusiasm did not necessarily have musical consequence. He set few of these poems: none of Jean Paul, Hoffmann, or Novalis, though five early settings of Eichendorff survive (some solo and choral settings also appeared later), three items of Mörike, one of Arnim, and

Hölderlin's "Schicksalslied."[77] Though Brahms did not possess the complete edition of Tieck's works until 1880, when it was presented to him by his friend Arthur Faber, he knew Tieck's "Magelone Romanzen" from at least 1847, when he read it to Lieschen Giesemann at Winsen. He possessed Uhland's *Alte hoch—und niederdeutsche Volkslieder* from 1857. He owned the complete works of Heine, Hebbel, and Kleist and the lyric poetry of Kerner, as well as works by Grabbe, Freiligrath, Immermann, Hegel, Schopenhauer, and Schlegel. But he possessed no Chamisso, though he did set one item for chorus. None of these poets was set early, and Heine was the most frequently set in later years, with six solo songs. Thereafter he set only a duet by Kerner and two choruses by Brentano. The works of Ludwig Hölty, six of whose lyrics he set, do not appear in Brahms's library.

Brahms also showed an early interest in the literature from which German Romantic poetry had sprung: the lyrics of Goethe, the plays of Schiller, the dramas of the Sturm und Drang movement. Brahms had a Goethe collection with eighteen listed items, including the complete poems and plays, many individual editions of each, Vischer's critical commentary of *Faust,* the correspondence with Zelter, and *Conversations with Eckermann.* His Schiller library contains ten items, including the correspondence with Goethe and with Körner. His library contains six items by Lessing, including several complete editions. He also owned the complete works of Wieland and F. W. Klinger's play *Sturm und Drang,* though no works of Klopstock (a fellow North German). Of these he set Goethe most often.

Brahms also read many foreign classics, and, as Geiringer stresses they were "only in good translations."[78] His library ranges from ancient Greek and Roman classics through Romance literature and modern classics. Of ancient writers he possessed works by Aeschylus, Apuleius, Catullus, Herodotus, Homer, Ovid, Plautus, Plutarch, Sophocles—some of these in editions by his friend Gustav Wendt. Of Romance literature he possessed Boccaccio's *Decameron,* Cervantes's *Don Quixote,* Dante's *Divine Comedy,* and Ariosto's *Roland.* His favorite foreign classics included much English literature, beginning with Shakespeare, of which he had individual editions of several plays. He obtained a complete edition in March 1854 and the sonnets in 1868. He also owned Byron's works, Thomas Moore's *Lalla Rookh,* Lawrence Stern's *Tristram Shandy,* Daniel Defoe's *Robinson*

Crusoe, Henry Thomas Buckle's *History of Civilization in England.* Ralph Waldo Emerson's *On Goethe und Shakespeare* was a present from Avé Lallemant.

By the time that Brahms had begun to develop his literary interests the great Romantic era was over. After 1848 new issues were current in the world, and new preoccupations and forms emerged in poetry and literature. Prominent among these was the Dialect Movement. The two great dialect writers of Brahms's time both wrote in Low German: Klaus Groth (1819–99) from Schleswig-Holstein, and Fritz Reuter (1810–74) from Mecklenburg. Brahms possessed the works of both in complete editions. He became well acquainted with Groth in 1856, and his library included no fewer than twelve items. Brahms drew frequently·on Groth's poetry in his musical settings for solo voice and piano, including some of his most personal settings, reflecting the deep affinity he felt for his fellow North German. The most striking settings are those for "Regenlied," which were incorporated into the G Major Violin Sonata. Theodor Storm (1817–88) was another North German poet, a native of Schleswig Holstein. Brahms knew him and possessed his poetry from as early as 1854, though he set only one poem. Brahms also was attracted by Berthold Auerbach's writings about the Black Forest, recommending that Clara read his collection of letters in 1884. "There is a great deal fine, thoughtful and refreshing in it," he commented.[79] The greatest literary figure of Brahms's Hamburg background was his older contemporary, the poet and dramatist Friedrich Hebbel. Brahms and Hebbel had in common a lower-middle-class upbringing and hard-won achievement, and both found in Vienna a second home. Brahms met Hebbel in the early 1860s, at end of Hebbel's life. Brahms possessed his complete works but set only three of his poems.

The two most important of the so-called social writers were Gottfried Keller (1819–90), the greatest Swiss poet of his day, and Gottfried Freytag (1816–95), founder of the German historical novel. Their work is thoroughly represented in Brahms's library, and he knew Keller personally, having met him in Zurich in the musical circle that included his friend of youth, Theodor Kirchner. Though not a musician, Keller was always stirred by Brahms's music, and Brahms was an enthusiastic admirer, collecting as many of his volumes as possible. He set three of Keller's poems. Paul Heyse was another Brahms favorite, a delicate lyric poet from Munich who enriched German literature with short stories, often with an Italian atmosphere. Brahms possessed several of his works, and he made several settings from the collection *Der Jungbrunnen*. Two writers report that Brahms also read the novels of Emile Zola (though none are in his surviving library), a striking choice because their strongly naturalistic character was considered very modern and, at least among musicians of the Bayreuth circle, unpleasant and disagreeable.[80] Brahms also took an interest in light and humorous literature. He owned more than twenty volumes of the satirical sheet *Kladderdatsch* and a short anthology of the writings of the popular humorist Wilhelm Busch.[81] He took a special enthusiasm in the satirical plays of the Viennese poet-actor Johann Nestroy. He owned seven of them, including the notorious *Judith und Holofernes* (a travesty on Hebbel's *Judith*), on the title page of which are noted the passages suppressed by the censor, a collector's item apparently obtained with great difficulty.[82]

Brahms's possession of many classic plays, including works by Goethe, Schiller, and Klinger, is evidence of his lively interest in the theater. He was among the most zealous of first-nighters at the Burgtheater in Vienna, and this interest was certainly related to his own creative curiosity toward drama in the theater. As Widmann recalls, "It gave him the greatest pleasure to analyse the merits and defects of any plot," and his critical attitude toward drama was based on thorough knowledge.[83]

The Visual Arts

As with his preferences in literature and drama, Brahms favored classic art. He found his greatest focus in painting of the Italian Renaissance, which he saw on his trips to Italy in later years. Widmann recalls:

> Probably the chief source of [his] love for Italy may be
> found in his quiet consciousness of an inner congeniality
> with the masters of the Italian Renaissance. Not that
> Brahms ever compared his creative work with that of
> these artists whose productions, whether in the province
> of architecture, sculpture or painting, were his delight!
> On the contrary, on those rare occasions when he spoke
> to some friend of his own works it was always with a
> touching modesty, ever showing the deepest veneration

for the great heroes of the past in every field of art. But such comparisons unconsciously suggested themselves when witnessing his rapt contemplation of the artistic treasures of Italy, or when listening to his enthusiastic praise of some characteristics of the Old Masters, characteristics which, in very truth, he himself possessed in a high degree; for instance, their conscientiousness of execution in minute details and their faithful industry in art. Brahms's especial delight was to discover gems of patient labor which would pass unnoticed by the ordinary tourist. For instance, in Santa Maria Maggiore at Bergamo, it gave him the greatest pleasure to note the beautiful Intarsia work, which is there applied not only to the backs of the choir stalls, but also to the seats themselves, these latter being usually kept covered with boards, which, however, the sacristan removed when perceiving the delight and insatiable interest with which the bearded stranger, whom he took for a "scultore," studied the upper part.
. . . There is no doubt that Brahms felt the art of the Renaissance akin to his artistic nature, though as I have already observed he was much too modest ever to acknowledge the analogy. And his interest in the art treasures of Italy was perfectly natural and spontaneous, not based upon any previous study of the history of Art. It is true he enjoyed the perusal of modern classical works on Italy, such as Jakob Burckhardt's *Cultur der Renaissance,* or the writings of Gregorovius, but this rather in remembrance of a just completed journey than in preparation. Likewise when visiting churches and museums, he did not often consult the guide books, preferring to rely on his own perception of what was most significant. He would walk rapidly through the galleries; where he paused one might be sure that there was true work of Art or something particularly original to be seen. Then he would beckon to his companion and draw attention to some fine details in the picture; but sometimes he preferred to stand alone before a painting, as the sight

of the most transcendent beauty easily moved him almost to tears. Altogether it did not need the tragically
sublime to move him deeply: pure beauty, if ever so simply expressed, could do this.[84]

As well as Burckhardt's *Die Cultur der Renaissance in Italien,* Brahms
also possessed Lübke's *Geschichte der Architektur, Geschichte der Renaissance
in Frankreich, Die heutigen Kunst, Kunsthistorisches Studien,* five books by
Hermann Grimm, including his *Lebens Michelangelos,* Wölfflin's *Renaissance and Baroque,* and the catalogue *Gemälde in den Loggien des Vatikans.*

In addition to the works of the High Renaissance and other epochs,
Brahms took a particular interest in the works of contemporaries. He was
most inclined toward Feuerbach and Max Klinger. The copies of his
friend Allgeyer's studies of Feuerbach's work in his library bear witness to
his knowledge of the paintings, and he had direct access to fine examples
of them in the gallery at Karlsruhe. Anselm Feuerbach, the nephew of
the philosopher Ludwig Feuerbach, was a major representative of the
movement known as Romantic Classicism. After early imitation of Courbet and Delacroix, Feuerbach became influenced by ancient and Roman
art and the Italian High Renaissance painters, developing his own style
into "idealized figure compositions" of a lyrical elegiac nature. His subjects were chiefly tragic figures of Greek mythology or Italian literature,
the most significant being the two versions of *Iphigenie* of 1862 and 1871,
The Judgement of Paris of 1870, and compositions on the Medea theme.

According to Specht, Brahms ("who had always been attacted by a
noble face and a sonorous voice") was also drawn to Feuerbach's very
appearance, his ideally handsome, fair-haired head.[85] Brahms frequently
commended Feuerbach's art to his friends and did all he could to encourage the antisocial painter, though his warnings as to the shallow nature of Viennese criticism were not heeded in the case of *The Battle of
the Amazons,* with sad consequences, for this painting represented a decisive failure for Feuerbach. Though Brahms spoke little of details, the
nature of the attraction can be deduced from his choral work *Nänie,*
whose text is on Thetis's lament for Achilles, which Brahms composed
to Feuerbach's memory and whose personal significance emerges from the
letter Brahms wrote to Feuerbach's stepmother. Specht sees Feuerbach as
a "transposition of one and the same artistic phenomenon as that of

Brahms, claiming that the maxims in Feuerbach's *Vermächtnis* would have been applauded by Brahms.[86]

In the debate on the claims of romanticism and classicism in painting, Brahms predictably was more drawn to the powerful restraint of the German Romans than to the brighter colors of the Nazarenes or the lavish richness of the interiors by Hans von Makart. However, he took a great interest in his prominent contemporaries, notably Arnold Böcklin and Adolf von Menzel. Böcklin, whose works existed in many versions, was widely admired by musicians, and some of his works influenced their compositions, most notably *The Isle of the Dead*. Brahms admired his work. Brahms knew Menzel personally, commending his work to Clara, to whom it was unfamiliar. Clara responded to Brahms, "I was very surprised by your remark about Menzel. Is he really such a great artist? I hardly know anything of his. If you have any time to spare do write and tell me something about him."[87] Brahms was very close to the artist (1815–1905), his elder by eighteen years, and admired him all his life. He quotes from Menzel in *Des Jungen Kreislers Schatzkästlein*. Stanford's recollection captures his respect even in the full maturity of his own achievement. "The last vision I have of him was sitting beside the diminutive form of the aged Menzel, drinking in like a keen schoolboy every word the great old artist said, with an attitude as full of unaffected reverence as of unconscious dignity." Specht considered Menzel, with Gottfried Keller, to be the figures "closest to Brahms in artistic and mental affinity."[88]

The significance of Klinger was different. He was highly receptive to music, and he included musical subjects in his work (a statue of Beethoven and an incomplete statue of Wagner are notable). But Brahms was his greatest love, and he saw Brahms as a progressive figure whose music could be realized visually with great subtlety, and in works of almost surreal character. He devoted an entire series of forty-one engravings to Brahms's works—the *Fantasias*—in addition to illustrations for Brahms's song volumes. The center of the *Fantasias* is a selection inspired by Brahms's *Song of Destiny*. Brahms was greatly impressed by them, and he wrote to Clara in 1894 that "they are not really illustrations in the ordinary sense but magnificent and wonderful fantasias inspired by my texts. Without assistance (without actual clarification) you would certainly often miss the sense and connection with the text. How much I should like to look them through with you and show you how profoundly he has grasped

the subject and to what heights his imagination and understanding soar."
To Klinger himself he praised the "rich, fantastic invention which is at
the same time so beautifully serious, of such significant depth, and allows
one to think and surmise further" even commenting that they show that
"all art is the same and speaks the same language."[89]

As with his literary interests, Brahms also enjoyed the lighter aspect of
visual art. Geiringer observes that "he had a particular liking for the
pictures of the spirited genre painter Chodowiecki, whose wealth of not
altogether spontaneous inspiration enchanted him; the presence in
Brahms's library of a quantity of the daintiest little almanacs is due merely
to their being illustrated with a few Chadowiecki etchings."[90]

FIVE · The Social Brahms

Friendship and Travel

16 · Friendship

The Hamburg Years

Brahms's bitter comment in his later years was prompted by the passing of many old friends. Despite his need for independence and his frequent tensions with his friends, he needed them and always preserved a friendship circle, whether in his daily contact with fellow musicians in Vienna or in maintaining his links with colleagues and their growing families. He settled easily into family situations, especially when they studied his needs. There is little record of childhood friendships that arose through his own family. Opportunities for friendships that would be vital to the development of the mature personality came first from his father's professional contacts. The first was in 1847, when Brahms was fourteen, with the Giesemann family of Winsen an der Luhe, near Hamburg. Adolf Giesemann, owner of a paper mill, was a keen musician who had met Jacob Brahms when Jacob played at the Alster Pavillion in 1846. A vacation was arranged for Brahms the following summer in return for his teaching piano to the daughter of the family, Lieschen. Brahms was warmly welcomed into this family, whose home became his own second home for many years. Here, outside the city, appears the first evidence of Brahms's passion for the open air; and his natural physical exuberance was soon in evidence. "He used to rise at four . . . and begin his day by bathing in the river. Joined not long afterwards by Lieschen he would spend a couple of delightful hours rambling about. . . . [He] soon gained flesh and colour." Although the delicate Johannes was picked on by the local boys (he preferred the company of the girls), he seems to have been contented, if largely self-absorbed, in this environment, and his musical talents were soon known in the neighborhood.[1]

Life robs one of

even more than

death does.

Life in Hamburg had encouraged Brahms to be inward-looking to preserve his world of imagination against the pressures of the routine music-making he had to undertake. Brahms would naturally have looked to fellow young musicians for friendship, particularly the pupils of Cossel and Marxsen, from the time he began lessons in the winter of 1840–41. His closest friendship was not with a pupil of either, however, but with Luise Japha,[2] who used the same practice studio as he at Baumgardten & Heins in Hamburg. Her attraction perhaps lay in her maturity—she was seven years Brahms's senior and had studied with different teachers. She tried to interest Brahms in Schumann's music, of which he knew nothing, and encouraged him to approach the couple when they played in Hamburg in 1850. Though this visit by the Schumanns had no immediate consequence for Brahms (his compositions were returned unopened), Luise studied with them from 1852. Because of his frequently withdrawn manner, Brahms found it difficult to capitalize on his contact with Japha in Hamburg. He spent some evenings at her home, but only her sister Minna warmed to him. An indication of why comes in a recollection of a member of the Japha circle who had been interested in hearing Brahms, then about eighteen, play the Scherzo in E flat Minor; he "accompanied [Brahms] on the way home and made repeated but quite hopeless efforts after sociability. Not one word would [Brahms] say," commenting to Luise in explanation that "one is not always inclined to talk . . . often one would rather not, and then it is best to be silent. You understand that, don't you?" Nonetheless, when Luise left for Düsseldorf in 1852, Brahms expressed to her sister his sense of impending loneliness.[3] This taciturn side is also confirmed in the case of another musician whom he had met while playing the piano in a restaurant at Bergedorf in the summer of 1846: Christian Miller. "Miller heard him there, and, fascinated by his performance, begged to be permitted to play duets with him. After this the two . . . met frequently until Miller left Hamburg to become a pupil at the Leipzig Conservatory. The companionship would seem to have been tolerated rather than actively desired by Johannes, who rarely spoke when out walking with Miller, but was accustomed to march along hat in hand, humming!"[4]

The vital professional contact of Brahms's early years—meeting Eduard Reményi and touring in 1853—never resulted in friendship, and the two went their separate ways after the visit to Liszt. For a time they held obvious attractions for each other: the contact offered Brahms an entirely new performing experience as partner of a virtuoso, and Reményi's playing of Hungarian melodies captivated Brahms and stimulated his imagination. But temperamentally they were poles apart. By contrast, the contact with Joachim, to whom Brahms next turned, introduced him to a much richer musical world, and Brahms was drawn to Joachim's personality and values. Brahms's only previous knowledge of him was as a visiting performer in Hamburg, when his playing had transported the younger man. Now Joachim himself was to be overwhelmed by Brahms's playing, and to recognize a kindred spirit and the beginning of a lifelong friendship. In the company of an already internationally known artist, Brahms was finally in the world to which he belonged, for Joachim's musical allegiances were similar. Friendships with leading musicians would now follow quickly as a result of Brahms's visits to Bonn and environs and eventually to the Schumanns' at Düsseldorf. Their response to his music and playing, their identification with his aims and values, forged an intimate relationship that transformed Brahms's fortunes as a composer. He revered his relationship with them both, and, with Joachim, they were his closest musical friends.

Schumann's death and the inevitable change in domestic as well as professional arrangements required that Brahms rethink his future as an independent musician. The post at Detmold, for which he had been recommended by Clara, helped broaden his outlook. Though he never settled, naturally finding the formality of court life not only against his nature but foreign to his experience, he found himself in an environment of young musicians and musical opportunities from which he could benefit. He quickly established friendships with members of the court orchestra and played chamber music. Again, the contact with nature had an immediate effect on his behavior, since the town was surrounded by countryside and hills. If he still remained taciturn and dreamy, he also developed a greater spontaneity in the company of Carl Bargheer and the von Meysenbug brothers. May summarizes records of his social life as follows: "The daily life . . . was one very much after his own heart. His mornings were sacred to work. Bargheer joined him at the Stadt Frankfurt for early dinner, and the afternoons were generally passed in exercise in the crisp autumn air of the Teutoburger Forest. There were games with Carl [von Meysenbug] and his younger brother Hermann; trials of strength with Bargheer, in which Brahms was invariably defeated, Sunday excursions with Carl Bargheer and others, which occupied the whole day and included an al fresco luncheon carried from Detmold, to which Brahms [would sometimes be able] to contribute an excellent bottle of Malvoisier: 'he was as happy as a king at these times, he loved beautiful nature so much' [recalled the court cellist Julius Schmidt]."[5]

He retained the post until 1859 but never lost touch with Hamburg, where he still lived for most of the year. Brahms's growing fame had opened up new contacts there and possibilities for friendship. He developed connections with various musical families who entertained him, provided him with an appropriate working environment, and helped him to continue his activity as a choral conductor through providing a context for his Frauenchor. The first such connection came through Friedchen Wagner, a piano pupil of his from 1856 who was the cousin of conductor G. D. Otten. Brahms became a friend of her family and was always welcome at the house, where, in 1859, he met Bertha Porubszky from Vienna, who was staying with her aunt, Augusta Brandt. Geiringer states that she was the first Viennese girl Brahms had ever met,[6] and he was very attracted to her. Another family contact was with the family of the actuary Johann Gottfried Hallier, friends of Clara Schumann, who lived at Eppendorf: Clara and her daughter Marie were guests of the Halliers in 1861.[7] There were regular music parties in their spacious drawing room. In 1861, Brahms rented a room from Frau Dr. Elisabeth Rösing (aunt of the Völkers sisters, who were prominent members of the Frauenchor), at her quiet house surrounded by a large garden at Hamm on the outskirts of the city. There he completed the Piano Quartet in G Minor, op. 25, and A Major, op. 26.

Vienna: A New Social World

When Brahms arrived in Vienna he had no plans for permanent residence and had few connections apart from Bertha Porubszky, who had returned from Hamburg, and his fellow Hamburg composer Carl Grädener, who had recently moved there. Brahms set about establishing contacts with the musical circle that would have known his work through publication. He first approached the leading piano teacher, Julius Epstein, who introduced Brahms to a number of leading musicians, including Joseph Hellmesberger, the leader of the Philharmonic orchestra. Brahms's first private performance, at which he played the piano quartets opp. 25 and 26 with Hellmesberger and members of his quartet, created a great impression, not least on Epstein, who then organized a successful public performance of op. 25 on 16 November. Another leading pianist associated with the Conservatory was Anton Door, whom Brahms distantly knew through acquaintance at a concert at Danzig in 1855.

The link to Brahms's first professional position in Vienna was through Joseph Gänsbacher, still an amateur musician practicing law, who was the moving spirit behind Brahms's election to the Singakademie conductorship the following autumn.[8] The leading resident composer on Brahms's arrival was Carl Goldmark, who was then thirty and had lived in Vienna since the age of sixteen. He was famed for his opera *The Queen of Sheba,* with its mastery of orchestral colors. He had an uneasy admiration for Brahms, which Specht described as his "embittered sympathy."[9] Brahms was often sarcastic to him, sensing his insecurity, though they remained quite close and regular companions over many years. A much easier friendship was with Gustav Nottebohm. A confirmed bachelor with, in Specht's words, a "morbidly exaggerated teutomania," Nottebohm seems to have encouraged Brahms into his bachelor habits and growing misogyny, and they socialized regularly over the years. Specht summarizes Kalbeck's view of him as a "distorting mirror" for Brahms's personality. But Brahms was devoted to him and traveled to Graz to be at the scholar's bedside in his last days, despite Brahms's usual inclination to distance himself from illness in others. Brahms even gave the funeral oration for Nottebohm.[10]

Friends later added to this Viennese circle were the pianist Ignaz Brüll, the scholars Carl Ferdinand Pohl and Eusebius Mandyczewski, and the critic Max Kalbeck. Brüll was perhaps Brahms's favorite musician in the later years in Vienna, and they often played duets. Brahms was always welcome in the hospitable Brüll home, and Brüll's tact resolved some social tensions in Brahms's relationships with his circle. Brüll visited Brahms during his last illness at the spa of Karlsbad near Vienna before his death.[11] Mandyczewski was another of the closest friends of the later years. This quiet and exceptionally modest man with an encyclopedic knowledge came from Eastern Austria and took care of the troublesome details of Brahms's life, correcting proofs, making copies, acting as his secretary. Hans Gál, speaking from personal acquaintance with Mandyczewski, describes him as "the only of Brahms's friends who claimed never to have experienced anything but kindness and consideration from him," adding, "but this was probably due largely to himself, a man of such mild and natural charm and strict objectivity that unfriendliness seemed impossible in his presence. Brahms valued the keen critical eye of his very much younger friend."[12] Kalbeck became part of Brahms's Viennese circle in about 1880. He was perhaps Brahms's most devoted admirer, and his four-volume biography of 1904–14, the first great monument to Brahms's achievements, was a labor of love for which he seems to have prepared during his years of acquaintanceship.[13]

Beyond his circle of professional colleagues, Brahms's social life in Vienna was marked by his close friendships with Eduard Hanslick and Theodor Billroth. Specht describes the group as "The Triumvirate."[14] Brahms had already met Hanslick 1856 at the Lower Rhine Music Festival at Düsseldorf. He met Billroth later, in 1865, not in Vienna, but as part of the circle of Theodor Kirchner at Zurich, where Billroth held a professorship of medicine. Musically Brahms was closer to Billroth, who had a wider musical knowledge and cultural perspective and was a committed amateur player of violin and viola for whom music was almost as important as his own profession. But Brahms knew nothing of him when he arrived in Vienna in September 1862. Hanslick was then the dominant figure in the public discussion of music. But Hanslick had his limitations and knew little of music before the Viennese classics, claiming that for him music began with Mozart. Indeed, he had great difficulty in coming to terms with Brahms's early works. Brahms's attraction was in seeming to represent a historical continuity from the classics, and he came to symbolize for Hanslick his musical opposition to Wagner. But he was a brilliant writer, and Brahms would scarcely have denied his support as he sought to establish himself, not least because of the appeal of a strong character who expressed himself honestly and went to lengths to understand and prepare the works he reviewed or lectured on.[15] Brahms later wrote Clara, "I can't help it, but I know few men to whom I feel as hearty an attachment as I do to him. To be so simple, good, honorable, benevolent, serious and modest and everything else as I know him to be, I regard as something very beautiful and rare." But they naturally disagreed over many musical issues. Brahms had first regarded Hanslick's treatise as full of inconsistencies in 1856,[16] and he could never share his opposition to Wagner's music. But from Brahms's first years in Vienna, when he clearly aligned himself with Brahms as the great composer of the future, not least through his review of the first (partial) performance of *A German Requiem* in Vienna in December 1867, the friendship deepened and was never threatened.

Billroth's calling to a professorship in Vienna in 1867 coincided with Brahms's growing attraction to Vienna as a permanent base. Billroth's villa in the Alserstrasse soon became a rendezvous point for leading Viennese musicians with whom Billroth shared his passion for music. They performed chamber music, and such distinguished artists as Gustav Walter sang to a small but select audience. Brahms's music was frequently given, with Billroth attempting the second viola part in the sextets and later the quintets, or second violin in the quartets. Their musical tastes coincided almost exactly. Billroth was one of the few among Brahms's friends who could match his range of musical and nonmusical knowledge. Billroth was a devotee of Beethoven who disliked Wagner. Although a musical amateur (though his talents had early been grounded in a sound piano technique and passable skills as a string player), he was of an artistic temperament for which music was a necessity. He immediately recognized Brahms's significance and eagerly welcomed his new works.[17] Brahms's final separation from Billroth, when Billroth's personality seemed to undergo a change after a serious illness, prompting manifestation of resentments about Brahms's personal manner which appear to have been long suppressed, was one of the many losses Brahms sustained in the few years before his death.[18]

The friendship with Billroth was symbolic of the circle in which Brahms now moved with his establishment in Vienna. He increasingly came to know the cultured Viennese families for which music was a necessary provision and where he was naturally welcomed. Some of these families became very close, providing something of a support structure in his last years. The Fabers were the first family Brahms got to know well, since Frau Faber (his Hamburg friend Bertha Porubszky), kept contact with him when he moved to Vienna and welcomed him to her new home, where he spent the Christmas of 1864. Arthur Faber, an Austrian industrialist,[19] became an equally close friend and was a regular member of the party, which included Nottebohm, that went for walks in the Wienerwald during the early Vienna years: he was present at Brahms's fiftieth birthday celebrations with Billroth and Hanslick. Bertha's connection with the Hamburg years gave their friendship a special value. Along with the Fellinger family, the Fabers were particularly active in attending to his needs in his last months. The Fellingers came into Brahms's circle as friends of Clara Schumann; he met them at Mürzzuschlag in 1885. Richard Fellinger was also an industrialist, and his wife, Maria, was a gifted sculptor. From 1890, the Fellinger home became ever more a substitute home for Brahms. Geiringer describes the relationship:

> Dr. Richard Fellinger, manager of the important indus-
> trial firm of Siemens and Halske, and his gifted wife . . .
> were among the master's most intimate Viennese friends.
> The sensitive and tactful manner of the Fellingers, who
> tried to divine the artist's every wish but never forced
> themselves upon him, was particularly soothing to the
> aging and lonely bachelor. He often invited himself to
> the Fellingers' house on Sunday, knowing that he could
> count on his favorite dishes; and in other respects he was
> not unwilling to be spoiled by his friends' affectionate af-
> terthought. Frau Fellinger knitted his stockings as his
> mother had done, and made the sorts of neckties he
> liked to wear. One day Herr Fellinger delighted Brahms
> by installing electric lighting in his room.[20]

His friendship was such that on one special occasion he completely surprised them by his unexpected arrival to take part in their silver wedding festivities in June 1896. Brahms met the family of Dr. Viktor Miller zu Aicholz some years earlier, and by 1882 the acquaintance had ripened into a firm friendship; this was strengthened by the fact that Miller had a house at Gmunden near Ischl, where Brahms spent later summers, beginning in 1882. Miller was one of Gmunden's most influential residents, and his villa there was a favorite meeting place for many musicians of the Brahms circle during the last fifteen years of Brahms's life. It was the Miller family who arranged for a carriage to be bought to take Brahms around Vienna and Gmunden, and Miller was the first to receive the news of Brahms's fatal illness. He was a pallbearer at the funeral. Miller established the first Brahms museum on the grounds of his villa.

"His attitude at the piano was precisely that of Professor von Beckerath's sketch." Brahms is recalled in the G Minor Rhapsody, op. 79/2, in a charcoal drawing by Willi von Beckerath (1896). (Brahms Institut, Lübeck, Sammlung Hofmann)

"I like to think of him best at the piano, playing his own compositions" (Ethel Smyth). Pencil sketch of about 1895 by Willi von Beckerath.

"Her lovely Italian and also German things you would never hear done more beautifully." A rare appearance by Brahms to accompany the mezzo soprano Alice
Barbi at the Bösendorfer Saal, Palais Lichtenstein, Vienna. Watercolor. (Österreichisches Nationalbibliothek, Vienna)

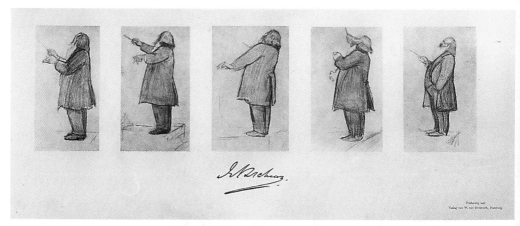

Ferdinand Schumann recalled the "concise, calm gestures, . . . amiable directions to the different instrumental groups." Drawings by Willi von Beckerath of Brahms conducting the Academic Festival Overture in February 1895. (Royal College of Music, London)

Gesellschaft der Musikfreunde.

Sonntag den 18. April 1875:

Viertes und letztes

Gesellschafts-Concert

im grossen Saale

unter der Leitung des artistischen Directors, Herrn

JOHANNES BRAHMS.

Mitwirkende:

Fräulein **Wilhelmine Tremel**, k. k. Hofopernsängerin,
Herr **Georg Henschel** aus Berlin,
Herr **Anton Schittenhelm**,
Herr **Dr. Ferd. Maas**,
Herr Director **Josef Hellmesberger**: Violindirigent,
„**Singverein**."

PROGRAMM.

Max Bruch:

„ODYSSEUS."

Scenen aus der Odyssee. — Für Soli, Chor und Orchester. *)

---

*) Bei der heutigen Aufführung entfallen: Nr. 5 (Penelopes Traum), Nr. 6 (Nausikaa) und das Duett in Nr. 10.

Streichinstrumente: Semböck.

Conducting the music of his colleagues. Brahms's last performance as musical director of the Gesellschaft der Musikfreunde was of Max Bruch's *Odysseus* on 18 April 1875. (Gesellschaft der Musikfreunde, Vienna)

"The haunt of no ordinary mere musician": Brahms in his library. (Brahms Institut, Lübeck)

Brahms reading in the library of Dr. Viktor von Miller zu Aicholz in Vienna.
Photo by Eugen von Miller zu Aicholz, 1894. (Gesellschaft der Misikfreunde,
Vienna)

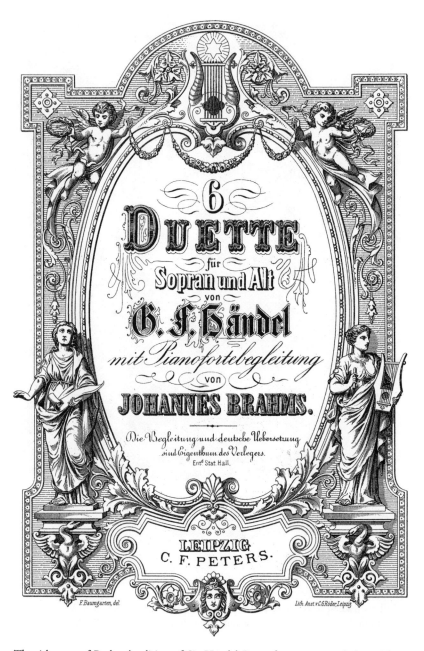

The title page of Brahms's edition of Six Handel Duets for soprano and alto, with his realization of the keyboard part. (Peters Edition, Leipzig, 1881)

COUPERIN's
WERKE

HERAUSGEGEBEN

von

JOHANNES BRAHMS

ERSTER THEIL

Clavierstücke

Livre I.

———

Mit der nächstjährigen Lieferung, welche Livre II der Pièces de
Clavecin enthalten wird, bildet diese zusammen den ersten Band der Werke Couperin's.
Haupttitel, Vorwort etc. werden bei jener zweiten Lieferung erfolgen.

The title page of Brahms's edition of Louis Couperin's "Pieces de Clavecin," Livre I, as Clavierstücke
in the *Denkmäler der Tonkunst* series edited by Friedrich Chrysander, vol. 4, 1871.

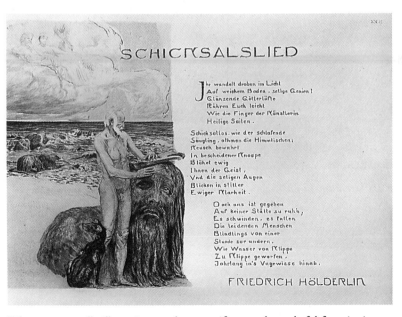

"They are not really illustrations . . . but magnificent and wonderful fantasias inspired by my texts." (Brahms to Clara Schumann). Max Klinger's evocation of
Brahms's *Schicksalslied,* part of the series of forty-one *Brahms Fantasies* (1885–94).

Clara Schumann at fifty-eight. Oil painting by Franz Lembach, Munich, 1878.

Brahms and Joachim. Photograph J. Reiner, Klagenfurt. (Gesellschaft der Musik-freunde, Vienna)

Robert and Clara Schumann. (Gesellschaft der Musikfreunde, Vienna)

Joachim and Clara in performance. Pencil sketch by Adolf von Menzel, inscribed "In Erinnerungen 20 December 1854."

Elisabet von Herzogenberg. A perceptive critic and close artistic friend, this accomplished musician received the dedication of the Rhapsodies, op. 79. Photograph from Brahms's own collection. (Brahms Institut, Lübeck, Sammlung Hofmann)

The surgeon Theodor Billroth at about the time he settled in Vienna in 1867 as director and professor of surgery at the Surgical Institute, University of Vienna. Photograph from Brahms's own collection. (Brahms Institut, Lübeck, Sammlung Hofmann)

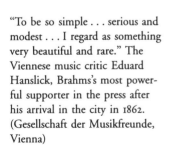

"To be so simple . . . serious and modest . . . I regard as something very beautiful and rare." The Viennese music critic Eduard Hanslick, Brahms's most powerful supporter in the press after his arrival in the city in 1862. (Gesellschaft der Musikfreunde, Vienna)

"After Bach and Beethoven, he is the greatest, the most exalted of all composers."
In the 1880s Hans von Bülow devoted himself and his Meiningen Hofkapelle Or-
chestra to achieving new standards of performance with Brahms's orchestral works.
Photograph taken in Berlin on 4 March 1889. (Brahms Institut, Lübeck, Sammlung
Hofmann)

"He is one of the few colleagues I can hold in limitless respect." Brahms's view of Johann Strauss, Jr., pictured here with Brahms on the veranda of Strauss's fashionable villa at Bad Ischl, where he was a regular guest, in 1894. (Gesellschaft der Musikfreunde, Vienna)

"I dwell with the greatest pleasure at Salzburgerstrasse 51." Brahms's modest summer lodgings at Bad Ischl from 1880–82 and 1889–94 as seen in a painting by Karl Blumauer, from Brahms's own collection (Österreichisches Nationalbibliothek, Vienna), and today, at the town limits (photograph by the author).

Friendships with the Conrats, Hornböstels, and Wittgensteins came late in Brahms's life. The Conrats were known by the young pianist Artur Schnabel; his biographer describes them thus: "Hugo Conrat [who wrote the German texts of the Zigeunerlieder, op. 103] was a prosperous merchant and a passionate devotee of the arts. His house on the fashionable Walfischgasse (close to the Opera House), was on Sunday afternoons during the winter, given over to convivial meetings for the performance of chamber music by professionals or amateurs, including the host himself." Schnabel often attended and played there, where he saw Brahms. "He mostly sat reading in the library, which was several rooms distant from the music room." Schnabel first entered the Brahms circle at the home of Frau von Hornböstel, formerly a singer and the guiding spirit of a private ladies' choir that rehearsed at her home. Its conductor was Eusebius Mandyczewski, who was Schnabel's teacher, and Schnabel was its accompanist from about the age of eleven (from which time he conceived his love of the *Liebeslieder* waltzes).[21] Brahms's friendship with the Wittgenstein family brings his social position into the clearest focus: for this family had not only great wealth and culture but creative significance. Wittgenstein was a millionaire industrialist with an interest in the arts that would come to fruition in his talented children, including the philosopher Ludwig and the pianist Paul. His house was the location of regular chamber music performances with players of Brahms's circle, including the violinist Marie Soldat, and the venue of an important event in later years, the first private performance of the Clarinet Quintet.[22]

Brahms had some Viennese friends in other locations, since, as members of the upper-middle classes, many had summer residences elsewhere. Along with Miller zu Aicholz, Karl Goldmark had connections in Gmunden, where he regularly stayed, and Ignaz Brüll had a house on the adjacent Lake Attersee. Brahms also liked to meet Johann Strauss at Ischl, where Strauss regularly played for the imperial court and had a residence. But Brahms had no interest in close contact with the higher social circles of the town, and so he lived modestly in a farmhouse on the outskirts, where he rented rooms.[23] In earlier years his friendship with Clara Schumann had introduced him to the spa of Baden Baden and the cultural circle there, which included members of royalty and diplomats from every part of Europe, as well as many artists, including the Russian playwright Ivan Turgeniev, the German painter Anselm Feuerbach, the French-born

Spanish actress Pauline Viardot Garcia, as well as Anton Rubinstein and Johann Strauss.[24] But musical friends with whom he could relax were more attractive to him. In nearby Karlsruhe he had developed firm friendships in his earlier years with the young court conductors Hermann Levi and Otto Dessoff and the engraver Julius Allgeyer, and at Zurich, directly accessible by train, as was Baden Baden, with Theodor Kirchner. In addition, friends from the Schumann years were Albert Dietrich at Oldenburg and Julius Otto Grimm at Münster in Westphalia, all of whom providing lodgings when Brahms required them.

Clara's home was to remain an anchor for Brahms for many years, even when, having given up the Baden house in 1874, she reestablished herself in Frankfurt in 1878 to teach at the new Conservatory of Dr. Hoch. Eugenie Schumann recalled, "When we lived in Frankfurt, Brahms visited us every year there . . . but in later years when he went to Italy every year, he came to the north but rarely."[25] While Clara was pondering her change of location, Brahms suggested she consider Leipzig. Although she had friends there, she decided on Frankfurt. Brahms's own early musical experiences in Leipzig had gone badly, but he was to have important friendships there in later years, for the city maintained its central importance in German musical tradition. Musicians came from all over Europe to study at the Conservatory and to participate in the musical life there, and the annual performance of Bach's *St. Matthew Passion* was the focal point of the musical year. Brahms was to meet many musicians of different backgrounds staying in Leipzig, including Grieg and Tchaikowsky. His strongest links were to the Herzogenberg family. Elisabet von Herzogenberg had, as Elisabet von Stockhausen, been Brahms's piano pupil in Vienna. She settled in Leipzig, where Brahms met her again in 1874. Heinrich von Herzogenberg studied at Graz under Nottebohm and had come to Leipzig as conductor of the *Bach Verein,* a position he held until 1885, when he was appointed head of theory and composition at the Berlin Hochschule. The couple's devotion to Brahms's music and their cultured home, in which he felt at ease, made their friendship very valuable, though Brahms had to maintain a polite distance from Heinrich's compositions, not least in view of their imitation of his own. The correspondence from this friendship, notably that with Elisabet concerning Brahms's piano music, is among the most revealing on his attitudes toward his own work. Elisabet's early death in 1892 was a great shock to

Brahms. Through this circle he also met the family of Julius Röntgen, a prominent young composer and conductor whose father was concert-master of the Gewandhaus Orchestra. He formed a firm friendship with Röntgen and invited him to visit him at his holiday home in Thun in 1888, as well as to visit in Vienna, where Brahms gave Röntgen and his sister the hospitality of his favorite restaurants.

Brahms's early connection with the Rhineland was stimulated shortly after his new links with Leipzig. When he made a concert tour in January 1880, visiting among other places the small town of Krefeld, which impressed him with its lively musical life, he formed a strong friendship with his host on that occasion, Rudolf von der Leyen. Brahms enjoyed the Leyens' friendly home and was to engage in much relaxed domestic music-making there over the years, not least with singers who were part of the family's circle, including Antonia Kufferath and Hermine Spies, whom Brahms met there in January 1883. It was to Leyen that Brahms would reveal some of the most profound evidence of his loneliness in later years; it was with members of this circle, the Wehrmanns, who were relatives of the Leyens', that Brahms, deeply distressed, stayed after Clara's funeral in 1896. Krefeld received its artistic recognition in 1885 when Brahms dedicated his *Tafellied*, "To the friends in Krefeld," on which occasion the work and some partsongs and other compositions were sung at the jubilee of the Krefeld Concert Society. The Leyens had many relatives in the Rhineland, and through them Brahms met the music-loving von Beckerath family, who lived near Wiesbaden. Alwin von Beckerath was an accomplished viola player in a quartet led by Richard Barth, a former pupil of Joachim, and Brahms greatly enjoyed the hospitality of von Beckerath and his wife, Laura. Brahms greatly appreciated the countryside around their home, but what drew him there in summer of 1883 to interrupt his pattern of Austrian vacations was his attraction to Hermine Spies, whom he had met at the Leyens and who lived nearby. Here Brahms completed his Third Symphony that summer.[26]

Of other places with special associations, Brahms took particular pleasure in his contacts with the ducal court of Meiningen. They came about through his longstanding acquaintance with Hans von Bülow. Bülow had been appointed director of music to the court in 1882 and set about building an orchestra of great distinction, drawing on Brahms's orchestral works in this task and bringing them to a new standard. The quality of the orchestra was a consequence of the deep artistic commitments of Duke Georg and his wife, the former actress Ellen Franz, who carried the morganatic title Baroness Heldburg, and many distinguished artists were visitors in Meiningen. Brahms became a welcome guest and was attracted by the relaxed atmosphere of the court, as well as by the high musical standards. He frequently was invited to stay at the Villa Carlotta, the ducal couple's residence on Lake Como. Indeed, the fact that Brahms could not visit Meiningen as often as they—and especially she—wished was the cause of a little irritation to the baroness, to which Brahms replied with rare frankness in 1887: "I imagine you must often consider me un-grateful or even disloyal and in a certain sense you are justified. It is so when I am offered the benefit of your great and bountiful generosity and kindness. I know how to appreciate them with all my heart, as you have seen for yourself and you cannot doubt. But often I must renounce them and you cannot understand my reasons. Now let me confess that in such a case I am by no means dishonest when not candid. The really truthful answer will not come out because I do not like to speak of myself or my idiosyncrasies. The confession is simple: that I need complete solitude, not only to achieve my best, but even to think of my work at all."[27]

Brahms's friends in other countries were limited to those in Switzerland and Holland; his Italian trips were not to visit friends, only those of his circle who stayed there. His early contacts with Switzerland had existed through the circle of Schumann's pupils. Brahms had been known there since 1853, when Dietrich had reported the talents of a new acquaintance in Düsseldorf to Theodor Kirchner, Emil Naumann, and others living in Zurich: both were aspiring composers named by Schumann in "Neue Bahnen" as worthy of attention. Though Brahms had visited Zurich with Clara in 1856, it was through his sustained work on *A German Requiem* there in 1866 that Brahms became closer to the circle around Kirchner. This included the conductor Friedrich Hegar and his wife, Albertine, a discerning interpreter of Brahms's songs. Brahms's music, especially the chamber music and piano duet music, became the focus of this musical community, which also included the highly talented German-Swiss composer Gustav Weber, who died early in 1887, and Robert Freund, the German-Hungarian pianist who was a pupil of Tausig and Liszt. But Brahms was to meet a wider circle, most significantly the surgeon Theodor Billroth, soon to move to Vienna in 1867;

through him Brahms came to know Billroth's friend Wilhelm Lübke of Stuttgart.[28]

Two other friendships with nonmusician artists associated with Switzerland were with the poets Gottfried Keller and J. V. Widmann. Brahms had a special kinship with Keller, the greatest Swiss poet of the period, since both had struggled from obscurity to fame. Keller, for his part, never missed a Brahms symphony performance. Though, by his own confession, he knew little of the technical aspects of music, Keller felt "particularly stirred and attracted by Brahms's music, which really had something new and individual to say to him." Throughout his life Brahms remained an enthusiastic admirer of Keller's poetry and repeatedly thanked Professor Jakob Bächthold of Zurich, who later wrote a biography of Keller, for every new and rare work of Keller's he found for him.[29] The friendship with Josef Viktor Widmann dated from 1874, when they met at the Zurich music festival at which Brahms's *Song of Triumph* was being performed. Brahms spent virtually the entire time in Widmann's company. Widmann's wide interests in matters of art and literature as well as religion (he was a Protestant pastor by training) naturally attracted Brahms's attention. However, as important as his stimulation of Brahms's responses on religion and politics was his role in advising on possible operatic subjects for composition and as potential librettist. He seems to have prompted the "second phase" of Brahms's lifelong interest in operatic composition.[30] More than to almost any other friend of later years, Brahms revealed his deepest thoughts to Widmann, not merely about artistic issues, but also about his youth and personality, even his compositional processes. It was on this basis that Widmann became a permanent member of Brahms's companions for his trips to Italy from 1888. It was also through a desire to be near Widmann that Brahms interrupted his routine of spending summers in Ischl to stay at Hofstetten on Lake Thun.

17 · Travel

The deep affinity that Brahms came to feel for Austria is well caught in his comment on returning to the country after the Italian holidays of his later years: "When I cross the Austrian border . . . I always feel like embracing every railway conductor."[31] Living in Vienna made it easy for him to travel to Italy, which he did almost annually from the late 1870s. But aside from this he traveled little outside Germany and Austria, German-speaking Switzerland, and Holland; much of his traveling was in the course of concert-giving. He never visited France or England, despite endless invitations. He made his first trip to Italy only after long having settled in Vienna. What drew him, apart from his love of the art treasures, was part of an increasing attraction to warmer climes and more spectacular scenery, a development of his growing desire for freedom to travel in the summer. During the part of the year when he was not working as performer or teacher in Hamburg, and more especially in Vienna, he found himself a location that gave independence and quiet, and the opportunity for walking. The sequence of these summer visits shows him gradually broadening his regional horizons.

Apart from the recreations of Hamburg and its immediate environs,[32] Brahms's upbringing had given no opportunity for travel. His first recital tour with Reményi in spring 1853 and its sequel opened up a completely new perspective; he traveled to Hanover, Weimar, Göttingen, and eventually to the Rhine, staying at Bonn, Mehlem, and Düsseldorf. Before he left Mehlem, his music-loving friends had encouraged him to share the local scenery,[33] which included the Drachenfels rock on the other side of the river near Königswinter with its magnificent view of the river. Brahms remained attached to this region, often returning during concert tours, as when he gave successful performances of the D Minor Piano Concerto in 1876 at Mainz and Coblenz. A particularly memorable stay was to come in 1883 when, in response to repeated invitations from Alwin von Beckerath, he spent the summer at Wiesbaden to complete the Third Symphony. He had the use of what Geiringer describes as a "wonderfully situated studio, high above the town."[34] Brahms's deep association with the north of Germany continued for many years. In 1853 his concert travels took him to Danzig; in 1876 he spent the summer on the Isle of Rügen, now having an added interest to him as the birthplace of his friend Theodor Billroth. He later wrote to Joachim, who was taking a holiday there in 1886: "Rügen will greatly please you: it is quite magnificent and once for a whole summer long—I endured it! I had to tell myself, unfortunately, that in spite of all its beauty I wouldn't go there again. One has to put up with too much discomfort and inconvenience which I, who have made my home in the south, am not used to any more."[35]

Before settling in Austria, Brahms had explored much of Germany, particularly the southwest around Karlsruhe and Baden Baden. He had first visited Karlsruhe in 1855 to see his friends Hermann Levi and Julius Allgeyer. He enjoyed pleasant accommodation in Karlsruhe, often staying with Allgeyer. But it was through Clara Schumann that his connections with this region were cemented. Since 1863 Clara had been established in the beautiful suburb of Baden Baden named Lichtental, on the edge of the Black Forest. Her garden backed on to the river Oos running down the Lichtentaler Allee, a park that runs down to the town. The following year Brahms was guest at the villa of Anton Rubinstein. In the summer of 1865 he made his own arrangements in Lichtenthal, renting two attic rooms in a house on the edge of the village, not far from Clara's house, with magnificent views into the wooded hills and valleys beyond. The house was owned by one Frau Becker, the widow of a lawyer. Brahms called this country house, situated on a rocky slope, "the beautiful house on the hill," and he told Florence May, who studied with him there, that the view was "unsurpassable."[36] There were many walks to be taken there, and many works were conceived and completed over the following decade, including the First Symphony, the *German Requiem,* and the Horn Trio. He returned to Lichtental intermittently, generally staying at the Hotel Bär, just a short distance from Clara's former dwelling. In 1889 he visited Clara when she stayed at the Parkhotel in Baden Baden, but he seemed to lose his feeling for the place when he found that some of his favorite trees had been cut down. Clara intended to go again in 1896, though she was prevented by her fatal stroke. Brahms had written her of his plans: "I heard that you intended to go to B[aden] Baden. Please let me know where you are planning to go and for how long. I have always had a sort of longing for Baden Baden anyway and would dearly love to see the beloved old landscape—and friend!"[37]

The composition of *A German Requiem* had been associated with locations other than Karlsruhe and Baden Baden: namely, Winterthur and Zurich in German-speaking Switzerland. Brahms's friends Kirchner and Allgeyer had encouraged him to travel since his first trip with Clara in 1856, and in 1866 he fulfilled an old promise to his publisher Rieter Biedermann to stay with him at Winterthur. After a short stay there,

Brahms spent the summer of 1866 on the Zurichberg. Brahms soon found friends in the artistic circles of Zurich. Apart from those mentioned, another interesting contact was with the Wesendonck couple, Mathilde now turning her musical support toward Brahms after the cooling with Wagner. In autumn Brahms was to make an extensive tour with Joachim. In 1874 he spent from early June until the end of September in a chalet near the Nidelbad by Rüschlikon, high above Lake Zurich, working toward the completion of the First Symphony (where he exchanged visits with Gottfried Keller and made the acquaintance of J. V. Widmann). Pohl's letter in reply to Brahms's own from Vienna describes the idyllic situation: "The man who calls me sits far away beside the lake of Zurich, admiring the view of the Nidelbad; he drives to Küssnacht, eats freshwater fish and crayfish in the 'Sun,' drinks the excellent red wine at Erlenbach, or even better, lakeside wine at Mariahalden—and saunters along the Horgen, which is one fragrant rose garden in June."[38]

From the later 1860s Brahms increasingly identified with Vienna, where he had now effectively settled, and which drew him inevitably toward the Austrian mountain scenery. In 1870 he passed through the town of Tutzing on the Starnberger lake, about an hour from Munich, with friends with whom he was staying for a Wagner performance in the city. In 1873 he decided to spend the summer there, a stay that represented an obvious step toward warmer climes, where he completed the "St. Antoni" Variations. He was a houseguest, with Levi and Allgeyer, of Conrat Amtmann. "Tutzing is far more beautiful than we first imagined," Brahms commented. "We have just had a gorgeous thunderstorm. The lake is almost black, but magnificently green along the shores; usually it is blue, though of a more beautiful and deeper hue than the sky. In the background there is a range of snow-covered mountains—one can never see enough of it."[39]

But two years later Brahms was drawn back to the southwest, where he settled down in the spring at Ziegelhausen on the right bank of the Neckar, a little above Heidelberg and opposite Schlierbach. He wrote to Reinthaler, "I am delightfully lodged and pass my time only too well, [with] Heidelberg, Mannheim and Karlsruhe all quite close at hand. You know the country, people and inns of Baden and can sing their praise." He there worked on the C Minor Piano Quartet and the B flat String Quartet and kept in touch with visiting musicians. "Levi and Dessoff were here today. Tonight Frank [a Viennese conductor working in Mannheim] is coming, tomorrow some charming lady singers from Mannheim. In short, life is only too gay."[40]

The completion of the First Symphony in 1876 represented a profound moment of achievement for Brahms. From now on he could relax after years of sustained thought and effort, and there appears in his outer life a more relaxed manner and in his choices of summer locations a new pattern of interest in which he systematically explored the mountain regions of Austria. He also showed a more complete happiness with Vienna. He loved his walks in the woods, parks, and, especially, the Prater, Vienna's unique amusement park, commenting that "it isn't really spring without a few evenings in the 'Prater.' "[41] He was also attached to some of the surrounding districts and spent the summer of 1882 at the village of Pressbaum, not far from the city, where he stayed with Brüll and completed the B flat Piano Concerto. Brahms's familiarity with the mountain areas of Austria dates from 1867, when he and his father walked through Styria and Carinthia in the Austrian Alps. Brahms was eager to show his father the area and climb mountains; Josef Gänsbacher accompanied them. Their walk included a long trek from Mürzsteg to Wildalpen, though the father let his companions climb the Hochschwab.

Four places were to be especially important in the future: the Carinthian spa of Pörtschach, where he spent three consecutive summers in 1877–79; the spa of Bad Ischl, where he spent 1880 and 1882, and to which he returned in 1889–96 as a final and most important summer location after Lichtental; Mürzzuschlag in Styria, where he stayed in 1884–85; and the village of Hofstetten on Lake Thun, about a mile from the Swiss town of Thun, where he spent three consecutive years 1886–88.

Brahms had intended to spend the summer of 1877 at Ziegelhausen, as he had in 1875. But he changed his mind in favor of Pörtschach, then a little-known lakeside spa on the northern side of the Wörthersee. There was already something of an artists' colony in the town, and Brahms was acquainted with some of the musicians, including a descendant of Schubert's friend Leopold Kupelwieser.[42] Brahms also met there his singer friend Luise Dustmann, whom he had known in Hamburg. He sang the praises of the location to many of his friends in letters, writing to Billroth, "I only wanted to stay for a day, and then as the day was beautiful, for yet another, but each was as beautiful as the last, so I stayed on. If you have looked up from this letter, you must have seen all the mountains around the blue lake are white and how delicately green the trees are."[43] Brahms lived modestly in a guest house at the very end of the town. It was quiet and led easily to long walks along the lake and to the wooded slopes. Music came easily here, notably the Second Symphony, Violin Concerto, Violin Sonata in G. Coincidentally, he met there, in a concert arranged by Dustmann, the young violinist destined to be one of his favorite players of the concerto when she later completed her training under Joachim. Her name was Marie Soldat. Brahms effectively discovered her in a concert in the town during his first summer there, and he subsequently helped to guide her career.[44]

Brahms did not stay beyond a third year at Pörtschach. Too many people had begun to take an interest in the town in the meantime, and he no longer had access to the garden overlooking the lake.[45] He now turned his attention to the Salzkammergut region, which he had visited as part of his 1867 tour with his father, when they included the Scharfberg in their itinerary. He now chose Bad Ischl. In contrast with Pörtschach, it was a highly fashionable and substantial spa patronized by royalty at the kaiser's summer lodge; a circle of artists was also resident there in the summer, including Johann Strauss, who played by royal request and had his own residence as well. The town was known appropriately as the Austrian Baden Baden. Brahms's 1880 lodging, on the Salzburgerstrasse, was a solid farmhouse situated a little above the road and the river that runs below it at a bend, giving magnificent views down the valley and over the town, which is built on the confluence of two rivers. He rented rooms from Engelburt Gruber, had excellent walks in the surrounding hills, and could escape from prying visitors with ease. It was to be his longest overall association with one location, 1880–96, including the consecutive years 1889–96. Goldmark had spent every summer in Ischl since 1871 and it was patronized by many of Brahms's Viennese friends. Brahms wrote to Billroth in 1880, "I must really praise Ischl, and it doesn't worry me in the least that one finds half of Vienna here. I dwell with the greatest pleasure at Salzburgerstrasse 51."[46] He wrote in identical terms to Elisabet von Herzogenberg "that half of Vienna that does at present come to Ischl does not spoil it for me—even the whole of Vienna would fill me with anything but repugnance. Indeed, half of Berlin or Leipzig would probably put me to flight, but half of Vienna is quite pretty and need not be ashamed of itself."[47] Before he returned in 1889, the summer of 1883 was spent at Wiesbaden at the home of Alwin von Beckerath. When Brahms came back to Ischl in 1889 after three summers in Thun, it was probably in conscious awareness that he was nearer to Vienna and to his circle of friends. He realized that he would have to break with distant Thun as he grew older. So the constant presence of the Viennese did not spoil it for him.

Brahms had intended to return to Ischl in the summer of 1884 after some days at Lake Como in the Villa Carlotta of the Duke of Meiningen, where he stayed intermittently after his friendship was established in 1882. But his summer visitors were disappointed, and he decided to make a change to the small town of Mürzzuschlag in the Styrian mountains, surprising his Viennese friends. Brüll remarked, "What a fellow he is! He means to take rooms in Ischl for the summer, then one morning he wakes up in Mürzzuschlag! I had been looking forward to our walks, on which I would not have disturbed the heavenly peace by a single sound . . . and now all my hopes are turned to water (hence all this rain)!"[48] The rain in Ischl may have accounted for Brahms's decision; also the fact that many Viennese were also resident in Mürzzuschlag. He had numerous visitors since the construction of the Semmering Pass enabled a direct rail connection: Brahms commented that he could now be within three hours of Vienna. The town, nestled deep in the mountains, offered quiet and the opportunity for many walks in the surrounding hills. The house was again situated at the end of the main street toward the edge of the town.

The preference for Austrian over Swiss mountain scenery that came about from the mid-1870s was set aside for three consecutive summers, 1886–88, when Brahms stayed at Hofstetten, on the shore of Lake Thun, backing on to the wooded mountainside. The reason was the friendship with Widmann, who lived in Bern. Geiringer observes of his accommodation at Bern that "from the windows of his rooms, which were situated on the Aar, Brahms enjoyed an indescribably beautiful view of the glaciers of the Bernese Oberland and we can understand why many of the compositions written here have something of an alpine majesty."[49] Brahms was able to indulge his passion for walking there, and he took many trips with Widmann.

Brahms's trips to Italy were generally made in addition to these long summer breaks for composition, and they represented the most outward sign of the new sense of freedom that came over him in his later forties. The trips combined all his pleasures—warmer climes, spectacular scenery, and fine cuisine—with the opportunity to experience some of the historical and artistic sites and associations with which he had long been acquainted through reading. For these explorations the company of like-minded male companions was essential to the now-confirmed bachelor. He preferred whenever possible to travel out of season, generally in the spring. Specht observes that "a spring without a visit to Italy he accounted lost."[50] Brahms first intended to visit in 1876, though he went instead to Ziegelhausen and Baden Baden. He apparently made eight trips to Italy: in 1878, 1881, 1882, 1884, 1887, 1888, 1890, and 1893. He took different kinds of trips with different groups of friends who changed over the years. Billroth was the most regular companion of the earlier years, Widmann of the latter, from 1888. The last trip was the most extensive, and Brahms fully intended something of the kind in the following year, though circumstances intervened.

The first visit, in the spring of 1878, was with Billroth and Goldmark, when they made a brief journey through southern Italy to Rome and Naples. The journey of April and May 1881, in which Billroth was joined by Nottebohm and Dr. Adolf Exner (a professor of law in Vienna) was through southern and central Italy (Palermo, Messina, Naples, Rome, Siena, Orvieto, Florence, Pisa). In spring 1884 he combined a visit with Rudolf von den Leyen to the Villa Carlotta (the summer home of the Duke of Meiningen) with a short tour through the southern Tirol (Trent, Rovereto), and, by way of the Lake of Garda, through northern Italy (Milan, Genoa, Turin). The fifth Italian tour, in the spring of 1887, was with Theodor Kirchner and the publisher Fritz Simrock, which took them from Innsbruck over the Brenner Pass to northern and central Italy: Vicenza, Verona, Venice, Bologna, Florence, Pisa, Genoa, Milan. The sixth tour, on which Widmann alone joined him for the first time in May 1888, took them through Venice, Bologna, Rimini, St. Marino, Ancona, Loreto, and the Umbrian Apennines (Spoleto, Terni) to Rome (Fracati, Tivoli, Porto d'Anzio, Nettuno) and back to Florence, Turin, and Milan. Their next tour together, the seventh, of 1890, was confined to northern Italy; the Lake of Garda, Parma, Bergamo, Cremona, Brescia, Vicenza, Padua, and Verona. For the eighth and last, in the spring of 1893, the two were joined by their Zurich friends Hegar and Freund. This, the most extensive trip of all, included Genoa, Pisa, Rome, Naples, Palermo (Mount Pelle-grino, Monreale), Girgenti, Catania, Syracuse, Taormina, Messina, re-turning by Naples.

There was no change in Brahms's lifestyle on these holidays. As at his apartment in Vienna, he preferred simplicity in accommodation and his eating arrangements, though he availed himself of the best he could find and always sought privacy. The recollections of Widmann give a picture of some of their experiences, beginning in 1888, when they traveled through the marches of Umbria on to Rome and back through Pied-mont.[51] Widmann had joined Brahms at Verona, their first goal being Bologna, where an international musical exhibition was being held which they wanted to visit. Brahms was wary of being recognized among mu-sicians and critics, and his fears turned out to be justified as he found himself being effusively hosted by the director of the Bologna Conser-vatory of Music, the composer Martucci.[52] The following day they went to Rimini, St. Marino, and Pesaro, where Brahms paid his respects to Rossini's birthplace. From Ancona they traveled to Loreto, where they observed a religious procession of peasants from the Abruzzi.

> From Ancona we went through the Umbrian Appenines
> into Roman territory. On the railway journey, which tra-
> verses the lovely valley of Clitumnus, Brahms frequently
> lamented that the railway ran past such interesting old
> towns as Fabriano, Gubbio and Trevi, the "Algiers of It-
> aly." "One should really do all this on foot," he said
> quite rightly. But some things we did enjoy as pedestri-
> ans. Spoleto, for instance, with its wonderful bridge, and
> Monte Luco, where formerly the Carmelite monks had
> their hermitages, now turned into villas; then Terni, with
> the majestic waterfall of Verlino. . . . In Rome we also
> went about much on foot. I specially recall to mind a
> long and fatiguing walk we took one morning along the
> Via Appia, when I suffered much anxiety on account of
> my companion, who, in accordance with his favourite
> habit, was carrying his hat in his hand and, beginning to
> get redder and redder with the burning sun and the exer-
> tion of walking along the dusty road. Fortunately we

came across an old inn, where one could obtain shelter from the heat and refresh ourselves with the white wine of the country.[53]

Their visits also included Tivoli and Hadrian's Villa. For their second journey, in the spring of 1890, they met at Riva on the Lake of Garda. They first visited Parma:

> As we were strolling along the streets under brilliant moonlight, upon turning a corner we suddenly found ourselves opposite the cathedral and Brahms was quite overwhelmed by the light of the beautiful marble facade with its fabulously romantic outline. It certainly is one of the most original edifices in Italy. . . . Next to the cathedral rises the gloomy and gigantic torrazzo, the highest tower in Italy. Brahms could hardly tear himself away from this beautiful sight and returning there later that same evening we watched the magical effects of the moonlight on this mighty edifice as it glided over the marbled surfaces and statues, the shadowy tirazzo seeming to reach into the heavens, the dark shadows in the vaulted porch alternating with bright patches of moonlight, the statues looking like the living figures of a dream of bygone days.[54]

In the spring of 1893, Widmann was joined by Friedrich Hegar and Robert Freund (from Zurich) as Brahms's companions. Brahms had met the party at Milan, intending that they should travel to Genoa, but they traveled instead by rail to Naples. They included a visit to Sorrento, where Hanslick was staying with his wife. Next they sailed to Sicily, going from Palermo to Girgenti. At Girgenti "we spent two mornings among the massive and awe-inspiring ruins: where the sight of Brahms sitting on the lowest steps of the temple of Juno, his bare head and silvery beard illuminated by the morning sun involuntarily."[55] Then to Catania from Syracuse, to Brahms's favorite spot, Taormina, where he had made a previous memorable visit with Billroth. "[Above all he enjoyed] the hours we spent in the ancient theatre. One day we ascended the hill to Mola, the former city of saracens, perched on rocky pinnacles. Uphill walking was rather difficult with Brahms but his downhill pace resembled that of a rolling ball, and his companions frequently found it hard work to keep up with him, as was also the case with us that afternoon as we were walking from Mola. Brahms was far ahead and, missing the way found himself on the edge of a quarry down which he clambered and probably would not have reached the bottom safe and sound had not a man who was working close by seen him and come to his aid."[56]

Brahms would doubtless have anticipated the continuation of these trips. But from 1894 his friendship circle began to shrink, first with the deaths of Bülow, Billroth, Spitta, then of Clara Schumann in 1896, followed within a year by that of Brahms himself.[57]

SIX · Brahms in Perspective

18 · Critical Reception During Brahms's Lifetime

If Brahms's views on his music and the musical world around him emerged only indirectly during his lifetime, the views of others toward him were much more immediate. After the appearance of Schumann's article "Neue Bahnen," Brahms's music began to attract attention. He soon was at the center of a controversy that continued long after his death. Given the consistency of his compositional philosophy, his music quickly became the focus of a much wider aesthetic debate on the nature of musical progress. There were three phases of reception: the gradual emergence of support for the music and positive critical reaction to it in his lifetime, the changing contexts of response in the broader musical world of the twentieth century, and further changes linking the post–World War II period to the present day.

Brahms entered the musical world as a Schumannite, known to the larger public only through Schumann's advocacy. With the publication and performance of his works and his appearances as a pianist, a growing circle of musicians had the chance to form its own opinions. Yet it was only after the publication of the Declaration of 1860 that attitudes toward Brahms's work began to polarize significantly as part of a general change in the musical climate that accompanied the emergence of Liszt's symphonic poems and the wider influence of Wagner's music dramas. In the earlier years a real relationship had existed between artists of different persuasions. Liszt and other supporters of the New German school regularly contributed to the *Neue Zeitschrift für Musik*, which, though founded and first edited by Schumann, was by this time in the hands of Franz Brendel, a strong advocate of Liszt's music. Schumann's 1853 article on Brahms thus

[Schumann's] article

had awakened

mistrust in numerous

circles.

appeared under Brendel's editorship.[1] Yet this represented no threat to Brahms, because Liszt was still supportive of Schumann and viewed his promotion of his young favourites with interest rather than animosity. It was only later in the decade that the *Neue Zeitschrift* effectively became an organ for the Liszt school, and even then Brendel sought to counter the growing antagonism.

Brahms certainly had more to fear from the conservative critics of Leipzig than from the Liszt circle. When the next occasion permitted the meeting of important musicians—in early December 1853, when Berlioz appeared at the Leipzig Gewandhaus—there was every reason for Brahms to attend and to participate in the informal music-making and socializing that accompanied the event. At an *at home* organized by Brendel (and attended by Berlioz) Brahms was persuaded to give the final item in the informal program, his Scherzo in E flat, op. 4, and an "andante" (apparently from the C Major Sonata, op. 1). The tone of a report of the occasion (written independently and sent to the *Neue Zeitschrift für Musik*), clarifies the reaction of his audience and shows the general appreciation of the delicacy of his position: the epigraph continues, "at all events [the article] had created a very difficult situation for the young man, for its justification required the fulfillment of great demands; and when the young, slender blond man appeared . . . few could have suspected the genius that had already created so rich a world in this young nature. . . . And when the young genius . . . presented his scherzo, flashing rushing, sparkling, [and] when afterward his andante swelled toward us in intimate, mournful tones, we all felt: 'Yes, here is a true genius, and Schumann was right.' "[2]

Brahms was further persuaded to give his first public Leipzig performance on 17 December, at one of the David Quartet concerts at the Gewandhaus, at which he again played the Scherzo and his complete Sonata in C Major. Ferdinand Gleich, the critic of the *Neue Zeitschrift für Musik,* a writer sympathetic to the New German school and influential on its behalf in Leipzig, commented:

> It was thought that Schumann had gone too far with his
> inspiring praise. . . . But all doubt has been dispelled by
> Brahms's public appearance, and we concur with all our
> heart and with the warmest satisfaction in Schumann's

opinion of the unassuming and richly endowed young artist. There is something forceful, something transporting in the works Brahms performed on this evening. A ripeness rare in one so young, a creative power springing spontaneously from a rich artistic mind, are revealed in them. We find ourselves in the presence of one of those highly gifted natures, an artist by the grace of God. Some roughnesses and angularities in the outward, very independent form of Brahms's compositions may be overlooked for the sake of the imposing beauty of their conception. His modulations are often of striking and new effect, they are frequently surprising, but always fine and artistically justifiable. Brahms's spirit is in affinity with the genius of Schumann. He will, advancing steadfastly and safely along "new paths," some day become what Schumann has predicted of him, an epoch-making figure in the history of art.[3]

Despite Gleich's sympathetic response, nothing more appeared on Brahms in the *Neue Zeitschrift* until 1855, when Richard Pohl, the pro-Liszt Weimar correspondent of the journal ("Hoplit"), wrote a long article covering the published works opp. 1–9, in which he apologized for the delay in giving them proper attention, admitting his reluctance to set himself against Schumann in disputing their quality. In voicing criticism of Schumann while defining Brahms's individuality, he reveals the emerging fault lines in the assessment of new music:

> Whoever asks the question is soon given the answer that "Brahms is the most talented and original of the Schumannites." Inasmuch as this is true we regret it. . . . Schumann cannot be carried further. . . . His very important individuality quite unquestionably possesses a high value, but only in its originality, not in the imitation. . . . Brahms is [however] no imitator of Schumann. He displays in the whole bent of his nature and creative activity an inner affinity with him which is more than mere sympathy, and has about it nothing forced or borrowed; but he possesses an element not in Schumann which makes

us believe that, if it is only given to him to attain full development, he will find his own paths. . . . The more he succeeds in freeing himself from the characteristic Schumann nature, the more may be looked to from his future. . . . Brahms is not free from Schumann's danger; he, also, has the subtle habit of mind, the tendency to the indefinite and misty, which characterize the romanticists. . . . He shares Schumann's strong faith, moreover, in impulses of genius and inspirations of the moment, to be followed without discrimination or resistance. . . . He sometimes introduces passages . . . which have neither antecedent nor consequence, and which cannot yet properly be called inspired. His work is inconsistent and defective in style. . . . He should have been regarded as an artist not yet mature.[4]

The first major test of Brahms's maturity as a developing composer came with the appearance of the Piano Concerto in D Minor, a work, by its scope and individuality, guaranteed to be controversial. It was first given publicly in Hanover on 22 January 1859 by Brahms, with Joachim and the Court orchestra. An observer of the concert, Dr. Georg Fischer, noted that "with all its serious striving, its complete rejection of triviality and its skilled instrumentation, the work appeared to have been conceived from the depths, yet was still difficult to understand, dry, and even really fatiguing in parts. But despite this, Brahms gave the impression of being a really sterling musician, and it was conceded without reserve that he is not only a virtuoso but a great artist of piano playing."[5] The critic of the *Neue Zeitschrift für Musik* (presumably Gleich) reacted similarly but indicated the larger opposition of most critics and audience members. Acknowledging again his respect for Schumann and for Brahms's disdaining of publicity, the critic wrote, "Notwithstanding its admitted lack of outward effect, we regard the poetic content of the work as an unmistakable sign of original creative power; and, in the face of the belittling criticism of a certain portion of the public and press, we consider it our duty to insist on the admirable sides of the work, and to protest against the not very commendable manner in which judgement has been passed upon it."[6]

When the work was given in Leipzig on 27 January 1859, the critics were harsher. Yet Ferdinand Gleich writing for *Leipziger Tageblatt* was not wholly dismissive. In expressing sympathy for Brahms's aims he also saw the composer as a modern figure in his handling of instruments. But, as with Pohl, reservations persisted.

> The work again suggests a condition of indefiniteness
> and fermentation, a wrestling for a method of expression
> commensurate with the ideas of the composer, which has
> indeed broken though the form of tradition but has not
> yet constructed another sufficiently definite and rounded
> to satisfy the demands of the aesthetics of art. . . . The
> first movement, especially, gives us the impression of
> monstrosity; this was less the case with the two others,
> although even there we were not able, in spite of the
> beauties they contain, to feel real artistic enjoyment.
> Brahms places the orchestra, as far as is possible in a
> concert piece, by the side of the obbligato instrument,
> and by so doing establishes himself as an artist who un-
> derstands the requirements of the new era. The treatment
> of the orchestra shows a blooming fancy and the most
> vivid feeling for new and beautiful tone effects, although
> the composer has not yet sufficient command over his
> means to do justice to his intentions. The work was re-
> ceived calmly, not to say coldly, by the public; we, how-
> ever, must acknowledge the eminent talent of the
> composer, of whom, though he is still too much ab-
> sorbed in his *Sturm und Drang* period, it is not difficult
> to predict the accomplishment of something great.[7]

A colder response came from Eduard Bernsdorff, the critic of the conservative *Leipziger Signale für die musikalische Welt*.

> It is sad but true that new works have had little or no
> success this season. Again at the fourteenth Gewandhaus
> concert . . . a composition was borne to its grave. This
> work, however, could not give pleasure. . . . Save in its se-
> rious intention . . . it has nothing to offer but waste and

barrenness. . . . Its invention is neither attractive nor
agreeable. . . . And for more than three-quarters of an
hour one must endure this rooting and rummaging, this
dragging and drawing, this tearing and patching of
phrases and flourishes! Not only must one take in this
fermenting mass; one must also swallow a dessert of the
shrillest dissonance and most unpleasant sounds. With
deliberate intention, Herr Brahms has made the principal
part in his concerto as uninteresting as possible; it contains no effective treatment of the instrument, no new or
ingenious passages, and wherever something appears
which gives promise of effect, it is immediately crushed
and suffocated by a thick crust of orchestral accompaniment.[8]

The only other major works to receive prominent public performances
by the time Brahms left for Vienna were the Serenade in D Major, op.
11, and the Serenade in A Major, op. 16. The D Major Serenade was first
given in its version for full orchestra on 3 March 1860 in Hamburg and
was received with indifference. Only under Brahms's friend Albert Dietrich at Oldenburg on 14 March 1862 was the work well received, partly
because of the enthusiam of members of the orchestra. "The whole made
the most satisfactory impression and carried the hearers away more and
more, especially from the fourth movement onward, and at the close the
applause reached a pitch of enthusiasm not hitherto experienced here."[9]
The op. 16 serenade, which was considered easier, was received with comparative favor in Brahms's own city on 10 February 1860. By the time
Brahms left for Vienna, the symptoms of increasing alienation between
the New German composers and Brahms's circle were becoming clearer.
The motives behind the Declaration of 1860 now led Brahms to increasing antipathy toward the works of Liszt, and, of equal significance for
musical life, the growing coolness of Joachim toward a musician to whom
he had once been so close.

The Emerging Master: Recognition and Reservation, 1862–76

When Brahms arrived in Vienna in late September 1862 he placed himself
not merely in a much richer musical environment but also in a sharper

critical forum, which was to work both for and against him. While he could hope for more sensitive acknowledgment of his musical aims because of the debt of his own work to Vienna's greatest composers, he could also anticipate the polemic for which the city was famed, not least in response to his North German compositional traits. The most important figure on the critical scene was Eduard Hanslick, the articulate opponent of Wagner and Liszt whose sympathy was vital in building Brahms's support base in Vienna. Hanslick had already widened the debate on the issues of musical meaning and value in 1854 with his book *Vom musikalisch-Schönen* (*On Beauty in Music*), establishing his own credentials as a proponent of "absolute" music. As chief critic of the *Neue Freie Presse* from 1865, his views were to gain force during a career that lasted beyond Brahms's death. But there were many shades of response to the emerging Brahms. Aligned most closely with Hanslick was Karl Eduard Schelle, who wrote for *Die Presse* in Vienna from 1864. He was a "loyal though unbiased supporter of Brahms," in the view of May. Ludwig Speidel, Hanslick's junior at *Die Presse* when Brahms arrived in Vienna, was at first a supporter, but he soon became, in the words of Goldmark, an "implacable enemy." Rudolf Hirsch, who made his debut as a Brahms critic in the *Wiener Zeitung* in 1863 as successor to Schelle, was an opponent from the start. The range of critics involved would widen with the growing musical debate.[10]

Hanslick had a special interest in Brahms, having followed his progress since their first meeting in 1856. He was present at Brahms's first appearances in Vienna, as pianist in his op. 25 piano quartet at a Hellmesberger Quartet concert at the Gesellschaft der Musikfreunde on 16 November 1862, and as soloist in his op. 24 variations on 29 November. As Hanslick observes, Brahms was effectively a stranger to the concertgoing public on his arrival in the city. "Of his larger works, not a single one had been heard previously in Vienna," and of the smaller pieces, only the (unpublished) series of Hungarian Dances had been introduced by Clara Schumann.[11] Hanslick's perspective was of Brahms as a Schumannite who had worked steadily over the years from his earliest piano works and songs up to the two substantial piano quartets and op. 24 variations, yet still remained something of a mystery. "Brahms's compositions hardly belong among those immediately enlightening and gripping works which carry the listener along with them in their flight. Their esoteric character, disdainful of popular effect, combined with their great technical difficulties make their popularization a much slower process than would have been expected after the delightful prophecy Schumann gave his favourite as a parting blessing. . . . From the two exuberant piano sonatas to the F sharp minor variations and since then to the piano quartets and Handel-Variations what progress there has been in the free secure command of technique and what a gain in self-control and formal clarity!" Hanslick conceived the connection as an essentially spiritual link, and he sets himself against Pohl's evaluation of 1855, though observing similar traits:

> Brahms is a significant figure of the present time, possibly the most interesting among our contemporary composers. In form and character he is closest to Schumann, though rather in the sense of an inner relationship than of actual formal modeling. . . . His music and Schumann's have in common above all purity and inner nobility. There is no seeking after applause in Brahms's music, no narcissistic affectation. Everything is sincere and truthful. With Schumann's music it shares to the point of stubbornness a sovereign subjectivity, the tendency to brood, the turning away from the outer world, the introspection far exceeded by Schumann in fullness and beauty of melodic ideas. Brahms often matches him in wealth of purely formal shaping. This is his greatest strength; the imaginative modernization of canon and fugue he has from Schumann. . . . His talent has thus far found variation the most congenial form. It requires above all richness of formal shaping and consistency of mood, which are just his most decisive virtues.[12]

But Hanslick also saw Brahms as standing at the parting of the ways, for he already viewed his development in relation to the trends that had prompted his own writings on absolute and programmatic music. Thus he still posed a problem for Hanslick:

> One cannot speak here of a beginner. But it is precisely in Brahms's latest works that one encounters question marks and puzzle-pictures that will be resolved only in

his next creative period. The solution will be decisive. Will his originality of invention and melodic power keep in step with the ultimate development of his harmonic and contrapuntal art? Will the natural freshness and youthfulness of his first works continue to bloom untroubled in the costly vase he has now created for them, indeed unfold even more beautifully and freely? Does the veil of brooding reflection which so frequently clouds his newest works presage a sudden burst of sunlight, or a thicker, less hospitable twilight? The future, the very near future will tell.[13]

In truth, Hanslick's admiration for Brahms yielded to love only in the most accessible works, or aspects of larger works. The more technically complex or ambiguous aspects of Brahms's language did not please him. Only in such classically oriented works as B flat Sextet and the serenades was he free of Hanslick's reservations. Given first in Vienna on 27 December 1863 by the augmented Hellmesberger Quartet, the Sextet was to be Brahms's first truly popular extended work. Hanslick responded that the work was conceived in that "clear, easily moving, inwardly blissful mood which is so winning in the D Major Serenade." Likewise of the A Major Serenade, given in Vienna on 8 March 1863 by the Philharmonic orchestra under Otto Dessoff; he later commented that the work is the "younger, tender sister of the serenade in D recently produced at the Gesellschaft der Musikfreunde. It is conceived in essentially the same peaceful, pleasurable dreamy garden mood."[14]

Hanslick's open support of Brahms inevitably attracted attention. Carl Goldmark recalls how the chief editor of *Die Neue Freie Presse* called in the critic Ludwig Speidel to confirm that Brahms was indeed a composer worthy of such praise.[15] But the resistance by many Viennese musicians to the novel aspects of Brahms's music (which had already manifested itself in open opposition by some members of the Philharmonic orchestra to rehearsal of the A Major Serenade for the 8 March performance) continued in subsequent reviews of his new works.[16] Even as accessible a work as the G Major Sextet drew reservations from Eduard Schelle when it was given by the augmented Hellmesberger Quartet in 1867: "The composer was certainly called for and applauded . . . but it was with a certain reserve. One felt distinctly that the public was not carried away by the work, but desired to do justice to so admirable an achievement. ... Brahms may be called a virtuoso in the modern development of the quartet style ... but only that can reach the heart which proceeds from the heart, and the Sextet comes from the hand and the head, whilst the warm pulsations of the heart are to be felt only at intervals."[17] As early as 1863, Hirsch, reviewing the op. 16 serenade in the *Wiener Zeitung,* could find nothing better to say of the work than that it should please those who were content with "modest gifts": "Brahms should be on his guard against excess of things. The exorbitant applause raised by his friends had the effect of procuring him very loud hisses from other parties." He retained this view in 1867 when commenting on the G Major Sextet: "We are always seized with a kind of oppression when the new John in the wilderness, Herr Johannes Brahms, announces himself. This prophet ... who ... has his energetic admirers in Vienna ... makes us quite disconsolate [with effects] that have neither body nor soul and can only be products of the most desperate effort. Such manifest, glaring artificiality is quite peculiar to this gentlemen."[18]

Alongside these varied criticisms were more lengthy and reasoned examinations of the music as published. The first complete survey of Brahms's work to appear in print was the series of articles by Adolf Schubring that appeared in *Neue Zeitschrift für Musik* in 1862. It was the most important part of a series, entitled "Schumanniana," commissioned by Brendel in 1860–62 on the pupils of Schumann.[19] Schubring was clearly sensitive to the lack of focus in the reactions to Brahms's music, partly because of Schumann's public claims and partly through the "musical fragmentation" that he noted in German musical life. He set about examining Brahms as a Schumannite, surveying the output from op. 1 to op. 18, the latter having just appeared in print. He divides the works into three groups: opp. 1–6, 7–10, and 11–18. His greatest preoccupation is with thematic process (*Thematische Arbeit*), a major feature of the Viennese classical tradition. Yet Schubring does not see Brahms as a mere epigone; other factors are at work. In the C Major Sonata, op. 1, one

> sees that Brahms is using the old thematic art of Haydn
> and Beethoven, and yet his work makes a thoroughly dif-
> ferent impression from theirs. Through the ascent of the

imitation even up to the seventh, the ninth, and the eleventh, it possesses an unusual character, the double counterpoint becoming ponderous and bloated through the addition of filler voices, or at least losing that transparent ease which alone is suitable to the nature of arabesques. And since Brahms has already employed the most natural and pleasing of his thematic intricacies in the first part, he must often have recourse to forceful and rough sonorities in order to bring about the necessary intensification in the development. Thus, especially in the development, . . . he has repeatedly overstepped the limits of beauty, and thus it has happened that in his first sonata movement Brahms has provided us with a truly magnificent and original, yet overloaded image, full of glaring contrast."

Schubring perceives a gradual clarification from the ferment of the early works through his analysis of the motivic working. Highly significant is his relating of Brahms in the last works to Beethoven, as well as Schumann, unusual by this date. It is only through his boundless confidence in Brahms's right to stand beside these composers that he can be so blunt in his comments on reception of the music achieved in the period 1854–61. "After seven years of work . . . to acquire the rich heritage of Beethoven and Schumann is truly worth the sweat of nobles."[20]

For Hanslick, however, it was not so much the working as the ideas themselves that called forth comment.

> Less admirable was the effect of the Piano Quartet in A.
> First, the themes are insignificant. In a number of cases,
> Brahms prefers themes whose contrapuntal capacity is far
> greater than their inner content. The themes of this
> quartet sound dry and flat. In the course of events they
> are given a wealth of inspired derivatives, but the effect-
> iveness of the whole is impossible without significant
> themes. Then too we miss the continuous stream of de-
> velopment. There is a continual pulling together and tak-
> ing apart, preparation without object, promise without
> fulfillment. In each of the movements we find incidental

episodic motives, but none which could carry the whole piece. . . . The Piano Quartet and other of Brahms's more recent works unhappily suggest Schumann's last period, just as his earliest works are reminiscent of Schumann's first period. Only for Schumann' s crystal clear, ripe middle period has his favorite pupil thus far offered us no companion piece.[21]

Interpretation of the kind of composer Brahms was and wherein lay his destiny was still wide open five years after his arrival in Vienna. It was with the completion of *A German Requiem* and eventually the First Symphony—premiered, respectively, in 1868 and 1876—that the measure of his technical achievement became clearer. With these works reactions sharpened between Brahms's adherents, led by Hanslick, who increasingly presented him as a custodian of traditional values, and the New Germans, who saw him as reactionary. Though rumors of a Brahms symphony in preparation had circulated since 1862, it was a work of a very different kind that came to fruition by 1868, though it reflected equally clear aspects of its composer's lineage: the preoccupation with choral music, which his Viennese audiences had come to know during his period as conductor of the Singakademie in 1863–64. The work was first made known in performance in incomplete form, when movements 1–3 were sung by the Singverein at a concert in memory of Schubert on 1 December 1867. Hanslick's response concerning technique and expression was largely unequivocal: "a work of unusual significance and great mastery, one of the ripest fruits to have emerged from the style of later Beethoven in the field of sacred music. . . . [Yet] the harmonic and contrapuntal art learnt by Brahms in the school of Bach and inspired by him with the living breath of the present, almost recedes for the listener behind the mounting expression from touching lament to annihilating death shudder [in the funeral march of the second movement]." Schelle found the first and second movements acceptable, but not the third: "Unfortunately, the third is extremely inferior . . . ; the text demanded a strong increase of effect, which the composer has been incapable of giving. The bass solo is not written gratefully for the voice, and there is much that is obtrusively bizarre and unedifying in the chorus. . . . The movement was a failure." Hirsch, in the *Wiener Zeitung,* gave the work a polemical emphasis, noting of the audience reactions that "in the interest of truth" the opposition party was in the majority.[22]

Important as the *Requiem* was for Brahms's creative development and professional status, Brahms's first symphony was to be a much more controversial work in political terms. It appeared in November 1876, the year of the first complete performance of Wagner's *Ring of the Niebelung*, and thus assumed added significance as an expression of Brahms's dedication to the symphonic tradition. As a symphony gathering together so many traditional features in such a masterly synthesis it provided an obvious context for debate and was more widely reviewed than any other of his works to date. Hanslick wrote with inside knowledge of.the years of preparation, noting Brahms's hesitation to produce his string quartets or a symphony and stressing his unwillingness to pander to popular taste, his unconcern for popular effects leaving, for Hanslick, the third movement "without charm." Respect for Brahms's aspirations was unanimous, showing that the composer had become a custodian of severe and rigorous approaches to composition. A lineage from Beethoven is now observed by all critics, and all cite a relationship between the main theme of the finale and that of Beethoven's *Freude* theme in the Ninth Symphony. For Hanslick the consequence was of mixed value, since he did not really warm to the result.

> If I say that no composer has come as close to Beethoven as Brahms in this finale, I don't mean it as a paradoxical pronouncement, but rather as a simple statement of indisputable fact. . . . Neither Mendelssohn nor Schumann approaches the late Beethoven in their symphonies. Beethoven's Third Period is not a prerequisite for their symphonies. Brahms quartets and the symphony, on the other hand, could not have been had it not been for Beethoven's last period. . . . Thus Brahms recalls Beethoven's style not only in his individually spiritual and transcendental expression, through the beautiful breadth of his melodies, the daring and originality of his modulations, and his sense of polyphonic structure, but also and above all in the manly and noble seriousness of the whole. . . . This strongly ethical character of Beethoven's

music, which is serious even in merriment . . . is also decidedly evident in Brahms. In the latter's newest works there is also a good deal of the late Beethoven's darker side. Beethoven's style toward the end was often unclear, confused, and arbitrary, and his subjectivity often descended into an ill-humored, brooding character. The beautiful clarity, the melodic charm, the estimable popularity of the first and second periods vanished. . . . Brahms seems to favor too one-sidedly the great and the serious, the difficult and complex, at the expense of sensuous beauty. We would often give the finest contrapuntal devices (and they lie bedded away in the symphony by the dozen) for moments of heart-warming sunshine.

Hanslick identifies three elements as aspects of this concentration: "which all play a great role in modern German music—for which Brahms has a conspicuous predilection: syncopation, suspension and the simultaneous employment of different types of rhythms. In these three points, and in particular regard to syncopation, he can hardly go further than he has recently gone."[23]

The sense that in this work Brahms had come to the end of a course of development rooted in Beethoven recurs widely. For Richard Pohl, the Ninth Symphony was the inevitable starting point. "That Brahms, who has established altogether the firmest direct link to Beethoven, would also sympathetically tend that way in the symphony too, was foreseeable; but which way he will now turn in his second symphony which is sure to come, we are all the more keen to find out after the impression of the first."[24] Friedrich Chrysander addressed the issue of the medium.

The reference to Beethoven, the linkage to the . . . Ninth is so obvious that we must presume it, with an artist like Brahms, not to be feeble, unproductive imitation, but conscious intention. And it is precisely this intention, this artistic will that invests the work with its historical significance. What is involved here is the problem of how to produce counterpart that can, without the aid of the human voice, match the manner and strength of the

Ninth Symphony. And insofar as this attempt has succeeded, it therefore signifies an attempt to lead back
from the symphony composed of instruments and voice
to the purely instrumental symphony. At the same time
it signifies an expansion of those effects that can be generated through purely instrumental means.[25]

Just how wide was the acceptance of the work is clear from the reaction
of the critic of the *Leipziger Nachrichten,* Alfred Dörfell, showing Brahms's
increasing support base in a city of which he was still very wary. Indeed,
he reveals a wider sympathy for the work as a whole:

Its effect on the audience was the most intense that has
been produced by any new symphony within our remembrance. Schumann in his time did not obtain such.
The composition is to be viewed and measured from the
standpoint of Beethoven's Ninth and of Schumann's Second symphony. To reach it, Brahms, well equipped and
daring spirit as he is, goes his own way. He is [as] great
in attack as his two predecessors and has the same wide
vision over the domain of spiritual-human existence. . . .
As regards uninterrupted energy of creative power, we
would give the palm to the first movement; the second,
with its fervor and longing, accords with it. To the third
we should gladly have listened longer. It supplied a counterpoise of sentiment to what had gone before which had
not been maintained long enough when the movement
closed. Of the finale we would almost venture to surmise
that it gave the composer the most trouble. Here he re-
linquishes his independence and flies to Beethoven in order to get new force for his climax. We do not regard
the resort to Beethoven as accidental but believe the
composer to have been well aware of it. He came, however, to one over whom he could not prevail.[26]

It is interesting that Brahms's chief opponent in Vienna, Hirsch, was
not drawn to criticize this link. Though still claiming that before the
finale "there is nothing that can be admired without reserve," he notes

that "with sure step . . . that reminds one of the majesty of Beethoven, the finale strides out . . . as a man who would get rid of pain by nerving himself to action. With the entry of the chorale the hearer experiences a sensation of brightness as at the rising of the sun after a night of sorrow. . . . Here is a truly great artistic achievement, the value of which is but slightly prejudiced by the consideration that the 'joy' theme has an un-mistakable resemblance as of son to father to that of the 'ninth Symphony.' "[27]

The Mature Master in Symphonies and Chamber Works, 1877–90

The successful reception of the First Symphony inevitably served as a focus of controversy, both as regards the future of Brahms's music and his place in modern music. Added to this, his prominent position in Viennese musical life, which had recently included the directorship of the Gesellschaft der Musikfreunde, made him the object of increasing opposition by those who saw his works as embodying a new musical orthodoxy. After so long a period of preparation for the First Symphony, Brahms's major orchestral works were now to follow regularly. The Second Symphony appeared in the following year, 1878. For Hanslick it was to be welcomed without reserve because it displayed many of the qualities of accessibility that he prized:

> This novelty was a great, unqualified success. Seldom has
> there been such a warm public expression of pleasure in
> a new composition. Brahms's Symphony No. 1, intro-
> duced a year ago, was a work for earnest connoisseurs . . .
> capable of pursuit of its minutely ramified excursions.
> The Symphony No. 2 shines like the warming sun on
> connoisseurs and laymen alike and it belongs to all those
> who long for good music, whether they are capable of
> grasping the most difficult music or not. . . . Among
> Brahms's compositions the closest to it in style and
> mood is the Sextet in B flat, the most popular of all his
> instrumental works—so popular indeed that subsequent
> complicated quartets have subsisted on its popularity.
> The new symphony is radiant with healthy freshness and
> clarity. It is readily intelligible, though it offers plenty to

listen to and think about. There is much in it that is new, yet nothing of the unfortunate contemporary tendency to emphasize novelty in the sense of the unprecedented. Nor are there any furtive glances towards foreign artistic fields, nor any shamefaced, even impudent begging from poetry or painting. It is all purely musical in conception and structure and purely musical in effect. It provides irrefutable proof that one (though not everyone to be sure) can still write symphonies after Beethoven and moreover in the old forms and on the old foundations.[28]

Hanslick could not refrain from drawing the two symphonies into the controversy with Wagner.

Richard Wagner and his disciples go so far as to not only deny the possibility of writing symphonies after Beethoven, but also the justification for the existence of purely instrumental music altogether. The symphony has become superfluous since Wagner transplanted it into the opera. The utmost concession is to admit the contemporary viability of Liszt's "symphonic poems" in one movement and with specifically poetic programs. This nonsensical theory has been cooked up for the domestic requirements of the Wagner-Liszt household. If any further contradiction is needed, there is none more brilliant than the long succession of Brahms's instrumental works, and particularly this second symphony. Its essential characteristic can best be defined as serene cheerfulness, at once manly and gentle, animated alternately on the one hand by pleased good humor and on the other by reflective seriousness. . . . The finale . . . is a far cry from the stormy finales of the modern school. Mozartian blood flows in its veins.[29]

But for Brahms's Leipzig supporter Dörfell, the change in character had the opposite effect. "The Viennese . . . are much more easily satisfied than we. We make quite different demands on Brahms, and require from him music which is something more than 'pretty' and 'very pretty' when he comes before us as a symphonist. Not that we do not wish to hear from him in his complaisant moods, not that we disdain to accept from him pictures of real life, but we always desire to contemplate his genius, whether he displays it in a manner of his own or depends on that of Beethoven. We have not discovered genius in the new symphony. . . . [Had we not known it was by Brahms] we should have recognized the great mastery of form, the extremely skillful handling of material, the conspicuous power of construction in short, which it displays, but we should not have described it as preeminently distinguished by inventive power."[30]

Hanslick, however, grew successively more pleased as the works seemed to reflect his values and taste; he now places them in the context of Beethoven's middle period:

> The Symphony No. 3 is really something new. It repeats
> neither the anguished song of destiny of the first nor the
> cheerful idyll of the second. Its prevailing mood is of self-
> confident, enterprising strength. The heroic element has
> nothing to do with anything military, nor does it lead to
> anything tragic, such as the funeral march of the *Eroica*.
> Its musical characteristics recall the healthy soundness of
> Beethoven's second period, never the strangeness of the
> last. And here and there are suggestions of the romantic
> twilight of Schumann and Mendelssohn. . . . For all their
> fundamental differences, Brahms's first and third sym-
> phonies are similar in one important respect; their re-
> spective middle movements appear rather too small-scaled
> in content as well as in extent for the imposing move-
> ments that adjoin them. The finale . . . is again an
> achievement of the first order. . . . The theme itself is not
> impressive, but immediately experiences the most aston-
> ishing development. . . . The orchestration is richer in
> novel and charming combinations than the earlier works.
> In ingenious modulations it is equal to the best of
> Brahms's works; and in the free association of contrary
> rhythms, of which Brahms is so fond and of which he is

such a master, it has the virtue of not seeking effects at the cost of intelligibility.[31]

The Fourth Symphony was more of a challenge for Hanslick, but his admiration for what it represented remained unreserved.

> What symphony of the past thirty or forty years is even remotely comparable with those of Brahms? Yet more symphonies are being composed these days than is generally appreciated. The . . . *Leipziger Signale* lists no fewer than nineteen performed for the first time last year. It looks as though Brahms's suggestions have stimulated production following the long silence that set in after Mendelssohn and Schumann. But not every pretty talent with a few piano pieces and songs ought to enter the field. The symphony demands complete mastery. It is the instrumental composer's severest test and his highest calling. Brahms is unique. . . . All [these virtues] are abundantly present in the Fourth Symphony. Indeed they even seem to have gained stature, not in melodic invention, perhaps, but certainly in the art of realization. . . . Independent of any direct model, they nowhere deny their ideal relation to Beethoven, a factor incomparably more obvious with Brahms than with Schumann. . . . There is no other modern work so productive to the musician as an object for study. [The] finale is like a dark well. The longer we gaze into it the more brightly the stars shine back.[32]

The extent of this support even exceeded that of others in Brahms's closest circle, Kalbeck proposing to him that he replace the variation finale with something more conventional.[33]

The Third and Fourth Symphonies appeared after Wagner's death. By this time an insurmountable barrier had developed between the adherents of Brahms and of Wagner. It had been growing ever since the publication of the Declaration, though at this time it prompted no significant response from other composers because Brahms was not yet a figure of international renown but an interesting and difficult new talent who had hitherto kept his thoughts private. Yet the ground had been prepared. Against the mounting literature and propaganda of Liszt and Wagner (Hanslick commented that their views "had the force of military commands") Brahms was placing nothing other than an increasingly powerful body of extended instrumental music whose presence denied the claims of the Music of the Future. Clearly a confrontation would emerge.

A confrontation did not arise with Liszt, who remained largely silent with regard to Brahms, despite the attacks of his adherents. His references were respectful and muted, and he clearly saw Brahms as worthy but as an unimportant epigone of the classics. But it was more difficult with Wagner. After the publication of the Declaration, Wagner's antipathy toward Brahms grew steadily, though it was not immediately apparent. Wagner was present at one of Brahms's early Vienna appearances, as shown, commenting that the op. 24 variations demonstrated "what could still be done in the old forms when someone comes along who knows how to handle them."[34] But by the late 1860s Wagner was commenting in the article "On Conducting," with obvious reference to Brahms, on the "intrinsic weakness of variation form as a structural principle, [wherein] strongly contrasted parts are placed side by side without link or reconciliation." The title *A German Requiem* was also an apparent irritant to Wagner in its implicit claim to a specifically German form of expression, and many comments in Cosima Wagner's diaries show a disparaging attitude toward Brahms as the latter gained prominence. Wagner never accepted the significance of Brahms's achievements within the sphere of the symphony, rather classing him as a mere "composer," as in the article "On Poetry and Composition" in June 1879: "Compose, compose, even when you have no ideas. Why is it called 'composing,' a putting together—if invention too is considered unnecessary. . . . I know a famous composer you can meet at concert masquerades, today in a ballad singer's disguise, . . . tomorrow in Handel's Hallelujah wig, another time as a Jewish Czardas player, and then again as a genuine symphonist decked out as No. 10" (references to *The Song of Triumph,* the Hungarian Dances, and the First Symphony, as designated by Bülow). For the Second Symphony Cosima Wagner's diary records Richard Wagner accusing Brahms of echoing Johann Strauss: "The symphony, with all its triviality blown up by orchestral effects, its tremolando theme, which might have come from the introduction to a Strauss waltz, we find utterly shocking."[35]

Wagner's criticism of Brahms went beyond the purely musical. He disdained the society that provided Brahms's work with such support. Brahms appealed to a highly educated liberal class whose strong musical cultivation emphasized musical knowledge, whether of the music of the past or of the intricacies of complex chamber music that was so often played in the homes of the educated. The achievements of Brahms were seen as analogous to those of the leading scientists and scholars who were his friends. But the music of Wagner, with its theatrical conception, symbolic meanings, and, for Brahms, frequently crude textual rhythms, belonged in a much more populist world of historical romanticism. But by the 1880s the dominance of Brahms's class was under threat. A populist and nationalist political movement that included open anti-Semitism was developing in Vienna. By 1897 it would lead to the election of Mayor Karl Lueger partly on an anti-Semitic agenda. It is against this political background that the remarkable animosity of the musical polemics of the last two decades of Brahms's life can better be understood.[36]

The intense opposition to Brahms manifested itself in association with two very different composers: Hugo Wolf and Anton Bruckner. The later extremes of Wolf's criticisms of Brahms are partly to be attributed to personal factors. His desire to study with Brahms indicates an admiration of the music—he especially liked the String Sextet in G and the Alto Rhapsody—and he wrote a prose poem about the F Major Quintet:

> The imagination of the composer revels in picturesque
> images; we find no trace of the frosty November mists
> that elsewhere brood over his compositions and stifle
> each warm tone from the heart before it can sound out—
> all is sunny, now brighter, now more dim; a magical em-
> erald green is diffused over this fairy-like picture of
> spring; everything grows green and buds, one really hears
> the grass growing—nature is so mysterious, so solemnly
> still, so blissfully transfigured—the composer could only
> by a sudden effort of will withdraw himself from this
> magic, so closely did the muse hold him under her spell.
> In the second movement the shadows sink lower. Eve-
> ning, and then night, shroud the fantastic creation that
> moved so wonderfully in the first movement. Deep med-

itation and silence. An animated form moves through the
deep solitude. It is as though glow-worms danced their
rounds, it flashes and sparkles so in the rushing figures of
the instruments. But the form disappears. The former silence returns, to be once again broken by a similar motive. In strange harmonies, that modulate between dream
and waking, this mysterious tone picture dies away.

But Wolf's receptivity to Brahms did not last, for "with a jerk [Brahms]
is sitting on the school bench at Altona and recalls in the finale with
much gladness his contrapuntal studies under Marxsen, whither, however,
we have no desire to follow him."[37]

Whenever Brahms displayed his constructive rather than purely poetic
skills, Wolf reacted. Thus, of the "St. Antoni" Variations and Fourth
Symphony, he wrote that "Brahms's variations . . . bear eloquent witness
to his peculiar gift of artistic manufacture. Herr Brahms understands the
variation of given themes better than anyone else. His whole works are
nothing but a great variation upon the works of Beethoven, Mendelssohn,
and Schumann. Striking is the crab-like retrogression of Brahms's productions. He has to be sure never been able to raise himself above the
level of mediocrity, but such nullity, emptiness and hypocrisy as prevail
in the E Minor Symphony have come to light in no other of his works.
The art of composing without ideas has decidedly found its most worthy
representative in Brahms." For Wolf, the true successor of Beethoven in
the symphonic realm was Liszt. Thus he responds to Brahms's Third
Symphony:

> As a symphony of Herr Dr. Johannes Brahms it is to
> some extent a capable, meritorious work; as a symphony
> of a second Beethoven it is a complete failure, since one
> must ask of a second Beethoven all that which is lacking
> in a Dr. Johannes Brahms—originality. Brahms is the ep-
> igone of Schumann and Mendelssohn, and as such [he]
> exercises about as much influence on the course of the
> history of art as the late Robert Volkmann, . . . which is
> to say, *no* influence at all. He [Brahms] is a proficient
> musician who knows his counterpoint, to whom occur
> ideas now and then good, occasionally excellent, now

and then bad, here and there familiar, and frequently no ideas at all. . . . Schumann, Chopin, Berlioz, and Liszt, the leaders of the revolutionary movement in music since Beethoven . . . have passed by our symphonist without trace; he was, or pretended to be, blind as the eyes of astonished mankind opened and overflowed before the radiant genius of Wagner, as Wagner, like Napoleon, borne on the waves of the revolution, led them into new channels by his despotic power, created order, and performed deeds that will live on eternally in the memory of mankind. But the man who has written three symphonies and apparently intends a further six to follow these cannot be affected by such a phenomenon, for he is only a relic from primeval ages and no vital part of the great stream of time. . . . As in those days people danced minuets, i.e., wrote symphonies, so Herr Brahms also writes symphonies, whatever may have happened meanwhile. He comes like a departed spirit back to his home, [staggering] up the rickety staircase.[38]

But by the time of Wagner's death the symphony was back on the agenda of modern composition, and Brahms's role in putting it there led the Wagnerians in Vienna to champion the cause of Bruckner partly in order to oppose him. Though Bruckner, who was nine years Brahms's senior and had produced his first symphony in 1860, must have had much resentment toward Brahms for the latter's influence in Vienna, he did not attempt to respond to the disparaging comments that had come from the Brahms circle. Rather, the battle was carried on by the supporters, Hanslick, Kalbeck, and others on the Brahms side representing the liberal papers and Theodor Helm of the *Deutsche Zeitung,* Hans Paumgartner of the *Wiener Abendpost,* and August Göllerich of the *Deutsches Volksblatt.*[39] Helm criticized Brahms more for his connection with the liberals than for his music, as in his criticism of the revision of the B Major Trio. "What stood there earlier . . . seemed to us the direct outpouring of a passionate youth's heart; what stands there now has been dictated by the technical artistic understanding of one who has since become a master but also a much more coolly thinking man." The 1890 premiere of the op. III String Quintet stimulated similar responses: "ingenious, full of interesting details. . . . Nevertheless, this creation of Brahms also bears the cool reflecting trait shared by Brahms, even if his faction conducted itself in the most enthusiastic manner. But enthusiasm is the very feeling that Brahms never arouses. The themes, although treated so effectively and elaborately, seem nonetheless more and more thought rather than felt, more constructed than discovered. One is so seldom in one's innermost soul touched by Brahms." A more pointed response was that of Göllerich, who criticized the accessible style of the Third Symphony. "One of the cleverest critics in Vienna [Ludwig Speidel], in an ingeniously appropriate way writes that when Brahms wants to be popular, he displays a kind of 'desperate naiveté.' We were reminded again of this choice expression while listening to the Andante of the [Third] Symphony—what wretched barrenness of ideas reigns in this *Zampa*-like movement, which does not even disdain the use of Jewish temple triplets simply to appear properly 'understandable.' "[40]

The Perspective of the 1890s

By the last years of Brahms's life the context of criticism was changing, especially for the younger generation. Dramatic music had not displaced instrumental music, and young composers had grown to maturity with the musical languages of Brahms and Wagner at the forefront of their experience. Some sober judgments indicate the different values that inspired support for the two traditions. On one side were the scholar Philipp Spitta and young critic Heinrich Schenker, and on the other was the Wagnerian conductor Felix Weingartner. Music scholars naturally were particularly admiring of Brahms's achievements. Spitta wrote in 1892:

> The musical politicians of our day call [Brahms] a reactionary. . . . Others say that Brahms demonstrates practically all that in these [that is, classical] forms something new can "still" be said. Not "still," but always—so long as our music remains will this be the case. For these forms are derived from the very inner nature of this music, and their outlines could not have been more perfectly conceived. Even those composers who think that they have broken them, and thereby have accomplished

an act of liberation, avail themselves of these forms insofar as they still have any desire at all to achieve a satisfying impression. They cannot do otherwise so long as
statement and contrast in music remain. They only do it
much worse than does he who enters into the inheritance from the past with full awareness and with the intention of employing it in the service of the beautiful.
Power, of course, is required: moreover, many ways lead
to the shrine. Weber and Schubert, Schumann and Gade
have in many ways loosened Beethoven's firm construction and are, in the matter of musical architectonics, unquestionably lesser masters. They seek to make up for
this deficiency through other, magnificent characteristics;
and no one for whom music is more than a mere sort of
arithmetic will be so pedantic as to look askance at their
weaknesses. But the assumption that their willfulness is
the signpost to new and higher goals is false. The foundations must remain fixed, and each one builds upon
them according to his needs. After Brahms, others will
come who will compose in ways other than his. His en-
deavor was toward concentration and indissolubly firm
integration, using all the means that are proper to the art
of music as such.[41]

Brahms's mastery of the symphonic and instrumental tradition had
particular significance for musical analysts. There is no clearer reflection
of the themes of the criticism offered during Brahms's lifetime than in
the obituary by Heinrich Schenker.

The moral of Brahms's works can be expressed more or
less as follows. Above all he proved that absolute music
must not be regarded as a territory that has been perma-
nently forfeited. It is true of course that Beethoven de-
marcated the boundaries of this territory, and his reign
was a veritable golden age, which will never come again;
but Schubert, Mendelssohn, and Schumann showed that
freedom of expression was still possible in the land of
Beethoven. All that is necessary . . . is the sense of one's

own individuality and a determination to make use of one's freedom of thought. . . . Brahms's chamber works will always preserve their immortality alongside Beethoven's. His quartets, quintets, and sextets, which brought him his great success, will soon have a second, even more beautiful service to perform for their creator. Brahms, like Haydn, Mozart, Schumann, and every other great figure of his art, will soon be numbered among the masters of the purest, most innocent simplicity, and the most beautiful melody. In place of the slanderous image of Brahms "the Brooder," which has been current in the recent past will appear that of a rapturous magician of melody—a Mozart of our time. It is now the task of his chamber music to awaken this feeling in the public. It was insufficiently appreciated during his lifetime how simple and melodious he is. Now everyone will have to see. . . . Some will say "he has also rejected our own time: one should not be allowed to flirt with old forms in a post-Beethoven symphony." And, yes, in a certain sense those who say this are correct. But nonetheless one has to admire the master's intelligence and instinct in this regard; since he found no dramatic subject to present from his own life, and knew in the long run that he lacked Beethoven's power to create symphonic peripeteia and catastrophe, he preferred to modernize older forms with an unerring and surpassing sense, rather than seeking from perplexity and pathological ambition to feign and stutter out symphonic magnitude like, for instance, Bruckner.[42]

But for Weingartner, such values were not by themselves convincing in the face of expressive limitations he found in Brahms: "Taken together [it is] I might say scientific music, composed of sonorous forms and phrases; it is not the language of humanity, mysterious, but still infinitely expressive and comprehensible; it is not the language which the great masters knew how to speak, and did; the language, in fact, which moves and stirs us up to the depth of our being, because [in it] we recognize our own joys and sorrows, our struggles and our victories. [Such] music is artistic [while Brahms's music] is artificial."

He also found Brahms to overwork certain devices in maturity, notably the use of triplets and syncopations. Yet in his change of heart in later years, in which he found a power of expression comparable with Wagner, Weingartner typified a reassessment observable in other critics: an initial perception of formalism yielding to a later appreciation of the musical content. He appreciated Brahms's importance when he met the composer in 1896 and pleased him with a performance of the Second Symphony. But though even then very fond of that piece, "I had obstinately hardened my heart against many of [Brahms's] works. I still saw in Brahms the man who had been destined to overthrow Wagner. I had not yet freed myself sufficiently from the spell of the Bayreuth magician to meet without embarrassment his great opposite number, though as a matter of fact, Brahms was nothing of the kind."[43]

Brahms Abroad

Brahms's music, with its distinctively German forms and techniques, traveled less easily than Wagner's music, which was of interest to wider audiences than the purely musical, not least in France. Brahms's impact on France would be insignificant until well into the twentieth century. During his lifetime Brahms's music traveled easily to German-speaking Switzerland and to Holland, where it had devoted supporters in influential positions. But these apart, it traveled chiefly to Great Britain and America, with their more extensive concert activity, still dominated in the later nineteenth century by émigré German musicians. Though considered difficult at first, Brahms's music found its greatest foreign markets in Britain and America. Brahms's friends traveled regularly to Britain to perform the music, and they helped to establish a strong support base. Brahms himself never took up repeated invitations to him to visit. The numerous German-trained performers and composers who settled in America took with them a Brahmsian tradition that formed a part of the country's rapidly developing instrumental and symphonic culture.

Indeed, credit for the first performance outside Germany of Brahms's first chamber work goes to America. In 1855 the Trio in B Major, op. 8, was performed by William Mason, a pupil of Liszt, in New York on 27

November at Dodsworth's Hall; the other players were Theodor Thomas and Carl Bergmann. In contrast, England heard only two unpublished minor piano pieces in a recital by Clara Schumann earlier in the same year at the Hanover Square Rooms.[44] It was in New York that the first orchestral work received a performance outside Germany; in February 1862, the second Serenade was given at the Philharmonic Society by Carl Bergmann. America prided itself on coming to terms with Brahms much sooner than England did, and a report, noted disparagingly in the *Musical Times*, stated that "in an English musical magazine [itself], Brahms's beautiful Variations for orchestra on Haydn's Choral St. Antoni should have been spoken of as a 'weariness to the flesh.' . . . 'Well, well! The British music writers are getting along, but it's slow work, my masters, slow work. Some day they will reach Tchaikowsky." The *Musical Times* responded: "For the information of American musicians and journalists generally we make this an opportunity for saying that as all English musicians and critics of standing have long ago recognized the genius of Brahms (this does not mean that he is fanatically worshipped nor that his faults are ignored), it is considered a sign of independence by a certain small clique of writers in this country to systematically attack that composer whenever it is possible to do so."[45]

Resistance in Britain is emphasized by the fact that only the adventurous German conductor August Manns performed an orchestral work by Brahms in the 1860s (at the Crystal Palace), but he presented it only in part (three movements of the Serenade in D Major in 1863). The prevailing attitude is clear from the reaction expressed in the first important article on Brahms—which was prompted by an article in the *Nieder-Rheinische Musik-Zeitung*—published in *The Musical World* on Brahms's birthday, 7 May 1864. It chides German critics for their too easy acceptance of Schumann's praise of Brahms, echoing the more conservative of their reactions. The critic writes that "it struck me that the composer's talent was wrapped up in, and smothered by, the fearful confusion of tone from all the four instruments, played together without calm, without cessation, and without any light spots of melody, that it is nearly impossible for anyone to think of comprehending the works as a whole, far less of having any pleasing or elevating effect produced upon his mind or imagination." Performances were slow to come in Britain. Only three years later, in February 1867, was the most accessible of Brahms's chamber works, the B flat Sextet, op. 18, first given. It was performed by Joachim's London Quartet, though May notes that it made "no impression."[46] A review of the work in score in the *Monthly Musical Record* of April 1871 shows a reluctant acceptance, and less concern for inherited elements than in Germany.

> The first thing that strikes us . . . is that Brahms is a very
> unequal writer. By far the best of the compositions be-
> fore us is the Sextet for stringed instruments. The ideas
> are original throughout, and often very striking, and the
> work is to a great extent free from that over-elaboration
> and diffuseness which seem to be Brahms's great fault.
> The opening movement is charming, from beginning to
> end. . . . The variations in D minor are very interesting.
> More generally, he is evidently a man who thinks for
> himself, his subjects are always unborrowed, but there is
> a want of clearness of form, and a tendency to over-
> development which seems more or less to characterize all
> the modern German school of composition, and which
> greatly impairs the effect of the whole.[47]

The reviews grew less stiff in the 1870s, though they still were reserved. An 1872 performance of the D Minor Piano Concerto, again arranged by Manns, drew no significant press response. But when *A German Requiem* was given at the Philharmonic Society on April 2, 1873, the reaction reflected the contrast between the powerful status of choral music and the oratorio tradition founded on Handel and Mendelssohn and the nascent orchestral tradition. "It is impossible in the space of these comments even to hint at all the extraordinary merit, technical and aesthetic, of the composition under our notice. . . . When the German Requiem becomes known, the lovers of music in England will feel, indeed, that their art has a living representative, that the greatest masters have a successor." The review in *Monthly Musical Record* was qualified, noting diffuseness, but it also stressed the abundance of ideas and the "harmonic and contrapuntal treatment of amazing skill." Instrumental music still found less support, with negative responses to both a second performance of the piano concerto and the D Major Serenade. Only with the "St. Antoni" Variations is any real enthusiasm to be sensed. The critic for the *Record* picked up on all the work's contrapuntal ingenuities, stressing that they were not in conflict with its beauty, and emphasizing the quality of its instrumentation.[48]

With the appearance of the First Symphony, critical reaction became much more positive. Although reservations about the difficulty of Brahms's language did not disappear, his stature—his technical mastery and high purpose—were widely acknowledged, as in Germany. "Whether as a whole it will ever be 'popular' in the sense in which that term is applied to the symphonies of Mozart and Beethoven may be doubted: Brahms's style is too reflective, at times too abstruse, to meet with universal appreciation. But the real traces of genius which abound in this symphony, and which become more apparent on each repeated hearing, are such as to secure for this great work a place in the esteem of musicians hardly second to that held by the symphonies of Schumann, with whom Brahms has much in common." Yet a reluctance to make unqualified comparison with Beethoven persists, the *Musical Times* commenting later that "many of the most distinguished German musical critics have spoken of the work as 'the greatest symphony since Beethoven; and although one might perhaps be inclined to dispute the literal accuracy of the statement and to point to Schumann's great symphonies in C and E flat in justification of a different opinion, there can be no doubt that Brahms's C Minor Symphony towers among contemporary works like Mont Blanc among the Alps. . . . It may be seen that [the C Minor and D Major Symphonies] occupy toward one another a position somewhat analogous to that held by Beethoven's C Minor and Pastoral Symphonies." Performances of Brahms's work were to remain relatively infrequent in Britain, but leading American orchestras, especially the Boston Symphony Orchestra, gave regular performances of the symphonies—almost one each year in Brahms's lifetime—and the press responded more positively. The critic in the *Boston Daily Advertiser* (18 January 1878) reflects the great expectations aroused by early reception in commenting: "Johannes Brahms is a modern of the moderns, and his C Minor Symphony is a remarkable expression of the inner life of this anxious, introverted, over-earnest age. . . . [But] we venture to express a doubt that this work demonstrates its author's right to a place beside or near Beethoven." Brahms's chamber works received frequent performance as well, perhaps most notably by the Kneisel Quartet of Boston.[49]

As in Germany, the pro-Brahms faction found opposition from the adherents of Wagner, though first-hand knowledge of Wagner's music was more difficult to obtain. A leading British Wagnerian was the young George Bernard Shaw, who found that his social ideals were perfectly interpreted in *The Ring*. But in disdaining Brahms's works he took a different line from many of the German critics. He praised the orchestral or instrumental ideas but belittled the extended structures: he saw Brahms as a "sentimental voluptuary with a wonderful ear" but "a child playing at being grown up," through his "brainless" discursiveness. His response to the choral works was more predictable, and he aimed his sharpest darts at the *German Requiem*, citing Brahms's presumed appeal to the academic mind in extensive *points d'orgue*. He was not the only outspoken critic: the views of his fellow Wagnerian and Fabian socialist John F. Runciman also pursue the theme of Brahms as miniaturist.

> The true Brahms, the Brahms who does not deceive
> himself, is the Brahms you may find in many of the
> songs, in some of the piano chamber music, in the
> smaller movements of his symphonies, and in certain
> passages of his overtures and I have no hesitation what-
> ever in asserting (though the opinion is subject to revi-
> sion) that his songs are much the most satisfactory things
> he did. Here, unweighted by a heavy sense of a mission,
> he either revels in making beautiful, though never su-
> premely beautiful—tunes for their own sake, or he actu-
> ally expresses with beauty and considerable fidelity certain
> definite emotions. Had he written nothing but such
> small things . . . his position might be a degree lower in
> the estimation of dull Academics who don't count, but
> he would be accepted at something like his true value by
> the whole world, and the whole world would be better
> for oftener hearing many lovely things. But merely to be
> a singer of wonderful songs was not sufficient for
> Brahms[—]he wanted to be a great poet, a new Beetho-
> ven. . . . If ever a musician was born a happy, careless
> romanticist, that composer was Brahms. . . . Much of
> Brahms's music is bad and ugly music, dead music; it is

a counterfeit and not the true and perfect image of life. . . . There are many of the songs in which Brahms's astonishing felicity of phrase, and his astounding trick of finding expression for an emotion when the emotion has been given to him enables him almost to work miracles![50]

Such views held no interest for the supporters of the emerging instrumental tradition, which was a key feature of the so-called English Musical Renaissance of the early 1880s. For the leading figures—especially in the conservatories and universities—Brahms represented a perfect model for the modern expression of their principles and values. The leading figures in this world were supporters of Brahms; for example, Hubert Parry, Charles Villiers Stanford, Henry Hadow, and H. C. Colles. For Colles, Brahms was not only a master composer but a custodian of old values in an increasingly threatening musical world, where the modernism of the Wagnerian theater had penetrated the concert hall through the symphonic poems of Richard Strauss.

It is now only ten years since Brahms's death and twenty-five since that of Wagner, yet music seems to have made immense strides and to have passed into channels not directly prophesied by either. Music drama has not advanced since *Tristan,* Italian opera has been rejuvenated, and German and French opera have progressed into characteristic channels. . . . Still less have the symphonies of Brahms found a successor. Instead, the principles of programme music, as formulated by Berlioz and Liszt, have been developed and pushed to their logical conclusion . . . in the works of Richard Strauss and others. As we sit in the concert room, our ears flooded with orchestral outpourings, we read in contemporary criticism that principles of tonality are now completely outworn, that we are emancipated into the realm of unrestrained chromaticism, of music in which emotional expression is at last unfettered by formal restraints and prohibitions. Brahms may well be seen as the last of a great tribe, born after his time, mighty, yet influencing little the art of the future.

Art moves so quickly that Wagner, the revolutionary of the [1870s], is now the idol of respectable, orthodox, and churchgoing English people; soon even Richard Strauss must vacate the rostrum and allow even more advanced demagogues to preach this gospel of freedom. But when the gospel is completely preached and heard by all, what then? At the rate of progress now in vogue, that must certainly be achieved before Brahms has lain in his grave a quarter of a century. Then, when we know that we can do everything in music; . . . when the composer has within his grasp effects of orchestral colour of which Brahms never dreamed, shall he not look at the scores of the first symphony, the piano quintet, the double concerto, and find there something majestic, a fundamental dignity, a nobility of conception which he lacks? When all artistic means are at the composer's disposal, comes the time for ordering, for selection amongst them. It is then that Brahms's influence will assert itself and his example become a guiding light. History repeats itself; our art has passed through such periods before, and probably must do so again.[51]

Long before Brahms's death, Edward Elgar, as an obscure young violin teacher in Malvern, wrote a prose sketch in response to Brahms's new Third Symphony, offering a composer's view in which he expressed the hope that his home town "would do itself honour by duly appreciating the classical composer *par excellence* of the present day, who, free from any provincialism or expression of national dialect, writes for the whole world and for all time—a giant, lofty and unapproachable." Elgar clearly regarded the work as a model of absolute symphonic composition. His intimate knowledge later emerged in informal lectures, in which he emphasized its thematic integration across movements. He comments that the movements are related to each other in the following way: "the 'motto theme' reappears in the last movement twelve bars from the end—the first subject proper of the first movement reappears in the last nine bars from the end." But he ventures further than any other writer of the time in observing that the "second theme of the second movement reappears as a subsidiary theme in the finale," commenting to the theorist Donald Francis Tovey of this relationship that "[it] is the tragic outcome of the wistful theme in the middle of the slow movement." Elgar also noted what he termed reminiscence phrases: "The opening theme of course suggests Mendelssohn—the passage which links it to the second subject suggests Wagner. The Andante suggests, momentarily, Zampa." Elgar's precise observations also illustrate another critical theme: reserve about Brahms's orchestration. He would have rescored some passages; his informal lecture was taken down as follows:

> Orchestration—noble and restrained: but there are curiously "casual" passages—ending *pp* [pianissimo] [which is] fiendishly difficult to get 'level'—doubling the third—where special effects are intended—such as 'solo' passages for any instruments—we must not cavil but accept what is given us, but where we see a tutti—full force and the effect is thin we may enquire where the disappointment lies. Similarly, when we see a chord, and know that this chord employs every instrument, and know also that a *pp* is required, we may enquire why the instruments are so arranged as to make it almost impossible to obtain a real *pp*. Final chords [of the] first movement, the third appears *nine* times, dull, heavy effect—the clearer you want the sound omit the third. . . . [The] third might be cut out of four or six places. Compare the last chord of all. Trumpet parts cruel. Second trumpet—long skips—open notes only.[52]

For the American writer James Huneker, the point was certainly to accept "what was given." In an article devoted to Brahms with the title "The Music of the Future," he admits that "[Brahms] is accused of not scoring happily. The accusation is true. Brahms does not display the same gracious sense of voicing the needs and capabilities of every orchestral instrument as have Berlioz, Dvořák, and Strauss. He is often very muddy, drab and opaque, but his nobility of utterance, his remarkable eloquence and ingenuity in treatment make you forget his shortcomings." But, as Huneker continues, "his mastery of material is as great as Beethoven's and only outstripped by Bach. . . . His contribution to the technics of rhythm is enormous. He has literally popularized the cross relation, re-discovered the arpeggio and elevated it from the lowly position of an accompanying figure to an integer of the melodic phrase . . . who shall carve from the harmonic granite imperishable shapes of beauty as did Johannes Brahms."[53]

Phillip Goepp reiterates this view: "There is a giant power, a reposeful mastery without strain, without the lack of a corresponding strength and breadth of feeling. . . . The manner of his writing is the result of his poetic personality." And in 1897, Theodor Thomas's comments anticipate Colles in pleading for time: "Brahms will be better appreciated when people have become more familiar with his music. It is true that he appeals much to the intellect—so did Beethoven and Bach and, therefore, he does not satisfy those who regard music as an amusement, or only as an emotional factor. He may, nevertheless, outlive his more popular contemporaries, because his music is freer from the influences of the times in which he lived than that of any other composer of his day."[54] Daniel Gregory Mason writes from a later vantage point, comparing Brahms directly with his peers:

Of all the figures of modern music, brilliant and varied as they are, impressing one with the many-sidedness and wide scope of the art, there is perhaps only one, that of Johannes Brahms, which conveys the sense of satisfying poise, self control, and sanity. Others excel him in partic-ular qualities. Grieg is more delicate and intimate, Dvo-rák warmer and clearer in colour; Saint-Saëns is more meteoric, Franck more recondite and subtle, and Tchai-kowsky more impassioned; but Brahms alone has Ho-meric simplicity, [exhibiting] the primal health of the well balanced man. He excels all his contemporaries in soundness and universality. In an age when many people are uncertain of themselves and the world . . . it is solac-ing to find so heroic and simple a soul, who finds life acceptable, meets it genially, and utters his joys and his sorrow with the old classic sincerity. He is not blighted by any of the myriad forms of egotism, by sentimentality, and by the itch to be effective at all costs, or to be "orig-

inal," or to be Byronic or Romantic or unfathomable.
He has no "message" for an errant world; no anathema,
either profoundly gloomy or insolently clear, to hurl at
God. He has rather a deep and broad impersonal love of
life; universal joy is the sum and substance of his expression.[55]

The heroism that Mason depicts is certainly not that associated with
Beethoven, which lay in its revolutionary agenda, its dramatizing of musical form and content: finally its appeal to most notably the verbal ethical
element in the "Freude" movement of the Ninth Symphony. Rather, at
the end of the century, heroism is proposed as consisting in the capacity
and will to hold the most basic elements of music together in meaningful
relationship in the face of an increasing reliance on text, program, and
orchestra. As Huneker adds, "[Brahms] restored to music its feeling for
form. He was the greatest symphonist in the constructive sense since
Beethoven."[56] Thus, a modernist as well as a traditionalist, Brahms already
eluded straightforward classification and evaluation.

19 · Reverence and Reaction in the Twentieth Century

This view of heroism seemed increasingly irrelevant in the new century.
For most of the younger critics and composers, the rapidly expanding
harmonic and orchestral resources made the idea of Brahms as a "musician of the future" difficult to take seriously. Understanding Brahms the
Modernist remained a specialist activity for the likes of Elgar. Though
the music would become increasingly familiar in the concert hall—indeed, it became a test of developing orchestral standards—its subtleties
remained the possession of a small group for years to come. Though his
hopes for a compositional reengagement with Brahms ultimately were not
so wide of the mark, Colles could hardly have anticipated the form they
were to take, or the musical result. For the moment, the most obvious
followers of Brahms were minor figures indeed. Much more noteworthy
were the efforts of scholars and friends in presenting to the public a mass

of posthumously released materials throwing invaluable light on the secretive master for later generations.

The Embodiment of a Brahms Tradition

By the turn of the century Brahms's art had taken strong root in the Germanic musical world. Modern concert life and rapid communications meant that the composer's reputation became more rapidly established than that of any of his predecessors, and he was probably more widely imitated in his maturity and after his death than any previous composer. Brahms's vast impact on the musical world led many close to him to wish to establish permanent expressions of his importance, to embody his achievements in the form of publications, societies, and special performances and festivals. The flow of publications began almost immediately after Brahms's death, with the reminiscences of Albert Dietrich, J. V. Widmann, and the choral conductor Julius Spengel. In the following years, other friends would produce their recollections, extended or brief: notable are those of Richard von den Leyen, Richard von Perger, Richard Fellinger, as well as the writings of Max Kalbeck.[57] For these figures Brahms was not only a towering composer whose acquaintance had transformed their lives, but a figure symbolic of German art and culture, representing spiritual as well as purely musical values. If the following words of Leyen seem rather inflated in their imagery and claims, the fact that Niemann was to use them to preface his biography of the composer shows the depth of the reverence of Brahms's circle for the values he embodied in changing times: "If ever our German nation is passing through a period of national mourning and tribulation—which God forbid for long years to come—then shall the children of Brahms's muse, like holy angels, droop their lily wands over mankind in its affliction, pouring a healing balm into their wounds, and thus aim in directing our mission in the life of nations towards new and glorious aims."[58]

The task of assembling and documenting Brahms's materials after his death found a focus in the creation of two societies: the Wiener Brahms Gesellschaft [Vienna Brahms Society] (1904–14), and the Deutsche Brahms Gesellschaft [German Brahms Society] (1906–193?). The Viennese society aimed to acquire Brahms's manuscripts, items from his library, and artifacts from his estate for permanent preservation in the Archive of the Gesellschaft der Musikfreunde, of which Eusebius Mandyczewski was archivist. Both Mandyczewski and Kalbeck served on the committee. In contrast, the German society, based in Berlin, was larger and had a more international membership and better financial resources to support its more ambitious aims. It achieved author's rights to all of Brahms's then known compositions, royalty rights to the performance of the music, and a large collection of correspondence. Under such figures as the scholar Max Friedländer, the conductor Fritz Steinbach, and the publisher Hans Simrock, it flourished until World War I and then existed sporadically until the collapse of the Weimar Republic. Its major achievements were the sponsorship of an "official" biography, by Max Kalbeck, and of sixteen volumes of correspondence, as well as the publication of some works unpublished in Brahms's lifetime that have since become familiar.[59] Kalbeck's biography appeared between 1904 and 1914, with all volumes going through revisions and the work achieving wide circulation. Its four extensive volumes were published as eight half-volumes combining biography with extensive discussion of the music. It represented at the time the most extensive biography produced for any major composer so soon after his death, and it immediately established itself as the most authoritative source for Brahms's life and works.[60] Although Kalbeck was part of the Brahms circle, his task in drawing together the information and filling the gaps in the recently published reminiscences was hardly easy. He had known Brahms only since 1874, and he drew on the information of no fewer than 127 of Brahms's acquaintances, sending some of them lengthy questionnaires that show how much basic information he had to establish from scratch.[61] The volumes of correspondence were edited by various members of the Brahms circle and by younger scholars with a special interest in or connections with the correspondents. Kalbeck's work included editing the letters to and from the Herzogenbergs, the correspondence with Widmann and with Adolf Schubring, as well as the lengthy correspondence with Simrock. Richard Barth edited the letters with his teacher Julius Otto Grimm; Joachim's letters were edited by his pupil, Andreas Moser; Wilhelm Altmann edited various collections of correspondence with musicians, and Leopold Schmidt likewise. From 1920, Carl Krebs edited the letters to Spitta and Dessoff, and Ernst Wolff the letters to Wüllner.[62] By the time the Kalbeck biography and the volumes of correspondence were finished, many of the chief participants in the

Brahms tradition were dead or very old. A new generation assumed the responsibility for making available the source materials through the remaining years up to the centenary of Brahms's birth, in 1933. The most important of these tasks was the creation of a collected edition of Brahms's works, which was edited by Eusebius Mandyczewski with the young Hans Gál. The *Johannes Brahms Sämtliche Werke* appeared in twenty-seven volumes between 1926 and 1928[63] and included many unpublished minor works and variant versions of published works. Its basis was the manuscripts, where available, and the many first editions corrected by Brahms himself. As in the case of the biography—and wholly consistent with the era of intensified musicological activity in which it was produced—the collected edition of Brahms's works appeared in closer proximity to the composer's death than did any other collected edition of a major composer's works. It was regarded as a model of reliability, in view of the close contact that Brahms had with his publisher and the knowledge of his methods by close colleagues, particularly Mandyczewski. Thus the critical assessment was supportive: "Singularly well performed applies not merely to the work of the editors, Hans Gál and Eusebius Mandyczewski, who have achieved a higher degree of completeness than most of their predecessors in the editing of German collected editions, but also, and above all, to the accuracy of Brahms himself, which gave them a definitive basis on which to work for the composer's finally corrected edition."[64]

In fact, the edition was by no means as reliable and comprehensive as was believed. Many factors served to limit its accuracy; some to do with circumstances—the withholding of sources by some individuals—some with the conclusions drawn by the editors as a result of the lack of materials (these limitations were aggravated by the now aging Mandyczewski, as Gál later reported).[65] A major task related to the creation of a reliable collected edition was that of assembling a comprehensive thematic index, listing all known works with their incipits and with dates of composition and of first performance. The first of these to appear independent of the customary intermittent publisher's catalogues (which included such information in brief) was that which formed the appendix to the biography of Brahms by Alfred von Ehrmann, which appeared in 1933. One of the two major outstanding volumes of correspondence, that with Clara Schumann, appeared in 1927; it was followed in 1935 by the correspondence with Theodor Billroth.[66] Along with the many brief reminiscences published in special issues of journals around 1933, these brought the bulk of Brahms's letter exchanges into the public domain by the centenary of his birth. The following years would be less striking for source material, but a steady trickle of complementary publications followed over the years, even into the postwar period.

Changing Attitudes of the Younger Generation

Brahms's mastery of instrumental forms meant that many young composers quickly became aware of his music through their training. Yet a typical pattern saw them move away toward the larger resources and greater freedoms of the programmatic work for large orchestra. The reactions of the two leading younger figures in the orchestral sphere, Richard Strauss and Gustav Mahler, typify this movement. Strauss had direct contact with Brahms through his position at Meiningen as Bülow's assistant from 1884, and possibly even earlier through his father, a leading orchestral musician of "conservative" inclinations at Munich. He seems to have developed an enthusiasm for Brahms and then grown out of it. Before being appointed to Meiningen he had reacted variously to the new Third Symphony, writing to his father in January 1884 after hearing a rehearsal in Berlin that his head was "still buzzing with all this obscurity. I candidly confess that I haven't yet understood it, but it is so unclear and wretched in its instrumentation that in the first and last movements I could only make out two coherent four-bar ideas." But Strauss changed his mind with repeated hearings, and by 1 February he had listened three times "and liked it better each time, so that I am now almost enthusiastic." His reservations, however, disappeared with the rehearsals and first performance of the Fourth Symphony at Meiningen on 25 October 1885. By then he fully shared Bülow's enthusiasm and declared the piece a "giant work, great in concept and invention, masterful in its form, and yet from A–Z genuine Brahms, in a word, an enrichment of our art."[67] Despite the rather sharp advice he received from Brahms on his own Symphony in F Minor, he retained respect for Brahms's judgment, and some of his works are Brahmsian in character. But in his maturity, when compositional interest had moved from the instrumental to the orchestral and then operatic spheres, his interest waned. On one occasion in his later years (he was tired and on edge), he even declared to Elisabeth

Schumann, "I much prefer Spohr. I always get so angry with Brahms.— he is over-rated, he doesn't have enough ideas."[68] There is certainly no evidence that the strong "classical" element in Strauss found any stimulus from Brahms: his classical world was that of Mozart.

Unlike Strauss, Mahler stayed in the symphonic milieu. Though he drew extra-musical influences into his symphonies, which went far beyond Brahms's in their length and orchestral scope, he shared many more musical elements with Brahms than did Strauss, not least the love of folksong, despite his very different treatment of it. He had much more to say on Brahms, whom he knew more closely than Strauss did, having cultivated an acquaintance since his first meeting in 1884 through regular visits in Brahms's last years. From these and his studies of the music he seems to have retained a largely ambivalent general attitude, now enthusiastic, now critical. Positive attitudes emerge from conversations with his brother on the subject of form in the symphony with regard to the works of Brahms and Bruckner: "In order to judge a work, . . . you have to look at it as a whole. And in this respect, Brahms is indisputably the greater of the two, with his extraordinarily compact compositions which aren't at all obvious, but reveal greater depth and richness of content the more you enter into them. And think of his immense productivity, which is also part of the total picture of an artist! With Bruckner, certainly, you are carried away by the magnificence and wealth of his inventiveness, but at the same time you are repeatedly disturbed by his fragmentary character which breaks the spell. . . . No it isn't enough to judge a work of art by its content; we must consider its total image."[69]

One aspect of content was the treatment of instrumentation. Bauer-Lechner observed of the Third Symphony, which Mahler conducted with the Vienna Philharmonic that "Mahler is delighted with the Brahms symphony. . . . Its one failing, he feels, is a lack of brilliance in the instrumental setting: but this might easily be taken care of with a few changes in the scoring." The desire to brighten Brahms's scoring was seemingly not unrelated to an observation of Brahms's artistic limitations: "Brahms is not concerned with breaking all bonds and rising above the grief and life of this earth to soar up into the heights of other freer and more radiant spheres. However profoundly, however intimately and idiosyncratically he handles the material, he remains imprisoned in this world and this life, and never attains the view from the summit. Therefore his works can never, and will never, exercise the highest, ultimate influence."[70] For Mahler only Beethoven and Wagner could fulfill this role.

Franz Schmidt, the outstanding Austrian composer to pursue less radical paths, was drawn to the romantic symphonic tradition of Bruckner rather than to Brahmsian "classicism" in maturity, though he knew both composers in their last years. It was the large paragraphing of Bruckner, rather than Brahmsian rhetoric, that remained his ideal. The Italian-German Ferruccio Busoni, another major figure of this generation active in German musical circles, might seem more likely to have been drawn to Brahms in light of his classical inclinations, his love of Bach, and because Brahms was one of his early supporters. Yet he seems to have had many reservations about Brahms's output as a whole. Although he admired some works, including the Violin Concerto, he noted of a group of five Lieder that "they never did live. Harmony . . . overlarded with platitudes. Nor could I find any relationship between the words and the music." The larger import of Busoni's *New Aesthetic of Music,* his belief in the power of music to "float on air" and to possess the "divine prerogative of buoyancy, of freedom from the limitations of matter," led him to a deep suspicion of any undue reverence for the traditional elements of the forms of "absolute music" and thus put him at odds with the Brahmsian view. Like Mahler, he finds no ultimate effect in Brahms's work because of the composer's commitment to formal working; he observes of the introduction and Allegro theme of the finale of the First Symphony that Brahms lacked Beethoven's "lust of liberation." Though, like Schumann in the transition to the Finale of the D Minor Symphony, Brahms is "seized [by the] boundlessness of this pan-art [of free, "absolute" instrumental music], the moment they cross the threshold of the *Principal Subject,* their attitude becomes stiff and conventional, like that of a man entering some bureau of high officialdom."[71] The classicism that Busoni espoused was found in Mozart and in Bach, but not in Brahms.

Brahms's Vienna was the focus of the musical culture as well as of the ambitions and education of many young musicians from eastern Europe, especially the Czech Lands and Hungary. Many composers destined to contribute to the nationalist musical movements came naturally into Brahms's orbit through their connection with the Vienna Conservatoire (as had Mahler, who shared teachers with some of them), not least through Brahms's contacts with Dvořák and through his own interests in folk music. Although Janáček, Novak, Suk, and Fibich all went through a Brahmsian phase, each moved away from Brahms's germanicism in their search for a national style. Indeed, on one occasion in the Leipzig Conservatoire, Janáček declared that Brahms left him cold. The composer who acknowledged Brahms most openly was the Hungarian Bela Bartók. His lifelong commitment to the classical tradition, both in his fascination with the use of strict traditional devices and with the variation of traditional forms, to say nothing of his deep knowledge of the literature as a player, gave him immense respect for Brahms. He includes Brahms with Beethoven and Mendelssohn as models for the form of violin concerto when modestly referring to his own first violin concerto. And this respect was not disturbed by his taking issue with Brahms and Liszt over the true folk status of the melodies they both set as Hungarian.[72]

A More Technical Interest by Austro-German Composers

For composers of the Strauss-Mahler generation, Brahms's importance was still considered in terms of the opposition of Brahms and Wagner regarding so-called absolute music and programmatic or dramatic music. They also were viewed as symbols of conservatism and progressiveness, respectively. But for composers of the generation born in the 1870s, who had matured under the influence of both, the issues were different. As Schoenberg put it, "What in 1883 [the year of Wagner's death] seemed an impassable gulf was in 1897 [the year of Brahms's death] no longer a problem."[73] Their concern was much more with the potentiality of the language that had been handed down to them. They were also significantly more interested in chamber music, a field in which Brahms was the acknowledged major modern master and one that he had largely restored to the forefront of musical concern. For such composers as Reger, Zemlinsky, and Schoenberg and his followers, Brahms became the chief model for the understanding of musical processes.

Though the music of Max Reger has, as a whole, failed to maintain the level of interest shown in the others mentioned, in the years immediately following Brahms's death it was more prominent than that of any of the others. This success was not simply a matter of fluency of technique, which enabled him to produce a large output. He was also seen as a major innovator by the Schoenberg school, and his music was more frequently performed in Schoenberg's Society for Private Musical Performances than that of any other contemporary figure. Reger had more direct access to the Brahms tradition than the others because he had been a pupil of Hugo Riemann, who had known Brahms much longer than Schoenberg's teacher Zemlinsky (who was, in any case, of Schoenberg's own generation). His world was essentially that of Mozart and Bach, drawing in complex chromatic harmonies directly from them rather than from Wagner. His chamber music reflects the influence of Brahms in its rich polyphony and developmental working, and he shared Brahms's passion for variation writing in which he followed Brahmsian methods. His view of Brahms as a progressive composer is evident in his reaction to the apparent view of Riemann, a theorist whose remarks in his obituary for Brahms Reger quotes in order to challenge them: "Brahms holds a strong and singular position. . . . He is as a living artistic potency, the complement of the historical developments of the blossoming Musikwissenschaft of the last decade." Reger thought this attitude entirely false.

> I believe that my [total admiration] toward Brahms, my
> glowing reverence for the great old masters is too well
> known, that I need to stress it here. But above all I pro-
> test here [most energetically] against the view of Brahms
> [as being understood] as a complement to the historiciz-
> ing tendency of the last decade of blooming Musikwis-
> senschaft! It is a big error if Herr Riemann believes that
> Brahms has therefore become the gnarled old oak tree
> who survives the storm of turmoil. . . . Brahms as the
> complement of the musicology of his time!! Now that is
> really nice! . . . It would be very sad for the immortality
> of a Brahms if he owed his immortality in the first place
> to the old masters, as Riemann believes. That is some-
> thing only gray theory could state, that has its lonely ex-
> istence apart from the golden stream of life, the
> powerfully pulsating heartblood of the music of our
> time. . . . [A composer like] Rheinberger has passed
> quickly. That which secures Brahms's immortality will
> never be just the "inclination" to the old masters, but
> only the fact that he knew how to release his newly

breathed spiritual moods on the basis of his own spiritual
personality! Therein lies the source of all immortality.[74]

Zemlinsky had access to Brahms through his contact with the Vienna
Conservatoire and his membership in the Vienna Tonkünstlerverein.
Brahms regarded his early works highly, recommending a String Quartet
in A Major, op. 4, and a Clarinet Trio in D Minor, op. 3 (written for
the same combination as his own op. 114) to his own publisher, Simrock.
In these works Brahms would clearly have seen his own values perpetuated
by the younger generation. In his early orchestral works Zemlinsky also
showed Brahmsian inclinations, employing a passacaglia in the finale of
the Second Symphony. In later years the influence of Mahler became
greater and his style was transformed as he found his true expressive world
in opera; Schoenberg thought him without equal in his day in satisfying
the demands of the theater.[75] His respect for Brahms would certainly have
been passed on to his pupil. But while many composers moved through
a Brahmsian stage as part of their development in the mastery of traditional forms, Brahmsian principles permeated Schoenberg's entire creative
outlook. Thus, when he was about fifty—at the time of the centenary of
Brahms's birth, when the composer's stock with composers and critics was
low—Schoenberg could give a radio broadcast that intimately associated
Brahms with his own works and cast Brahms in the role of a progressive
composer. Writing to Hans Rosbaud concerning the radio program, he
commented, "Here I'd probably have something to say that only I can
say. For though my exact contemporaries and those who are older than
I, also lived in Brahms's time, they aren't 'modern.' But the younger
Brahmsians can't know the Brahms tradition from first hand experience,
and anyway they mostly tend to be 'reactionary.' But: what I have in
mind is the theory of composition, not anecdotes!"
Elsewhere he stressed the values of traditional musical craft embodied
in Brahms's music. "Living in the proximity of Brahms, it was customary
that a musician, when he heard a composition for the first time, observed
its constructions, was able to follow elaborations and derivation of its
themes and its modulations, and could recognize the number of voices
in canons and the presence of the theme in a variation. . . . This is what
music critics like. Hanslick, Kalbeck, Heuberger, Speidel, and amateurs
like the renowned physician Billroth were able to do."[76] Judged by the

criteria of this elevated musical society, Brahms was for Schoenberg a difficult modern composer, certainly not one to be looked down on nor adversely compared with Wagner. Schoenberg allied himself with Brahms in sharing these values and in presenting Brahms in an entirely new perspective.

Taking the previous generation of Mahler and Strauss as his starting point in the article later drawn from the broadcast, he states that "their example helped us to realize that there was as much organizational order, if not pedantry in Wagner as there was daring courage, if not even bizarre fantasy in Brahms." He casts Brahms as an advanced composer, exploring every remote possibility of his material, extending the norms of musical form richly, relative to his means, and displaying the vital "responsibility to his materials," which was clearly such a part of Schoenberg's own philosophy. Brahms is portrayed as the composer of "music for adults" who can take in rapid changes and developments and does not need empty repetitions. Brahms's innovations are seen as extending to harmony, theme, and rhythm. His harmonic methods are seen as being as daring as those of Wagner, if different; in the sphere of phrasing he grows further than any other composer of his time toward an "unrestricted musical language" through his use of a process of motivic development without parallel, which has intimate relationship with Schoenberg's own concept of "developing variation," and which he illustrates in precise detail. In this sphere Brahms is seen as upholding principles manifest in Mozart's chamber music and to be maintained in Reger's music. In the rhythmic sphere he comments that when Brahms writes twos or fours against threes, "this was probably the start of the polyrhythmic structure of many contemporary scores." Perhaps most significant of all, Schoenberg sees Brahms as master of the long-term relationship, the anticipation of later events and the integration of the whole, which was for Schoenberg the sign of greatness in music. Thus, he cites examples of the unity achieved between the theme of the first movement of the Fourth Symphony, constructed in a way that can be interpreted as a series of falling thirds, and the finale, where this sequence provides the content of one of the variations and thus unveils further unsuspected links to the first movement.[77]

Schoenberg's teaching, the roots of which are evident in his earliest music, was passed directly to his pupils: Alban Berg, Anton Webern, Egon Wellesz, and Erwin Stein. Berg's early songs are deeply Brahmsian in form and style, and his Twelve Variations on an Original Theme, written for Schoenberg in 1908 though unpublished by Berg, likewise draws on Brahmsian examples, notably the "St. Antoni" Variations, as well as on his general style in their use of thirds and sixths. Brahms was one of Berg's favorite composers, and he greatly admired the symphonies. Brahms's trios, especially opp. 8 and 101, were frequently played at the Berg home. But the young critic's highest compliment was saved for *A German Requiem*, of which Berg noted on his duo copy "This is Music! Truly a higher revelation!" Brahms's work had a lasting effect on Berg, who retained a commitment to its values of detailed structural organization, even in the sphere of expressionist opera. Adorno implies that Berg continued to strive for the "step by step" quality of Brahms's themes through his work. Webern's music, lacking the dramatic aspect of Berg, lent itself to Brahms's influence as filtered through Schoenberg in perhaps more obvious ways. His first published work was a passacaglia for orchestra, obviously inspired by the finale of Brahms's Fourth Symphony, and he clearly saw Brahms in an even broader historical perspective through his interests in fifteenth-century music, also noting the closing bars of *Song of the Fates* as almost atonal. "See how the cadences carry the music far away from tonality." Wellesz was particularly sensitive to the thematic working in the course of a piece, directly relating Schoenberg's concept of liquidation in his first string quartet to Brahms's example. He emphasizes the dominant position of Brahms in the Vienna of Schoenberg's youth and of his role in what he designates as Schoenberg's path to twelve-note music, commenting bluntly that the "composer who influenced him decisively throughout his life, and whom he rated highest among modern composers, was Brahms."[78]

Fuller evidence of Schoenberg's early teaching seems to emerge in the discussion of Brahms's Fourth Symphony by another of his pupils, Erwin Stein.

> First of all, listen to the theme itself, how its wavy line is
> produced by the alternation of thirds and sixths (i.e, har-
> monic inversions of thirds); how the sixths are widened
> into octave leaps and thus stretch the melodic curve
> more tightly until the theme comes to dwell on the C
> for its motivic play; how with diminishing tension, the

basic motive [now in fourths] descends stepwise in dimi-
nution; how this descent becomes a motive itself [that is,
to play a decisive role in the course of the movement].
. . . Listen to the wealth of shapes which grow from the
simple motive of a third and of which we have only outlined a small part. And now for the ensuing restatement;
as a logical result of preceding events, the theme reappears in a varied form, broken up into octave figurations.
. . . The succession of thirds [of the first subject] remain[s] the most important formative principle of the
movement. . . . And in the first movement itself we may
finally remind ourselves of the famous recapitulation
where, with the most tender sonorities the theme is created anew out of its basic idea. . . . This is a true "factuality" (*Sachlichkeit*), the ability to keep to the "subject,"
to say much about the same thing. . . . Economy of material in the Brahmsian sense presupposes the material's
transformability. Brahms has indeed considerably widened
the concept of variation, more particularly outside the
field of variation form proper. . . . His melodies move
more freely in musical space than those of his predecessors and contemporaries.[79]

These observations and many other examples scattered through
Schoenberg's writings provide evidence of a more detailed analysis than
that supplied by any other writer. A comparison of the analyses of two
British musicians equally supportive of the view of Brahms as a modern
composer—Charles Villiers Stanford and C. A. Abdy Williams—also
shows a changing perspective in the years after Brahms's death. Stanford's
analysis of the "St. Antoni" Variations in a text published in 1911 outlines
the contrapuntal devices and the relation of the theme to the variations
in general terms, thus reinforcing the view of Brahms as a clever traditionalist. In contrast, Williams, writing in 1909, deals with the phrase and
rhythmic structure of numerous works, including the whole of the Second
Symphony, discussed bar by bar to show the irregularities and the overlap.
But even though he outlines the effects in detail he does not point to the

determining processes, since phrasing is considered apart from motive; in this connection lies the key to Schoenberg's approach.[80]

Brahms in a Changing World

The attraction of both Brahms and Wagner for younger composers declined after World War I as part of a reaction against Romanticism. New musical values came to dominate, whether constructivist principles like the twelve-note method or the many varieties of neoclassicism, giving new emphasis to music of French, Italian, Russian, and Spanish origin. It is ironic that so few adherents of the supposedly new principles of serialism could have realized its debt to Brahms through the thinking of Schoenberg. It was at this time just after World War I that the deeper continuity of interest in Brahms became clearer. Many composers still found in the variety and technical resource of his instrumental works features of interest for themselves; in this he was more relevant than Wagner. A view of what Brahms had to offer younger German composers by comparison with his contemporaries was offered Weissmann in 1926.

> Those who believe [the] nonsensuous quality to be the most valuable element in the German race, look to Brahms. They believe that if in the vaporous and sultry atmosphere which predominated in the "new" music of his day, a man like Brahms could yet attain astonishing success, it is because he has contributed to music something fundamental and necessary. In his name they too, claim to be moderns. . . . Neither the old school nor the new school disputes the lasting value of Bach; both, indeed, claim descent from him. Polyphony must be saved, though modern tone color has struck at its roots. In modern German music, as opposed to other music, there is already a tendency to return to polyphony, which must surely result in a deeper and more intellectual development of the art. . . . The disciples of Brahms believe that they hold the key to the situation. Brahms rediscovered and reestablished the ground plan of music, and the middle class and academic elements in the Germanic and

kindred races rallied to him. A nontheatrical composer feels the influence of Brahms just as surely as a prospective opera composer succumbs, at least temporarily, to Wagner. Brahms assimilated much of Bach and Beethoven; his creative gift, if forceful, was narrow; he had not their breadth of outlook; but only a powerful substitute for compositional originality could have brought about the amazing reaction against Wagner for which he was responsible. . . . His followers have a yet narrower sense of vision; nevertheless they possess ability and sincerity, virtues which, with a measure of truth, they sometimes deny to those of the opposite school.

[In comparison with some of Brahms's followers,] the Hungarian, Ernst von Dohnányi, has achieved somewhat more under the Brahms influence, his versatility and executive virtuosity giving him a special capacity for assimilating form; but even he in all his work, operatic and otherwise, has produced only a few concert pieces of value, such as his Rhapsodies for the pianoforte and a violin concerto. Neither Wilhelm Berger's refinement, nor that jovial Rhinelander Ewald Straesser's attempts to break through academic conventions in symphony and chamber music, display originality; nor do Otto Taubmann's German Masses, beautiful as they are in parts, help to solve the problem of modern choral music. The work of the prototype has been too powerful for those industrious and imitative followers. . . . The spirit underlying the forms of nondramatic music needs renewal. Will this renewal come from Germany? It is clear that the time has come to put into practice that cult of Bach to which lip service has been paid for a number of years. The idolisation of Brahms, a pensive reflection of Bach, exaggerated as it has been during the last two decades, is an important sign of the times.[81]

Despite Brahms's historicist credentials, there was little place for him in the esteem of the neoclassicists of the 1920s and 1930s. The call was

"Back to Bach," not "Back to Brahms." The weight and richness of his music made it an inappropriate model for composers of the period. Yet even such figures as Hanns Eisler and Paul Hindemith still acknowledged Brahms's skills. Indeed, Eisler was a "notorious Brahmin" as a student, commenting of his music that "here I found rounded forms, shapely themes," models which anticipated his later devotion to music made from simple and popular resources. Though Hindemith was less openly acknowledging of Brahms in youth than in maturity, his critical response to a performance of the Second Symphony under Mengelberg reveals his respect: "I'm no great Brahms admirer—but anything more unBrahms-like it's impossible to imagine: first movement brutal or sentimental, without any feeling, the splendid second movement distorted and robbed of all its swing, the third just empty notes and the coda of the finale a timpani concerto with orchestral accompaniment. Horrible!"[82]

Hindemith's response is a reminder that, during the years following the pioneering performances of Bülow and Richter, the Brahms symphonies had become a prominent vehicle in the rapid development of orchestral performance standards, providing complex scores that tested every department of the orchestra to the full, as well as its ensemble. Wilhelm Furtwängler, conductor of the Berlin Philharmonic from 1922–54, was one of the leading interpreters of Brahms in the interwar period. He was invited by the German Brahms Society to give the address on the occasion of the Brahms Festival in Vienna in May 1933. Furtwängler began by placing Brahms in the broad perspective of the major composers of his time:

> If we ask ourselves today who was the last German com-
> poser to leave an indelible mark on the work of music,
> the answer would have to be—if we exclude the incom-
> parable figure of Wagner—Brahms. . . . Indeed, apart
> from the internationally minded and internationally suc-
> cessful Richard Strauss, no German composer who came
> after him, not his contemporary Bruckner, nor Pfitzner,
> nor Reger, has succeeded to such an extent in making
> himself known beyond the frontiers of his native country.
> . . . . Its impact and importance are still growing—more
> accurately, has started to grow again. . . . As this notion

increasingly took hold of the minds of the general public, as the victory of Wagner's music became complete at the end of the nineteenth century, and as figures such as Richard Strauss began to appear, . . . Brahms was finally banished to the background. He became regarded in many circles as *passé*, reactionary, of no relevance to the future, and was thrown onto the scrap heap. But as time went on, people began to observe, to their astonishment, that whereas most of the modern "music of the future," loudly trumpeted and lavishly promoted, began to collect dust in a remarkably short time, the tranquil music of Brahms, dismissed as way behind the times, not only retained its pristine vigor undiminished but even began to shine forth with a new radiance. . . . There has been much talk in modern aesthetics of the concept of Objectivity, "factuality." . . . In a sense I would call Brahms the "objective" composer *par excellence.* In an age obsessed with the creation of "effect" through the build-up of tension, through the instrumentation, through drawing on the forces of nature etc.—when composers, great and small alike, seized every available opportunity to achieve such "effects," Brahms looked studiously in the opposite direction. He uses the orchestra with a restraint derived from the classical composers, ignoring the developments which came with Wagner . . . and which exercised such a fascination on his contemporaries. He keeps to his concise, small-scale forms—They are controlled by a strict inner logic such as is found only in the very greatest. The artistic utterance says no more than the object—i.e., the world embodied by the work in question—requires. All alien thoughts are dismissed. . . . In return, what Brahms says, he says clearly, fully and consistently—because he has something to say.[83]

But Berg places these comments in a broader perspective, one that serves to show just how specialized and little known were the views emanating from Schoenberg and his pupils and how easy it was to use

Brahms for a conservative cultural agenda, on grounds of the nature of his achievement—thus, how differently the same achievement might be interpreted: "It was a Nazi-inspired speech on *German* music, which, he implied, had found its last representative in Brahms. Without mentioning any names he betrayed the whole of post-Brahmsian music, especially Mahler and the younger generation (like Hindemith). There was no reference at all to the Schoenberg circle as even existing. It was horrible having to put up with all this and witness the frenzied enthusiasm of the idiot audience. Idiotic not to realize how the Brahms *a cappella* songs which followed made nonsense of Furtwängler's tendentious twaddle."[84]

Responses in France and Elsewhere

With the twentieth century came a fundamental shift in the locus of musical modernism. Despite Schoenberg's far-reaching formal developments, inspiration at the time was drawn as much from France and its musical links with Russia and Spain as from Germany. French responses to Brahms and those French-inspired composers focus these changing values. From the first appearance of Brahms's music in the 1860s there was stiff resistance. Brahms never inspired the interest of Wagner, even in purely musical rather than literary terms. On the contrary; as Brahms's music gained a wider audience at the turn of the century, the term Nouveau Classicisme was coined as a derogatory reference to modern German instrumental music, of which Brahms was regarded as the chief representative.

Reactions were naturally modified by the particular interests of musicians, as in the case of chamber players seeking new repertoire. For them his works were obviously important from early on by virtue of their scope and commitment to the medium. Notable early supporters were the members of the quartets founded in about 1870 by Jules Armingaud and Charles Lamoureux. But critics were harsh. A review of the Piano Quintet in *La Revue et Gazette musical* in February 1870 stated, "We should be sorry for Brahms if he had to be judged by this work alone; it is tortured, laboured, and the exaggerated . . . sonorities seem to demand an orchestra; the work does not breathe, except perhaps in the scherzo." But Brahms's chamber music obviously became part of the inheritance of aspiring composers in these forms. Thus Vincent d'Indy was astonished to discover, even in 1888, when Franck was planning a string quartet, that he found the piano in his studio "littered with the scores of quartets by Beethoven, Schubert, and Brahms."[85] It is likely that the young Fauré knew the first two Brahms piano quartets, for they were among the works sent to the Paris publisher Jacques Mayo in the 1860s. *A German Requiem* was also known in 1875 when it received a Paris performance, and it is likely that Franck's own choral work *Les béatitudes* was influenced by it, in light of the textual parallels and the fact that Franck sent a copy to Brahms via D'Indy (though without a good response from Brahms). French attitudes by the turn of the century may be summarized in the views of Vincent D'Indy, who sees Brahms in much the terms of Liszt and the New Germans, as seeking to follow Beethoven: "Brahms, himself, in spite of a sense of development which may be compared, without exaggeration, to that of Beethoven, did not understand how to benefit by the valuable lessons left by the latter for future generations, and his weighty symphonic baggage must be regarded as a continuation rather than a progress."[86]

Attitudes changed slowly in the twentieth century, though signs of a more deep-rooted interest emerge from some writers and performers. The first biography in French, by Hugues Imbert, appeared in 1906, and various performers, chiefly the pianist Alfred Cortot, cultivated the music. Setting aside the highly subjective objections of Debussy, who loathed much German music and mentioned Brahms only in the context of neo-Beethovenianism (Vallas recalls that Debussy mentioned Brahms only casually in connection with his neo-Beethovenianism and with his Violin Concerto, which Debussy considered "very tiresome").[87] Though Ravel's views were more sympathetic, they follow those of D'Indy in objecting to Brahms's developmental working:

> This is what appears most clearly in the majority of Brahms's works. It is evident in the Symphony in D Major, which was recently performed at the Lamoureux concerts. The themes bespeak an intimate and gentle masculinity; although their melodic contour and rhythm are very personal they are directly related to those of Schubert and Schumann. Scarcely have they been presented than their progress becomes heavy and laborious. It seems that the composer was ceaselessly haunted by the desire to equal Beethoven. Now the charming nature

of Brahms's inspiration was incompatible with his vast, passionate, almost extravagant developments, which are the direct result of Beethovenian themes, or rather, themes which spring from Beethovenian inspiration. This craft, which his predecessor Schubert was deprived of *naturally*, was acquired by Brahms through study. He did not discover it within himself. . . . With Brahms, a clear and simple inspiration, sometimes playful, sometimes melancholy; learned developments which are gradiloquent, complicated and heavy.

Ravel compared Brahms's concerto methods with his own as follows: "I set out with the old notion that a concerto should be a divertissement. Brahms's principle about a symphonic concerto was wrong, and the critic who said that he had written a concerto 'against the piano' was right. Mozart's piano concertos and Mendelssohn's Violin Concerto are absolutely perfect." Surprisingly, the one area that Ravel singles out directly for praise is Brahms's "extremely brilliant" orchestration.[88]

In France and in other Latin countries the coolness toward Brahms continued. Its nature is clarified in a 1929 article by Jean Delaincourt:

French audiences are said to be unfair to Brahms. In German circles and in circles that are under German influences it is sometimes believed that we Frenchmen object to Brahms because his music calls for too great an effort of attention. This is not true. His grandeur wearies us because it strikes us as turgid. We find him tedious at times because he consistently avoids indulgence in relaxation. He was a great inventor of melodies, but he never rests content with melodies; he must stretch them and drape them in heavy folds. To his creations he gives false dimensions, making them appear laboured, but not actually expanding them. He arranges, he repeats, but he never makes real headway. His misfortune was that he was born in a time of great symphonists, and believed that salvation was not to be found except in their wake. He has written impressive things; but often he irritates us by being untrue to himself and borrowing an idiom alien to his nature in order to serve gods that are not really his.[89]

Brahms's smaller-scaled work fared better, as in the response of the classically inclined Poulenc, who appreciated the skill and economy of Brahms's scoring in the violin sonatas. "How beautiful Brahms's sonatas are! I did not know them very well. One cannot achieve a proper balance between two such different instruments as the piano and violin unless one treats them absolutely equally. The prima donna violin above an arpeggio piano accompaniment makes me vomit."[90]

That Ravel's views might have been even more sympathetic had he possessed a wider acquaintance with the music seems implicit in the valuable light thrown on the response of the Latin composers by Manuel de Falla, the Spanish nationalist composer and contemporary of Ravel. He notes not merely the characteristics of Brahms's keyboard writing but has knowledge of Brahms's musical interests when he comments that "these Scarlattian qualities are the saving graces of the best contemporary music. What might not have happened to Brahms (I am Northern enough to be able to bear the sound of his name, without the familiar, supercilious Latin gesture of disgust) . . . if he had come across the Santini manuscript of Scarlatti earlier in his life! . . . As it is, even Brahms could write passages (for example, in the Intermezzo, op. 116, no. 4) which, without being a direct imitation, show his mind working in the same way as Scarlatti's."[91] The general lack of interest in Brahms mentioned by Falla was probably strongest in Italy, the country of Scarlatti's birth, where the musical culture offered little opportunity for a general knowledge of Brahms's art. Brahms's acknowledgment of Verdi's greatness was strikingly reciprocated at the time of Brahms's death, when Verdi sent a letter-card to the Musikverein in Vienna marked "Condolences on the death of your great composer, Brahms."[92] But aside from this and the enthusiasm of Brahms's younger contemporary Guiseppe Martucci, interest varied, perhaps depending on circumstances of contact, as in the case of Alfredo Casella. Casella came to know Brahms's music (ironically in Paris) through his contact with Georges Enesco, the leading Romanian composer of his generation. Enesco had absorbed the music of Brahms through his training and passed it on to many other musicians. Casella comments, "My great intimacy with Enesco . . . was highly beneficial to my musical development. . . . From him I learned to know and under-stand—and therefore to love—the music of Schubert and Brahms. This was especially important in the latter case, as the Hamburg master was then completely misunderstood and undervalued in France, where he is far from being understood even today [1939]."[93]

Brahms was also of variable interest in northern countries beyond the German sphere. The symphonists Sibelius and Nielsen both went to Vienna as students. Sibelius gained a letter of introduction to study with Brahms from Busoni, though he apparently never visited the composer. Brahms got to hear that the young Sibelius had written a good string quartet, and he was charmed by one of his songs, but he was unwilling to teach at this very late stage of his life.[94] The remarks of Levas from personal contact with Sibelius late in his life summarize his outlook: "So far as Brahms, his wife's favorite composer, was concerned, he regarded him as an epigone of Beethoven, a fact that was bound to reduce Brahms's significance in his eyes. In any case he did not appreciate him in the same way that he appreciated Mozart and Beethoven—not to speak of Bach. He once said to me that Brahms became clearer in old age—from which it is to be understood that in his youth Brahms had seemed to lack clarity. . . . Sibelius in fact seldom had anything to say about Brahms, and even less about his contemporary and rival Anton Bruckner."[95] He did acknowledge the precedent of Brahms's Violin Concerto, which he did not hear until he had finished his own, declaring, "I have heard the Brahms violin concerto which is good. But so different (too symphonic) from mine." The virtuoso in him resisted Brahms's handling of the solo role, though in fact he soon revised his own concerto to reduce the virtuoso dimension. Nielsen developed an admiration for Brahms early on, as well as for Bach and Mozart, and he went to Vienna to meet him. He left a revealing description of the composer. Brahmsian aspects are notable not merely in his student works, such as his String Quartet in F Minor, but clearly in his first symphony, in which Simpson observes many links to Brahms.[96] Indeed, his continued devotion to the symphony and variations in traditional form shows him as a successor of Brahms to a much greater extent than is Sibelius.

In Russia there was no foundation for an appreciation of Brahms comparable with that laid by Schumann and Liszt, both of whom had visited the country, the latter taking great interest in Russian nationalist composers.[97] With the exception of some favorable comments by Cui and an interest in the D Minor Piano Concerto by Taneyev (though presumably for its pianistic interest, for he later expressed distaste for Brahms), the views of younger Russians were similar to those of Tchaikowsky, and he seems to have held no interest whatever for a progressive such as Alexander Scriabin. Stasov recalls in an essay published in 1889 the views of Liszt in old age: "He feels that at the present time there are no outstanding composers in Germany. [But] we, in Russia, have outstanding composers, who have said *something new* and have advanced art. Liszt spoke with special warmth about Balakirev's *Islamey.*"[98] Only in the more classically inclined approach of Rachmaninov is there some obvious interest and enthusiasm for Brahms. Thus, in criticizing the unfortunate first performance of Rachmaninov's First Symphony in 1906, the critic observed that it "is the product of a composer who has not yet fully found himself. At this point he could become either a musical crackpot or a Brahms." Rachmaninov himself was always sympathetic to Brahms the symphonist, as he was to many German classical composers, taking great interest in performances by Nikisch in Leipzig and Berlin while he was studying in Germany, as when he noted of a performance by the Berlin Philharmonic on 2 December 1908: "Yesterday . . . I heard the Philharmonic concert, at which Nikisch conducted the Brahms Second Symphony. And what a beautiful symphony!" As a pianist he played more Brahms than was customary in the Conservatoire programs; his remarkable capacity to master new works in a short time is illustrated in the case of Brahms's Variations and Fugue on a Theme of Handel, which Alexander Siloti required him to learn on short notice, and in three days he was playing "like a master."[99]

Stravinsky's view of Brahms is of interest in light of his strong historical knowledge and inclinations. Like those of Mahler, his views varied in different contexts. He had come to know Brahms's music well from youth through his uncle, a keen musician, and even began a symphony influenced by Brahms in his youth. In some comments he seems to regard Brahms as predictable and boring, and he was certainly averse to too much sentiment, as in response to Koussevitzky's view that Brahms had more feeling than Beethoven: "[He] is . . . right, but beware—*unfortunately* for Brahms and *fortunately* for Beethoven."[100] Yet Stravinsky clearly had great interest in the techniques of Brahms the composer, seeming to echo that of Schoenberg when he remarks in two separate comments in the 1920s and 1930s: "I have great feeling for Brahms. . . . You always sense the overpowering wisdom of the great artist even in his least inspired works. . . . What the public likes in Brahms is the sentiment. What I like has another, architectonic basis."[101] Brahms took on special interest when Stravinsky turned his attention to classical forms, especially to variations and to a symphony, and he claims to have "steeped" himself "in the variations of Beethoven and Brahms," including the "St. Antoni" Variations.[102]

Attitudes in England and the United States tended to be more generalized, following party lines with less individuality of response and fewer obvious tensions. In England the Royal College of Music was to be the focus for these tensions since so many of the leading composers and important pupils taught and studied there. The influence of Parry and Stanford brought with it a devotion to Brahmsian values, which were retained by many of their pupils. Stanford was considered by a composer of the younger generation, Eugene Goossens, to be the "finest interpreter of Brahms that he had ever heard." The young Vaughan Williams was thus initiated into a Brahmsian world that, to judge from a later comment, he too accepted as modern: "In 1891 when I first went to Parry, [he] introduced me to Wagner and Brahms—which was quite contrary to curricula then obtaining in academies." The influence also extended to Cambridge through Stanford, which he had entered in 1892. Williams acknowledges Brahms's stature in commenting on the attitude of the young student of his day that "if he favors the 'classical' school, he thinks it only becoming to make a show of exercising Brahmsian self-restraint, without considering what a storehouse of invention Brahms possessed out of which to deny himself." He clearly knew Brahms's music well, and he even commented on the skill of Brahms's folksong arrangements, a subject of interest to Williams. Yet respect never changed to affection in later years as he moved away from the Brahmsian qualities occasionally to be found in his early works. A younger pupil of Stanford's, John Ireland, was one of the few composers to keep any Brahmsian elements in his works, which incline more toward the instrumental and song forms employed by Brahms than do the songs of his contemporaries. He retained a devotion to Brahms's music, commenting, "I have always felt a deep affection for his works."[103]

The greater appeal of non-German music undermined any real curiosity about Brahms's music. The English critic Cecil Gray even used this inclination as a means of distinguishing between German composers: "In Bach, Beethoven, and Mozart it is the strong Italian substratum of thought that chiefly holds me; it is the comparative absence of that element in Brahms, Schumann, and Bruckner which repels me."[104] Gray criticized the Fourth Symphony as "morose and ascetic." This view prompted a response by the critic J. H. Elliot in 1929 who, in citing the criticism of "flat-footed pedantry," reveals another critical image that echoes earlier observations. His response was to question the grounds on which such an attitude could persist, save through irrelevant comparison with music devoted rather to the "picturesque." He challenges the view of Brahms as a "dual personality," one who never resolved the tensions between the desire to be evocative and romantic in his songs and to write purely instrumental works. He sees Brahms as achieving the balance and as being at his strongest when essaying in larger forms. He draws particular attention to the Fourth Symphony:

> The austerity ascribed to certain of Brahms's symphonic
> music can be conceived only as a misapprehension aris-
> ing either from cursory listening or from a preoccupation
> with structural values alone. To impute austerity to the
> Fourth Symphony is to admit that formal considerations
> still obscure the issue in the mind of the critic. The
> point is not so much whether the Finale is a passacaglia
> as whether it is the proper vehicle of the emotional con-
> dition which prompted it. Had Brahms been consciously
> obsessed with formal conventions he would certainly not
> have employed a form so apparently foreign to the sym-
> phonic condition. The result is, humanly speaking, per-
> fect. The formal trend of that massive movement serves
> inimitably the noble, triumphant mood—exultant rather
> than stern—which informs it; the whole conception is
> permeated with an electric vitality that is every whit as
> potent as that of Wagner in his most dynamic moments,
> and is certainly more subtle and rarefied. The musical
> and emotional subtlety is, moreover, common to

Brahms's symphonic music generally; it is essentially natural and characteristic, and cannot be regarded in any sense as a failure, either complete or comparative.[105]

Such reasoning was arid for those seeking new musical forms, or those who were inspired by other sources. Constant Lambert, who was interested in Russian and French ballet music, commented that Brahms's symphonies "command at least our respect"; this may be regarded as quite complimentary relative to his general outlook. A more positive view is offered by Arthur Bliss (who was on the staff of the RCM), a composer inspired by new European developments yet a Brahms enthusiast who played the piano music. He still identified among the beneficial influences of the new school in England that they "killed off the pseudo intellectuality of the Brahms camp followers, with their classical sonatas, concertos and variations, and other 'stock in trade.' "[106]

But German classicism continued to provide a starting point for most English composers, even if they soon turned elsewhere. The young Benjamin Britten was thoroughly familiar with Beethoven and Brahms yet soon felt that they had " 'let him down.' . . . He had expected so much from [them]." He later developed a noted aversion to Brahms, criticizing his orchestration and lack of spontaneity, a view to which only such works as the *Liebeslieder* waltzes found exception, played by him at the Aldeburgh Festival. The more developmental side repelled him, a view captured in his comment that "it is not bad Brahms I mind, it's good Brahms I can't stand." He attributed the weaknesses to personal reasons, finding an exception in the D Minor Piano Concerto and suggesting that "after Schumann's death something went out of him."[107] His older contemporary Michael Tippett found much more stimulus in the German symphony, though it was in the dramatic manner of Beethoven rather than in the manner of the "lyrical symphonists," including Brahms. He did find a performance of the Second Symphony valuable in contemplating symphonic composition, and, like Britten, found special interest in the D Minor Piano Concerto.[108]

As in Britain, Brahms's status had a profound impact on the development of American musical life in public concerts and at universities and conservatories, especially on the East Coast. The influence of Horatio Parker, professor of music at Yale University, was particularly strong. His students, including Charles Ives and Carl Ruggles, were destined to be important in the development of native music in the early years of the twentieth century. For Parker, like Stanford and Parry, Brahms was a model for modern orchestral and symphonic composition. Thus, for example, he required that Ives revise the second movement of his second symphony "à la Brahms" (which he apparently did). One of Ives's tasks as a student was to write his own setting of texts that had been set by Brahms and Schumann ("Feldeinsamkeit" and "Ich grolle nicht"). Parker's own teacher George Whitfield Chadwick wrote in a strongly Germanic style, and his Third Symphony was commended by the *Boston Globe* as the "best that has been written since Brahms." Even Ives retained a great regard for the German classics throughout his life, his favorite work being Mozart's G Minor Symphony. Though he admired certain other composers (Elgar, Franck, D'Indy), he had contempt for Strauss and Wagner and was undecided about Reger and Mahler. Yet he retained great regard for Brahms. His nephew recalls that "I have a book of his entitled *From Grieg to Brahms* and in it are many passages of Brahms that he underscored."[109]

Carl Ruggles held a similar regard for the German classics, noting as late as 1931 the importance of Brahms in relation to phraseology as part of an ascription of technical influences to different composers—Beethoven, Mozart, Bach, and Wagner. His orchestral work *Suntreader* (1931) has been likened to the opening of Brahms's First Symphony.[110] The centenary year 1933 gave the occasion for summarizing American attitudes. An article on contemporary American music in the *Musical Quarterly* that year comments that "not long ago there was a movement to promote the appreciation of Brahms, with the result that everyone now likes Brahms, or says he does. Liking him has its advantages, but we are only now emerging from the aping of his mannerisms." Yet it was immigrant European figures like Schoenberg who found more interest than native composers, typified in Virgil Thomson's response to a review of Hindemith's Symphony by Ernst Krenek: "I am going to use your reference about the 'masterful retreat into the heavily fortified Brahms line.' . . . Conservative as it is, the Hindemith Symphony has a certain workmanship interest. In view of the kind of contemporary music commonly appearing before us, a Brahms Fifth, as you call it, does present a slightly greater musical interest than the more usual Humperdinck Fifteenth."[111]

20 · Toward a New Evaluation of Brahms

The Postwar Situation: Brahms and the Progressives

The survival of Brahms's music through changing times had shown him to be no epigone of the classics. The position of classic-by-association that had been conferred on Brahms in the partisan disputes of his time now yielded to one of genuine acknowledgment of the individuality of his achievements within a revered tradition. Thus he remained of interest to the younger generation even though his language was now far removed from theirs. Karlheinz Stockhausen, in seeking to contrast his new vision of the potential of musical organization with that of Schoenberg (which he sees as standing at the end of a tradition) thus suggests, in analyzing motivic materials, that one "[take a theme] by Beethoven . . . [and] why not [one by] Brahms too" to illustrate the point. But status as a classical composer also opened Brahms's work to the possibility of radical creative reinterpretation in the form of parody by composers exploring new aesthetics of musical collage or music theater. In 1971–72, Mauricio Kagel, a leading composer of the absurdist music theater, produced his own orchestral version of Brahms's *Variations and Fugue on a Theme of Handel,* op. 24, for piano. Titled *Variationen ohne Fuge,* the Brahms work is used as a source for the kind of "meta-collage" previously employed by Kagel in his Beethoven-derived work *Ludwig Van.* This theatrical approach shared little with *Sinfonia,* the more famous synthetic work of the Italian Luciano Berio, which uses several Brahms extracts in its third movement and in which materials from other classical and romantic symphonies were drawn into relationship with the scherzo of Mahler's Second Symphony. As Berio comments, "The Mahler movement . . . is treated like a container—rather a generator, within whose framework a large number of musical references and characters is proliferated. They go from Bach to Schoenberg, Beethoven to Strauss, Brahms to Stravinsky, Berg to Boulez, the different musical characters always integrated into the flowing harmonic structure of Mahler's scherzo." But Berio's feeling for Brahms also appears in a more focused manner in his sensitive arrangement for orchestra of the Clarinet Sonata in F Minor, op. 120, no. 1, with its realization of the effect of piano pedaling and introductory passages to the first and second movements.[112]

Less radical responses to Brahms's music are found in Eastern European musical traditions after World War II, suggesting the longer continuation of a traditional creative link. The Polish composer Witold Lutoslawski acknowledged the direct influence of Brahmsian finale form in his First Symphony, whose "Toccata" finale is "modeled directly on the large sonatina form (i.e., sonata without development) which Brahms chose for the finales of his first and third symphonies."[113] The Hungarian György Ligeti also acknowledges Brahmsian precedent in taking a uniquely Brahmsian genre—"the very, very beautiful work of Brahms" as the model for his own trio for horn, violin, and piano—and dedicating his work to Brahms. Though in France general resistance to Brahms remained after the war, the remark of Honegger in 1950—"today he is admitted to the same rank as Beethoven or Berlioz"—shows the changing effect of familiarity through concert performance, the broadening of traditions long established by specialists.[114] Brahms's symphonies were increasingly programmed by French conductors, though the most individual performances remained of the Second Symphony, notably in the reading of Pierre Monteux. Indeed, this new interest in Brahms provides the background to the title of François Sagan's novel *Aiméz vous Brahms?*[115] in the form of a casual remark by way of invitation to a concert: when the recipient, the protagonist of the story, listens to a recording of a Brahms concerto, she dismisses it as too romantic, which in cultural context means sentimental and old-fashioned. For the radical young composers, resistance remained predictably absolute. Despite Pierre Boulez's wide interest in Wagner, Mahler, and the Second Viennese School, his writings are notable for their paucity of references to Brahms, who was clearly in no sense a progressive composer for him—he characterizes Brahms as "boring" and predictable. His guarded attitude to Schoenberg, first expressed in the article "Schoenberg is Dead," meant that, for Boulez, Brahms was even more completely dead; indeed, Robert Craft recalls the young composer harmonizing Schoenberg in the style of Brahms (as if to make this point) when in the company of Stravinsky.[116]

But French music also offers a strikingly different point of view from an equally radical composer, albeit of an older generation, Edgard Varèse: he still finds in Brahms's compositional ethos features retaining their validity for a modern composer. In his teaching Varèse always took a series of classes on orchestration, which included examples from Brahms's First

Symphony, and a pupil recalled that "after quoting Brahms's definition of composition—the 'organization of disparate elements'—[he] went on to attack the neoclassicists and the return to Bach, or to Mozart, or to Debussy." Of orchestration he commented that "the orchestra, in the present sense of the word, like the virtuoso, is finished. Therefore orchestration, as we call it, must revert to its original meaning; must become part and parcel of the substance itself. From this it follows that Rimsky-Korsakov was a poor orchestrator and Brahms a good one. The composition itself is the orchestration. You can't write a piece of music and then say that you will orchestrate it; both processes must be accomplished in the one stroke, for orchestration is the response to the musical content of the work."[117]

More unexpected interest in Brahms emerged in the case of the American Elliott Carter. As a young composer in late 1920s and 1930s, Carter naturally came into contact with the Brahmsian orthodoxy in America and clearly got to know the music well, not least through observing its value in the eyes of his hero Charles Ives. Though choosing a quite different musical path and specifically classifying Brahms as a "reactionary" in comparison with Beethoven as a "progressive," Carter could still admit the quality of Brahms's music, arguing that a composer as such is not good or bad according to these designations. It was in connection with Stravinsky's criticism of Schoenberg's piano writing in his Piano Concerto that Stravinsky recommended that Carter study etudes. Carter did this, especially Brahms's *51 Keyboard Exercises* (*51 Übungen für Klavier*), to which he had been introduced by Jean Casadesus: "I found them very entertaining because they have things like three against five and so on. So I guess my Piano Concerto comes from these as much as anything."[118] In these and other such rhythmic features emerges a structural rather than stylistic link with Brahms that recalls Stravinsky's own explanation of his interest in the composer.

The Emerging Discipline of Music Analysis

If Brahms's music held little interest for the successors of the Second Viennese School after the war, the attitude of their contemporaries in the field of analysis was entirely different. Compositional systemization had found its counterpart in a newly rigorous attitude toward music analysis and criticism. Brahms was to be a primary figure within this new tradition. Schoenberg rather than the theorist Heinrich Schenker would be the main agent of the postwar interest, because translations of Schenker's works came much later to the English-speaking world, where they attracted interest through the teachings of his pupils, who had immigrated to America. The publication of the revised and translated version of Schoenberg's article "Brahms the Progressive" in 1950 suddenly revealed to the general public a new facet of Schoenberg, a supposedly revolutionary composer. But it was not this article alone that stimulated thinking on the role of transformation and variation in the structure of classical works and their relation to serialism. Schoenberg's German pupil Josef Rufer used his teacher's article "Composition with Twelve Tones" (published in the same volume as "Brahms the Progressive") as the basis of a book of that name, whose introduction draws out Schoenberg's links to German instrumental tradition, with particular reference to structural unity, especially the use of a basic motive or *Grundgestalt* in organizing an entire tonal work. Among the examples, predominantly drawn from Beethoven, is one from Brahms not used by Schoenberg, though also from the A Minor Quartet, op. 51/2, the slow movement theme of which he analyzes at length.[119]

Schoenberg was not the only analyst to stress the vital role of thematic process in Brahms. In 1950 the Viennese critic Rudolf Réti wrote a book titled *The Thematic Process in Music,* which did not mention Schoenberg yet dealt with issues that reflected similar concerns. Réti sought to explain the pervasive unity he found in the Austro-German tradition in terms more detailed than those of formal structure, concluding that a background thematic contour ensured a deeper unity intended by the composer and specific to every work. His primary example is Schumann's piano cycle *Kinderszenen,* which thus appears as a set of variations on a basic contour. Likewise, by simple manipulations of figures he found in Brahms's seemingly contrasted rhapsodies op. 79, nos. 1 and 2, a shared and complementary contour. Where he differed most from Schoenberg was in his broader view of linking contour, Schoenberg's preoccupation being with the thematic process at the most detailed level. Though Réti does make passing references to thematic process, it is the larger thematic contrasts of a work that he finds interesting, as in the case of the first movement of the Second Symphony: "The mechanism of Brahms's orchestral technique is largely based on [the] art of cutting out particles of one theme, changing their tempo and rhythm and integrating them, and linking them to other themes. Brahms almost regularly delineates the secondary parts, with which he accompanies the second subjects in his symphonies with figurations that are differently accentuated particles from the same work's first theme. If we single out certain notes, the first theme comes to the fore; if we single out others, the second theme appears. . . . [Thus] the second theme is also accompanied by parts of the first."[120]

Later writers benefited from both these emphases—the sense of continuity and overall unity in Schoenberg, the process of detailed derivation of contrasted ideas in Réti. The English writer Alan Walker reached the most radical conclusion based on his response to Schoenberg's ideas in his article "Brahms and Serialism" in 1958. Many of his ideas were based on those of his teacher Hans Keller, the chief advocate of Schoenberg in postwar Britain. Though Keller had little interest in Brahms as a composer, Walker used Brahms to develop Keller's ideas (which also related to those of Réti), concerning the "unity behind surface contrasts." Thus, Walker contends that the opening three-note motive in the Second Symphony "pervades the entire work. A stepwise curve, a falling fourth, a rising third, from these primitive elements Brahms builds one of his mightiest structures. Time and again they turn up as part of the content of his symphony. But they also play a deeper role. They express the background drive against which some of the work's other extreme contrasts unfold."[121] Like Erwin Stein, Walker saw Brahmsian motivic variation in especially strong terms in the Fourth Symphony, but he went much further in seeing Brahms's Fourth Symphony as a "proto-serial" work.

There are two things that I seek to show in this article. The first is that the attitude of mind which led Schoenberg to invent his twelve-note system had already made itself manifest *on a conscious level* in Brahms; and the second is that 20th-century serial techniques enable us to see the music of the great composers, especially the music of Brahms, in a new and significant light. "Brahms the Progressive" reveals a comparatively unknown aspect of this composer, but rather tantalizingly ignores the logical conclusion of the argument it represents. For example, Schoenberg knew Brahms's E Minor Symphony well enough to point out the vital connection between the outer movements and it is inconceivable to me that having got this far he failed to recognize the embryo serialism that occurs throughout the work. Serialism is a conscious attempt on the part of twentieth-century composers to do what pre-nineteenth-century composers did intuitively. It is a deliberate act of unification. All great works of art represent a unity and it matters little whether this was brought about by a flash of inspiration, hard work, or the detached application of serial techniques. . . . The existence of strict serialism is due to evolution not revolution, and a careful examination of the music of Bach, Mozart, Beethoven and Brahms will reveal many of the acorns from which Schoenberg's oak trees were later to spring. For a number of reasons, the music of Brahms offers the best demonstration of this fact, but the main reason is that he was one of the first composers to do his musical thinking out loud. His unifying technique lies near the surface of his music as it were, and it will be a comparatively simple matter in my musical examples to let Brahms draw my conclusions for me.[122]

Similar conclusions were reached by Theodor Adorno, who viewed Schoenberg's achievements from another perspective. His book *Philosophie der neuen Musik* of 1948 sees the essential dialectic of twentieth-century musical development as residing in the attitudes of two major figures: Schoenberg as a progressive and Stravinsky as a reactionary.

In Brahms the development—as the execution and transformation of the thematic material—took possession of the sonata as a whole. Subjectification and objectification are intertwined. Brahms's technique unites both tendencies, forcing the lyric intermezzo and academic structure into meaningful union. While still composing within the total framework of tonality, Brahms by and large rejects conventional formulae and fundamentals, producing a unity of the work which—out of freedom—is constantly renewed at every moment. He consequently becomes the advocate of universal economy, refuting all coincidental movements of music, and yet developing the most extreme multiplicity, the result from thematic material the identity of which has been preserved. This indeed is his greatest accomplishment. There is no longer anything which is unthematic; nothing which cannot be understood as the derivative of the thematic material, no matter how latent it may have become. Schoenberg develops the tendencies of Beethoven and Brahms; in so doing he can lay claim to the heritage of classical bourgeois music—in a sense very similar to that in which dialectical materialism is related to Hegel. . . .

In Beethoven and still more completely in Brahms the unity of the motivic-thematic manipulation is achieved in a type of balance between subjective dynamics and traditional "tonal" language. The subjective approach to composition forces the conventional language to speak again, without varying it by means of its intervention as language. The alteration of language was accomplished along Romantic Wagnerian lines at the expense of objectivity and the binding force of the music itself. This alteration has shattered motivic-thematic unity in the art song and substituted for them leitmotiv and programmatic content. Schoenberg was the first to reveal the principles of universal unity and economy of material which Wagner had discovered as new, subjective and emancipated. His works offer definite proof that the more consequently adhered to the nominalism of musical language inaugurated by Wagner, the more perfectly this language is to be mastered by rational means.[123]

Schenker's theories complement Schoenberg's on theme and motivic process in the field of harmony and tonality. Like Schoenberg, Schenker based his theories on the study of classic and Romantic music. Also like Schoenberg, he gave a great deal of attention to the music of Brahms, whom he saw likewise as representing the climax of this tradition. The obituary quoted above represents the views of the young composer/theorist, but his views never changed as he devoted himself to the development of his theories of tonal coherence. He parallels Schoenberg in finding ever new evidences of the value of his theories as he developed them, and Brahms remained a prime means of this demonstration, though the character of the demonstration changed over the years. Thus, in the first volume of *Neue Musikalische Theorien und Phantasien: Harmonielehre*, his interest lies in both thematic links and the extension of the tonal system through enrichment from church modes, citing many examples from Brahms. The basic preoccupation with the avoidance of ornament that he shares with Schoenberg has similar relevance to Brahms, and examples serve to show this, most notably the collection of octaves and fifths made by Brahms from works from the Renaissance to his own day, and in which he sought to show when these intervals were acceptable and when not. Schenker transcribed these and added an explanatory commentary as to their significance.[124]

Alongside these established methods, a broadening interest in Brahms's techniques and stimuli became apparent. In the 1957 article "The Structural Origin of Exact Tempi," Allen Forte sought to demonstrate the "inter relatedness of tempo, rhythm and melody in a single composition, the Variations of a Theme of Haydn op. 56a and 56b. The thesis . . . is that the various tempi are derived from rhythmic configurations, which are, in turn, conditioned—if not totally determined—by basic melodic-rhythmic patterns unique to this work." This effectively draws a postwar compositional concept—the total integration of the parameters of a work—into the analysis of a nineteenth-century work, further highlighting the architectonic aspect of the music. The strikingly constructivist aspects of the late Piano Pieces, opp. 116–119, naturally have special interest. In an early and important text on the interpretation of music in terms of the principles of semiology (1975), Jean Jacques Nattiez uses the Intermezzo in C Major, op. 119, no. 3, to demonstrate the capacity of the music to be reduced to a small number of related shapes that ensure its continuity and coherence. Alongside this "structuralist" view analysis has also sought to reveal the fuller extent of the historical origins of Brahms's music, anticipating later trends. In a study of the Intermezzo in B Minor, op. 119, no. 1, Brian Newbould sees its use of descending fifth progressions as masking a fundamental chaconne structure, thus proposing the penetration of a principle demonstrated in many variation movements into the most intimate of Brahms's forms of expression.[125]

1983 and Beyond: Brahms the Postmodernist

The sesquicentenary year of Brahms's birth provided a focus for the clarification of changing attitudes since the centenary of 1933. One dimension of the view was by now predictable: the acceptance of Brahms's classic status, the acknowledgment by critics and analysts as well as performers of his vast creative achievement. The unpredictable element was related to a fundamental change in musical values only then becoming apparent: the reaction against Modernism. Brahms's classic status has been expressed in two ways: in the desire of scholars to produce more accurate and comprehensive musical editions and supporting material, and in the desire to reexamine the music even more precisely for construction and for relation to historical models. The current undertaking of a second collected edition of his works, reedited from a much larger spread of sources than the 1926–28 edition, now coincides with the second collected editions of the works of Schumann and Mendelssohn, and it also appears closer in time to new collected editions of Bach, Haydn, Mozart, Schubert, and Beethoven.[126] An essential part of the preliminary research for this edition has been the preparation of a thematic index, along the lines of the Haydn, Schubert, and Beethoven indexes, adding much more information on source location and compositional background than previous catalogues.[127] And in consequence of this work, much more comprehensive bibliographies have recently appeared, as have studies concerning editorial methods and problems. Research on Brahms thus stands ready for a mastery of its source materials on a par with that for any great composer to date. Yet the context in which research will take place has altered significantly with changes in the musical attitude to the past. With the end of postwar Modernism and a new interest in and rapport with the vast world of music of the past made available especially through recordings in the twentieth century, Brahms has come increasingly to be seen not simply as a follower of the classics, however resourceful, but as a pioneer anticipating this new world in his devotion to the study and understanding of past music. A nascent postmodernist, perhaps. Thus the recent view of Northcott:

By contrast [with Wagner] . . . Brahms seems to have
worked from the apprehension that after Schubert and
Mendelssohn, the great central tradition of composition
had somehow got lost and was only to be found again, if
at all, through a conscious effort of historical synthesis.
Hence not only the unprecedented analytic insight he
brought to the music of the past but his concern with
manuscripts, scholarship, the whole paraphernalia of scientific musicology as it was emerging in his lifetime. . . .
Must one concede that, in anticipating the self-conscious
and compound spirit of so much twentieth-century art
from Picasso to T. S. Eliot, the first truly modern composer was not Stravinsky, Schoenberg, Debussy or even
Wagner, but Brahms? And how on earth is this to be
squared with his apparent accessibility to the ordinary
music lover. One answer would presumably lie in the
many levels his music works on at once, somehow fusing
together angular lines or teasing cross rhythms, which, in
isolation, might seem to pre-echo Schoenberg or even Elliott Carter, in an assuaging flow. Does this in turn possibly explain his increasing attraction now? For if Brahms
might be said not only to have anticipated some of the
problems of Modernism but also their resolution, then
he could well have a special message for these ambiguous
times which, for want of a better term, we have settled
to call Post-modern.[128]

The implication of the view of Brahms as a model is pursued by
Burkholder, who sees in his very position an example for the modern
composer.

Far from needing to be saved from the back benches of
progress, Brahms can be characterized as the most modern and indeed the most imitated of composers of the
latter nineteenth century, the composer whose approach
to music has become most typical of later generations of
composers. Brahms is the single most important influence on twentieth-century classical music—not in the

way it *sounds*, but in how we think about it, how composers think about it, how music behaves, why it is written, and how composers measure their success. . . . I want to redefine modernism in music and to begin the modernist movement in music with Brahms. . . . What is most radical about Brahms's music is that he faced head on the problems of writing for a concert audience familiar with the music of the past, the problem that has been the principal concern of serious composers since his time. . . . Brahms's fundamental importance for the music of the past one hundred years is this: he has provided the model for future generations of what a composer is, what a composer does, why a composer does it, what is of value in music, and how a composer is to succeed. . . . In this respect the music of the future has belonged not to Wagner but to Brahms. . . .

It is the change in the orientation of serious music, the change in the purpose of composition, which has been of greatest importance, rather than the changes within the language of music itself. The music that resulted from a confrontation with Wagner, from Strauss to Debussy, evolved a new language where orchestral colour, striking dissonant chords, new scales and modes, and characteristic rhythmic patterns assumed increasing structural weight and the old foundations of tonal centres and thematic repetitions gradually lost their importance. This process was relatively untroubled, as it has had almost nothing to do with modernism. When new resources were called into play for programmatic, pictorial or coloristic reasons, there was no potential limit for the evolution of the musical language or for its comprehensibility. Even works which transcended tonality, such as Stravinsky's early ballets, found enthusiastic audiences. . . . While Wagner and Liszt provided new musical tools, Brahms helped establish the framework for using these tools, and his assumptions concerning what music is and does have been played out in succeeding generations. Thus it was

Brahms the traditionalist rather than Wagner the revolutionary who created and confronted the central problem for composers of the twentieth century: the integration of a progressive musical language with an allegiance to the tradition of Bach, Mozart, Haydn and Beethoven. There are no Wagners now, except perhaps composers who write movie music—I am thinking here of the contemporary American Gesamtkunstwerk called *Star Wars,* and the music for it by John Williams. But there are hundreds of Brahmses, composers who look to the classical music of the past as source and measure of their own "classical" music and who seek . . . "a place beside or near Beethoven."[129]

Thus the view of Colles and other critics might seem to have come full circle in vindicating Brahms's position and outlook. Because, as an instrumental composer, he represented the musical mainstream, his problems were essentially the problems of later composers who wished to relate to the great tradition that, far from being usurped by Modernism, was actually being reborn through burgeoning concert life, broadcasting, and recordings. In summarizing the apparent paradoxes that so confused critics conditioned to a dualist polarity between Modernism and Tradition— Brahms the "difficult epigone," Brahms the "cerebral sentimentalist," Brahms the "alienated conformist"—Peter Gay not only proposes that Brahms's position lies beyond either classification, but he also points to the requirements of any future music that may seek to regain the qualities embodied in Brahms's music. His conclusion has lost none of its force for current musical culture: "Brahms, in his aspirations, his culture, above all his compositions, embraced, without strain, many of the polarities we have been taught to see as unchangeable, and unchangeably opposed to one another. The lesson of his reputation is the urgent need to restore our sense of complexity about Modernism."[130]

Notes

ONE · *Brahms the Man*

1 · Physical Appearance, Temperament, and Personality

Epigraph: Adelina de Lara, *Finale* (London, 1955), 48. De Lara (1872–1961) was a pupil of Clara Schumann's in Frankfurt from 1886–91. She continued to play into her advanced years, when she made some recordings. Her own estimate of Brahms's age as being "about forty" when she first met him is obviously mistaken.

1. Albert Dietrich, *Erinnerungen an Johannes Brahms, besonders aus seiner Jugendzeit* (Leipzig, 1899), 4.

2. "Aus der Zeit des jungen Brahms. Nach Erinnerungen von Elisabeth Proffen, geb. Rösing," *Zeitschrift für Musik* 94 (1927): 417. Frau Dr. Elisabeth Rösing was the widow of Dr. J. G. H. Rösing and aunt of the Völkers sisters, leading members of Brahms's Hamburg Frauenchor (Hamburg Ladies' Choir).

3. J. V. Widmann, *Johannes Brahms in Erinnerungen* (Berlin, 1898), 17.

4. George Henschel, *Musings and Memories of a Musician* (London, 1918), 123–24. Ignaz Brüll (1846–1907).

5. Widmann, *Erinnerungen*, 43.

6. "Dieser kleine, rundliche Herr." Gustav Jenner, *Johannes Brahms als Mensch, Lehrer und Künstler. Studien und Erlebnisse von G. Jenner* (Marpurg, 1905), 3.

7. Eugenie Schumann, *Erinnerungen* (Stuttgart, 1927), 191.

8. Henschel, *Musings and Memories*, 46.

9. C. V. Stanford, *Studies and Memories* (London, 1908), 108–9.

10. Dietrich, *Erinnerungen*, 4.

11. Henschel, *Musings and Memories*, 98.

12. Walter Niemann, *Brahms* (Berlin, 1920), 152.

13. E. Schumann, *Erinnerungen*, 263.

14. Quoted in Niemann, *Brahms*, 156.

15. Kalbeck, *Johannes Brahms*, 3:207.

16. Richard von Perger, *Brahms* (Leipzig, 1908), 66. Von Perger (1854–1911) was a conductor and composer of Brahmsian inclination. He was first active in Rotterdam, then became conductor of the Gesellschaft concerts in Vienna and director of the Conservatory.

17. Kalbeck, *Johannes Brahms*, 1:477.

18. Brahms's charitable nature was captured in "Brahms and the Beggar," the popular silhouette by Otto Böhler (Breitkopf & Härtel).

19. Henschel, *Musings and Memories*, 111.

20. "Du, Glücklicher!" Quoted in Richard Heuberger, *Erinnerungen an Johannes Brahms*, ed. K. Hofmann, 2nd ed. (Tutzing, 1987), 21.

21. E. Schumann, *Erinnerungen*, 259–60.

22. Quoted in Edward Speyer, *My Life and Friends* (London, 1937), 67.

23. Letter of 20 October 1854. *Briefe von und an Joseph Joachim*, ed. Johannes Joachim and Andreas Moser (Berlin, 1911), 1:218.

24. Letter of 3 January 1856. *Briefe von und an Joseph Joachim*, 303.

25. Undated letters (placed 27 November 1894 and 12 May 1895 by the editor) in Alfred Orel, *Johannes Brahms und Julius Allgeyer, Eine Künstlerfreundschaft in Briefen* (Tutzing, 1964), 126.

26. E. Schumann, *Erinnerungen*, 251.

27. Letter of "Easter Monday, April, 1872." *Schumann–Brahms Briefe*, 2:8.

28. Eduard Hanslick, *Die Neue Freie Presse*, 1 July 1897, quoted and trans. in Florence May, *The Life of Brahms*, 2 vols., 2nd ed. (London, 1948), 2:654.

29. Quoted in Niemann, *Brahms*, 154. Philipp Spitta (1841–94).

30. Quoted in the English version of Niemann, *Brahms* (trans. C. A. Phillips as *Brahms* [New York, 1929]), 179. Karl Goldmark, *Erinnerungen aus meinem Leben* (Vienna, 1922), 89.

31. Hans Gál, *Johannes Brahms, His Work and Personality* (Frankfurt am Main, 1961), trans. J. Stein (London, 1963), 59.

32. Letters of 3 February "1855" and September 1890. *Clara Schumann–Johannes Brahms, Briefe aus den Jahren 1853–1896*, hsg. Berthold Litzmann, 2 vols. (Leipzig, 1927), 1:70, 2:422.

33. Widmann, *Erinnerungen*, 130.

34. Rudolf von den Leyen, *Johannes Brahms als Mensch und Freund* (Düsseldorf, 1905), 26.

35. Kalbeck, *Johannes Brahms*, 4:406.

36. Leyen, *Johannes Brahms*, 96–97.

2 · *Upbringing and Education*

37. May, *Life of Brahms*, 1:54–55.

38. Niemann, *Brahms*, 17.

39. I have omitted from the above quotations the passages that stress the squalor of the dwelling at the time of the descriptions given, since they imply the condition of the Brahmses' dwelling and neighborhood at the time of the composer's birth. Although it is impossible to know the state of the dwelling when Brahms was a child, the evidence suggests that the family attempted to keep its various homes in good order. Karl Geiringer comments that the parents "were always eager to add to the comfort of their home as far as lay in their power . . . [and] were always fond of keeping songbirds—once there is even mention of a nightingale—and wherever possible the room was adorned with flowering plants in whose welfare the whole family took the liveliest interest." See Geiringer,

Brahms, His Life and Work, 2nd ed., trans. H. B. Weiner and B. Miall (London, 1948), 11.

40. Details of Brahms's baptism are given in Kalbeck, *Johannes Brahms,* 1:13.

41. As noted by Klaus Groth. See Heinrich Miesner, *Klaus Groth und die Musik: Erinnerungen an Johannes Brahms* (Heide, 1933), 30–35.

42. La Mara [Maria Lipsius], *Johannes Brahms* (Leipzig, 1921), 9–10.

43. Ibid., 10. Niemann, *Brahms,* 16.

44. Unpublished letter of Christiane Brahms to Johannes Brahms of 6 January 1865. Kurt Hofmann, *Johannes Brahms und Hamburg,* 2nd ed. (Reinbek, 1986), 19.

45. Geiringer, *Brahms,* 9.

46. Ibid., 6.

47. Elizabeth Wilhelmine Luise ("Elise") Brahms, 1831–92. Geiringer (*Brahms*) quotes from a number of early letters from Elise (1831–92). Brahms helped Fritz (1835–85) to obtain a position as piano teacher to Countess Ida von Hohenthal, which explains the dedication of the Piano Sonata in F Minor op. 5 to von Hohenthal. Geiringer, *Brahms,* 39.

48. Brahms took a room for his father so that Johann Jacob could live apart from his wife, who stayed at the family home with Elise. Geiringer, *Brahms,* 87. The effect of the separation on Brahms can be gauged from the concern expressed by Clara in her reply to his letter (lost) of 19 July 1864. *Schumann–Brahms Briefe,* 1:457–59. (Karoline Brahms, formerly Schnack [1824–1902]; Fritz Schnack [1851–1919]).

49. Henschel, *Musings and Memories,* 118.

50. Unpublished letter of "1864." Quoted in Geiringer, *Brahms,* 83.

51. Henschel, *Musings and Memories,* 117.

52. Letter to his father of 21 October 1865. Kurt Stephenson, *Johannes Brahms' Heimatbekenntnis in Briefen an seine Hamburger Verwandten,* ed. Kurt Stephenson (Hamburg, 1948), 70.

53. Letter of 23 July 1867. Quoted in Stephenson, *Johannes Brahms' Heimatbekenntnis,* 86–87.

54. Unpublished letter of 3 September 1867. Quoted in Geiringer, *Brahms,* 97–98.

55. Letter of 22 August 1867. *Johannes Brahms im Briefwechsel mit Joseph Joachim,* 2:42 (*Bw* 6).

56. Letter of 4 March 1872 to Karoline Brahms. Quoted in Stephenson, *Johannes Brahms' Heimatbekenntnis,* 133–35.

57. Noted in Geiringer, *Brahms,* 87.

58. Recorded by the English musician John Farmer, who was present at the performance. Quoted in Geiringer, *Brahms,* 100.

59. *A German Requiem* (Ein deutsches Requiem) has long been associated with Brahms's feelings about his mother. For example, the text of the fifth movement includes the words "thee will I comfort even as a mother comforts," and Brahms is known to have told Hermann Deiters that he was thinking of his mother while composing the movement. In addition, consistent work is known to have

been under way soon after her death. However, there is little documentation on the origins of the work. On the issues relating to the background of the *Requiem,* see Michael Musgrave, *Brahms: A German Requiem* (Cambridge, 1996), 9–13.

60. May, *Life of Brahms,* 1:53. This, however, cannot have been strictly true. She is recalled as having returned from the theater only shortly before suffering her fatal stroke "one evening in the last week of January" 1865. See May, *Life of Brahms,* 2:362.

61. Geiringer, *Brahms,* 3–77.

62. Kalbeck, *Johannes Brahms,* 1:15–16.

63. Von den Leyen stresses the importance of his access to the Bible in his formal education (*Johannes Brahms als Mensch und Freund,* 32).

64. Brahms was confirmed at the St. Michaeliskirche in 1848. He was prepared by Pastor Geffcken, described by Kalbeck as a distinguished hymnologist and a compiler of the "neuen Hamburgische Gesangbuch," begun in 1843 (*Johannes Brahms,* 1:18–19). Brahms stresses his early knowledge of the Bible in correspondence with Adolf Schubring, humorously confirming his suitability to act as godfather to Schubring's child. "I was baptized, learned by heart the catechism according to Luther, also read the Bible diligently." Letter of July 1856. *Briefwechsel mit Schubring* (*Bw* 8), 188. For a view stressing Schumann's influence on Brahms's Bible reading, see Daniel Beller-McKenna, "Brahms, Schumann and the Bible," *Newsletter of the American Brahms Society* 13 (1995): 1–4.

65. It is impossible on the basis of the limited available evidence to gauge the full scope of Brahms's activities as an entertainment pianist. The long-held belief that he played in low-class taverns from childhood—and the picture of exploitation drawn from it—must ultimately have stemmed from repeated statements by Brahms himself in later years (allied to the impression of poverty given by the later condition of the dwelling of his birth). For example, he said to the choral conductor Siegfried Ochs, when challenged for his tactlessness, "Where should I have learnt tact? In my youth I had to play in sailor's taverns in order not to go hungry, and there one learns nothing good" (Siegfried Ochs, *Geschehenes, Gesehenes* [Leipzig, 1922], 298); or, more veiled, to Clara Schumann, as recorded by her daughter Eugenie: that, when he was a "mere boy" he "saw things and received impressions which left a deep shadow on his mind" (*Erinnerungen,* 247). However, close witnesses of his youth denied any knowledge of exploitation; see, for example, Frau Cossel and Christian Otterer to Florence May (*Life of Brahms,* 1:71). Given such evidence, along with the good character of the locations at which he is know to have performed, and Brahms's parents' concern for the education of their children, Kurt Hofmann has recently argued that Brahms greatly exaggerated his youthful experiences and that the economic circumstances have been misinterpreted. The Brahms family always lived in the

Hamburg Neustadt, near the Alster lake, quite separate from the St. Pauli dockland area. During Brahms's childhood they belonged to the working class, but there was never any question of poverty or dependence. See Hofmann, *Brahms in Hamburg*, 12–13, and, more extensively, "Brahms the Hamburg Musician, 1833–1862," in *The Cambridge Companion to Brahms*, ed. Michael Musgrave (Cambridge, 1998), 4–15.

66. Quoted in Niemann, *Brahms*, 31.

67. May's description of the apartment in which Brahms was born suggests that there was hardly room for a piano. The repeated reminiscence of Lieschen Giesemann (quoted by Geiringer) of the "charming pastel portrait of Christiane Brahms as a young girl . . . which was hung in the place of honor over the piano in every home they had" can relate only to the homes with which she was familiar from 1847. Letter from Elise Denninghof, 25 September 1889. Geiringer, *Brahms*, 11. By the time he met Luise Japha in the later 1840s, however, he had begun to use a studio in Hamburg.

68. Otto Cossell, 1813–65.

69. The letter is reproduced in facsimile by Kalbeck, *Johannes Brahms*, 1:24, facing.

70. La Mara, *Johannes Brahms*, 10–11.

71. Quoted in May, *Life of Brahms*, 1:69. This was apparently the arrangement of the Rondo from Weber's piano sonata op. 24, which later appeared in the Studies for Piano as no. 2. See Margit L. McCorkle, *Johannes Brahms, Thematisch-Bibliographisches Werkverzeichnis* (Munich, 1984), 616.

72. May, *Life of Brahms*, 1:85–87.

73. La Mara, *Johannes Brahms*, 12–13.

74. Friedrich Wilhelm Grund (1791–1874) was cofounder and director of the Philharmonic Concerts and founder and conductor of the Singakademie (both 1828). Georg Friederich Otten (1806–90) founded his Musikalische Gesellschaft in 1843, the year Carl Voigt (1808–79) founded his Cäcilienverein.

75. Unpublished letter of 11 June 1853. Geiringer, *Brahms*, 29.

76. Joachim spent summer vacation at Göttingen so that he could attend university lectures in philosophy and history. Geiringer, *Brahms*, 32.

77. Unpublished letter of 23 July 1853. Geiringer, *Brahms*, 33.

78. Letter from Joachim to Brahms's parents of 25 July 1853. Quoted in Geiringer, *Brahms*, 33–34.

79. Jacob's reply of 1 August 1853 is published in *Briefe von und an Joseph Joachim*, 1:68.

3 · The Critical Stages of Brahms's Life and Ambitions

80. Joachim quoted and trans. in May, *Johannes Brahms*, 1:108–9.

81. The cooling of Joachim's friendship with Liszt is documented in his letters. See *Briefe von und an Joseph Joachim*, vols. 1 and 2, various entries.

82. Letter of 29 June 1853, *Briefe von und an Joseph Joachim* (Berlin, 1911), 64–65. "Johannes Kreisler" was the chief character in Hoffmann's fantastic tale *Kater Murr*. E. T. A. Hoffmann (1776–1822).

83. W. J. von Wasieleski, *Aus siebzig Jahren: Lebens Erinnerungen* (Stuttgart, 1897), 143–44. Wasieleski (1822–96) was a violinist, conductor, and writer of music histories, theoretical works, a biography of Schumann (1858, 2nd ed. 1869, 3rd ed. 1880).

84. Commerzienrath Theodor Deichmann was a rich and influential merchant, and his home at Mehlem, opposite Königswinter on the Rhine, was a meeting place for many artists and musicians. Ferdinand Hiller (1811–85); Karl Reinecke (1824–1910); Franz Wüllner (1832–1902).

85. Kalbeck, *Johannes Brahms*, 1:55.

86. Berthold Litzmann, *Clara Schumann. Ein Künstlerleben, nach Tagebüchern und Briefen* (Leipzig, 1901, 1906–9), 280–81. Litzmann lists all the early entries concerning Brahms from Schumann's *Tagebücher*.

87. "Neue Bahnen," *Neue Zeitschrift für Musik* 39 (1853):185.

88. See Eugenie Schumann's account of Brahms's first visit in *Ein Lebensbild meines Vaters* (Leipzig, 1931), 357.

89. Quoted in Kalbeck, *Johannes Brahms*, 2:430.

90. Dietrich, *Erinnerungen*, 1–2.

91. Letter of September or October 1853. *Bw* 5, 8.

92. Letter of December 1853. *Schumann–Brahms Briefe*, 1:3–4.

93. Bülow gave the first public performance of a published Brahms work other than by the composer when he played the first movement of the Piano Sonata in C Major, op. 1, on 1 March 1854 in Hamburg. Noted in *Hans von Bülow: Briefe und Schriften*, ed. Marie von Bülow (Leipzig, 1896–1908), 6 [Briefe 5], 141.

94. Letter of September 1856. *Brahms im Briefwechsel mit Grimm*, 44–45 (*Bw* 4).

95. Clara Schumann had many connections in aristocratic musical and social circles, and she knew Princess Frederike, the sister of the Prince of Detmold. See Willi Schramm, *Brahms in Detmold*, ed. with new commentary by Richard Müller Dombois [*Sonderveröffentlichen der Naturwissenschaftlichen und historischen Vereins für das Land Lippe*, Bd. 33] (Hagen, 1983), 15–20. Clemens August Kiel (1813–71).

96. Carl Louis Bargheer was the pupil of Spohr, David, and Joachim. Letter of 5 December 1857. *Bw* 5, 187.

97. Letter of 18 June 1859. *Bw* 5, 241.

98. Brahms appears to have borne no grudge against Stockhausen, and the two gave many recitals together. Stockhausen sang in the first performance of *A German Requiem* in April 1868 at Bremen. Brahms was godfather to one of Stockhausen's children.

99. Letter of 18 November 1862. *Schumann–Brahms Briefe*, 1:413.

100. On Bertha Porubszky's friendship with Brahms, see Geiringer, *Brahms*, 63–64, 66, 71, 117.

101. Letter to Julius Otto Grimm of November 1862. *Bw* 4, 110.
102. Letter of November 1862. Reproduced in facsimile in Heinrich Reimann, *Johannes Brahms* (Berlin, 1919), 32.
103. Letter of 26 March 1863. *Bw* 8, 196.
104. Letter of 25 November 1863. *Schumann–Brahms Briefe*, 1:432–33.
105. Letter to Adolf Schubring of 28 or 20 June 1865. *Bw* 7, 207.
106. For details of Brahms's later invitations to Sonderhausen and the Thomaskirche, see May, *Life of Brahms*, 2:515, and Geiringer, *Brahms*, 126–27.
107. Letter of 17 October 1876. *Billroth und Brahms in Briefwechsel*, ed. Otto Gottlieb-Billroth (Berlin, 1935), 222–23.
108. Letter of 11 December 1890. *Johannes Brahms Briefe an Fritz Simrock*, 2:35–36. Hereafter *Bw* 12, ed. Max Kalbeck, Berlin, 1919.
109. Letter of 27 April 1894. Kalbeck, *Johannes Brahms*, 4:345.
110. Letter of August 1894. *Schumann–Brahms Briefe*, 2:562.
111. Letter of 17 September 1894. *Bw* 12, 15.
112. Widmann describes the event in his *Erinnerungen*, 16.

4 · *Professional Outlook and Relationships*

113. Letter of 11 October 1882. *Johannes Brahms Briefe mit P. J. Simrock und Fritz Simrock*, 2:224. Hereafter *Bw* 10.
114. *Briefe von und an Joseph Joachim*, 1:65.
115. Confirmed in Brahms's letter to Schumann of 29 November 1853. *Schumann–Brahms Briefe*, 1:3.
116. Brahms retained the same publishers for opp. 16–46. Breitkopf & Härtel (opp. 24, 29–31); Rieter Biedermann (opp. 22, 23, 32–35, 37, 39, 41, 43–45); with Spina (opp. 27–28); Cranz (op. 42). Simrock published the revised version of op. 8. On Brahms's relationship with the publishing house Simrock, see *Bw* 9–12, Introduction, and Kurt Stephenson, *Johannes Brahms und Fritz Simrock, Weg einer Freundschaft* (Hamburg, 1961).
117. Letter of February 1870. *Bw* 9, 92.
118. Letter of April 1869. *Bw* 9, 73–74.
119. Letter of 1 April 1888. *Bw* 11, 181–82.
120. Letter of 5 April 1895. *Bw* 12, 170. Brahms did have investments of his own. His objection was to the nature of this one, not, seemingly, the principle.
121. Quoted in Widmann, *Erinnerungen*, 98.
122. Letter of 24 April 1877. *Schumann–Brahms Briefe*, 2:95.
123. Letter of 1 April 1854. *Bw* 5, 31–32.
124. Letter of 16 February 1855. *Bw* 5, 85.
125. Brahms sought Joachim's advice on the solo part, making alterations as a result, though these were almost exclusively to reduce the difficulty of the solo part. Brahms rarely changed his original views on matters of musical substance. The autograph score with consequent annotations is reproduced in facsimile: *Con-*

certo for Violin, op. 77. A Facsimile of the Holograph Score (Washington, D.C.: Library of Congress, 1979).

126. Hans von Bülow, *Ausgewählte Schriften, 1850–1892* (Leipzig, 1911), 2:169.

127. Letter to Marie Schanzer (Bülow's fiancée) of 23 May 1882. *Bülow: Briefe und Schriften*, 7 [Briefe 6]:176.

128. Fritz Steinbach (1855–1916) was appointed to Meiningen as conductor of the court orchestra in 1886. His performances in London with this orchestra in 1902 set new standards for orchestral performance in Britain, especially of works by Brahms. In that year he succeeded Wüllner as kapellmeister and director of the conservatory in Cologne.

129. Dessoff gave the Serenade in A on 8 March 1863. Otto Dessoff (1835–92).

130. Letter (dated by Kalbeck as 13 October 1876). *Bw* 16, 144.

131. Letter of [late] October 1892. *Schumann-Brahms Briefe*, 2:486.

132. Letter of 12 October 1864. Clara Schumann, *Ein Künstlerleben*, 3:164.

133. Letter of 18 August 1866. Ibid., 3:190.

134. Letter of 29 April 1864. *Bw* 6, 32.

135. Because the D Minor Concerto had been poorly received and had, according to its publisher, few prospects as a repertory work, the full score was not published until 1874, fifteen years after its first performance. Other performances entrusted to Levi included, most notably, the first complete performance of *The Song of Triumph*, op. 55, with Stockhausen as soloist, on 5 June 1872 at Karlsruhe.

136. Symphony No. 2 was first given on 30 December 1877 and No. 3 on 2 December 1883, both at the Gesellschaft der Musikfreunde, Vienna. Hans Richter (1843–1916).

137. Letter of 12 March 1868. *Bw* 3, 15.

138. Letter to Hans von Bülow of "between 17/28 March 1887." Bülow, *Briefe und Schriften*, 8 [Briefe 7]:94–95.

5 · *Brahms's Mode of Life*

139. Although Niemann draws from Jenner, *Johannes Brahms*, 26–27, some of his description is his own, and seems to suggest his own knowledge of the apartment, which he could still have visited until 1908 when it was demolished. Niemann, *Brahms*, 139–45.

140. Jenner, *Johannes Brahms*, 26–27.

141. Ibid., p. 26.

142. The Red Hedgehog (Zum roter Igel) was Brahms's favorite eating place. It was in the center of Vienna and had been a famous meeting place for artists since the 1830s. It was adjacent to the old Musikverein building (1831). The present building dates from 1870.

143. Niemann, *Brahms*, 149–50. Ludwig Rottenberg (1864–1932) was an opera director in Frankfurt from 1893 to 1926. He was a pupil of Mandyczewski, and his

compositions include lieder and one opera. Jenner's comment (*Johannes Brahms,* 20) seems to suggest that gossip had circulated that Brahms's death was the result of heavy drinking. The group also included Daniel Spitzer (1835–93), a Viennese critic and satirist famous for his epigrams. For twenty years he had a column in the *Neue Freie Presse,* "Vienna Walks," in which he attacked the corruption of Parliament and the greed of the capitalist classes in Austria, as well as Wagner. See Frank Field, *Karl Kraus: The Last Days of Vienna* (London, 1967), 15.

144. Widmann, *Erinnerungen,* 54–56.
145. Geiringer, *Brahms,* 168–69.
146. Letter of 22 July 1886. Quoted in *Billroth und Brahms in Briefwechsel,* 390.
147. *Brahms im Briefwechsel mit Heinrich und Elisabet von Herzogenberg,* 1:200 (*Bw* 1).
148. See also Daniel Beller-McKenna, "Brahms on Schopenhauer: The *Vier Ernste Gesänge,* op. 121, and Late Nineteenth-Century Pessimism," in *Brahms Studies I,* ed. David Brodbeck (Lincoln, Neb., 1994), 1:170–90; David S. Thatcher, "Nietzsche and Brahms: A Forgotten Relationship," *Music and Letters* 54 (1973): 261–80.
149. Widmann, *Erinnerungen,* 152–54.
150. Letter of 21 July 1896. *Brahms im Briefwechsel mit Heinrich und Elisabet von Herzogenberg,* 2:275, note.
151. Letter of c. 9 October 1867. *Johannes Brahms im Briefwechsel (mit Karl Reinthaler u.a.)* 3:10 (*Bw* 3).

6 · *Brahms and Women*

152. Letter of 24 February 1863. *Bw* 6, 2.
153. Widmann, *Erinnerungen,* 48.
154. Letter of August 1890. *Schumann–Brahms Briefe,* 2:419.
155. Reported by Widmann, *Erinnerungen,* 28.
156. Ibid., 45.
157. "Children, Church, Kitchen": William II's axiom that women are out of place save in the nursery, church, and kitchen. Ethel Smyth, *Impressions That Remained,* 2 vols. (London, 1919), 1:263–64. Smyth's relationship with Elisabet von Herzogenberg was seemingly the most important aspect of her experience in Leipzig. See also *Impressions,* 266–77.
158. Gál, *Johannes Brahms,* 89.
159. Letter of May 1887. *Schumann–Brahms Briefe,* 2:315–16.
160. Brahms's relationship with Clara is discussed in Nancy Reich, "Brahms and Clara Schumann," in *Brahms and His World,* ed. Walter Frisch (Princeton, 1990), 37–48.
161. Letter of 31 May 1856. *Schumann–Brahms Briefe,* 1:188–89.

162. Letter of 19 June 1854. Arthur Holde, "Suppressed Passages in the Brahms–Joachim Correspondence Published for the First Time," *Musical Quarterly* 45 (1959):314.
163. E. Schumann, *Erinnerungen*, 245–48.
164. Smyth, *Impressions*, 1:264.
165. Walter Hübbe, *Brahms in Hamburg* (Hamburg, 1902), 23–24. Geiringer refutes this oedipal view, citing Brahms's physical attraction to young female singers and disputes the views of Schauffler and Hitschmann (Geiringer, *Brahms*, 332). R. H. Schauffler, *The Unknown Brahms*, 252–85. Eduard Hitschmann, "Johannes Brahms und die Frauen," *Psychoanalytische Bewegung*, 5/2:97–129.
166. Letter of 13 November 1867. *Schumann–Brahms Briefe*, 1:568.
167. Letter of 13 September 1892. C. Schumann, *Ein Künstlerleben*, 3:558.
168. Quoted in Gál, *Johannes Brahms*, 93–94. *Robert Schumann's Werke, hsg. von Clara Schumann*, 34 vols. plus supplementary volume (Leipzig, 1879, 1881–93).
169. Quoted and trans. in May, *Life of Brahms*, 2:425.
170. C. Schumann, *Ein Künstlerleben*, 3:497.
171. Marie Schumann, Preface to *Schumann–Brahms Briefe*, vol. 1. Marie Schumann (1841–1929) was the eldest daughter of the Schumanns. She assembled the Schumann–Brahms correspondence, which was edited by Berthold Litzmann.
172. Letter of 19 March 1874. *Schumann–Brahms Briefe*, 2:45.
173. Letter of 10 April 1896. *Bw* 6, 285.
174. C. Schumann, *Ein Künstlerleben*, 3:609.
175. Brahms claimed that his final illness arose from a chill caught at Clara's funeral (Widmann, *Erinnerungen*, 119–20). However, as Widmann observes, the ailment probably began earlier.
176. Brahms met her in summer 1858. See Emil Michelmann, *Johannes Brahms, Jugendliebe* (Göttingen, 1930).
177. *Schumann–Brahms Briefe*, 1:297.
178. Quoted in Geiringer, *Brahms*, 60.
179. Ibid. See also Michelmann, *Agathe von Siebold, Johannes Brahms: Jugendliebe*.
180. Quoted in Kalbeck, *Johannes Brahms*, 1:330.
181. C. Schumann, *Ein Künstlerleben*, 3:230. Ibid., 1:232. Julie Schumann (1845–72) was the third daughter of the Schumanns; she died three years after her marriage to Count Radicati di Marmorito.
182. Letter to Joachim of 9 November 1862. *Bw* 5, 320.
183. "Guten Abend, Gute Nacht," op. 49/4. Friedländer states that it was written in July 1868 in celebration of the birth of the second son of Bertha Faber. Brahms wove a popular dance by A. Baumann, which she used to sing, into the accompaniment. The published piece bore the dedication "To B. F., Vienna." Max Friedländer, *Brahms Lieder* (Berlin, 1922), trans. C. L. Leese as *Brahms's Lieder* (Oxford, 1928), 79.
184. Marie Luise Dustmann (born Meyer, 1831–99) was a German soprano attached to the Vienna Hofoper from 1857–75 and who also taught at the Vienna Con-

servatoire. She encouraged Brahms to move to Vienna. On Ottilie Hauer (1836–1920), see Ottilie von Balassa, *Die Brahms Freundin Ottilie Ebner* (Vienna, 1933), 38–44. The quote is from Geiringer, *Brahms*, 71.

185. Speyer quoted in Gál, *Johannes Brahms*, 102. Widmann, *Erinnerungen*, 46–47.

186. Unpublished letter from Elise Brahms of 26 April 1883. Quoted in Geiringer, *Brahms*, 153.

187. Quoted in Heinrich Miesner, *Klaus Groth und die Musik* (Heide, 1933), 93. Letter to the daughter of Albert Dietrich, quoted in Geiringer, *Brahms*, 153–54. Hermine Spies (1857–93).

188. Letter of "end of February 1890." *Schumann–Brahms Briefe*, 2:406. "Von ihren schönen italienischen Sachen und auch deutsche Lieder ... kannst du nicht schöner hören."

189. Richard Specht (*Johannes Brahms, Leben und Werk eines deutschen Meisters* [Hellerau, 1927], 317) also notes that she threw the first handful of earth on Brahms's coffin. Geiringer, *Brahms*, 196.

190. *Johannes Brahms in Briefwechsel mit Heinrich und Elisabet von Herzogenberg* (*Bw* 1 and 2), ed. Max Kalbeck (Berlin 1912). Julius Epstein (1832–1918).

191. Letter of 31 January 1877. *Bw* 1, 16.

192. Mathilde Wesendonck (1828–1902) was a German poet and an author. She settled in Zurich with her husband in 1852. Five of her poems were set by Wagner as the "Five Wesendonck Lieder" (none by Brahms). Letter of 12 June 1867. Geiringer, *Brahms*, 86.

T W O · *Brahms the Composer*

7 · *The Young Composer's Outlook*

Epigraph: Florence May, *The Life of Brahms*, 2 vols., 2nd ed. (London, 1948), 1:3.

1. The "Erklärung" (Declaration) was published in the *Berliner Musik-Zeitung Echo* on 6 May 1860.

2. In "Neue Bahnen," *Neue Zeitschrift für Musik* 39:18 (28 October 1853), 185.

3. Brahms claimed to have been barely acquainted with Schumann's music before summer 1853. He wrote to Joachim that "only since my absence from Hamburg and especially during my stay at Mehlem did I get to know and revere Schumann's works. I ought to do penance for this." Letter dated by editor as "beginning October?" *Bw* 5, 9. However, Brahms must have known some of Schumann's music through his friend Luise Japha, already an enthusiast, since Brahms sent a parcel of his compositions to the Schumanns when they were visiting Hamburg in 1850. See May, *Life of Brahms*, 1:91–92.

4. The Kreisler persona is presented in the stories "Kater Murr" and "Kreisleriana" and in the novel *Kreislers musikalische Leiden* (Berlin, 1810). See also S. Kross, "Brahms and E. T. A. Hoffmann," *Nineteenth-Century Music* 5 (1982):193–200.

5. *Des Jungen Kreislers Schatkästlein*, ed. C. Krebs (Berlin, 1909). The editor has indexed the subject-content of Brahms's individual fascicles in the following categories: Gott-Glaube-Religion; Natur-Tod; Lebensweisheit-Moral; Frauen-Liebe; Politik; Kunst, Kunsturteil-Kritik; Dichtung-Literatur-Schriftstellerei; Musik. Geiringer assembled other quotations of the period under the title *Brahms zweites Schatzkästlein des Jungen Kreisler.* See *Neue Zeitschrift für Musik* 100 (1933):443–46. Another notebook compiled by Brahms during his youth is transcribed and discussed in George Bozarth, "Johannes Brahms's Collection of Deutsche Sprichworte (German Proverbs)," *Brahms Studies I,* ed. David Brodbeck (Lincoln, Neb., 1994), 1:1–29.

6. Johann Paul Friedrich Richter (1763–1825) was known as "Jean Paul." "Novalis" was a pen name for F. L. von Hardenberg (1772–1801).

7. "O Musik! Nachklang aus einer entlegnen, harmonischen Welt! Seufzer des Engels in uns!" *Schatzkästlein* no. 6.

8. "Die Natur ist eine Äeolsharfe, ein musikalisches Instrument, dessen Töne wieder Tasten, wieder Töne höherer Saiten in uns sind." *Schatzkästlein* no. 466.

9. "O Töne, ohne Worte, sprecht zu den Herzen ihr, erreget allgewaltig der Seele Tiefen mir." *Schatzkästlein* no. 369.

10. "Die Musik und Poesie mögen wohl ziemlich eins sein und vielleicht ebenso zusammengehören wie Mund und Ohr, da der erste nur ein bewegliches und antwortendes Ohr ist." *Schatzkästlein* no. 464.

11. "Wer sein Leben höher achtet als seine Kunst, wird nimmermehr ein Künstler." *Schatzkästlein* no. 129. Sigismund Neukomm (1778–1858) was an Austrian composer, pianist, and scholar.

12. "Künstler sollen nicht Diener, sondern Priester des Publikums sein." *Schatzkästlein* no. 229.

13. "Ich kann mein Werk nicht nach der Mode meisseln und zuschneiden, wie sie's haben wollen: das Neue und Originelle gebiert sich selbst, ohne dass man daran denkt." *Schatzkästlein* no. 402.

14. "Der Erzeuger des Kunstwerkes der Zukunft ist niemand anderer als der Künstler der Gegenwart, der das Leben der Zukunft ahnt, und in ihm enthalten zu sein sich sehnt. Wer diese Sehnsucht aus seinem eigensten Vermögen in sich nährt, der lebt schon jetzt in einem besseren Leben, nur einer aber kann dies; der Künstler." *Schatzkästlein* no. 212. [From "Opera und Drama," in Richard Wagner's *Sämtliche Schriften und Dichtungen,* 12 vols. (Leipzig, 1911), 4:229.]

15. "Das Technische einer Kunst muss eigentlich in frühern Jahren ordentlich erlernt werden. Regt sich erst der Geist von innen heraus, so muss die Sorge für äussere Darstellung beseitigt sein." *Schatzkästlein* no. 539.

16. "Theorie und Praxis wirken immer aufeinander. Aus den Werken kann man sehen, wie es die Menschen meinen, und aus den Meinungen voraussagen, was sie tun werden." *Schatzkästlein* no. 544.

17. "Zwischen Theorie und Praxis, Regel und Beispiel, Gesetz und Freiheit bleibt immer ein unendlicher Bruch übrig, und vielleicht ist eben dieser Bruch mehr

Wert als das Ganze. Das Schöne wäre vielleicht nicht mehr schön, wenn irgendein Denker das Geheimnis enträtselte." *Schatzkästlein* no. 500.

18. "Wenn man die Kunst in einem höheren Sinne betrachtet, so möchte man wünschen, daß nur Meister sich damit angäben, daß die Schüler auf das strengste geprüft würden, daß Liebhaber sich in einer ehrfurchtsvollen Annäherung glücklich fühlten. Denn das Kunstwerk soll aus dem Genie entspringen, der Künstler soll Gehalt und Form aus der Tiefe seines eigenen Wesens hervorrufen." *Schatzkästlein* no. 622.

19. "Wir sind nur Originell weil wir nichts wissen," quoted in Karl Geiringer, trans. M. D. Herter Norton, "Brahms as a Reader and Collector, *Musical Quarterly* 19 (1933):168.

20. "Die Form ist etwas durch tausendjährige Bestrebungen der vorzüglichsten Meister Gebildetes, das sich jeder Nachkommende nicht schnell genug zu eigen machen kann—Ein höchst törichter Wahn übelverstandener Originalität würde es sein, wenn da jeder wieder auf eigenem Wege herumsuchen und herumtappen wollte, um das zu finden, was schon in grosser Vollkommenheit vorhanden ist." *Schatzkästlein* no. 482.

21. Quoted in Gustav Jenner, "War Marxsen der rechte Lehrer für Brahms?" *Die Musik* 12 (1912–13):78.

22. Richard Heuberger in *Erinnerungen and Johannes Brahms*, 2nd. ed., ed. K. Hofmann (Tutzing, 1976), 95.

23. Jenner, "War Marxsen der rechte Lehrer," 77–83.

24. Gustav Jenner, *Johannes Brahms als Mensch, Lehrer und Künstler. Studien und Erlebnisse von G. Jenner* (Marburg, 1905), 24.

25. Joseph Sittard was a Hamburg music and theater historian. He delivered the memorial address at a Brahms concert given in Hamburg after the composer's death. Quoted and translated in May, *Life of Brahms*, 1:158. Eduard Marxsen, *Hundert Veränderungen über ein Volkslied.* The concerto dedication read, "Seinem teuren Freunde und Lehrer Eduard Marxsen zugeeignet" [to his dear friend and teacher Eduard Marxsen].

26. May, *Life of Brahms*, 1:155.

27. Ibid, 158.

28. Quoted in ibid., 1:70.

29. Quoted in La Mara, *Johannes Brahms*, 10th ed. (Leipzig, 1921), 11–12, 15–16.

30. Letter of 5 November 1853. *Schumann–Brahms Briefe*, 1:1.

31. "Neue Bahnen," 185–86. Schumann founded *Neue Zeitschrift für Musik* in 1834. In 1845 it was bought by Franz Brendel, who edited it from 1845–68.

32. Letter of 16 November 1853. *Schumann–Brahms Briefe*, 1:1–2.

8 · The Years of Study

33. Schumann refers to Sonatas for Violin and Piano and String Quartets in "Neue Bahnen." The early choral piece does not survive. See further George S. Bozarth,

"Paths Not Taken: The 'Lost' Works of Johannes Brahms," *Music Review* 50 (1989–90):185–205.

34. Letter of 26 February 1856. *Bw* 5, 120.

35. Letter of 24 March 1856. *Bw* 5, 123.

36. For example, letters of 19 October 1856, 5 December 1857. *Bw* 5, 159, 189. The exchange foundered by 1858, though Brahms attempted to revive it in 1861. The counterpoint exchange is discussed by David Brodbeck in "The Brahms-Joachim Counterpoint Exchange, or Robert, Clara and 'the best harmony between Joseph and Johannes,'" *Brahms Studies I*, ed. D. Brodbeck, 1:30–80.

37. Letter of 26 April 1856. *Briefe von und an Joseph Joachim*, 1:339.

38. Letter of 27 April 1856. *Bw* 5, 133–34. Letter of 4 May 1856. *Bw* 5, 137.

39. Quoted by Arnold Schoenberg in *Style and Idea: Selected Writings of Arnold Schoenberg*, ed. L. Stein (London, 1975), 67. Brahms made a feature of writing canons and fugues with answers by inversion or augmentation, sometimes combining features. He points out to Joachim that the "answer" of the Fugue in A flat Minor for organ is in inversion, and he even quotes it to him. *Bw* 5, 140.

40. The theme of the Variations on a Theme of Schumann, op. 9, was taken from Albumblatt no. 1 of *Bünte Blätter*, op. 99.

41. Letter of June 1856. *Bw* 5, 146–47. Letter of 20 August 1876 *Bw* 1. 7–8. For further discussion of variation technique, including the Nottebohm variations on a theme of Bach and Herzogenberg's variation on a theme of Brahms, see Elaine R. Sisman, "Brahms and the Variation Canon," *19th Century Music* 14 (1990):132–53.

42. Berthold Litzmann, *Clara Schumann: Ein Künstlerleben, nach Tagebüchern und Briefen* (Leipzig, 1901, 1906–9), 2:316–17.

43. Letters to Joachim (27 July 1854), *Bw* 5, 52, and to Schumann (30 January 1855), *Schumann–Brahms Briefe,* 1:69. Letter of 7 February 1855. *Schumann–Brahms Briefe,* 1:76. Letter to Joachim of "April 1856." *Bw* 5, 124. Clara's diary entry for 1 October 1856. Litzmann, *Ein Künstlerleben,* 3:12.

44. Letter of 12 December 1856. *Bw* 5, 164. Letter of 30 December 1856. *Schumann– Brahms Briefe,* 1:198. Letter of "beginning January" 1857. *Bw* 5, 166.

45. Letter of 19 June 1854. *Bw* 5, 43.

46. Hans Gál, *Johannes Brahms, His Work and Personality* (Frankfurt am Main, 1961), trans. J. Stein (London, 1963), 114.

47. Letters of 12 December 1856, 24 February 1858, and [beginning] "January" 1857. *Bw* 5, 164, 195, 166.

48. Letter of 20 April 1857. *Bw* 5, 176. Letter of 9 December 1857. *Schumann–Brahms Briefe,* 7, 211. Letters of 26 November 1858, *Bw* 5, 217; 28 January 1859, *Bw* 5, 228–29.

49. Letter of 3 September 1862. *Schumann–Brahms Briefe,* 1:407.

50. Letter of 18 December 1862. *Schumann–Brahms Briefe,* 1:418. Letters of 5 November 1862, 15 April 1863. *Bw* 5, 316, and *Bw* 6, 9.

51. Letter of 22 July 1864. *Schumann–Brahms Briefe*, 1:461. Carl Tausig (1841–71) was a Polish composer-pianist, a protégé of Liszt. He became close friends with Brahms in 1863 and gave the premiere of the Sonata in F Minor for Two Pianos, op. 34b, with Brahms, who composed the Variations on a Theme of Paganini, op. 35, with Tausig in mind.

52. Letters of 9 November 1864, 22 July 1865. *Bw* 7, 11, and *Bw* 9, 11. In 1828 Schubert composed the String Quintet in C with two cellos (it was not published until 1853).

53. May asserts the original version as an octet for wind and strings on the authority of Carl Bargheer, who was seemingly knowledgeable about its composition. May, *Life of Brahms*, 1:234; see also Carl Bargheer, *Erinnerungen an Johannes Brahms in Detmold, 1857–1865* (Typescript in Lippische Landesbibliothek, Detmold, 2182–84), 10. However, internal evidence suggests that the work is more likely to have been a nonet, or to have quickly become one, because its five wind instruments are an essential part of the musical thought, as is a four-part string group. Kalbeck, *Johannes Brahms*, 4 vols. (Berlin, 1904–14), 1:317, 352. The revisions are outlined in McCorkle, *Werkverzeichnis*, 32.

54. Letter of 8 December 1859. *Bw* 5, 221. This letter is misdated in *Bw* 5 as 1858.

55. Letter of 25 December 1859. *Bw* 5, 251.

56. The allegro of the first movement was complete in some form as we know it by 1862. See Clara's letter to Joachim of 1 July 1862. Litzmann, *Ein Künstlerleben*, 3:123. The autograph is lost, and the edition was made from a copy. See further *32 Stichvorlagen von Werken Johannes Brahms*, Kulturstiftung der Länder, Patrimonia 107 (Kiel, 1995), 36–38. Brahms's revision of the second movement of Symphony no. 1 and other changes are discussed in Robert Pascall, *Brahms's First Symphony Andante—the Initial Performing Version: Commentary and Realization*, Papers in Musicology no. 2, Department of Music, University of Nottingham (Nottingham, 1992), *Johannes Brahms Neue Ausgabe Sämtliche Werke, Serie 1 Orchester Werke, vol 1, Symphonie Nr. 1* (Munich, 1996), ix–xviii. James Webster discusses the background to the Piano Quartet op. 60 in "The C Sharp Minor Version of Brahms's Op. 60," *Musical Times* 121, no. 1644 (February 1980):89–93.

9 · The Mature Compositional Outlook

57. Jenner, *Johannes Brahms*, 24. Brahms's comment obviously refers to the fact that his father wanted him to become a performer rather than a composer.

58. May, *Johannes Brahms*, 2:638.

59. Jenner, *Johannes Brahms*, 22.

60. George Henschel, *Musings and Memories of a Musician* (London, 1918), 108.

61. Jenner, *Johannes Brahms*, 5. H. C. Colles, *Walford Davies* (London, 1942), 41–43. Henry Walford Davies (1869–1941) was an English composer, organist, and educator.

62. Jenner, *Johannes Brahms*, 13. Letter to Elisabet von Herzogenberg, 29 April 1879. *Bw* 1, 96.

63. Eusebius Mandyczewski, "Die Bibliothek Brahms," *Musikbuch aus Österreich* (Vienna, 1904), 7–17. Eusebius Mandyczewski (1857–1929).

64. Henschel, *Musings and Memories*, 112.

65. Jenner, *Johannes Brahms*, 40. This covering of middle parts was frequently observed, as by Henry Walford Davies, *Walford Davies*, 43.

66. Heuberger, *Erinnerungen*, 14.

67. Jenner, *Johannes Brahms*, 40, 38.

68. Heuberger, *Erinnerungen*, 94. Hugo Riemann, "Johannes Brahms und die Theorie der Musik; ein paar kleine Erinnerungen," *1. Deutsche Brahms-Fest Programmbuch* (Munich, 1909), 62. Eugenie Schumann, *Erinnerungen* (Stuttgart, 1927), 250–51. Jenner, *Johannes Brahms*, 12–13.

69. Letter to Elisabet von Herzogenberg, 29 April 1879. *Bw* 1, 96–97. With reference to musical grounding generally, Brahms praised the early encouragement of violin playing in Austrian villages and also the singing of the Mass in benefiting sight-reading (in conversation with Widmann). Widmann, *Erinnerungen*, 70–71.

70. Riemann's references to his *Grundriss der Kompositionslehre*, Part 1 (*Musikalische Formenlehre*) (Leipzig, 1889) as distinct from his later *Grosse Kompositionslehre*, 3 vols. (1902–13). Riemann, "Johannes Brahms," 62.

71. His collection of octaves and fifths in the work of classical and modern composers was edited and published as *Oktaven und Quinten und Andere*, ed. Heinrich Schenker (Vienna, 1933), translated and transcribed by Paul Mast as "Brahms's Study Octaven und Quinten," *Music Forum* 5 (1980). Brahms knew Schenker's early critical writings and reputedly commented that "nowadays [he is] the only one that writes about *music*." Quoted by Michael Mann, "Schenker's Contribution to Music Theory," *Music Review* 10 (1949):8.

72. Henschel, *Musings and Memories*, 113.

73. Letter of 15 January 1866. *Bw* 8, 214–15, note.

74. Jenner, *Johannes Brahms*, 35–36. Josef Lewinsky (1835–1907) was the leading tragic actor in Vienna during Brahms's period.

75. Heuberger, *Erinnerungen*, 14.

76. Jenner, *Johannes Brahms*, 31, 30.

77. Ibid., 37; Henschel, *Musings and Memories*, 112.

78. Heuberger, *Erinnerungen*, 14; Jenner, *Johannes Brahms*, 41, 142.

79. Henschel, *Musings and Memories*, 87.

80. Letter of 27 January 1860. *Schumann Brahms Briefe*, 1:294.

81. Letter of 28 April 1894. *Bw* 12, 126.

82. Letter to Fritz Simrock of 28 April 1894. *Johannes Brahms Briefe an Fritz Simrock* 2:126 (*Bw* 12).

83. Letter of 27 September 1894. *Bw* 6, 273.

84. A. Kretzschmer, *Deutsche Volkslieder mit ihren Original-Weisen*, vol. 1 (Berlin,

1840); A. Wilhelm von Zuccalmaglio, *Deutsche Volkslieder mit ihren Original-Weisen,* vol. 2 (Berlin, 1840); Friedrich Nicolai, *Eyn feyner, kleyner Almanach* (Berlin, 1877–88).

85. Quoted in Friedländer, *Brahms's Lieder,* 204.

86. Letter of 29 June 1894. *Brahms Briefwechsel,* 3:125–26.

87. Friedländer, *Brahms's Lieder,* 204.

88. Friedländer, *Brahms's Lieder,* 204.

89. *Deutscher Liederhort; Auswahl der vorzüglicheren Deutschen Volkslieder nach Wort und Weisen aus der Vorzeit und Gegenwart.* Franz M. Böhme, 3 vols. (Leipzig, 1893–94). See also Friedländer, *Brahms's Lieder,* 205.

90. Friedländer, *Brahms's Lieder,* 204–6. The folksong polemic is discussed in Imogen Fellinger, "Brahms beabsichtigte Streitschrift gegen Erk-Böhmes Deutscher Liederhort," in *Kongressbericht, Brahms Kongress Wien 1983,* ed. Otto Biba and Suzanne Antonicek (Tutzing, 1988), 139–54.

91. Widmann, *Erinnerungen,* 37.

92. Letter of 26 November 1871. *Bw* 9, 109.

93. Quoted by Widmann, *Erinnerungen,* 23.

94. Heuberger, *Erinnerungen,* 49. Edward Devrient was director of the court theater at Karlsruhe, where he worked with Hermann Levi.

95. Quoted by Widmann, *Erinnerungen,* 37–38.

96. Letter of "January 1869." Alfred Orel, *Johannes Brahms und Julius Allgeyer, Eine Künstlerfreundschaft in Briefen* (Tutzing, 1964), 59.

97. Undated letter (entered between 7 February and 17 June 1870) in Orel, *Johannes Brahms und Julius Allgeyer,* 62–63.

98. Widmann, *Erinnerungen,* 31–50.

99. Jenner, *Johannes Brahms,* 6–7.

100. Ibid., 8.

101. Comment to Levi. See Kalbeck, *Johannes Brahms,* 1:165: "Ich werde nie eine Symphonie komponieren! Du hast keinen Begriff davon, wie es unsereinem zu Mute ist, wenn er immer so einen Riesen (Beethoven) hinter sich marschieren hört."

102. Karl Goldmark, *Erinnerungen aus meinem Leben* (Vienna, 1922), 85.

103. Letter of 22 November 1876. Quoted in Litzmann, *Ein Künstlerleben,* 3:343.

104. Bargheer, *Erinnerungen an Johannes Brahms in Detmold,* 52. Brahms notified Joachim of the new title, "Symphony Serenade" (letter of 25 December 1859, *Bw* 5, 251), which appears in the autograph score but is then deleted to restore "Serenade."

105. Letter of 19 June 1863. *Bw* 8, 200. For discussion of Schubert's influence on Brahms's chamber works of the early 1860s see James Webster, "Schubert's Sonata Form and Brahms's First Maturity," *Nineteenth-Century Music* 2 (1978–79): 18–35, and *Nineteenth-Century Music* 3 (1979–80):52–71; and Michael Musgrave, *The Music of Brahms,* rev. ed. (Oxford, 1994), 102–6. David Brodbeck discusses a Brahms Schubert edition of the period in "Brahms's Edition of Twenty Schu-

bert Ländler: An Essay in Criticism," *Brahms Studies, Analytical and Historical Perspectives,* ed. George S. Bozarth (Oxford, 1990), 229–50.

10 · Attitude to Contemporaries

106. Henschel, *Musings and Memories,* 119. May, *Life of Brahms* (London, 1948), 1:22.
107. Henschel, *Musings and Memories,* 110.
108. Henschel remarks that "thus he went on. It was no longer modesty, it was humility, and I took care not to disturb his mood by a single word." Henschel, *Musings and Memories,* 119.
109. Ethel Smyth, *Impressions That Remained* (London, 1927), 1, 105. Smyth saw Brahms comment to Herzogenberg after the slow movement conducted by Reinecke and later asked her about it.
110. Letter of 28 January 1859. *Bw* 5, 228–29.
111. Letter of 25 October 1859. Quoted in Kalbeck, *Johannes Brahms,* 1:396.
112. As reported by William Mason, who was present with Karl Klindworth, Eduard Reményi, Joachim Raff, and Dionysus Pruckner. William Mason, *Memories of a Musical Life* (New York, 1901), 128–9.
113. Mason, *Memories of a Musical Life.* There is no evidence that Brahms actually slept. Mason admits to being out of immediate sight of Brahms (130). When he asked Klindworth to corroborate his recollections of the meeting, he did so in every detail, but said nothing of this event. Even Reményi, who had every interest in blaming Brahms, holds back in his reminiscences. "Brahms calmly slept in a *fauteil,* or at least seemed to . . . claiming he was 'overcome with fatigue.'" Gwendolyn Hack, *Edouard Reményi, Musician, Litterateur, and Man: An Appreciation* (Chicago, 1906), 89. Whatever his state, Brahms clearly caused deep offense at the time.
114. Kalbeck, *Johannes Brahms,* 53.
115. Ibid., 33.
116. Letter of [7] August 1859. *Bw* 5, 243–44. At this stage Brahms apparently wanted Joachim to write the Declaration.
117. Letter of "July 1857." *Bw* 5, 186.
118. Letter of 27 January 1860. *Schumann–Brahms Briefe,* 1:294–95. Gottfried August Bürger (1747–94).
119. The expression Music of the Future probably was inspired by Wagner's pamphlet "The Artwork of the Future" (1849). The term New German School was coined by Brendel in *Neue Zeitschrift für Musik* in 1859.
120. The course of events is mainly to be followed through the correspondence with Joachim and Grimm (*Bw* 3, 5–6). Though profoundly interested in Wagner, Brahms became increasingly alienated from Liszt.
121. Letters of 21 March, 23 March 1860. *Briefe von und an Joseph Joachim,* 2:80, 82. Joachim states that "Kirchner, Grädener, Bargiel, Dietrich, Wüllner have consented, and I intend to write also to Gade, Rietz, and Hiller. I should also like

to ask Herr von Saran" (August Friederich Saran, 1836–1922, author of a study of Franz's work.)

122. *Berliner Musik-Zeitung Echo,* May 1860. For discussion of the background see Imogen Fellinger, "Brahms und die Neudeutsche Schüle," in *Brahms und seine Zeit* (Hamburg, 1984), 159–69.

123. Quoted in Kalbeck, *Johannes Brahms,* 1:403. The unheard-of theories were probably Liszt's ideas about program music as published in Brendel's *Neue Zeitschrift für Musik* in the preceding years.

124. Richard Wagner, "Aufklärungen über das Judenthum in der Musik," *Sämtliche Schriften und Dichtungen,* ed. H. von Wolzogen and R. Sternfeld, 12 vols. (Leipzig, 1911), 7:245. The parody is quoted and translated in May, *Life of Brahms,* 1: 271. (See further Fellinger, "Brahms und die Neudeutsche Schüle," 166.) The parody adds perspective to the event. Brahms is clearly seen by his opponents as the instigator and Joachim as disloyal to his colleagues.

125. Letter of 8 May 1860. Bülow, *Briefe und Schriften* 4 (*Briefe,* 3), 317.

126. Franz Brendel, the editor of *Neue Zeitschrift für Musik,* founded the *Allgemeine Deutsche Musikverein* in 1861 to further his pacific aims. See pp. 213–24 for press reactions to Brahms's early work.

127. Letters of April 1869, 25 December 1871. *Bw* 7, 46, 34; *Bw* 3, 42.

128. Letter of 28 March 1870. *Schumann–Brahms Briefe,* 1:617.

129. From "Recollections of G Schönaich," published in Kalbeck, *Johannes Brahms,* 2:116–17. Heuberger recalls Brahms as remarking that "I often had contacts with Wagner" (*Erinnerungen,* 39).

130. Letter of 29 December 1862. *Bw* 5, 326. Peter Cornelius (1824–74) was a German composer, poet, and critic.

131. Quoted by Heuberger, *Erinnerungen,* 180.

132. Widmann, *Erinnerungen,* 83. Gustav Wendt, philologist, 1827–1912.

133. Leyen, *Johannes Brahms,* 58.

134. See E. Schumann, *Erinnerungen,* 250–51.

135. Quoted in Kalbeck, *Johannes Brahms,* 3:409, note.

136. Heuberger, *Erinnerungen,* 23.

137. See also Specht, *Johannes Brahms,* 207. Of the various references to Brahms's "best of all Wagnerians," the most notable is in Specht, *Johannes Brahms,* 285. Specht recalls Brahms stating that he had said it directly to Wagner. When he said it to others, especially young composers, it was clearly a way of defending himself against Wagner worship.

138. Quote in Gál, *Johannes Brahms,* 144.

139. Heuberger, *Erinnerungen,* 43.

140. Letter of 28 March 1870. *Schumann–Brahms Briefe,* 1:617.

141. Henschel, *Musings and Memories,* 106. Henschel tried to encourage Brahms to attend *The Ring of the Niebelung* the following year, in August 1876. Brahms declined and stated that he had repeatedly heard *The Rhinegold* and *The Valkyrie* at Munich.

142. Letters of 6 June 1875, 26 June 1875. *Selected Letters of Richard Wagner,* trans. and ed. S. Spencer and B. Millington (London, 1987). Discussion of Brahms's musical relation to Wagner has recently focused on Symphony no. 3. See David Brodbeck, "Brahms, the Third Symphony, and the New German School," in Walter Frisch, ed., *Brahms and His World* (Princeton, 1990), 65–80; A. Peter Brown, "Brahms's Third Symphony and the New German School," *Journal of Musicology* 2 (1983):451–52; Robert Bailey, "Musical Language and Structure in the Third Symphony," in Bozarth, *Brahms Studies,* 405–22.

143. He looked to Hiller for performance opportunities. Hiller gave an early performance of *A German Requiem* in Cologne in 1869. Ferdinand Hiller (1811–85).

144. Richard Specht gives a full portrait of Goldmark's relation to Brahms in Viennese musical life (*Johannes Brahms,* 197–202).

145. Conversation of 6 April 1896 in which Brahms "doubted that [*Das Heimchen am Herd*] would hold its place in the repertory." Heuberger, *Erinnerungen,* 102. Goldmark's quotations are in his *Erinnerungen,* 89.

146. Letter of "June 1895" [after 12 June]. *Schumann–Brahms Briefe,* 2:587. Max (Karl August) Bruch (1828–1920) was a German composer and conductor, chiefly of symphonic works, concertos, and choral works. He studied with Hiller and Reinecke in Cologne.

147. Quoted by Speyer, *My Life and Friends,* 67, 64.

148. Specht, *Johannes Brahms,* 285–86. Brahms's use of the term "swindle" makes interesting comparison with his comments on Liszt in the suggestion of short-changing or counterfeiting in the artistic product.

149. Quoted in Gál, *Johannes Brahms,* 153.

150. Letter of 12 January 1885. *Bw* 2, 53.

151. The scores are listed in Alfred Orel, "Johannes Brahms' Bibliothek," in Kurt Hofmann, *Die Bibliothek von Johannes Brahms* (Hamburg, 1974), 150.

152. Quoted in Specht, *Johannes Brahms,* 214.

153. Though the predominant waltz influence in Brahms is from Schubert, the Strauss influence is apparent in pieces such as "Am Donaustrande" (*Liebeslied-erwalzer* no. 9) and the first subject of the Second Symphony.

154. Specht, *Johannes Brahms,* 178. Kemp specifies Baden Baden. Peter Kemp, *The Strauss Family: Portrait of a Musical Dynasty* (Tunbridge Wells, 1985), 99.

155. May, *Life of Brahms,* 1:23 (May's own recollection). She lived nearby during her studies with Clara Schumann. Max Graf, *Legend of a Musical City* (New York, 1945; repr. New York, 1969), 102.

156. Quoted in Kemp, *Strauss Family,* 99.

157. Recollection of 28 November 1887. Heuberger, *Erinnerungen,* 157.

158. Quoted in Kemp, *Strauss Family,* 99.

159. Letter of 2 October 1880. *Bw* 10, 158.

160. Heuberger, *Erinnerungen,* 159. Fuchs (1847–1927) composed chamber, orchestral, and piano music. He is chiefly noted for his five orchestral serenades (he was

known as "Serenaden Fuchs"), one of which was dedicated to Brahms. He also was a professor at the Vienna Conservatoire.

161. Richard Strauss (1864–1949): German composer and conductor. His father, Franz Strauss (1822–1905), was a leading horn player of his generation, styled by Bülow as the "Joachim of the horn." For forty-two years he was a member of the Munich Hofkapelle Orchestra. He was devoted to the Viennese classics.

162. Richard Strauss, "Erinnerungen an Hans von Bülow," in *Betrachtungen und Erinnerungen,* ed. W. Schuh (Zurich, 1949), 165. Richard Strauss, *Briefe and die Eltern, 1882–1906,* ed. W. Schuh (Zurich, 1954), 148.

163. Heuberger, *Erinnerungen,* 118, 154.

164. Mahler (1860–1911) was an Austrian composer and conductor who often visited Brahms in his later years. Their first meeting is described in Edward R. Reilly, *Gustav Mahler and Guido Adler: Records of a Friendship* (London, 1982), 23, 131, note.

165. Quoted by Specht, *Johannes Brahms,* 259.

166. Hugo Wolf (1860–1903) was an Austrian critic and the composer of songs and one opera. Quoted in Kalbeck, *Johannes Brahms,* 3/2:84. The earlier version, published in *Ein Musikbuch aus Österreich* in 1904, is part of a sharp reaction by Kalbeck to the reprinting of anti-Brahms reviews by Wolf from 1884–87 in the *Wiener Salonblatt* at the time. He was forced to withdraw the most offensive comments by threat of legal action from the Wolf family. See Frank Walker, *Hugo Wolf: A Biography,* 2nd ed. (London, 1968). Wolf's reticence can be understood. He could not afford Nottebohm's fees.

167. Noted by Walker, *Hugo Wolf,* 87.

168. Heuberger, *Erinnerungen,* 41, 45.

169. Ibid., 181.

170. Ibid., 35, 149.

171. Antonin Dvořák, [4] Moravian Duets [to folksong texts], c. 1879 (Berlin, 1879).

172. Letter of shortly after 23 January 1878 in reply to Dvořák's dedication to him of the Quartet in D Minor, op. 16. Otakar Sourek, *Antonin Dvořák: Letters and Reminiscences,* trans. R. F. Samsour (Prague, n.d.), 42–43.

173. E. Schumann, *Erinnerungen,* 264.

174. Heuberger, *Erinnerungen,* 47.

175. Comment to the cellist Robert Hausmann (1852–1909). May, *Life of Brahms,* 2: 663.

176. Heuberger, *Erinnerungen,* 101, 122.

177. Ibid., 80.

178. Edvard Grieg (1843–1907). Recollected by Julius Röntgen (1855–1932) in his *Grieg* (The Hague, 1930), 25. Röntgen was a professor at the Leipzig Conservatory and leader of the Leipzig Gewandhaus Orchestra. He settled in Amsterdam as a composer and conductor, and he directed the Amsterdam Conservatory from 1914. Heuberger, *Erinnerungen,* 168.

179. See Modeste Tchaikowsky, *The Life and Letters of Peter Ilich Tchaikowsky*, trans. and ed. Rosa Newmarch (London, 1906), 240–41. Rosa Newmarch, *Tchaikovsky: His Life and Works* (London, 1900), 190. A. Brodsky, *Recollections of a Russian Home: A Musician's Experiences* (London, 1914), 159–66.

180. David Brown, *Tchaikovsky*, vol. 2: "The Crisis Years" (London, 1982), 242.

181. Quoted in May, *Life of Brahms*, 2:604; see also Alexandra Orlova, *Tchaikovsky, a Self-Portrait*, trans. R. M. Davison (Oxford, 1990), 231.

182. See Brown, *Tchaikovsky*, vol. 4: "The Final Years, 1885–93," 177, 129. The criticism began with Tovey. See Edward Garden's comments in *Tchaikovsky* (London, 1973), 119, 128.

183. Specht, *Johannes Brahms*, 313.

184. Heuberger, *Erinnerungen*, 94. Luigi Cherubini (1760–1842) was an Italian composer, theorist, and teacher. He directed the Paris Conservatory from 1822–42. J. F. F. Halévy (1799–1862); Daniel Auber (1782–1871); Ambroise Thomas (1811–96).

185. Heuberger, *Erinnerungen*, 54, 94–95; *Billroth und Brahms Briefwechsel*, 348. Georges Bizet (1838–75). Leo Delibes (1836–91) was a French composer and organist. His output, almost entirely for the stage, includes operas, operettas, and, notably, symphonic ballets, of which genre he is often regarded as the founder.

186. Heuberger, *Erinnerungen*, 52, and Kalbeck, *Johannes Brahms*, 4:48–49. Charles Gounod (1818–93); Jules Massenet (1842–1912).

187. Specht, *Johannes Brahms*, 339.

188. Hector Berlioz (1803–69). Letter of 6 November 1855. *Schumann–Brahms Briefe*, 1:145.

189. Heuberger, *Erinnerungen*, 159.

190. Widmann, *Erinnerungen*, 130–31.

191. Heuberger, *Erinnerungen*, 62, 20.

192. Brahms's reaction is quoted by Widmann, *Erinnerungen*, 132, note.

193. Bülow's letter to Verdi was dated 7 April 1892. Bülow, *Briefe und Schriften* 8, [*Briefe*, 7], 386–87. Verdi's reply follows on pp. 387–88. Friedrich Hegar (1841–1927).

194. Widmann, *Erinnerungen*, 133–34. Heuberger, *Erinnerungen*, 181.

II · Brahms Reflects on His Achievement

195. Smyth, *Impressions That Remained*, 266.

196. Jenner, *Johannes Brahms*, 29–30.

197. Henschel, *Musings and Memories*, 118.

198. Moritz Hauptmann (1792–1868) was a scholar, composer, conductor, and member of the committee of the *Bach Gesellschaft*. Henschel, *Musings and Memories*, 109.

199. Specht, *Johannes Brahms*, 382.

200. Kalbeck, *Johannes Brahms*, 4:348.

201. For other younger composers influenced by Brahms see Walter Frisch, "The 'Brahms Fog': On Analyzing Influences at the Fin du Siècle," in Frisch, *Brahms and His World,* 81–94.

THREE · *Brahms the Performer*

12 · Brahms the Pianist

Epigraph: "Neue Bahnen," in *Neue Zeitschrift für Musik* 39, no. 18 (28 October 1853), 185–86.

1. Ibid.
2. Albert Dietrich, *Erinnerungen an Johannes Brahms, besonders aus seiner Jugendzeit* (Leipzig, 1899), 2–3.
3. Walter Hübbe, *Brahms in Hamburg* (Hamburg, 1902), 11. Eduard Hanslick, *Aus dem Konzertsaal, Kritik und Schilderungen, 1848–1868* (Vienna, 1897), 288–90.
4. J. V. Widmann, *Johannes Brahms in Erinnerungen* (Berlin, 1898), 17–18.
5. Florence May, *The Life of Brahms,* 2 vols., 2nd ed. (London, 1948), 1:21.
6. Gustav Ophuls, *Erinnerungen an Johannes Brahms* (Berlin, 1921), 19 ("So etwas wie rauschenden Orchesterklang hervorzuzauben"). Adelina de Lara, *Finale* (London, 1955), 49. Ferdinand Schumann, "Brahms and Clara Schumann," trans. J. Mayer, *Musical Quarterly* 2 (1916):514–15. Ferdinand Schumann (1877–1952) was the first son of the Schumanns' second daughter, Elise. Rudolf von den Leyen, *Johannes Brahms als Mensch und Freund* (Düsseldorf, 1905), 61. Anton Rubinstein (1829–94).
7. Letter to Rieter-Biedermann of 29 August 1860. *Brahms im Briefwechsel mit Breitkopf und Härtel u. a.,* 14:48 (*Bw* 14). ("Noch dazu gehören die tüchtigern Pianisten jetzt fast durchweg der neudeutschen Schüle an, die sich vielleicht nicht um meine Sachen bekümmert.")
8. Willy von Beckerath's drawings are based on his acquaintance with Brahms's playing from the 1880s, though some were executed after Brahms's death. See also Kurt Stephenson, *Johannes Brahms und die Familie von Beckerath* (Hamburg, 1979). Ethel Smyth, *Impressions That Remained,* 2 vols. (London, 1919), 1: 266. Dietrich, *Erinnerungen,* 3. F. Schumann, "Brahms and Clara Schumann," 508.
9. C. V. Stanford, *Pages from an Unwritten Diary* (London, 1914), 200.
10. Letter from Bülow to Hermann Wolff, 20 October 1881: Hans von Bülow, *Briefe und Schriften,* ed. Marie von Bülow (Leipzig, 1895–1908), 7 [*Briefe,* 6], 98. May, *Life of Brahms,* 1:30. Eugenie Schumann, *Erinnerungen* (Stuttgart, 1927), 269.
11. De Lara, *Finale,* 49. Leonard Borwick (1868–1925). See H. Plunket Greene, "Leonard Borwick: Some Personal Recollections," *Music and Letters* 7/1 (1926): 22.
12. Hanslick, *Aus dem Konzertsaal,* 288.
13. La Mara, *Brahms,* 18. May, *Life of Brahms,* 1, 5. E. Schumann, *Erinnerungen,* 268–69, 269–70.

14. George Henschel, *Musings and Memories of a Musician* (London, 1918), 55. May, *Life of Brahms*, 1:69; 1:17.

15. Letter of 20 August 1855. *Schumann-Brahms Briefe*, 1:132.

16. May, *Johannes Brahms*, 1:18.

17. Ibid, 1:18–19. The different types of pianos played by Brahms are discussed in George S. Bozarth and Stephen H. Brady, "The Pianos of Johannes Brahms," in *Brahms and His World*, ed. Walter Frisch (Princeton, 1990), 49–64.

18. May, *Life of Brahms*, 1:13.

19. Quoted in Heinrich Schenker, *L. van Beethoven, Die letzten [fünf] Sonaten von Beethoven: Kritische Ausgabe mit Einführung und Erläuterung* [op. 110] (Vienna 1913–21), 78, note. May, *Life of Brahms*, 1:5–6.

20. May, *Life of Brahms*, 1:61.

21. After giving solo and chamber contributions to concerts by various performers in 1847–48, Brahms performed his first solo recital on 21 September 1848. The program is listed in Kalbeck, *Johannes Brahms*, 1:44. Brahms's knowledge of Chopin is difficult to ascertain until much later, when he edited for the Breitkopf & Härtel edition.

22. E. Schumann, *Erinnerungen*, 228–31. *51 Übungen für Klavier*, mainly dating from the 1860s, published in 1893.

23. May, *Life of Brahms*, 10–11.

24. The event is described in ibid., 1:99.

25. The first performance of op. 25 is an exception. Clara played in its first performance on 16 November 1861 in Hamburg.

26. F. Schumann, "Brahms and Clara Schumann," 512. Ferdinand Schumann comments that "his by no means technically perfect playing only lessened the effect."

27. Noted by Karl Geiringer, *Brahms, His Life and Work*, 2nd ed., trans. H. B. Weiner and B. Miall (London, 1948), 94.

28. E. Schumann, *Erinnerungen*, 269–70, Sonata for Violin and Piano in D Minor, op. 108, bb. 155–81, first given on 21 December 1888 by Brahms and Jeno Hübay. The work is dedicated to Hans von Bülow.

29. This was doubtless prompted by his own very recent success with the medium of clarinet duo sonata, which he effectively inaugurated with the two sonatas opp. 120, 1 and 2, completed in this year (1894), and in turn by the stimulus of the playing of Richard Mühlfeld. These works had been preceded by works for clarinet and other combinations: the trio for clarinet, cello, and piano, op. 114, and the quintet for clarinet and strings, op. 115. F. Schumann, "Brahms and Clara Schumann," 508. Richard Mühlfeld (1856–1907).

30. Max Graf, *Legend of a Musical City* (New York, 1945; repr. New York, 1969), 105. Max Graf (1873–1958).

31. Ibid., 104. Gustav Walter (1834–1910).

32. Antonia Kufferath (1857–?) was a soprano for concerts and oratorios. She was a

pupil of Julius Stockhausen and Manuel Garcia and was admired by Clara Schumann. She married Edward Speyer in 1885. Her performances are discussed in Edward Speyer, *My Life and Friends* (London, 1937), 64, 71.

33. Graf, *Legend of a Musical City,* 103.

34. Ibid. Brahms's emphasis on the bass is also stressed by De Lara, *Finale,* 50. "He was furious if one's basses were weak."

13 · *Brahms the Conductor*

Epigraph: Letter of Levi to Brahms. 14 July 1870. *Bw* 7, 65.

35. Quoted in May, *Life of Brahms,* 1:75.

36. Brahms's greatest enthusiasm for conducting manifested itself in connection with his Symphony No. 4, which he conducted frequently with the Meiningen orchestra in 1885–86 and on tour in Germany and Holland.

37. Willi Schramm, *Brahms in Detmold,* ed. with new commentary by Richard Müller Dombois (Hagen, 1983), 31.

38. The work of the choir is discussed in Sophie Drinker, *Brahms and His Women's Choruses* (Meiron, 1952).

39. May, *Life of Brahms,* 1:80.

40. Hancock lists Brahms's performances of early music in Virginia M. Hancock, *Brahms's Choral Compositions and His Library of Early Music,* UMI Studies in Musicology, no. 76 (Ann Arbor, 1983), 209–11.

41. May, *Life of Brahms,* 1:80.

42. Recounted to Florence May by the court cellist Julius Schmidt. May, *Life of Brahms,* 1:227.

43. First published complete in Walter Hübbe in *Brahms in Hamburg.* Brahms still retained his youthful pseudonym, "Johannes Kreisler, Jr.," in endorsing the document.

44. See Hancock, *Brahms's Choral Compositions,* 126. May suggests that the Byrd was taken from a collection of English madrigals edited by J. J. Maier (*Life of Brahms,* 2:351). The full title is "Auswahl englisher Madrigale für gemischten Chor von Julius Jos. Maier," 3 vols. (Breslau, n.d.).

45. The Singakademie was founded in 1858.

46. Brahms subscribed to the *Bach Gesellschaft* edition from 1857 through the agency of Princess Frederike at Detmold and later took over the subscription himself. Carl von Winterfeld, *Johannes Gabrieli und sein Zeitalter* (Berlin, 1834).

47. Quoted from the review of an unnamed critic in May, *Life of Brahms,* 2:346.

48. Hirsch's review is quoted and translated in May, *Life of Brahms,* 2:349. Hanslick, *Aus dem Konzersaal,* 315–17.

49. Johann Ritter von Herbeck (1831–77) was an Austrian conductor and composer who succeeded Hellmesberger as conductor of the Gesellschaft der Musikfreunde in 1859. He became director of the Hofoper in 1870 but resigned in 1875 and

resumed the Gesellschaft concerts after Brahms's resignation. Hanslick reviewed this concert in *Aus dem Konzertsaal,* 269–74.

50. Letter of 25 November 1863, *Schumann-Brahms Briefe,* 1:433. Stockhausen had been appointed to the conductorship of the Hamburg Philharmonic Concerts in autumn 1862.

51. Letter of 25 October 1872 to Wilhelm Lübke. *Briefe von Theodor Billroth,* 7th ed. (Hanover, 1906), 149–50.

52. May lists all the concert programs (*Life of Brahms,* 2:466–95). They are discussed in further detail in Maria Komorn, *Johannes Brahms als Chordirigient in Wien und sein Nachfolger* (Vienna, 1928), 30–62.

53. See Maria Komorn, "Brahms as Choral Conductor," *Musical Quarterly* 19 (1933): 155.

54. See Henschel, *Musings and Memories,* 54–55. "The [concert] went off beautifully. Brahms had trained the chorus with infinite care and conducted with great earnestness." Henschel also sang the title part in Bruch's *Odysseus* in another concert.

55. The two harmonizations are published in *Neue Zeitschrift für Musik* 100 (1933): Notenbeilage no. 5.

56. Listed in Richard von Perger, *Geschichte der K. K. Gesellschaft der Musikfreunde in Wien, 1 Abteilung, 1812–1870* (Vienna, 1912), 62.

57. See Komorn, *Brahms als Nachfolger,* 73. Wilhelm Furtwängler (1886–1954): German conductor whose posts included the Vienna Philharmonic, Leipzig Gewandhaus, and Berlin Philharmonic Orchestras, as well as the Bayreuth Festival. He also had visiting conductorships, including the New York Philharmonic. He excelled in the German classical repertory and Wagner.

58. Unnamed Viennese critic quoted in May, *Life of Brahms,* 2:489.

59. Letter of 14 July 1870, *Bw* 7, 65. Brahms had conducted *A German Requiem* complete in Karlsruhe in April 1869.

60. Wichtgraf quoted (from personal contact?) by Niemann, *Brahms,* 166. Bernhard Vogel, *Johannes Brahms. Sein Lebensgang und eine Würdigung seiner Werke* (Leipzig, 1888), 17–18. F. Schumann, "Brahms and Clara Schumann," 513.

61. Smyth, *Impressions That Remained,* 179. The performance took place at the Leipzig Gewandhaus on 10 January 1878. Its shortcomings are described in Kalbeck, *Johannes Brahms,* 3:181–82. Richard Specht, *Johannes Brahms* (Hellerau, 1928), 148–49.

62. Stanford, *Pages from an Unwritten Diary* (London, 1914), 201–2. Richter is named as the conductor in C. V. Stanford, *Interludes: Records and Reflections* (London, 1922), 30.

63. Letter of "February 1880" in connection with a performance of the *Requiem* in London by the Bach Choir conducted by Otto Goldschmidt. Henschel, *Musings and Memories,* 313–14.

64. Letter of 20 January 1886. *Bw* 6, 205.

65. Letter of 30 October 1881. *Bw* 10, 192. As the editor of the letters points out, however, Brahms's reference to the existing marking is itself inaccurate (the first

edition is marked "poco sostenuto"), which adds an interesting dimension to the issue of the meaning of his typical markings and their importance.

66. Siegfried Ochs, *Der deutsche Gesangverein für gemischten Chor* (Berlin, 1926), 3: 159. Siegfried Ochs (1858–1929).

67. Henschel, *Musings and Memories*, 83. The passage in question was to the text "And behold now the heavens opened wide." See George Henschel, *Recollections of Brahms* (Boston, 1907), 18–19.

FOUR · *Brahms the Music Scholar and Student of the Arts*

14 · Reading and Scholarship in Brahms's Life

Epigraph: Max Kalbeck, *Johannes Brahms*, 4 vols. (Berlin, 1904–14), 4:275. The reference is to *H. Schütz: Sämtliche Werke*, ed. Philipp Spitta et al. (Leipzig, 1885–91), and the *J. S. Bach Werke* (*Bach Gesellschaft* edition), 1851–99.

1. Karl Geiringer, "Brahms as a Reader and Collector," *Musical Quarterly* 19 (1933): 158.

2. Florence May, *The Life of Brahms*, 2 vols., 2nd ed. (London, 1948), 1:78–79. Kalbeck, *Johannes Brahms*, 1:36–37.

3. Letter to Dietrich of "Düsseldorf 1854" [between 19 March and 21 July 1854] quoted in Albert Dietrich, *Erinnerungen an Johannes Brahms, besonders aus seiner Jugendzeit* (Leipzig, 1899), 18.

4. Kurt Hofmann, *Die Bibliothek von Johannes Brahms, Bücher und Musikalien Werkverzeichnis* (Hamburg, 1974), 156.

5. The first copy appears to have been made by 17 January 1853. See Virginia M. Hancock, *Brahms's Choral Compositions and His Library of Early Music*, UMI Studies in Musicology, no. 76 (Ann Arbor, 1983), for details of all Brahms's Abschriften; copies commissioned by Clara are noted on 32, 75, 174, 184. See further "Brahms's Links with German Renaissance Music: A Discussion of Selected Choral Works," in *Brahms 2: Biographical, Documentary, and Analytical Studies*, ed. Michael Musgrave (Cambridge, 1987), 95–110, and "The Growth of Brahms's Interest in Early Choral Music . . . ," *Brahms: Biographical, Documentary, and Analytical Studies*, ed. Robert Pascall (Cambridge, 1983), 27–40.

6. Kalbeck, *Johannes Brahms*, 1:318.

7. Noted in Karl Geiringer, *Brahms, His Life and Work*, 2nd ed., trans. H. B. Weiner and B. Miall (London, 1948), 101, note. The *Requiem* was given its first Karlsruhe performance on 10 March 1869 under Hermann Levi.

8. Letter of 17 January 1864. *Bw* 8, 201.

9. Letter of 21 October 1854. *Clara Schumann–Johannes Brahms, Briefe aus den Jahren 1853–1896, hsg. Berthold Litzmann*, 2 vols. (Leipzig, 1927), 1:22.

10. Letters of 16 February 1869 and 26 March 1863. *Johannes Brahms im Briefwechsel mit Joseph Joachim*, 8:216, *Bw* 8, 196. Schubring's relationship with Brahms is discussed in Walter Frisch, "Brahms and Schubring, Musical Criticism and Politics at Mid-Century," *Nineteenth-Century Music* 3 (1984):271–81. See also p. 222–

23 for extracts from Schubring's published analyses. Theodor Avé Lallemant (1806–90).

11. Friedrich Chysander, *Das Autograph des Oratoriums Messias*, Deutsche Handel Gesellschaft (Hamburg, 1892). Karl Franz Friedrich Chrysander (1826–1901).

12. Otto Jahn (1813–69). May, *Life of Brahms*, 1:276.

13. Otto Jahn, *W. A. Mozart*, 4 vols. (Leipzig, 1856–59); 2nd ed., 2 vols. (1867); 3rd ed. (ed. Deiters [1889–91]).

14. J. P. Gotthard was instrumental in obtaining through Spina of Vienna the publication of Brahms's setting of Psalm 13, op. 27, and his four vocal quartets, op. 28, in February 1863. See also David Brodbeck, "Brahms's Edition of Twenty Schubert Ländler: An Essay in Criticism," *Brahms Studies I* (Lincoln, Neb., 1995), ed. D. Brodbeck, 229–50.

15. Ferdinand Schubert (1794–1859) was the elder brother of Franz Schubert, second son of the family.

16. Geiringer, *Brahms*, 70. [Carl] Gustav [Martin] Nottebohm (1817–82).

17. *Ludwig van Beethoven; Thematisches Verzeichniss*, ed. G. Nottebohm (Leipzig, 1868). This is the second and greatly expanded edition of the Breitkopf and Härtel *Thematisches Verzeichniss* of 1851; *Ein Skizenbuch von Beethoven*, 1865; *Beethoveniana*, 1873; *Zweite Beethoveniana* (edited from articles in *Musikalisches Wochenblatt* by E. Mandyczewski), 1887. *Thematisches Verzeichniss der im Druck erschienenen Werke von Franz Schubert*, ed. G. Nottebohm (Vienna, 1874).

18. Described by Hancock, 62, 66.

19. Letter of 20 August 1876. *Bw* 1, 7–8. See the discussion of Nottebohm, *Variationen über ein Thema von J. S. Bach* (piano, four hands) in Elaine Sisman, "Brahms and the Canon."

20. Carl Ferdinand Pohl (1819–87). *Die Gesellschaft der Musikfreunde und ihr Conservatorium in Wien*, 1871; *Denkschrift aus Anlass des 100 jährigen Bestehens der Tonkunstler Societät in Wien* (Vienna, 1871); C. F. Pohl, *Haydn and Mozart in London*, 2 vols. (Vienna, 1867); with F. X. Haberl, A. Lagerburg, and R. Eitner, *Bibliographie der Musiksammelwerke des 16 und 17 Jh.* (Berlin, 1877); C. F. Pohl, *Joseph Haydn*, 2 vols. (Berlin, 1875–82), vol. 3 by Hugo Botstiber (Leipzig, 1927).

21. Geiringer, *Brahms*, 108, 166. For example, Brahms came to know the "Choral St. Antoni," attributed to Haydn, through Pohl, which was presented to Brahms in 1870; Brahms used it for the orchestral variations op. 56.

22. Eusebius Mandyczewski, *Franz Schubert. Kritische durchgesehene Gesamtausgabe* (Leipzig, 1885–97). *49 Deutsche Volkslieder mit Klavierbegleitung von Johannes Brahms*, 7 vols., ed. E. Mandyczewski (Berlin, 1894). *Johannes Brahms Sämtliche Werke*, 26 vols., ed. E. Mandyczewski and H. Gál (Wiesbaden, 1926–28).

23. *J. S. Bachs Werke*, 2 vols. (Leipzig, 1873–80); *Heinrich Schütz, Sämtliche Werke*, ed. Friedrich Chrysander and Philipp Spitta (Leipzig, 1885–94). This quarterly was one of the first to discuss "early music." Their relationship is documented in *Bw* 16, preface.

24. Letter of "end of January 1886." *Bw* 3, 79–80. See Otto Biba "New Light on the Brahms Nachlass," in *Brahms 2*, 39–47. The library is listed in Hofmann, *Die Bibliothek von Johannes Brahms*.

25. Geiringer, "Brahms as a Reader and Collector," 162.

26. Ibid., 161–62.

27. Ibid, 163. Brahms's Schubert manuscripts are further described in Otto Biba, *Johannes Brahms und Franz Schubert* (Vienna, 1997), and his Beethoven manuscripts, in Michael Ladenburger and Otto Biba, *Brahms und Ludwig van Beethoven: Zeugnisse einer künstlerischen Auseinandersetzung* [Exhibition Catalogue, Beethoven-Haus, Bonn) Bonn, 1997).

28. Letter of 16 October 1891. *Schumann-Brahms Briefe*, 2:467–68.

29. *Bach Gesellschaft Ausgabe*, vols. 1–46 (Leipzig, 1851–91); supp. vol. 1926.

30. Brahms discusses his reasons in a letter to Julius Allgeyer of 27 February 1869 (Alfred Orel, *Johannes Brahms und Julius Allgeyer, Eine Künstlerfreundschaft in Briefen* [Tutzing, 1964], 51) and in correspondence with Hermann Levi (*Bw* 7, 37–39 and notes).

31. Quoted by Max Graf, *Legend of a Musical City* (New York, 1945; repr. New York, 1969), 114.

32. *Handel Gesellschaft Ausgabe*, vols. 1–96 and supplementary vols. (Leipzig, 1858–1902). Vol. 32 (1870): Italian Duets nos. 1c, 9–14, 24, and Trios nos. 1, 2 with piano accompaniment. In a second edition of 1880, Brahms added a further six duets, nos. 15–20. Brahms also published the latter independently.

33. Quoted in Kalbeck, *Johannes Brahms*, 2:405.

34. *Denkmäler der Tonkunst IV.* "Clavierwerke."

35. Summarized in Imogen Fellinger, "Brahms's View of Mozart," in *Brahms: Biographical, Documentary, and Analytical Studies*, 46.

36. Letter of 18 December 1880. *Bw* 3, 174–76.

37. *W. A. Mozarts Werke, Kritisch durchgesehene Gesamtausgabe*, ed. L. von Köchel (Leipzig, 1877–83; supp. vols. 1877–1910).

38. *Mozart Requiem K. 626* (full score), ed. Richard Maunder (London, 1988), introduction. Franz Xavier Süssmayr took down the dying Mozart's instructions for completion of the Requiem.

39. George Henschel, *Musings and Memories of a Musician* (London, 1918), 103. Letter of 24 May 1876. *Bw* 6, 113.

40. *W. A. Mozarts Werke*, ser. 24, no. 1. "Requiem von W. A. Mozart" (Revisionsbericht). See also Fellinger, "Brahms's View of Mozart," 48–50.

41. Letters of 26 March 1863 and 19 June 1863. *Bw* 8, 196, *Bw* 8, 199–200.

42. Brahms's editions of Schubert are listed in Margit L. McCorkle, *Johannes Brahms, Thematisch-Bibliographiches Werkverzeichnis* (Munich, 1984), 636–47. *Bw* 14, 77.

43. *Franz Schuberts Werke*, ed. E. Mandyczewski and J. Brahms (Leipzig, 1885–95), "Revisionsbericht" to ser. 1, Symphonien.

44. *Chopin Werke*, ed. Bargiel, Brahms, Liszt, Reinecke, Rudorff (Leipzig, 1878–80), 13 vols. and supp. vol. The markings are noted in Karl Geiringer, "Brahms as Musicologist," *Musical Quarterly* 64, no. 4 (Fall 1983), 468.

45. *Robert Schumanns Werke*, ed. C. Schumann (Leipzig, 1881–93), ser. 1–14 (31 vols).

46. Letters of "April 1888" and 10 October 1891. *Schumann-Brahms Briefe*, 2:340–41, 464–65. He had planned this edition in June 1888 (2:347–48, 464). For discussion of Brahms's role in the Schumann edition and his other Schumann editing, see Linda C. Roesner, "Brahms's Editions of Schumann," in *Brahms Studies*, 251–82.

47. *Robert Schumanns Werke*, ser. 3, *Klavierwerke, Anhang*. Reprinted as *Piano Music of Robert Schumann*, ed. Clara Schumann and Johannes Brahms, ser. 3 (New York, 1980), 210.

48. This work, subsequently known as the *Missa Canonica* (Canonic Mass) was first published complete in 1983. See Brahms, *Missa Canonica*, ed. Otto Biba (Vienna, 1983). This work and its relation to the motet op. 74/1 are described and discussed in Robert Pascall, "Brahms's Missa Canonica and Its Recomposition in the Motet "Warum," op. 74, no. 1, in *Brahms 2*, 111–43.

49. Quoted in the preface to Brahms, *Ein deutsches Requiem* (Eulenburg ed. no. 969). For a discussion of the background to this quotation see Michael Musgrave, *Brahms: A German Requiem* (Cambridge, 1996), 26–34.

50. Brahms explains this origin in a letter to Joachim of 13 April 1863. *Bw* 6, 7.

51. Geiringer, *Brahms*, 251. Brahms completed his Variations on a Theme of Haydn ("St. Antoni Chorale") in 1873. The complete divertimento from which the movement was taken was published as *Divertimento* from *Feld-Partita für 8-stimmigen Bläserchor* (Hoboken no. 11/16), ed. K. Geiringer (Leipzig, 1933). Despite the title of Brahms's work, the authorship of the theme has long been disputed since his death.

52. Recalled by Kalbeck, *Johannes Brahms*, 3:454.

53. Siegfried Ochs, *Geschehenes, Gesehenes* (Leipzig, 1922), 299–300. Symphony No. 4, bb. 1–8 of the finale.

15 · *A Student of History and the Arts*

54. J.V. Widmann, *Johannes Brahms in Erinnerungen* (Berlin, 1898), 23.

55. Geiringer describes his first acquaintance with the Brahms holdings of the Gesellschaft der Musikfreunde as its librarian. See Karl Geiringer with Bernice Geiringer, *This I Remember* (Santa Barbara, 1993). His study of Brahms, written with his wife, Irene Geiringer, included many unpublished Brahms letters held in the archive.

56. Geiringer, "Brahms as a Reader and Collector," 158. For a wide-ranging discussion of Brahms's cultural life in Vienna see Leon Botstein, "Time and Memory:

Concert Life, Science, and Music in Brahms's Vienna," in *Brahms and His World*, ed. Walter Frisch (Princeton, 1990), 3–22. Theodor Engelmann (1843–1909) was a physiologist and professor at the Universities of Utrecht and Berlin.

57. Geiringer, "Brahms as a Reader and Collector," 166.

58. Eduard Hanslick, *Am Ende des Jahrhunderts* (Berlin, 1899), 394–95.

59. Ignazy Jan Paderewski (1860–1941). Ignace Jan Paderewski and Mary Lawton, *The Paderewski Memoirs* (London, 1939), 107.

60. Ethel Smyth, *Female Pipings in Eden* (London, 1933), 65–66. Adolf Wach (d. 1926) was a professor of law and a jurist. He was married to Lilli Mendelssohn, Felix Mendelssohn's youngest child (born 1846).

61. Geiringer, "Brahms as a Reader and Collector," 160.

62. Brahms made one recording for the Edison recording company of the opening section of the Hungarian Dance, set 1, no. 1, in the possession of the Phonogrammarchiv of the *Österreichischen Akademien der Wissenschaften*.

63. Karl Lueger (1844–1910) was an Austrian politician. He was cofounder and leader of the Austrian Christian Social Party in 1889. As mayor of Vienna (beginning in 1897) he modernized the city. His strong anti-Semitic and nationalist demagogy appealed to the lower-middle and artisan classes; Emperor Franz Joseph I deferred ratification of Lueger's 1895 electoral victory as mayor until 1897 on grounds of the anti-Semitic campaign. On hearing of Lueger's election, Brahms is recorded by Specht as declaring, "Next week I shall have myself circumcised." See Richard Specht, *Johannes Brahms, Leben und Werk eines deutschen Meisters*, 179. Georg Ritter von Schoenerer (1843–1921) was an Austrian political extremist and the founder of the Pan German Party.

64. Hans Gál, *Johannes Brahms, His Work and Personality* (Frankfurt am Main, 1961), trans. J. Stein (London, 1963), 51–52.

65. George Henschel, *Personal Recollections of Johannes Brahms* (Boston, 1907), 43.

66. Walter Niemann, *Brahms* (Berlin, 1920), 141.

67. Widmann, *Erinnerungen*, 85. Niemann, *Brahms*, 142.

68. Gustav Jenner, *Johannes Brahms als Mensch, Lehrer und Künstler. Studien und Erlebnisse von G. Jenner* (Marpurg, 1905), 53. A photograph of Brahms's collection of lead soldiers appears in Geiringer, *Brahms*, 96 facing.

69. Niemann, *Brahms*, 142.

70. Quoted in Widmann, *Erinnerungen*, 113. Adolf Menzel (1815–1905) was the leading historical painter of his time, noted for brilliant re-creations of Prussian historical scenes, including musical ones, with striking use of light and shade. Anselm Feuerbach (1829–80), Arnold Böcklin (1827–1901), Max Klinger (1857–1920). Paul Heyse (1830–1914) was a prolific German lyric poet, dramatist, essayist, and novelist who won the Nobel Prize for literature in 1910; Brahms set some of his poems. Gustav Freytag (1816–95).

71. Widmann, *Erinnerungen*, 113. Geiringer, "Brahms as a Reader and Collector," 159. The nonmusical library is listed in Hofmann, *Die Bibliothek von Johannes*

Brahms, which is the source for the following discussion. By "paternal relative" Geiringer is probably referring to Brahms's grandfather.

72. See *Billroth und Brahms im Briefwechsel,* ed. Otto Gottlieb-Billroth (Berlin, 1935), 339. See the collection *Brahms Texte,* ed. Gustav Ophuls (Berlin, 1898).

73. Its relation to the *Four Serious Songs* is discussed in Daniel Beller-McKenna, "Brahms on Schopenhauer," in *Brahms Studies,* 170–88. Brahms's editions of the Bible are listed in Hofmann, *Die Bibliothek von Johannes Brahms,* 10–11.

74. Brahms met Bettina von Arnim at the Schumanns' house on 28 October 1853, when the composite "F A E" ("Frei aber Einsam") Sonata was performed for Joachim. He remained in contact with her in the following months and dedicated to her the Songs, op. 3. Von Arnim (1785–1859, born Brentano), an essayist, was the sister of the Romantic poet Clemens Brentano and the widow of Achim von Arnim, also a Romantic poet. As a child she corresponded with Goethe. Her daughter Gisela was a close friend of Joachim's at Göttingen in the 1850s and was acquainted with Brahms. Niemann, *Brahms,* 143. Brahms's visit to Daumer is described in Kalbeck, *Johannes Brahms,* 2:136–37. Friedrich Daumer (1800–75).

75. Geiringer, "Brahms as a Reader and Collector," 159–60.

76. Letters of 15 August 1854 and 15 August 1855, *Schumann-Brahms Briefe,* 1:9, 126.

77. "Mondnacht" is the only survivor of many Eichendorff settings claimed by Brahms. See Ludwig Finscher, "Brahms's Early Songs: Poetry versus Music," in *Brahms Studies,* 331–44.

78. Geiringer, "Brahms as a Reader and Collector," 160.

79. Theodor Storm (1817–80) was a German poet and prose writer. Letter of 1 October 1884, *Schumann-Brahms Briefe,* in reply to letter of 29 September 1884. *Schumann-Brahms Briefe* 2:283. The work referred to is Berthold Auerbach, *Briefe an seinen Freund Jakob Auerbach. Ein Denkmal,* 2 vols. (Frankfurt am Main, 1884). Auerbach (1812–82) was a German novelist noted chiefly for his tales of village life. He began publishing his Black Forest stories in 1843. Friedrich Hebbel (1813–63).

80. H. H. Stuckenschmidt, *Arnold Schoenberg,* trans. H. Searle (London, 1977), 357–58.

81. Geiringer, "Brahms as a Reader and Collector," 161.

82. See *Billroth und Brahms im Briefwechsel,* 415.

83. Widmann, *Erinnerungen,* 37.

84. Ibid., 128–31.

85. Specht, *Johannes Brahms,* 330.

86. Ibid. *Ein Vermächtnis von A. Feuerbach,* ed. H. Feuerbach (Berlin, 1912). Brahms's interest in visual arts is discussed with illustrations by Leon Botstein in "Brahms and Nineteenth Century Painting," *Nineteenth Century Music* 14 (1992):154–68.

87. Letter of 30 January 1896, *Schumann-Brahms Briefe,* 2:614.

88. C. V. Stanford, *Studies and Memories* (London, 1908), 116; Specht, *Johannes Brahms,* 328.

89. Letter of 4 January 1894. *Schumann-Brahms Briefe,* 2:538–39. *Johannes Brahms an Max Klinger* (Leipzig, 1924), 5, 7. Klinger's Brahms-Denkmal (1905–9) stands in the Musikhalle, Hamburg.

90. Geiringer, "Brahms as a Reader and Collector," 161.

FIVE · *The Social Brahms: Friendship and Travel*

16 · Friendship

Epigraph: Quoted by Richard Specht, *Johannes Brahms: Leben und Werk eines deutschen Meisters* (Hellerau, 1927), 263.

1. See Florence May, *The Life of Brahms,* 2 vols. (London, 1948), 1:74. May notes that Brahms used to take a dummy keyboard into the fields with his reading for the day.

2. Later Frau Dr. Luise Langhans-Japha (1826–1910), a well-regarded pianist and composer who was successful in Paris. She gave the French premiere of the quintet op. 34 at her concert at the Salle Erard, Paris, on 24 March 1868. See May, *Life of Brahms,* 2:411.

3. Ibid., 92, 95. These observations make interesting comparisons with other examples of similar behavior; see pages 94, 117–18, 304.

4. Ibid., 71.

5. Ibid., 225–26.

6. Karl Geiringer, *Brahms: His Life and Work,* 2nd ed., trans. H. B. Weiner and B. Miall (London, 1948), 64.

7. May, *Johannes Brahms,* 1:283.

8. Brahms later dedicated the cello sonata op. 38 to Gänsbacher, a sign of esteem explained by the fact that Gänsbacher had helped Brahms find Schubert manuscripts, most notably that of the song "Der Wanderer." Anton Door (1833–1919).

9. Specht, *Johannes Brahms,* 199–200.

10. Ibid., 192–95. Specht's view of Nottebohm's personality is influenced by others, since he admits that he did not know him personally. See also Max Kalbeck, *Johannes Brahms,* 4 vols. (Berlin, 1904–14), 2:109–11. Brahms carried the expense of Nottebohm's funeral: Geiringer, *Brahms,* 145.

11. The relationship is discussed by Specht, *Johannes Brahms,* 202–5.

12. Hans Gál, *Johannes Brahms, His Work and Personality* (Frankfurt am Main, 1961), trans. J. Stern (London, 1963), 84.

13. He is discussed by Specht. Specht, *Johannes Brahms,* 205–10.

14. Ibid., 190.

15. Brahms even assisted by playing musical examples at the piano during his first years in Vienna.

16. Letters of 27 August 1895 and 15 January 1856. *Schumann-Brahms Briefe,* 2:596, 1:168.

17. Billroth was the author of a book of musical aesthetic: C. A. T. Billroth, *Wer ist musikalisch?* ed. E. Hanslick (Vienna, 1896).

18. There are, by comparison with those with Billroth, very few letters between Hanslick and Brahms. Some are included in his reminiscences *Am Ende des Jahrhunderts,* and some are translated into English in "Eduard Hanslick: Memories and Letters," trans. Susan Gillespie, in Walter Frisch, ed., *Brahms and His World* (Princeton, 1990), 163–84.

19. Arthur Faber (c. 1839–1907).

20. Geiringer, *Brahms,* 156–57.

21. Viktor Miller zu Aicholz (1845–1910). César Saerchinger, *Arthur Schnabel: A Biography* (London, 1957), 28–29. Arthur Schnabel, *My Life and Music,* with an introduction by Edward Crankshaw (London, 1961), 16.

22. Ludwig Wittgenstein (1889–1951), Paul Wittgenstein (1887–1961). The musical interests of the family are discussed in Brian McGuinness, *Wittgenstein: A Life; Young Ludwig* (Los Angeles, 1988), 19.

23. The address was 51 Salzburgerstrasse.

24. Pauline Viardot Garcia (1821–1910) was a French-born mezzo soprano, composer, and teacher of singing, the daughter of Manuel Garcia. She was one of the greatest vocal artists of the century, and it was for her that Berlioz prepared his alto version of Gluck's *Orfeo* (*Orphée*) in 1859.

25. Eugenie Schumann, *Erinnerungen* (Stuttgart, 1927), 263–64.

26. Brahms's relations with the von Beckerath family are described in Kurt Stephenson, *Johannes Brahms und die Familie von Beckerath* (Hamburg, 1979). Richard Barth (1850–1923) was a violinist and the music director at the University of Marburg and, later, in Hamburg. His relationship with Brahms is documented in Kurt Hofmann, *Johannes Brahms in den Erinnerungen von Richard Barth: Barths Wirkung in Hamburg* (Hamburg, 1779). Hermine Spies (1857–93).

27. Letter of 11 August 1887. *Brahms im Briefwechsel mit Herzog Georg II. von Sachsen Meiningen und Helene Freifrau von Heldburg,* edited by Herta Muller and Renate Hofmann (Tutzing, 1992), 75–76. This appears in the *Neue Folge,* edited by Kurt and Renate Hofmann as *Bw* 17.

28. Gustav Weber (1845–87) was a Swiss organist, conductor, and composer. He studied with Vincenz Lachner and Carl Tausig. Robert Freund (1852–1936) was a pianist who was a member of the party accompanying Brahms to Italy in 1893. Wilhelm Lübke (1826–93) was a professor of art history at Zurich, Stuttgart, and Karlsruhe. He was a close friend of Billroth from his Zurich period.

29. Walter Niemann, *Brahms* (Leipzig, 1920), 122–23. Gottfried Keller (1819–90) was a Swiss poet. Jakob Baechtold, *Gottfried Kellers Leben, Sein Briefe und Tagebücher* (Berlin, 1894).

30. They met on 11 July 1874 at the house of a mutual friend through the mediation of Hermann Goetz, who was prevented by illness from attending. Widmann

explains that he had heard Brahms play as early as 1865 in a chamber concert. See Widmann, *Erinnerungen*, 16.

17 · Travel

31. Comment to Eusebius Mandyczewski quoted in Gál, *Johannes Brahms*, 48.
32. Every week Brahms traveled back to Hamburg by steamboat for two days to continue his lessons with Marxsen. See May, *Life of Brahms*, 1:77.
33. Kalbeck, *Johannes Brahms*, 1:104–5.
34. Geiringer, *Brahms*, 154.
35. Letter of 2 August 1886, *Bw* 6, 214.
36. May, *Life of Brahms*, 1:20. The connection with Baden Baden is documented by Renate Hofmann and Kurt Hofmann, *Johannes Brahms in Baden Baden* (Baden Baden, 1996).
37. Letter of 8 May 1896, *Schumann-Brahms Briefe*, 2:619.
38. Letter from Pohl of 16 June 1874, quoted in Geiringer, *Brahms*, 119.
39. Letter to Levi of "May 1874," *Bw* 7, 134.
40. Letter of "June 1875," *Bw* 3, 59–60.
41. Quoted in Geiringer, *Brahms*, 121.
42. Leopold Kupelweiser (1796–1862) was an Austrian painter who later became a professor at the Kunstakademie in Vienna.
43. Letter of 6 May 1878 to Billroth. *Billroth und Brahms im Breifwechsel*, ed. Otto Gottlieb-Billroth (Berlin, 1935), 263.
44. Marie Soldat (1863–1955). Brahms regarded the violinist (despite her diminutive stature) as an outstanding performer of his Violin Concerto. For an account of their relationship see Michael Musgrave, "Marie Soldat: An English Perspective," in *Geschichte des Konzerts* (Bonn, 1988), 319–30.
45. In 1877 he resided at Schloss Leonstein, and in 1878–79 at Gasthof Werzer.
46. Letter of apparently between 26 April and 29 June 1880, *Billroth und Brahms im Briefwechsel*, 297.
47. Letter of 14 July 1880, *Bw* 1, 142.
48. Unpublished undated letter of Ignaz Brüll to Brahms of summer 1884. Quoted in Geiringer, *Brahms*, 156.
49. Geiringer, *Brahms*, 161.
50. Specht, *Johannes Brahms*, 183.
51. Widmann, *Erinnerungen*, 125–74.
52. Giuseppe Martucci (1856–1909) was an Italian composer, pianist, and conductor. His choral and orchestral works are particularly influenced by Schumann and Brahms.
53. Widmann, *Erinnerungen*, 154–55.
54. Ibid., 159.
55. Ibid., 168.
56. Ibid., 170.

57. Clara Schumann died in June 1896. Brahms's symptoms of "jaundice" appeared by August, and he declined steadily after the new year, being confined to bed in his last few days. His condition was cancer of the liver, of which his father had also died. He died early on 3 April 1897, about a month before his sixty-fourth birthday.

SIX · *Brahms in Perspective*

18 · *Critical Reception During Brahms's Lifetime*

Epigraph: From an "An Open Letter to Franz Brendel" of 5 December 1853 by Arnold Schloenbach, *Neue Zeitschrift für Musik*, 39/24 (9 December 1853), 257.

1. Franz Brendel (1811–68) was a music historian and critic. He edited *Neue Zeitschrift für Musik* from 1845–68. He was founder and editor of *Anregungen für Kunst, Leben, und Wissenschaft* (1859) and *Allgemeine Deutsche Musikalische Union* (1861).
2. Schloenbach, "Open Letter." The description seems to relate to the Andante of the Sonata in C, op. 1, rather than to the Andante con espressione of the Sonata in F sharp Minor, op. 2.
3. "Kleine Zeitung," *Neue Zeitschrift für Musik*, 40/1 (1 January 1854), 8.
4. "Johannes Brahms von Hoplit." Part 1 appeared in *Neue Zeitschrift für Musik* on 6 July 1855, 13–15, part 2 on 7 and 14 December 1855 (253–55 and 261–64, respectively). Quotes from 14 December 1855, 262–63. Richard Pohl (1826–96) was a prominent German music critic and thoroughgoing advocate of Wagner, Liszt, and Berlioz. He was editor of *Neue Zeitschrift für Musik,* translator of Berlioz into German, and author of connecting texts for Schumann's *Manfred* and Liszt's *Prometheus.* The journal noted the appearance of the works, and Pohl acknowledged that the editor had passed them to him.
5. Georg Fischer, *Opern und Konzert im Hoftheater zu Hannover bis 1866* (Hanover, 1899), 323.
6. "Kleine Zeitung," *Neue Zeitschrift für Musik*, 50/4 February 1859, 74.
7. Quoted and translated in May, *Life of Brahms*, 1:247. The work was conducted by Julius Rietz (1812–77), scholar, music director, and member of the editorial board of the *Bach Gesellschaft* edition. Ferdinand Gleich (1816–98).
8. *Leipziger Signale für die musikalische Welt,* 3 February 1859, 71–72. Eduard Bernsdorff (1825–1901) was a Leipzig-based critic and contributor to the *Signale* who remained resistant to Brahms's music.
9. Reported in the *Oldenburger Zeitung,* March 1862. Quoted in May, *Life of Brahms*, 1:295.
10. Ludwig Speidel (1830–1906) was a music critic in Vienna, chiefly for the *Wiener Fremden-Blatt.* Goldmark points out that the alienation was more of a personal than professional nature: he was offended by a "brusque remark" made by Brahms. He admired Brahms as a composer: Karl Goldmark, *Erinnerungen aus meinem Leben* (Vienna, 1922), 85. Rudolf Hirsch (1816–72) was a music critic in

Vienna, chiefly for the *Wiener Zeitung, Wiener Abendblatt,* and *Wiener Abend-post.* Quoted and translated in May, *Life of Brahms.* Karl Eduard Schelle (1816–82) was a Vienna-based critic of the circle that supported Brahms's emerging work.

11. Review of the concert of 16 November 1862 in *Die Neue Freie Presse.* Published in Eduard Hanslick, *Aus dem Konzertsaal, Kritik und Schilderungen, 1848–68* (Vienna, 1897), 285. Brahms's performance is described on p. 126.

12. Ibid., 285–87.

13. Ibid., 286.

14. Ibid., 329, 320.

15. Goldmark, *Erinnerungen,* 86.

16. A strikingly similar incident of resistance by the orchestral players, here in connection with the D Major Serenade, rehearsed by the Philharmonic in 1869 under Herbeck, is recorded in Kalbeck, *Johannes Brahms,* 2:331.

17. *Die Presse,* February 1867. Quoted and translated in May, *Life of Brahms,* 2:385–86.

18. *Wiener Zeitung,* March 1863. Quoted and translated in May, *Life of Brahms,* 2: 340, 386.

19. Adolf Schubring wrote under the initials D. A. S. His Brahms articles appeared under the title "Schumaniana Nr. 8," in several issues of *Neue Zeitschrift für Musik:* 21 March 1862, 93–96; 4 April 1862, 109–12; 11 April 1862, 117–19; 18 April 1862, 125–28.

20. *Neue Zeitschrift für Musik,* March 1862, 96, and 18 April 1862, 128. These passages are included in a discussion of Schubring's criticism by Walter Frisch in "Brahms and Schubring: Musical Criticism and Politics at Mid-Century." *Nineteenth-Century Music 7/3* (Summer 1983), 276, 278.

21. Hanslick, *Aus dem Konzertsaal,* 287–88.

22. Ibid., 476–77. Schelle noted and translated in May, *Johannes Brahms,* 2:395–96.

23. Eduard Hanslick, *Concerte, Komponisten, Virtuosen, 1870–1885* (Berlin, 1886), 165–69.

24. Richard Pohl, *Musikalisches Wochenblatt* 7 (1876):657.

25. Friedrich Chrysander, *Allgemeine Musikalische Zeitung* 13 (1878):94.

26. Alfred Dörffel (1821–1905). *Leipziger Nachrichten,* November 1876. Translated in May, *Johannes Brahms,* 2:511. The symphony was given in Leipzig for the first time on 18 January 1877 by the Leipzig Gewandhaus Orchestra.

27. Quoted and translated in May, *Life of Brahms,* 2:510.

28. Hanslick, *Concerte, Komponisten, Virtuosen,* 224–27.

29. Ibid., 361–66.

30. Quoted and translated in May, *Life of Brahms,* 2:524–25.

31. Eduard Hanslick, *Cooncerte Komponisten Virtuosen,* 362–65.

32. Eduard Hanslick, *Aus dem Tagebuch eines Meister (Der Moderne Oper VI) Kritiken und Schilderungen* (Berlin, 1892), 203–4.

33. Kalbeck, *Johannes Brahms,* 3:452–54.

34. Liszt placed Brahms with Joachim Raff and others (as did Wagner): he commented to Stasov that "[they] are all good musicians, they have written good works, but they have said nothing new, they have not advanced art." Vladmimir Stasov, *Selected Essays on Music,* trans. F. Jonas (London, 1968), 182. Wagner's quote is in Kalbeck, *Johannes Brahms,* 2:117.

35. Richard Wagner, *Sämtliche Schriften und Dichtungen,* 12 vols. (Leipzig, 1911):7 ("On Conducting"), 293; 10 ("On Poetry and Composition"), 148. Joseph Joachim Raff (1822–82) was a German teacher and composer of more than three hundred works. He was first attracted by the styles of Mendelssohn and Schumann and then allied himself with Liszt after Mendelssohn's death, becoming his assistant at Weimar from 1850. He was a prolific and popular composer of works of eclectic character, including eleven symphonies, much chamber music, and a vast quantity of piano music. In 1877 he became director of the Hoch Conservatory in Frankfurt. *Cosima Wagner's Diaries,* 2 vols. (1878–83), ed. and annot. M. Gregor Dellin and D. Mack, trans. G. Skelton (London, 1978), 2:25.

36. See also Margaret Notley, "Brahms as Liberal: Genre, Style and Politics in Late Nineteenth-Century Vienna," *Nineteenth-Century Music* 17 (1993): 107–23.

37. *Wiener Salonblatt,* 23 March 1884. Quoted and translated in Frank Walker, *Hugo Wolf,* 2nd ed. (London, 1968), 157–58.

38. Quoted and translated in Walker, *Hugo Wolf,* 155–56. Robert Volkmann (1815–83) was a prominent German composer of chamber piano and orchestral music (admired by Brahms) who lived in Vienna from 1854–78.

39. Theodor Helm (1843–1920) was a Viennese writer on music and a jurist. Hans Paumgartner (1843–96) was a Viennese critic. August Göllerich (1859–1923).

40. *Deutsche Zeitung,* 6530 (Morgen Ausgabe, 4 March 1890), 2; *Wiener Abendpost,* 19 November 1890; *Deutsche Volksblatt* 1/83 (Morgen Ausgabe, 28 March 1889), 1. These passages are discussed by Margaret Notley, "Brahms as Liberal," 120, 122. The Zampa reference is to the melodic parallel with Herold's overture of this name, the passage in question b.40 of Brahms's second movement, which recurs in the finale at b.18. By apparent coincidence, the musical analogy is also drawn independently by Edward Elgar. See note 52.

41. Philipp Spitta, *Zur Musik* (Leipzig, 1894), 416–17. the finale b. 18.

42. Heinrich Schenker, "Johannes Brahms," *Die Zukunft* (Berlin, 8 May 1897), 261–57.

43. Felix Weingartner, *The Symphony Writers Since Beethoven,* trans. A. Bles (London, 1897), 60–61. He describes performing Brahms's Second Symphony and meeting the composer in F. Weingartner, *Buffets and Rewards: A Musician's Reminiscences,* trans. M. Wolff (London, 1937), 221–37.

44. Clara's London recital of 17 June 1856 included a *Sarabande* and a *Gigue* "in the style of Bach." The New York performance was long regarded as the world premiere.

45. *Musical Times* 19 (1878):603.

46. Manns gave only movements 4–6; the performance took place on 25 April 1863. *Musical World* (7 May 1864): 298; May, *Life of Brahms,* 2:386–87.

47. *Monthly Musical Record* 1 (1871): 48–49.

48. G. A. Macfarren, Program Notes to the Philharmonic Society performance of 2 April 1873; *Monthly Musical Record* 3 (1873):46; *Monthly Musical Record* 4 (1874):60.

49. *Musical Times* 19, no. 423 (1878):551. The Crystal Palace Orchestra under Manns gave the second English performance of no. 1, and the first English performance of no. 2. First performances of Brahms are listed in Michael Musgrave, *The Musical Life of the Crystal Palace* (Cambridge, 1994), 222–26. On Boston performances, see H. Earle Johnson, *Symphony Hall, Boston* (Boston, 1950), 324–25; and *Boston Daily Advertiser,* 18 January 1878. Quotation from J. Peter Burkholder, "Brahms and Twentieth-Century Classical Music," *Nineteenth-Century Music* 8 (1984):75–83. May claims that performances by the Kneisel Quartet given also for the "European circle of music lovers" were "greatly appreciated" by Brahms (*Life of Brahms,* 1:296).

50. Quotations from George Bernard Shaw, *Shaw's Music* (London, 1979), 2:916, 3:402, 2:376. John Runciman, "A Note on Brahms," in *Old Scores and New Readings: Discussions of Musical Subjects* (London, 1899), 241–45.

51. H. C. Colles, *Brahms,* 2nd ed. (London, 1920), 159–61.

52. Edward Elgar (1857–1934). Sketch quoted by Jerome Northrop Moore, *Edward Elgar* (Oxford, 1984), 117. Elgar's lecture is reprinted as "Brahms's Symphony No. 3" in *A Future for English Music and Other Lectures,* ed. Percy M. Young (London, 1968), 99–103. D. F. Tovey, *Essays in Musical Analysis,* vol. 1 [symphonies] (London, 1935), 112. The reference is to Herold's overture *Zampa.* See note 40.

53. James Huneker, *Mezzotints in Modern Music* (New York, 1899; 3rd ed., 1905), 5, 7–8.

54. Philip H. Goepp, *Symphonies and Their Meaning: First Series* (Philadelphia, 1897), 376. Theodor Thomas (1835–1905) was a German-born violinist and conductor who pioneered chamber music concerts in New York and subsequently conducted both the New York Philharmonic Orchestra and his own symphony, and later directed the Chicago Symphony Orchestra. Theodor Thomas, "Johannes Brahms: His Individuality and Place in Art: A Symposium." *Music: A Monthly Magazine Devoted to the Art, Science and Technic of Music* 12 (Chicago, 1897), 60–61.

55. Daniel Gregory Mason, *From Grieg to Brahms* (New York, 1927), 175–76.

56. Huneker, *Mezzotints,* 5.

57. Albert Dietrich, *Erinnerungen an Johannes Brahms* (Leipzig, 1898); J. V. Widmann, *Johannes Brahms in Erinnerungen* (Berlin, 1898); the books of Widmann and Dietrich were printed together in the English translation as Albert Dietrich and J. V. Widmann, *Recollections of Johannes Brahms*, trans. Dora E. Hecht (London, 1899). Julius Spengel, *Johannes Brahms Characterstudie* (Hamburg, 1898). Rudolf von den Leyen, *Johannes Brahms als Mensch und Freund* (Düsseldorf, 1905). Richard von Perger, *Johannes Brahms* (Leipzig, 1928). Richard Fellinger, *Klänge um Brahms* (Berlin, 1933).

58. Leyen, *Johannes Brahms*, 98–99, as translated by C. A. Phillips in Niemann, *Brahms*, n.p.

59. Max Friedländer (1852–1934) was a scholar of German lieder and folksongs— interpreter, publisher, collector, editor—and was acquainted with Brahms. Hans Simrock (b. 1861) was first president of the society and head of the house of Simrock from 1901. Fritz Steinbach (1855–1916) was a German conductor and composer. See the discussion in Donald M. McCorkle, "Five Fundamental Obstacles in Brahms Source Research," *Acta Musicologica* 48 (1976):253–72. Examples of publications by the society are the song "Regenlied"; the "Sonatensatz" from the "F A E" Sonata; "Ellens Zweiter Gesang" (Schubert), arranged for orchestra; and two cadenzas to Beethoven's G Major Concerto.

60. Max Kalbeck, *Johannes Brahms*. See Thomas Quigley, *Johannes Brahms: An Annotated Bibliography of the Literature Through 1982* (Metuchen, 1990), 9–13, for details of the dates and editions of Kalbeck's *Johannes Brahms*. For details of the editions of the first series of the *Brahms Briefwechsel*, 16 vols. (Berlin, 1904–21), see Quigley, *Johannes Brahms*, 127. The sequence has recently been extended through a *Neue Folge* [New Series]: see note, comprising vols. 17–19.

61. Listed in the preface to Kalbeck, *Johannes Brahms*, 1:viii–x.

62. *Bw* 1 and 2 (with Heinrich and Elisabet von Herzogenberg), ed. Max Kalbeck; *Bw* 8 (with J. V. Widmann, E. and F. Vetter, and A. Schubring), ed. Max Kalbeck; *Bw* 9–12 (with Simrock), ed. Max Kalbeck; *Bw* 4 (with J. O. Grimm), ed. Richard Barth (1850–1923; German violinist, conductor, and writer on music); *Bw* 5 and 6 (with Joseph Joachim), ed. Andreas Moser (1859–1925; German violinist, author and editor, pupil, and biographer of Joachim). *Bw* 3 (Reinthaler, Bruch, et al.), ed. Wilhelm Altmann (1862–1951; German musicologist, director of the Music Section of the State Library in Berlin, 1915–27); *Brahms Bw* 7 (Levi, Gernsheim, Hecht, and Fellinger), ed. Leopold Schmidt; *Bw* 16 (Philipp Spitta and Otto Dessoff), ed. Carl Krebs; *Bw* 15 (with Franz Wüllner), ed. Ernst Wolff (Berlin, 1922).

63. *Johannes Brahms Sämtliche Werke* (Wiesbaden, 1926–28), 27 vols.

64. "The First Editions of Brahms," *Music Review* 1/2 (1940), 123–24.

65. Ibid. Gál was consulted by Donald M. McCorkle regarding his role in the edition.

66. Alfred von Ehrmann, *Johannes Brahms: Weg, Werk und Welt* (Leipzig, 1933). *Clara Schumann-Johannes Brahms Briefe*, ed. B. Litzmann (Leipzig, 1927; reprint, 1989); *Billroth und Brahms im Briefwechsel*, ed. O. Gottlieb-Billroth (Berlin, 1935).

67. Letters of "6 January 1884," 1 February and 25 October 1884. *Richard Strauss Briefe and die Eltern, 1882–1906*, ed. W. Schuh (Zurich, 1954), 32, 38, 63–64.

68. Kurt Wilhelm, *Richard Strauss: An Intimate Portrait* (London, 1989), 166.

69. Quoted by Natalie Bauer-Lechner, *Gustav Mahler*, trans., annot., and ed. P. Franklin as *Recollections of Gustav Mahler* (London, 1980), 37. Bauer-Lächner (1858–1921) was the leader of an important all-women string quartet in Vienna.

70. Bauer-Lächner, *Gustav Mahler*, 142–43.

71. Franz Schmidt (1874–1939). Ferruccio Busoni (1866–1924). *Entwurf einer neuen Aesthetik der Tonkunst* (Trieste, 1907), trans. Theodore Baker as *Sketch of a New Aesthetic of Music* (New York, 1911), 4, 7–8.

72. Vitezslav Novák (1870–1949) and Josef Suk (1874–1935) were pupils of Dvorák. Zdenek Fibich (1850–1900) was a pupil of Moscheles, E. F. Richter, and Jaddasohn at the Leipzig Conservatory (1865–67). Leos Janácek (1854–1928) spent 1879–80 at the Leipzig and Vienna conservatories. Hans Hollander, *Leos Janácek: His Life and Work*, trans. P. Hamburger (London, 1963), 38. The playing of Bela Bartók (1881–1945) is recalled as follows: "He was perhaps not sentimental enough for Schumann and the 'romantic' Brahms, but in the more classical Brahms—and of course in the Hungarian sections of the E flat Rhapsody, etc.— his playing was superb!" Quoted in Halsey Stevens, *The Life and Music of Bela Bartók*, rev. ed. (London, 1964), 39. See *Bela Bartók Essays*, selected by B. Suchoff (London, 1976), various entries, and *Bela Bartók Letters*, ed. P. Demeny (New York, 1971), 201–4, for his views on Brahms's "Hungarian" idiom.

73. Arnold Schoenberg, *Style and Idea*, (London, 1975), 399.

74. Max Reger (1873–1916) was a German composer, organist, pianist, and teacher. He was a pupil of Hugo Riemann, and from 1911–13 he conducted the Meiningen Court Orchestra. See p. 81 for his personal contact with Brahms. Riemann is quoted in Max Reger, "Degeneration und Regeneration in der Musik," *Neue Musik-Zeitung* 29 (1907):51. Josef Rheinberger (1839–1901) was a prolific German composer of instrumental music noted for his organ works, including twenty sonatas and two concertos.

75. Alexander von Zemlinsky (1871–1942). Schoenberg, *Style and Idea*, 80. Zemlinsky's brief recollections of Brahms are published in translation in "Alexander von Zemlinsky and Karl Weigl: Brahms and the Newer Generation: Personal Reminiscences," in Frisch, *Brahms and His World*, 105–210. For broader discussion of Brahmsian influence among younger Viennese composers and other Austrians and Germans, see Frisch, "The Brahms Fog," in *Brahms and His World*, 81–102. Clarinet Trio in D Minor, op. 3 (1897), and String Quartet in A Major, op. 4 (1896).

76. Letter of 7 January 1933. Arnold Schoenberg, *Briefe*, trans. and ed. Erwin Stein (London, 1964), 170. "New Music, Outmoded Music," in *Style and Idea*, 121.

77. The lecture was "completely reformulated" and published in English as "Brahms the Progressive" in the collection of essays titled *Style and Idea* (London, 1950), 52–101, the precursor of the expanded 1975 volume of this title (398–441). "Developing Variation" is not specified in "Brahms the Progressive" but associated with Brahms in *Style and Idea* (1975): 80; it is defined in *Fundamentals of Musical Composition*, ed. L. Stein (London, 1967), 9 ff. The term is applied to a range of Brahms's works in W. Frisch, *Brahms and the Principle of Developing Variation* (Berkeley, 1984). See further, Michael Musgrave, "Schoenberg's Brahms," in *Brahms Studies*, ed. George S. Bozarth (Oxford, 1990), pp. 123–28. Schoenberg's reference to Brahms's rhythm appears in *Style and Idea* (1975): 131. The critical climate of the Brahms-Wagner controversy is outlined by Christoph Wolff in "Brahms, Wagner and the Problem of Historicism in Nineteenth-Century Music," Bozarth, *Brahms Studies*, 9–12.

78. Alban Berg (1885–1935). Quoted by Rosemary Hilmar, *Alban Berg, Leben und Wirken in Wien bis seinen ersten Erfolgen als Komponist* (Vienna, 1978), 173–74. Theodor Adorno, *Alban Berg: Master of the Smallest Link*, trans. J. Brand and C. Hailey (Cambridge, 1991), 25. Anton Webern (1883–1945). Anton Webern, *The Path to the New Music*, ed. W. Reich, trans. L. Black (London, 1963), 46. Egon Wellesz (1885–1974). Egon Wellesz, *The Origins of Schoenberg's 12-Note System* (Washington, 1958), 4.

79. Erwin Stein (1886–1958) was an Austrian writer on music and an editor. He was a pupil of Schoenberg from 1906–10 and an ardent supporter of the twelve-note method. A close friend of Berg and Webern, he immigrated to England in 1938. Erwin Stein, *Orpheus in New Guises* (London, 1953), 96–98.

80. Charles Villiers Stanford (1852–1924) was a professor of music at the University of Cambridge and a professor of composition at the RCM. C. V. Stanford, *Musical Composition* (London, 1922), 53–69. C. F. Abdy Williams, *The Rhythm of Modern Music* (London 1909), 210–36.

81. Adolf Weissmann, *The Problems of Modern Music* (London, 1925), 116–18. Erno von Dohnányi (1877–1960), Wilhelm Reinhard Berger (1861–1911), Ewald Straesser (1867–1945), Otto Taubmann (1859–1929).

82. Hanns Eisler (1898–1962). Quoted in Albrecht Betz, *Hanns Eisler, Political Musician*, trans. Bill Hopkins (Cambridge, 1992), 22. Paul Hindemith (1895–1963). Letter to Emmy Ronnefeldt of "May 1917" quoted by Geoffrey Skelton, *Paul Hindemith: The Man Behind the Music, a Biography* (London, 1975), 42.

83. Wilhelm Furtwängler 1886–1954. *Furtwängler on Music*, ed. and trans. R. Taylor (London, 1991), 97–99.

84. Letter of 17 May 1933, in *Alban Berg, Letters to His Wife*, ed., trans., and annot. by Bernard Grun (London, 1971), 413. Yet Furtwängler had conducted the first performance of Schoenberg's Variations for Orchestra and was a supporter of the composer.

85. The Armingaud Quartet was founded in 1855; its members were Armingaud and Eduard Lalo, violins; Mas, viola; and Léon Jacquard, cello. The Lamoureux

Quartet originated in the Séances Populaires de Musique de Chambre, with Lamoureux and Eduard Colonne, violins, Adam and Pilet, viola and cello. A new quartet was founded in 1872. Quoted in J. M. Nectoux, *Gabriel Fauré: A Musical Life,* trans. R. Nichols (Cambridge, 1991), 87. Vincent d'Indy, *César Franck,* trans. R. Newmarch (London, 1909), 184.

86. Stated in Nectoux, *Gabriel Fauré,* 86. (There are strong stylistic links between the style of Fauré's first Piano Quartet in C Minor, op. 15 [1876–79] and the Brahms piano quartets.) D'Indy, *César Franck,* 87. D'Indy took the copy of *Les béatitudes* to Brahms on Franck's behalf in 1873: "[Brahms] laid the book down ... with an air of supreme boredom, without so much as glancing at the reverential dedication which our dear, good Franck had inscribed on the first page." Ibid., 112.

87. Hugues Imbert, *Johannes Brahms, Sa vie et son oeuvre* (Paris, 1906). Alfred Cortot (1877–1962) rarely played Brahms in public, but he played much Brahms for his own pleasure and owned several manuscripts at different times in his life. They are listed in Margit L. McCorkle, *Johannes Brahms, Thematisch-Bibliographiches Werkverzeichnis* (Munich, 1984). Cortot edited the Piano Pieces, op. 117 (Editions Curci, Milan, n.d.). Claude Debussy (1862–1918). Leon Vallas, *The Theories of Claude Debussy,* trans. M. O'Brien (London, 1929), 150.

88. Maurice Ravel (1875–1937). Arbie Orenstein, *A Ravel Reader* (New York, 1990), 344–45, 494. This is an adaptation of the more familiar remark that Brahms's violin concerto was a "concerto against the violin."

89. "L'Ami du Peuple," 6 May 1929, quoted in *Musical Times* 70, no. 1037 (1929): 608.

90. Francis Poulenc (1899–1963). Francis Poulenc, *Echo and Source: Selected Correspondence, 1915–1963,* trans. and ed. Sidney Buckland (London, 1991), 130.

91. Manuel de Falla (1876–1946) refers to one of two Scarlatti manuscripts of the Abbé Santini, which was owned by Brahms. He does not indicate whether he knew of Brahms's great interest in Scarlatti, whose sonatas he often played and even enshrined a sonata opening in a song accompaniment. Quoted in J. B. Trend, *Manuel de Falla and Spanish Music* (New York, 1929), 150.

92. Giuseppe Verdi (1813–1901). I am indebted to Pierluigi Petrobelli for providing me with this information and Drotto Biba for providing a copy.

93. Georges Enesco (1881–1955). Alfredo Casella (1883–1947). Alfredo Casella, Music in My Time: The Memoirs of Alfredo Casella, trans. and ed. Spencer Norton (Norman, Okla., 1954), 51.

94. Jean Sibelius (1865–1957). Santeri Levas, *Sibelius: A Personal Portrait,* trans. Percy M. Young (London, 1972), 64.

95. Quoted in Erik Tawaststjerna, *Sibelius,* 2 vols. Trans. Robert Layton (Berkeley, 1976), 1:1865–1905.

96. The description of Brahms is quoted in Robert Simpson, *Carl Nielsen, Symphonist* (London, 1979), 19.

97. The Schumanns' visit to Russia from January to May 1844 during which they

visited Mitau, Riga, St. Petersburg, and Moscow was received with enthusiasm and did much to promote Schumann's music.

98. Stasov, *Selected Essays in Music*.

99. J. Bertensson and J. Leyda, *Sergei Rachmaninov: A Life in Music* (New York, 1956), 72, 154. Alexander Siloti (1863–1945) was a pupil of Liszt. Quoted in Victor I. Seroff, *Rachmaninoff* (New York, 1950), 40.

100. Letter of Stravinsky to Robert Craft of 6 June 1948 (relating to an interview between Stravinsky and Koussevitzky), in *Stravinsky, Selected Correspondence,* ed. R. Craft (London, 1982), 1:342.

101. V. Stravinsky and R. Craft, *Stravinsky in Pictures and Documents* (London, 1979), 204.

102. E. W. White, *Stravinsky: The Composer and His Works* (London, 1979), 390.

103. C. H. H. Parry (1848–1918) wrote "Elegy for Brahms" in 1897 and delivered a memorial address for him at the Royal College of Music. Eugene Goosens (1893–1962) attended the RCM from 1907–c. 1912. Quoted in R. Vaughan Williams and G. Holst, *Heirs and Rebels* (London, 1959), 28, 95, 98. Ralph Vaughan Williams (1872–1958). John Ireland (1879–1962). Quoted in Jean Longmire, *John Ireland, Portrait of a Friend* (London, 1969), 130.

104. Cecil Gray, *Musical Chairs* (London, 1948), 19.

105. J. H. Elliott, *Musical Times* 70, no. 1036, (June 1929):554.

106. Constant Lambert, *Music Ho: A Study of Music in Decline* (Harmondsworth, 1948), 230. Arthur Bliss (1891–1975). *As I Remember* (London, 1970), 250.

107. The expression as used in a letter from Sir Peter Pears to me. I owe to Rosamund Strode the recollection of Britten playing the *Liebeslieder* with Josef Krips. His response to a Brahms performance by Clifford Curzon and other observations are found in *Remembering Britten,* ed. A. Blyth (London, 1981), 52, 88, 171.

108. Notes to the complete recording of the Tippett Symphonies (Decca LP, 1984: 440921DM3). Michael Tippett, *Moving into Aquarius* (London, 1953), 108.

109. Horatio Parker (1863–1919) was an American composer, church musician, and teacher. He studied first at the Munich Hochschule für Musik. Charles Edward Ives (1874–1954) was an American composer and businessman. Quote from David Wooldridge, *Charles Ives: A Portrait* (London, 1975), 86–87, 167. Interview with Brewster Ives in *Charles Ives Remembered: An Oral History* by Vivian Perlis (New Haven, 1974), 79. Carl Ruggles (1876–1971). George Whitfield Chadwick (1854–1931), quoted in Gary E. Clarke, *Essays on American Music* (Westport, Conn., 1977), 76. Daniel Gregory Mason, *From Grieg to Brahms: Studies of Some Modern Composers and Their Art* (New York, 1902).

110. For example, by Malcolm MacDonald: "The tremendous opening of the First Symphony . . . [is] surely re-created in personal terms at the beginning of Carl Ruggles's tone-poem *Suntreader*" (*Brahms* [London, 1990], 416).

111. Randall Thompson, "The Contemporary Scene in American Music," *Musical Quarterly* 18 (1932):9. Letter from Virgil Thompson to Ernst Krenek of February

1942, in *Selected Letters of Virgil Thomson*, ed. T. Page and V. W. Page (New York, 1988), 177.

20 · Toward a New Evaluation of Brahms

112. Karlheinz Stockhausen (b. 1928) quoted in Mya Tannenbaum, *Conversations with Stockhausen*, trans. D. Butchart (Oxford, 1987), 70. Mauricio Kagel (b. 1932) was an Argentine composer, filmmaker, dramatist, and performer. His approach to music derives from expressionism, surrealism, and dadaism. The work is discussed by Werner Klüppelholz, *Mauricio Kagel, 1970–1980 (Cologne, 1981), 74–100*. Luciano Berio (b. 1925) discusses the quotations in the *Sinfonia* in *Luciano Berio: Two Interviews*, trans. and ed. David Osmond Smith (London, 1985), 106–7. *Johannes Brahms: Sonate in F Minor for Clarinet (or Viola), Instrumented by Luciano Berio for Full Orchestra*, Universal Edition (Vienna, 1986).

113. Stated in Stephen Stucky, *The Music of Witold Lutoslawski* (London, 1981), 30. This interpretation is incorrect. The form is that of a conflated or reordered development and recapitulation in which the development begins with the first subject in the home key but leads to development and later recapitulation of the rest of the exposition.

114. György Ligeti (b. 1923). The Trio is inscribed "Homage to Brahms," though "[what is remembered] from Brahms is perhaps only a certain smilingly conservative compartment—with distinct ironic distance." Some parallels between the works are discussed in Paul Griffiths, *Gyorgy Ligeti* (London, 1997), 105. Arthur Honegger, *I Am a Composer*, trans. W. O. Clough (London, 1966), 19.

115. François Sagan, *Aimez vous Brahms?* (Paris, 1959).

116. Pierre Boulez (b. 1925). "Schoenberg is Dead," *Score* 6 (1952):18–22. Boulez's most extensive published writings appear in *Orientations, Collected Writings*, ed. J. J. Nattiez, trans. Martin Cooper (London, 1968). Robert Craft (b. 1923) recalls Boulez improvizing a "funny Brahms accompaniment to the beginning of the second movement of Schoenberg's Violin Concerto." Craft, *Stravinsky: The Chronicle of a Friendship, 1948–1971* (London, 1972), 61.

117. Edgar Varèse (1883–1965) quoted in Fernand Ouellette, *Edgard Varese*, trans. D. Coltman (London, 1968), 146, 125 from "Varese and Contemporary Music," *Trend* (May–June 1934):124–28.

118. Elliott Carter (b. 1908) quoted in Allen Edwards, *"Flawed Words and Stubborn Sounds": A Conversation with Elliott Carter* (New York, 1971), 70.

119. Josef Rufer, *Composition with Twelve Tones* (London, 1954), preface. Schoenberg analyzes the second movement of Brahms's A Minor Quartet, op. 51, no. 2, in "Brahms the Progressive," *Style and Idea*, 429–31.

120. Rudolf Réti, *The Thematic Process in Music* (London, 1961), preface, 78, 20. The lack of comment is unusual. Reti reviewed Schoenberg's piano pieces when they were published.

121. Alan Walker, "Brahms and Serialism," *Musical Opinion* 82, no. 973 (October 1958):17–21. Hans Keller (1919–85) did not regard Brahms highly. He noted to me Brahms's "tendency to interrupt a melody abruptly in order to avoid what he might have thought of as sentimental writing." Alan Walker, *An Anatomy of Musical Criticism* (London, 1966); *A Study in Musical Analysis* (London, 1962). Walker, "Brahms and Serialism," 19.

122. Walker, "Brahms and Serialism," 18.

123. Theodor Wissengrund Adorno (1903–69), *Philosophie der neuen Musik* (1949), trans. A. G. Mitchell and W. V. Bloomster as *Philosophy of Modern Music* (London, 1973), 56–58.

124. Heinrich Schenker, *Harmony* (part 1 of *Neue Musikalische Theorien und Fantasien: Harmonielehre*), trans. E. M. Borgese. (Chicago, 1954; rev. ed., Cambridge, Mass., 1973). *Brahms Octaven und Quinten u. A.*, ed. H. Schenker (Vienna, 1933), transcribed by Paul Mast, "Brahms's Study Octaven und Quinten," *Music Forum* 5 (1980).

125. Allen Forte, "The Structural Origin of Exact Tempi in the Haydn Variations," *Music Review* 18 (1957):138; Jean Jacques Nattiez, *Fondemonts d'une Sémiologie de la Musique* (Paris, 1975), 297–317; Brian Newbould, "A New Analysis of Brahms's Intermezzo, op. 119/1," *Music Review* 38 (1977):33–43.

126. *Johannes Brahms Neue Ausgabe Sämtlicher Werke* (Munich, 1997–).

127. Margit L. McCorkle, *Johannes Brahms, Thematisch- Bibliographisches Werkverzeichnis* (Munich, 1984). Elsewhere *Werkverzeichnis*. On Haydn see *Thematisches Bibliographisches Werkverzeichnis*, ed. A. von Hoboken (Mainz, 1957–71). On Schubert see *Franz Schubert. Thematisches Verzeichnis Seiner Werke* (Kassel, 1978). On Beethoven see *Das Werk Beethovens*, ed. G. Kinsky and H. Halm (Munich, 1955).

128. Bayan Northcott, "Once and Future Master," *The Independent*, 30 March 1991, 29.

129. See Burkholder, "Brahms and Twentieth-Century Classical Music," 75–83.

130. Peter Gay, "Aimez vous Brahms? On Polarities in Modernism," in Gay, *Freud, Jews, and Other Germans* (New York, 1978), 233.

Index

Busoni, Ferruccio, 112, 254, 269
Buxtehude, Dietrich, 154, 157
Byrd, William, 139
Byron, George Gordon (Lord Byron), 60, 178, 248

Caldara, Antonio, 139
Callot, Jacques, 177
Cambridge (England), 172, 271
Carissimi, Giacomo, 154
Carter, Elliott, 277, 284
Casadesus, Jean, 277
Casella, Alfredo, 268–69
Catullus, 178
Celle, 21, 133
Cervantes, Miguel, 178
Chadwick, George Whitfield, 274
Chamisso, Adalbert von, 60, 178
Cherubini, Luigi, 40, 70, 87, 114, 118, 142, 143
Chodowiecki, Daniel, 184
Chopin, Fryderyk, 131, 158, 160–62, 165, 235, 310
Chrysander, Friedrich, 153, 154, 158, 159, 162, 168, 170, 226, 314
Clementi, Muzio, 17, 131, 132
Colles, H. C., 244, 247, 248, 286
Cologne, 30, 38, 134, 166, 294, 306
Como, Lake, 198, 205
Conrat, Hugo, 76, 195, 202
Corelli, Arcangelo, 154
Cornelius, Peter, 41, 99, 102, 305
Cornet, Madame Adele Passy, 19
Corsi, Bernardo, 152
Cortot, Alfred, 266
Cossel, Otto, 17, 18, 64, 131, 152, 188, 290, 291
Couperin, François, 154, 162
Courbet, Gustave, 182
Craft, Robert, 276
Cramer, J. B., 17, 18, 131
Cranz, August, 161, 293
Cui, Cesar, 270
Czerny, Karl, 17, 130, 131

Dante, 178
Danzig, 191, 200

Daumer, Friederich, 82, 177, 318
David, Ferdinand, 214, 292
Davies, Henry Walford, 77
Debussy, Claude, 266, 277, 284, 285
Deichmann, Theodor, 22, 292
Defoe, Daniel, 178
Deiters, Hermann, 85, 155, 289
Delacroix, Eugène, 182
Delaincourt, Jean, 267–68
Delibes, Leo, 114, 308
Denninghof, Elise, 291
Dessau, 30, 153
Dessoff, Otto, 37, 55, 196, 202, 221, 250
Detmering, Philipp, 12
Deutsch, Otto Erich, 156
Deutsche Volksblatt, 235
Deutsche Zeitung, 235
Devrient, Edward, 87, 303
Dietrich, Albert: as friend and supporter of Brahms, 3, 5, 23, 96, 122, 196, 198, 249; as performer of Brahms's works, 102, 143, 218
Döhler, Theodor, 19
Dohnányi, Ernö, 262
Door, Anton, 42, 44, 191
Dörfell, Alfred, 227
Durante, Francesco, 152
Düsseldorf, 23, 30, 31, 152, 188, 189, 192, 200
Dustmann, Luise, 53, 203, 204, 296
Dvořák, Antonín, 110–12, 159, 246, 247, 255

Ebner, Dr. Edward, 54
Ebner, Ottilie. *See* Hauer, Ottilie
Eccard, Johann, 139, 140
Eckermann, J. P., 62, 91, 178
Ehrmann, Alfred von, 251
Eichendorff, Joseph von, 60, 177, 318
Eisler, Hanns, 263
Eitner, Robert, 156
Elgar, Edward, 245–46, 248, 274, 325
Eliot, T. S., 284
Elliot, J. H., 272–73
Emerson, Ralph Waldo, 179
Endenich, 24
Enesco, Georges, 268–69

Munich, 39, 100, 179–80, 202, 252, 305, 307

Murzzuschlag, Styria, 203, 205

Musical Quarterly, 274

Musical Times, 240, 242

Musical World, 241

Nattiez, Jean Jacques, 282

Naumann, Emil, 198

Nestroy, Johann, 180

Die Neue freie Presse, 219, 221

Neue Zeitschrift für Musik, 65–66, 94–97, 213–16, 222, 299, 304–5

"New Germans," 213–19, 224, 232, 266, 305

New York, 239–40

Newbould, Brian, 282–83

Nicolai, Friedrich, 85, 303

Niedelbad, Ruschlikon, 202

Nielsen, Carl, 269

Niemann, Walter, 6, 9, 11, 42, 174, 175, 176, 249

Nietzsche, Friedrich, 45, 105

Nikisch, Arthur, 270

Nissen, Johanna Henrika Christiane. *See* Brahms, Johanna Henrika Christiane

Northcott, Bayan, 283–84

Nottebohm, [Carl] Gustav [Martin], 42, 80, 155–59, 170, 191–93, 206, 300, 307, 314, 319

Novák, Vitezslav, 255, 327

"Novalis" (F. L. von Hardenberg), 60, 61, 177

Ochs, Siegfried, 147, 168, 169, 290

Ophuls, Gustav, 123, 309

Otten, Georg Dietrich, 19, 153, 190, 291

Otterer, Christian, 290

Ovid, 178

Paderewski, Ignazy [Ignace] Jan, 171, 172

Palestrina, Giovanni Pierluigi da, 138, 139, 142, 152

Parker, Horatio, 273

Parmigianino (Mazzuoli, Francesco), 10

Parry, Hubert (Charles Hubert Hastings), 244, 271, 274

Paumgartner, Hans, 235, 324

Percy, Thomas (Bishop Percy), 60

Perger, Richard von, 7, 44, 249, 287

Pfitzner, Hans, 263

Picasso, Pablo, 284

Plautus, 178

Plutarch, 178

Pohl, Carl Ferdinand, 156, 157, 159, 169, 170, 191, 202, 321

Pohl, Richard ("Hoplit"), 106, 215, 217, 226, 314, 322

Pomerania, 85, 86

Pope, Alexander, 60

Portschach, 44, 203, 204

Porubszky, Bertha, 28, 53, 93, 190, 193, 194, 292

Poulenc, Francis, 268

Praetorius, Michael, 138

Die Presse, 219

Pruckner, Dionysus, 304

Rachmaninov, Sergei, 270

Raff, Joachim, 304, 324

Raphael, 40

Ravel, Maurice, 266–67, 268

Reger, Max, 255, 256–57, 258, 263, 274

Reinecke, Karl, 23, 96, 113, 292, 304, 306

Reinthaler, Karl Martin, 38, 98, 158, 159, 295

Reményi, Ede (born Hoffmann, Eduard; generally known as Reményi, Eduard [or Edouard]), 19, 20, 21, 22, 94, 133, 188, 200, 304

Réti, Rudolf, 278–79

Reuter, Fritz, 179

Rheinberger, Joseph, 103, 143, 256

Rhineland, 22, 51, 85, 86, 197, 200, 292

Richter, Hans, 38, 146, 263, 312

Richter, Johann Paul Friedrich ("Jean Paul"), 60, 177, 298

Riemann, Hugo, 40, 80, 81, 256

Rieter Biedermann, Melchior, 33, 160, 161, 164, 165, 201, 293, 309

Rietz, Julius, 103, 143, 304, 322

Vallas, Leon, 266
Varèse, Edgard, 276
Vaughan Williams, Ralph, 271
Verdi, Giuseppe, 110, 115, 116, 268, 308
Viardot Garcia, Pauline, 196
Vienna
  Brahms's contact with and social life
    in, 10, 14, 15, 28–31, 39–44, 53–55,
    152, 173, 187–94, 202–3, 207–8,
    294
  musical institutions of: Conservatory,
    28, 43, 80, 137, 191, 254, 297, 307;
    Singakademie, 29, 34, 139–41, 145,
    153, 161, 191, 224; Gesellschaft der
    Musikfreunde, 30, 34, 112, 138, 228;
    Singverein, 34, 38, 87, 115, 141–43,
    145, 153, 161–63, 167, 219, 224;
    Philharmonic Orchestra, 37, 43,
    146, 155, 190, 221, 253; Tonkün-
    stlerverein, 43, 44, 257; Court
    Opera, 53, 115, 297
  musical life of, 37, 101, 153–55, 164,
    170, 254
  Brahms's works performed in, 73,
    147, 221–22, 227–28
  Brahms as performer in, 131, 133, 137,
    140–41
Vienna University, 157
Vinci, Leonardo da, 40
Viotti, Giovanni Battista, 6
Vischer, F. T., 178
Voigt, Carl, 19, 291
Völkers, Elisabeth (Betty), 190
Völkers, Marie, 190
Volkmann, Robert, 103, 143, 234
Voss, H. V., 17

Wach, Adolf, 172
Wackenroder, Heinrich, 60
Wagner, Cosima, 232
Wagner, Friedchen, 190
Wagner, Richard: Brahms's attitude to
  and knowledge of, 34, 37, 60–62,
  87, 96, 115, 159, 160, 298, 304;
  works and performances of, 38, 56,
  225; outlook, influence, and writings of, 59, 88, 173, 213, 244, 284;

  attitude toward Brahms, 97–102;
  Brahms's music compared with,
  118, 229, 232–33, 235–36, 239, 258,
  261–63, 272, 285–86, 306
Walford Davies, Henry, 301
Walsh, John, 168
Walter, Gustav, 135, 193
Walter, Johann, 156
Walther, Johann G., 159
Wasielewski, Wilhelm Joseph von, 22,
  292
Weber, Carl Maria von, 18–19, 60, 87,
  237, 291
Weber, Gustav, 198, 320
Webern, Anton, 258, 259
Wehrmann family, 197
Weimar, 20, 22, 200, 250
Weingartner, Felix, 236, 238–39, 324
Weissmann, Adolf, 261
Wellesz, Egon, 258
Wendt, Gustav, 63, 99, 171, 178, 305
Wesendonck, Mathilde, 56, 202, 297
Wesselburen, 12
Wichtgraf, Geheimrat, 144
Widmann, Josef Viktor: acquaintance
  and friendship with Brahms, 3–4,
  10, 42–43, 46–47, 86–89, 151, 175,
  199, 202, 205–6, 249–50; opinions
  of Brahms, 54, 123, 170, 174, 296;
  as Brahms's librettist, 99; visits to
  Italy with Brahms, 180, 207
Wieland, Christoph Martin, 178
Wiener Abendpost, 235
Wiener Salonblatt, 307
Wiener Zeitung, 219, 222, 224
Wiesbaden, 197, 200, 205
Williams, John, 286
Winsen an der Luhe, 17, 136, 138, 152,
  187
Winterfeld, Carl von, 140, 153
Winterthur, 88, 201
Wittgenstein, Ludwig, 195
Wittgenstein, Paul, 195
Wolf, Hugo, 108, 109, 110, 233–34,
  307
Wolff, Ernst, 250
Wolff, Hermann, 309